Bhagat
Singh

Bhagat Singh

A LIFE in REVOLUTION

SATVINDER JUSS

PENGUIN
VIKING
An imprint of Penguin Random House

VIKING

USA | Canada | UK | Ireland | Australia
New Zealand | India | South Africa | China | Singapore

Viking is part of the Penguin Random House group of companies
whose addresses can be found at global.penguinrandomhouse.com

Published by Penguin Random House India Pvt. Ltd
4th Floor, Capital Tower 1, MG Road,
Gurugram 122 002, Haryana, India

Penguin
Random House
India

First published in Viking by Penguin Random House India 2022

Copyright © Satvinder Singh Juss 2022

The views and opinions expressed in this book are the author's own and the
facts are as reported by him which have been verified to the extent possible,
and the publishers are not in any way liable for the same.

ISBN 9780670095230

Typeset in Adobe Caslon Pro by Manipal Technologies Limited, Manipal
Printed at Replika Press Pvt. Ltd, India

www.penguin.co.in

This is a legitimate digitally printed version of the book and therefore might not
have certain extra finishing on the cover.

In memory of Hartej

Contents

PART 3: A LIFE IN REVOLUTION

PART 4: THE ASSASSINATION

PART 5: 1928, THE NAUJAWAN BHARAT SABHA

PART 6: THE ASSEMBLY BOMB SPEECHES

PART 7: JUDICIAL REPRISALS

The desire to live is natural. It is in me also. I do not want to conceal it. But it is conditional. I do not want to live as a prisoner or under restrictions . . . Yet, one thing pricks me even today. My heart nurtured some ambitions for doing something for humanity and for my country. I have not been able to fulfil even one-thousandth part of these ambitions. If I live I might perhaps get a chance to fulfil them. If ever it came to my mind that I should not die, it came from this end only.[1]

An excerpt from Bhagat Singh's last letter to the convicts of the Lahore Conspiracy Case, dated 22 March 1931, the day before his execution.

I am, after all, a human being
and nothing more.
And no one can claim to be
more than that.
(Bhagat Singh, 'Why I Am an Atheist', 1931)

Acknowledgements

This book is about Bhagat Singh, the unacclaimed hero of the Indian freedom struggle. It is a sequel to my recent book *The Execution of Bhagat Singh: Heresies of the Raj*, but unlike that book, which focussed to a substantial degree on the trial proceedings leading up to the execution of Bhagat Singh, this one sets out to examine the wider aspects of his life in revolution. The original materials in this book that I consulted during my research are from the Lahore Archives at the offices of the Punjab Civil Secretariat in the tree-lined precincts of Anarkali, where, just as the gardeners outside tend to the flowers, the officials tend to the priceless documentation inside with meticulous care and attention. What follows is the fruit of my labours, a result of the unstinting assistance that I have received there. Needless to say, I alone remain responsible for what unfolds in the pages here and all errors are mine alone. Although this is my second book on this subject, the more I have researched and written the more I have realized that even after almost a hundred years after the death of Bhagat Singh, I am only scratching the surface. But history has to be rewritten in every generation, as Christopher Hill once explained, because although the past does not change, the present does. So, the writing of history is a continual process, and I would hope, therefore, that the reader will follow through with some of the sources cited and participate in casting further light on the life and death of a person whom *India Today* has described as 'the greatest Indian'.

I remain indebted to all those who have helped me during my own journey. In Lahore, I am grateful to Mohammad Abbas Chugtai, the director of the Punjab Archives Department, to Fakir S. Aijazuddin, to Furrukh Khan and Faisal Mahmood Khan. In Britain, I am most grateful to Dr Chris Moffat, Professor Kim Wagner, Dr Mark Condos, Sir Stephen Sedley, Sir Anthony Holland, Sardar Gulzar Singh Sahota. For strategic support, I am most thankful to Ghoghi. In India, M.M. Juneja and Professors Chaman Lal and Malwinder Jit Singh Waraich have always been ready to provide any information that I have asked for. Harpreet ('Harry') Bhinder of Mohali has been excellent in reading the manuscript and giving me the benefit of his detailed insights.

Finally, my heartfelt thanks must go to my publishers: Meru Gokhale for encouraging me to write a Penguin book on the 'life in revolution' of Bhagat Singh; to Shaoni Mukherjee for her eye for detail during the editorial stage, for which this work is all the better; and to Shubhi Surana for overseeing the publication process so professionally and thoroughly.

Prologue

Kisi ko ghar se nikalte hi mil gai manzil
Koi hamari tarah umr bhar safar mein raha

Some found their destiny at their doorstep.
Others like me were fated to be in the wilderness all their lives.

—Ahmed Faraz

The majestic but forlorn nineteenth-century building of Bradlaugh Hall, now derelict, sad and destitute, still stands behind the district courts of Lahore. Here, the National College, founded by Lala Lajpat Rai, practising the novelty of using books written in the English language, once schooled its 200 Hindu, Muslim and Sikh students. One such student was the nineteen-year-old Bhagat Singh, who established the Naujawan Bharat Sabha (Young Society of India) at Bradlaugh Hall in 1926. He was just coming to the end of his four-year tenure there, from 1922 to 1926. And the Sabha for him was to be the public face of the Hindustan Republican Association.

Bradlaugh Hall, however, has an illustrious past unknown to most Lahoris even today. If Bradlaugh Hall could speak, it would tell its own wistful story—a story of how in 1915 the Ghadar Party had its base here. With its enviable position in the heart of Lahore, Bradlaugh Hall had by the 1920s become the centre of political activity and had come to be known as such throughout India. From Pandit Jawaharlal Nehru to Quaid-e-Azam Muhammad Ali Jinnah and from Allama Muhammad Iqbal to Subhas Chandra Bose, all addressed their followers from Bradlaugh Hall. It was a bastion of art, literature and high culture. Cowasjee and Habib Seth, the two Parsi theatrical companies, performed here. *Mushairas* and stage dramas flourished in its large open spaces. F.E. Chaudhary, Lahore's first and all-time great news photographer, who died just before his 105th birthday in 2013, lamented the passing of its days of glory in his *Abb Woh Lahore Kahan*. Affectionately known as 'Chacha', he had much to lament about. He had seen the city's spiralling descent into decline and decay during his own lifetime.

The year 1921, when Bhagat Singh entered the National College, Lahore, was also the year when the Tilak School of Politics was founded on the same site. It was to be the turning point in Bhagat Singh's life. It was there that his intellectual transformation took place at the hands of such revolutionary teachers as Bhai Parmanand, Principal Chhabil Das and Professor Jaichandra Vidyalankar, who taught in the English medium. Vidyalankar at his home introduced Bhagat Singh to Sachindra Nath Sanyal, who went on to become the political guru of Bhagat Singh. These stalwarts rejected Gandhian non-violence in favour of a revolutionary overthrow of imperialism at a time of escalating anti-government feelings in Punjab. Bhagat Singh left National College, Lahore, in 1923 and fled for Kanpur without completing his degree when he came under family pressure to get married. In the process, he became the most famous icon of revolutionary pre-Independence India.

But then there was a reason why Bhagat Singh returned to Lahore to found the Naujawan Bharat Sabha at Bradlaugh Hall in 1926. A year earlier, the revolutionary movement had been all but vanquished when in 1925 ten men had ransacked the official treasury on a train in Lucknow which had been collecting monies from railway stations *en route*. Their purpose was to use the money thus looted from the train to fund the purchase of weaponry that they desperately needed to take on the British Raj. They were in a struggle for national freedom. However, those who had masterminded the robbery, namely Ram Prasad Bismil and Ashfaqullah Khan, were tracked down, tried and sentenced to be hanged for their troubles. This was what became known as the Kakori Conspiracy Case of 1925. With this the leadership of the revolutionary movement had been destroyed in one stroke.

Never one to give up, and rather like in Faiz's famous Partition poem, Bhagat Singh must have at this stage gritted his teeth and chastened himself with the words, '*Chale chalo keh woh manzil abhi nahin aayi,*' (Walk on, walk on, fellow traveller, for our destiny still lies ahead), because for him the leadership vacuum created an opportunity not to be missed. He was barely out of his teens then. And here he was proposing a new brand of politics, one which was the very antithesis of Gandhian satyagraha. A muscular revolutionary resistance against the imperialist Raj as opposed to Gandhi's passive non-cooperation was going to have to be the way forward. Bhagat Singh's politics was to stand for revolutionary violence, whereas Gandhi stood for non-revolutionary non-violence. In the popular mind, these positions came to be seen as two polar opposites. They predominate in the popular narrative of how the battle for Indian Independence was fought. The two traditions are two rival approaches in pre-independent India's quest for freedom. They incorporate contrasting strategies of resistance. The popular notion, however, is a gross simplification of the truth. And, here is why.

It is certainly true that Gandhi consciously stood for non-violence, but for him non-violence was a fetish. Bhagat Singh and his fellow revolutionaries took a much more practical, sophisticated and nuanced approach. While Gandhi drew from Indian mysticism, Bhagat Singh fervently rejected such unrealism, choosing instead to draw from a far wider range of sources. True it was that he sought inspiration from Indian revolutionaries such as Guru Gobind Singh and Shivaji, but he also learnt from Lafayette, Garibaldi and George Washington. In fact, the establishment of Naujawan Bharat Sabha, to bring Punjab's youth under one socialist non-religious banner, was inspired by Giuseppe Mazzini's Young Italy Movement in 1831. He realized that the foreign yoke of colonial oppression could not be lifted by turning the other cheek. Gandhi, of course, chose not to see this and strongly disapproved of Bhagat Singh's errant ways. When the young revolutionaries had the temerity to deviate from Gandhi's chosen path, he refused them support at all costs and thereby curried favour with the British. The revolutionaries in turn castigated him for his dogmatic adherence to utopian non-violence.

When twenty-four of the revolutionaries were tried in the Lahore Conspiracy Case 1931, they explained their approach to violence on the very first day of their trial by a special tribunal. This was on

5 May 1930 at Poonch House, where the Punjab Civil Secretariat offices are currently located in Lahore. Violence, they declared, was *not* a matter for them. It was up to their oppressors. They were merely reacting to their oppressors. In a four-page petition signed by five of the under-trials,[1] they made it clear that the special tribunal had no jurisdiction even to try them. They stood for a radical change, and colonial rule in India was the very negation of the principles of justice. So, every effort had to be made to bring about its end. This was morally justified because the government of the day was 'a pack of exploiters' who were only in control because they wielded the power of the sword against people and had 'predatory motives'. This government used the language of law and order. Their design, however, was to ignore the law and always to crush all those who opposed them. They forgot that people had inalienable rights. Indeed, if the choice lay with the revolutionaries, they would rather not use any violence at all. The revolutionaries lived by altruistic principles. They were lovers of peace. For the peace to be genuine and permanent, however, it had to be based on justice and equity. It had to be real and effective and could not be artificial and illusory. The government of the day could not impose it at the point of bayonets. Bombs and pistols were a matter of 'a terrible necessity' only. Violence for the sake of violence was not what the revolutionaries wanted. However, does the evidence support this thesis? It does if one looks at what Bhagat Singh was indicted for. The fact is that there were only ever two instances of purported violence on his part. One caused no human casualties, while the other did. Both are worthy of consideration.

The first was the throwing of two smoke bombs in the Central Legislative Assembly in Delhi on 8 April 1929. The aim was to prevent the passing of two government bills. The protest would 'make the deaf hear'. The act was carefully calculated not to injure anyone. In this, Bhagat Singh drew from the identical actions of the French anarchist Auguste Vaillant in 1893. He too had thrown a weak home-made device from the public gallery in the French Chamber of Deputies. His action caused only slight injuries to twenty deputies. He too had wanted only 'to make the deaf hear' in revenge for the execution of the fellow anarchist Ravachol. At his execution by guillotine, Vaillant had boldly proclaimed, 'Long live anarchy!' Bhagat Singh too employed the slogan '*Inquilab zindabad*' at his trial. And if Vaillant in 1893 wanted to cause maximum shock with minimum damage, then so too did Bhagat Singh in 1929. The fact that Bhagat Singh did not wish to cause physical injury to anyone but merely to draw attention to the iniquity of the two bills being passed showed how sophisticated and trailblazing he was when barely out of his teenage years.

Bhagat Singh's second act, however, did cause death. But it was deliberately calculated to do so to restore the honour of Punjab. It arose from the police beating and death of Lala Lajpat Rai. This had to be avenged, so an assassination was planned. Lala Lajpat Rai was no minor figure but a towering giant of the Independence Movement. He belonged to the trinity of early revolutionary leaders known as 'Bal, Pal, Lal', who consisted of *Bal* Gangadhar Tilak, Bipin Chandra *Pal* and *Lala* Lajpat Rai. All three had broken away from the Congress Party. Affectionately called '*Punjab Kesari*', Lala Lajpat Rai ('Lalaji') had set up the National College in Bradlaugh Hall to provide an alternative education centre to British institutions. When Lalaji was killed by police batons in what had been a peaceful demonstration, Bhagat Singh had to act. The policeman J.P. Saunders was shot on 17 December 1929 to avenge the death of Lalaji. It was a revenge attack. Immediately after the attack, the Hindustan Socialist Republican Association published a notice signed off by Bhagat Singh in which he described the assassination as a 'retaliatory action of none but a decisive nature' for the 'most dastardly attack made on the great old man of India' which 'hereby is avenged'. It was therefore as clear in its intent of settling a score as it was decisive.

This is how the shooting of J.P. Saunders was designed to salvage the honour of the people. Yet, Bhagat Singh was not left untouched by the death. He spent the following day in great anguish, and his writings show that he regretted taking a life. One of the Lahore Conspiracy accused later wrote how 'Bhagat Singh remained upset for some days'[2] after the murder. To him, violence was justified but only when it was a matter of moral necessity.

No one recognized this more clearly than Jawaharlal Nehru. He wrote, 'Bhagat Singh did not become popular because of his act of terrorism, but because he seemed to vindicate, for the moment, the honour of Lala Lajpat Rai; and through him of the nation.' This is why, '[w]ithin a few months, each town and village of the Punjab and to a lesser extent in the rest of northern India, resounded with Bhagat Singh's name' so that, '[i]nnumerable songs grew up about him, and the popularity that the man achieved, was something amazing'.[3]

Asaf Ali, his one-time lawyer who went on to become independent India's first ambassador to the USA, explained how after interviewing Bhagat Singh, he 'found him extremely human and gentle' being 'one of the gentlest and the most affectionate in temperament, the very antithesis of a hard and blood-thirsty revolutionary' so that 'had he been spared he would have been an outstanding personality in any field of life'.[4] Jaidev Gupta, Bhagat Singh's friend, also attested to his gentleness when he recalled much later that, 'had you the fortune of seeing him you would have never forgotten the broad charming smile and pleasing manners with which he would have received you'.

We can compare such impeccable moral coherence of Bhagat Singh's outlook with that of Mahatma Gandhi's doctrinaire belief in non-violent satyagraha at all costs. Gandhi insisted on non-violence even when it made no sense. This is why in the long run it did not work and he had to give it up. Nothing illustrates this better than the violent Chauri Chaura incident of 1922 in Uttar Pradesh. A large group of volunteers was participating in a protest against high food prices. The group was part of the non-cooperation movement of Mahatma Gandhi himself. During the protest, however, the police overreacted. They beat up the demonstrators and arrested their leaders. Then they locked them up at the Chauri Chaura police station. Two days later, on 4 February, there was a peaceful march against police brutality at the local marketplace. This is when police reaction got even worse—they fired on the gathered crowd.

An enraged mob now set the police station on fire and burned twenty-three policemen alive in the process.

What did Mahatma Gandhi do? His immediate concern was to appease the rulers of the Raj. So, a week later, on 12 February 1922, he called off the entire non-cooperation movement. This was just as it was beginning to become effective. He took the decision without consulting anyone. This left many stunned. Others in the non-cooperation movement, such as Jawaharlal Nehru, Sardar Patel and Rajendra Prasad felt positively aggrieved and let down. Gandhi's betrayal left them in a political vacuum. A party founded in 1885 as an organization representing Indian elites and comprising upper castes and classes was not unknown to benefit from colonial rule, while still protesting against the iniquities of the British Raj. Even for them this betrayal was a bit much. The non-violent resistance movement became discredited. Into the vacuum created by Gandhi poured in the angst of a new revolutionary politics. At its helm stood none other than Bhagat Singh.

The publication of this book is timely for this reason. It coincides with the hundred-year anniversary of the 1922 schism in Indian politics. This is when many split from Gandhi and when Bhagat Singh actively began advocating the overthrow of colonial rule by revolution. It is the decisive moment when he totally distanced himself from Mahatma Gandhi's creed of non-violence. Bhagat Singh's pursuit of India's freedom would take a different course, which we may reflect upon in the 75th year of Indian independence in 2022.

In fact, compared to the actions of Mahatma Gandhi over the 1922 Chauri Chaura incident, Bhagat Singh's throwing of two bombs into the Central Legislative Assembly on 8 April 1929 with B.K. Dutt 'to make the deaf hear' was a highly sophisticated and strategic act. It came in the form of a spectacular demonstration of the rejection of continued British occupation in India, but it did so without causing any lasting personal damage to anyone. In the ensuing trial, Bhagat Singh would have escaped with a long prison sentence, but unfortunately for him, it was the police investigations that followed the bomb blast, which then revealed that members of the Hindustan Socialist Republican Army (HSRA) had also been behind the 17 December 1928 assassination of a British official, J.P. Saunders. Sadly, for Saunders, he was mistaken for his boss, J.A. Scott, the superintendent of police who had been in charge when the nationalist figure, Lala Lajpat Rai, was assaulted in October 1928 by police batons. However, although the 1929 manifesto of the HSRA had proclaimed that 'Revolution is Law, Revolution is Order and Revolution is the Truth' in consequence of which 'the youths of our nation have realised this truth', what was meant by 'revolution' was not that it was a single event but an immutable, imperishable and perpetual quest for rebirth, recovery, and regeneration of the present. This meant that it need not be violent. Saunders' assassination was not violence as a political philosophy. This is why it was universally applauded in India. Bhagat Singh's immense popularity immediately thereafter showed him to have vindicated the honour of the Indian people. He alone took the step that he did with Sukhdev and Rajguru. No one else in the Congress Party did.

The Lahore Conspiracy case that followed became one of the most controversial trials of British India. Twenty-four members of the HSRA were initially charged with conspiracy against the government. When Bhagat Singh was moved from the Delhi prison to Mianwali Jail, he objected to the inequalities of treatment between European inmates and Indian inmates. He demanded parity in standards of food, clothing and toiletries. He also demanded to be treated as a political prisoner, with books and a daily newspaper being made available to him and others. He and his fellow prisoners also objected to manual labour and other undignified work. These demands were set out in a 24 June 1929 letter to the Home Member. In protest for these demands a hunger strike followed. After sixty-three days, one of their number, Jatindra Nath Das, died on 13 September 1929. The hunger strikers became household names. Uproar engulfed the country. Bhagat Singh went 116 days without food, surpassing a previous record held by the Irish hunger strikers. It took a heavy toll on him as his weight fell dramatically and he lost 14 lbs (6.4 kg) from his pre-strike weight of 133 lbs (60 kg).

In the trial that followed, the accused were able to roundly denounce British authority. The proceedings were daily reported in the Lahore-based paper *The Tribune*, whose editor was sympathetic to their cause. Congressmen too rallied to support them. The defiance and bravery of the accused were carefully showcased in the newspapers. Though debilitated by hunger, they still ran rings around the magistrate, undermining his authority and exposing the proceedings to ridicule.

The trial began as a normal one. It was before a regular magistrate and was presided over by Rai Sahib Pandit Sri Kishen. He started hearing the case on 10 July 1929. The trial carried with it a right of appeal for the accused against conviction. The appeal would go before a regular high court judge in Lahore. The trial even ran for ten months, during which time the hunger strike was called off on 5 October 1929. Over 200 witnesses were examined. But then it ended abruptly. The Governor-General Lord Irwin decided that these normal proceedings should be transferred to a 'special tribunal' (which was to become a blue-print for modern-day terrorist trials before special courts). In this way, the magistrate's trial was dramatically halted. This is despite the fact that it had been running for close to a year. How did Lord Irwin manage this stupendous feat?

He managed to do so because the governor-general signed off the Lahore Ordinance III of 1930 on 1 May 1930 from his Simla residence. Yet, under Section 72 of the Government of India Act, this could only be done if there was an 'Emergency', and the ordinance had to be for the 'peace and good governance' of India or any part of it. None of these conditions existed when the regular trial before a magistrate was so precipitously abandoned. The ordinance was not approved by the Central Assembly or the British Parliament. There was to be a three-judge special tribunal. It was not to sit in the regular courtrooms but at Poonch House. It was also not allowed to run the trial for another ten months to complete the remaining witnesses. Instead, it was mandated to complete the hearing within a fixed period of six months. This is because the Section 72 power of the Government of India Act could only be exercised as an 'emergency' for six months. After this, the tribunal would be functus officio. This is how the Lahore Conspiracy Case began on 5 May 1930. The 457 prosecution witnesses who were due to give evidence thereafter were not presented for cross-examination to the defence counsel. Only one of the five 'approvers' (i.e., 'super-grasses') was presented for cross-examination. Within two-weeks, two of the three judges had been sacked. Justice Coldstream was removed because he presided over the police beating of defendants in court when he took grave exception to their singing a revolutionary song in court. Justice Agha Haider, the only Indian judge, was sacked for not supporting such brutality. When prosecution counsel Carden Noad went to see him at his house (itself a breach of etiquette), Agha Haider reprimanded him with the words, 'I am a judge, not a butcher.' The Lahore Bar condemned the proceedings. They made it clear that the ordinance was ultra vires and invalid. There was 'no justification whatsoever for depriving the High Court of its power of hearing the appeal from the final order of the Special Tribunal . . .' Unsurprisingly, for five months, from May 1930 until the sentence of death on 7 October 1930, the accused refused to attend court. In the end, when the tribunal judgment came and handed down the sentence of death, it could not be challenged. There was no right of appeal to the Lahore High Court.

The full implications of the Lahore Ordinance III of 1930 have rarely been understood. It was never meant for the creation of a judicial tribunal. The power did not exist in the ordinance for this to be done. Lord Irwin must have known that. But the reasons Lord Irwin gave for promulgating the ordinance were poor. His statement only has four paragraphs. He begins by reasoning that '[t]wo of the accused had resorted to hunger strike before commencement . . .' and that '[a] number of others followed the same course shortly afterwards with the result that by the 26 July 1929, the case had to be adjourned owing to some of the accused being unfit to attend Court' (at para. 2). Trial courts, however, have to deal with all kinds of disruptive behaviour. This can come from intrepid lawyers or from obstructive defendants. Not infrequently, it is both. Some of it is quite unruly. None could remotely have been said to lead to an 'emergency' where 'peace and good governance of British India' was at stake in this case. Lord Irwin knew this. This is why his statement of reasons ends rather lamely with the explanation that the special tribunal is necessary 'to deal with wilful obstruction'. If going on a hunger strike is wilful obstruction, then that is the right of every political prisoner. It was not new. And it was certainly not 'wilful obstruction' even in the Lahore Conspiracy Case. It had been tried by the Irish freedom-fighters when they too had taken up the cudgels against British rule. Indian revolutionaries actually took their inspiration from them. These reasons were so poor that they stood to be immediately challenged as irrational and unsustainable. The Lahore Bar did exactly that. And yet, it did not end there. Lord Irwin took the step of transposing the existing proceedings into a special tribunal to take place away from the regular courts at Poonch House, near the tomb of Anarkali in Lahore. Such an exercise of power under Section 72 was simply impermissible as this section does not provide for a judicial tribunal to be created for six months, and certainly not when 457 witnesses have to be heard!

Lord Irwin's actions, therefore, amounted to a gross abuse of power. The Section 72 power was designed to deal with an 'emergency', which had to threaten the 'peace and good government' of British India. It was meant for riots, revolts and civil disturbances, such as the one in 1919 in Punjab, (as depicted so memorably in Pandit Pearay Mohan's *The Punjab 'Rebellion' of 1919 and How it was Suppressed*). The grant to the governor-general of an exceptional power is to deal with an extenuating situation. In such a situation he may impose a curfew and restrict civil liberties. Whatever he does, however, he can only do for a period of six months. After that, he must return everything to normalcy. This is de rigeur under the statute. Had Section 72 been intended to authorize the creation of a judicial tribunal in an emergency situation, it would have stated so and that would have been *without* a six-month time restriction. Otherwise, the six-month limit makes no sense. What if a six-month judicial tribunal is set up, but after which 'peace and good government' are still not restored because the 'emergency' continues? Does the special tribunal have to abort proceedings nevertheless because six months have come and gone? What if the remaining 457 witnesses cannot be heard in six months, as in Bhagat Singh's case in which Rai Sahib Pandit Sri Kishen had heard only some 200 witnesses in ten months of hearings, because there was just not enough time to hear them all? What then? The question deserves an answer because this is exactly what happened in Bhagat Singh's case. The 457 witnesses could not be heard because there was no time to hear them all in six months. In the end, all that this exercise of Section 72 did was to deprive the accused of due process and the right to a fair trial.

This is how the law in Bhagat Singh's case was used coercively by the colonial authorities for the purposes of an extrajudicial execution. It was a case of colonial coercive legalism. The rule of law was suspended but its rubric was retained. What is the consequence of such an illegality? Should the verdict be set aside after all these years? If so, by which court and where? And should the Indian government be involved? Or, should there be an apology? If so, by whom and to whom? None of the original participants are alive, and there are no living persons with rights to vindicate. Yet, the issue may still be worth considering. There is a case for saying that, rather than an apology being demanded, Bhagat Singh's conviction and sentence should be set aside by virtue of the grant of a royal pardon. He was convicted and hanged in the face of gross procedural irregularities and denial of due process and natural justice. Judicial orders that he be allowed interviews with his father and his legal advisers to best prepare his defence were deliberately flouted by the jail authorities under blatant government pressure so that in the end he and others on trial simply stopped attending court. On the face of it, the rule of law was preserved, but underneath it all it had been hollowed out through a relentless abuse of executive power by the colonial state. Letters and petitions produced in this book, previously never published, show the remorseless determination by which he continued to bring these concerns before the court but to no avail. The law on the grant of a royal pardon is such that it has been well established in the UK for thirty years. It is clear in its intent, 'that it is an error to regard the prerogative of mercy as a prerogative right which is only exercisable in cases which fall into specific categories', in that '[t]he prerogative is a flexible power and its exercise can and should be adapted to meet the circumstances of the particular case'. This is why in the UK the High Court case of *ex p. Bentley [1993] EWHC Admin 2*, Lord Justice Watkins was able to rule that '[t]he prerogative of mercy can no longer be regarded as no more than an arbitrary monarchical right of grace and favour' and that '[i]t is now a constitutional safeguard against mistakes'. Bhagat Singh's hanging was a clear mistake of law.

Does it matter, however, if the condemned have long since been executed? It would appear not, because under the common law '. . . there is no objection in principle to the grant of a posthumous conditional pardon where a death sentence has already been carried out' because '[t]he grant of such a pardon is a recognition by the state that a mistake was made and that a reprieve should have been granted'.

One person at the time who recognized the travesty of justice in the Lahore Conspiracy Case 1931 and was also prepared to publicly say so was Jawaharlal Nehru. In a speech in Allahabad on 12 October 1930, he unequivocally lambasted the judgment of the special tribunal and its sentence of death. His caustic words did not spare the viceroy and governor-general of India either. It was an unsettling time. But Nehru was unafraid.

Three Round Table Conferences were planned between 1930 and 1932 by the British government with the Indian National Congress. They were to consider constitutional reform in India. All of this was to happen against the background of the visit of the Simon Commission to Lahore, when on 30 October 1928 Lala Lajpat Rai was pummelled by police batons. His death on 17 November 1928 led to Bhagat Singh seeking retribution in the awful murder of J.P. Saunders on 17 December 1928. Nehru was aware of all this when he ventured to openly support the violent actions of Bhagat Singh and his comrades in carrying out the assassination. He had the temerity to ask of the viceroy whether, '[i]f England were invaded by Germany or Russia, would Lord Irwin go about advising the people to refrain from violence against the invader?'. He had no compunction in telling him that '[w]hether I agree with him or not, my heart is full of admiration for the courage and self-sacrifice of a man like Bhagat Singh' because '[c]ourage of the Bhagat Singh type is exceedingly rare' so '[i]f the Viceroy expects us to refrain from admiring this wonderful courage and high purpose behind it, he is mistaken'. In this way, the suave and urbane Nehru was able to justify the use of 'violence against the invader', which the Indian revolutionaries fighting for Indian freedom were deploying, but attracting so much opprobrium for, and not least from Gandhi. An appeal lay to the Privy Council in London. It was on a point of law only for what was a capital offence. Six days before the appeal was heard, Jawaharlal's father, Motilal Nehru, sent a message from Simla from his sick bed. On 6 February 1931, five days before the Privy Council hearing date, he quietly passed away. His petition pleading on behalf of the condemned men was not even admitted to a regular hearing by the Board of the Privy Council.

On a misty February morning in far-off London, a tenacious forty-four-year-old British lawyer, D.N. Pritt, disembarked from a taxi in Downing Street to appear before the Privy Council to plead against the death sentence on Bhagat Singh, Sukhdev and Rajguru. It was the last straw. Pritt knew he had an uphill struggle as the five-member panel of the Board of the Privy Council was not sympathetic. Educated at Winchester College, he had turned against the establishment. He was to go on to argue a string of revolutionary cases, from the Meerut Conspiracy Case in 1933 (for which his grateful clients gave him a silk gown which is still in his chambers in London), to Ho Chi Minh in 1932, to Jomo Kenyatta and the Mau Mau in 1952 (which is why there is today a 'Dennis Pritt Road' named in Nairobi after him). Highly respected, he could get away with saying things in the apex court which others could only have dreamt of. On one occasion when faced with a relentless judicial onslaught, he quipped: 'I will answer your Lordships's questions if

I can have the courtesy of two minutes without interruption.' On another occasion, frustrated, he sniped at the court: 'It's apparent that your Lordships have not taken in a word I have been saying. I shall have to start again. May it please your Lordships'. Perhaps his most noteworthy sally is when in the 1930s the UK authorities unlawfully detained a Russian ship carrying arms for the elected republican government in Spain, which was facing a fascist rebellion. Pritt spent a fruitless day before the Chief Justice of Gibraltar (known to be a fascist sympathizer) trying to get the ship released. When the judge rose at the end of the day, Pritt remained seated:

CJ: Mr Pritt, I am leaving the court.
DNP: I am very pleased to hear it.
CJ: It is customary, Mr Pritt, for counsel to rise as a mark of respect.
DNP: That is why I am remaining seated.

On the occasion of D.N. Pritt's defence of Bhagat Singh, however, he did not fare so well. The judges' attitude towards Pritt ranged from apoplectic outrage to haughty contempt. Pritt argued that the reasons given for the ordinance by Lord Irwin could not in law be justified. At the end, in *Bhagat Singh v. The Kings Emperor 1931*, without even calling upon the government lawyer to respond, Lord Dunedin handed down a one-and-a-half-page judgment in which he ruled that 'although the Governor-General thought fit to expound the reasons which induced him to promulgate this Ordinance, this was not in their Lordships opinion incumbent on him as a matter of law'. This was quite simply wrong. Even at the best of times, it would have been a proposition of dubious legal validity to say that the giving of reasons for an emergency ordinance was not even necessary. Bhagat Singh, Sukhdev and Rajguru mounted the gallows the following month on 23 March 1931. When they did so, they acquired the status of martyrdom.

In this way, Bhagat Singh differed once again from Gandhi in his belief in 'martyrdom'. For him, it was the ultimate sacrifice to be prepared to lay down one's life for a just cause. When he was just eight years old, Bhagat Singh was witness to the First Lahore Conspiracy Case of 1915. This is when on 17 November 1915, seven Ghadar martyrs were executed inside Lahore Prison. One of these was the nineteen-year-old Kartar Singh Sarabha, whose photograph Bhagat Singh carried in his pocket. Bhagat Singh's own execution now provided the nationalists' cause with a martyr at a time when few prominent figures gave their lives. It is the symbolic value of such martyrdom that has through time proved to be of inestimable value.

Gandhi was derided for failing to save these young men whom he described as 'deluded patriots'. He had meetings with Lord Irwin but did not insist on clemency. Deluded or not, the fact remains that Bhagat Singh forged a new ideological pathway as never before. Indian revolutionaries had hitherto only rejected the twin evils of capitalism and colonialism. Bhagat Singh wanted to do more. He rejected religion because it alienated the masses. But the rejection of religion for Bhagat Singh also had instrumentalist objectives. It served his socialist agenda of denouncing another towering edifice of oppression, namely, casteism. In this way, Bhagat Singh linked capitalism with casteism. He was the first revolutionary to do so. Yet, he was only twenty-three years old at the time of his execution. From the time he left National College in Lahore, the period of his activism was just seven years, from 1924 to 1931.

Today Bhagat Singh has achieved the unique distinction of being the only person who unites India and Pakistan in his vision of what they stand for as independent nations. His death anniversary on 23 March is celebrated as 'Bhagat Singh Day' in Pakistan every year. There are poems and songs recited in his name on the very spot where he was hanged. When there are causes to fight for, student demonstrations and protests carry banners dedicated to him.

Pakistan has long been in search of suitable icons. For a long time, one such was thought to be Zulfikar Ali Bhutto, the man accredited with democratizing and empowering Pakistan's poor in the 1970s. Bhutto was progressive, socialist and liberal. However, he made the cardinal error of appeasing his right-wing religious opponents by defining a Muslim in Pakistan's 1973 Constitution making Ahmedis outcasts. Bhagat Singh avoided such pitfalls, which is why some three-quarters of a century after his hanging, the high court in Pakistan was presented with a petition on 3 February 2016 to set aside the verdict of death on Bhagat Singh. That petition is still pending.

In India too, Bhagat Singh has been remembered during the largest labour protest in human history, when no less than 1,25,000 farmers protested in retaliation to the passing of three ordinances on agricultural marketing. These were passed by the Modi government on 5 June 2020. Aimed at 'modernizing' Indian agriculture by opening it up to market forces, they brought about the biggest popular revolt against the government. What has been most interesting, however, is that along the several kilometres between the Tikri border in Delhi and Haryana's Bahadurgarh, where Punjab and Haryana's farmers have found a new cultural unity, it has been the name of Bhagat Singh that has been ringing out in musical performances, songs and dances—a sobering reminder perhaps of the words of the poet Faiz Ahmed Faiz: *'Vo intizar tha jis ka ye vo sahar to nahin'* ('This is not the dawn we were waiting for'). What that dawn could have been is what this book is about. India deserves an answer after 75 years. And it lies in the now-forgotten story of Bhagat Singh.

Satvinder S. Juss
Vaisakhi, 2022

PART 1

KHATKAR KALAN, BANGA AND LAHORE

Ishrat-e-qatra hai dariya mein fana ho jaana
Dard ka had se guzarna hai dava ho jaana

The drop's joy is to perish in the ocean
as pain's joy is to become a potion.

—Mirza Ghalib

1

1840, Fateh Singh

Bhagat Singh was born on 27 September 1907 in a small village by the name of 'Banga'. It was then the Lyallpur district of undivided Indian Punjab. Today it is located in Pakistan under the new name of Faisalabad. The old name still persists though, and many continue to refer to it as Lyallpur district. Bhagat Singh's origin lay, however, in the Jalandhar district in his family's ancestral village of Khatkar Kalan, and this continues to remain on the Indian side of Punjab. Banga in Pakistan is not to be confused with Banga in India. The former is situated roughly 20 km from both Faisalabad and Jaranwala, and 133 km from Lahore. Banga town, just outside the village of Khatkar Kalan in India, is 8 km from Nawanshahr district, which was formed in 1995 from the districts of Hoshiarpur and Jalandhar in Indian Punjab. Nawanshahr in turn was renamed on 27 September 2008 as Shahid Bhagat Singh Nagar on the 101st birth anniversary of Bhagat Singh by Chief Minister Prakash Singh Badal. The two towns of Banga are manifestations of two representations of Bhagat Singh's life—one in Pakistan and one in India.

So Bhagat Singh was born in Banga on the Pakistan side even though there is also a Banga on the Indian side. In his birth, therefore, as in everything else that Bhagat Singh did in his short life, he made it possible for the two countries of India and Pakistan to be able to lay a claim on his person despite the communal bloodshed that accompanied Independence in 1947 that pitched one community against the other. No other political leader, before Partition or since, has been able to achieve such a feat.

And yet, Bhagat Singh's anomaly did not rest there. His father, Sardar Kishan Singh, and his mother, Mata Vidyavati were both staunch 'Arya Samajhis' (which in Sanskrit means 'Society of Nobles'). The Arya Samaj was founded in 1875 by Swami Dayananda Saraswati. It was dedicated to reforming modern Hinduism by consecrating the Vedas, eliminating caste and idolatry and emphasizing the scriptures of the Hindus. The movement believed that scripture alone was demonstrative of a revealed truth. The family had a strong political streak, and in this sense, Bhagat Singh's destiny appears to have been written earlier than he could himself have willed.

Opinions may differ as to whether the timing of his birth was auspicious. His father and two of his uncles, Ajit Singh and Swaran Singh, having just been released by the British for anti-government activities for their audacious protests against the Punjab Land Colonisation Bill 1906, were comfortably arriving home from jail as he was just arriving into this febrile world from his mother's womb. The 1906 bill was pernicious. A farmer dying without an heir would see his land being sold off by the government to wealthy and powerful land developers or zamindars. Oddly, this group had an unwavering allegiance to the British. Less than a half score years earlier, the Punjab Land Alienation Act 1900 had already succeeded in causing immense resentment amongst the elite urban classes. Bhagat Singh's family would now take up the cudgels against the British Government on behalf of the dispossessed farmers. This is how the Colonisation Bill would become the catalyst for the beginning of the freedom movement in Punjab. Bhagat Singh would ride on that wave because throughout his life he held an unalloyed adoration for the sacrifices of his uncles.

Bhagat Singh's father was Kishan Singh, the eldest amongst three siblings. His paternal uncles were Ajit Singh, who was next in line, followed by Swaran Singh, the youngest of the three brothers. They belonged to a middle-class family of Sandhu Jats and were relatively well-off. Nevertheless, they were heirs to the radical politics of Bal Gangadhar Tilak, Bipin Chandra Pal and Lala Lajpat Rai (the trio known as 'Lal-Bal-Pal') which preceded the Gandhian politics of non-violent passive resistance to the British. The two older Sandhu brothers stood in fierce opposition to the leadership of the Indian National Congress and were adept at garnering local support whenever the need arose. Both were radical politicians in their own right. The influence of both on Lal-Bal-Pal is clear from an article in Urdu that Bhagat Singh himself wrote, aptly titled 'Emergence of the Punjab in the Freedom Movement'.[1] There he emphasized how Punjab became a cauldron of radical politics in the early years of the twentieth century, long before Gandhianism was popular. In particular, Bhagat Singh highlights the extremist influence on his family elders of Bal Gangadhar Tilak. He refers to 'their enthusiasm at the 1906 Congress Convention in Calcutta', as a result of which 'Lokmaniya was pleased and in bidding them adieu, gave them the responsibility of strengthening the movement in the Punjab'.

When the two Sandhu brothers returned to Lahore, they immediately 'started a monthly newspaper called *Bharat Mata* to propagate their ideas'. However, they were short of money and had no financial backing from the rich. So they undertook to do everything themselves. They rang a bell and brought together a crowd in the market. There they gave a lecture 'on how foreigners had destroyed India's industry and commerce'. There followed an announcement. Within a week, a meeting would be held at the offices of the *Bharat Mata* to consider the struggle for Indian Independence. The meeting on Sunday went well. It was thereafter decided that meetings would be held every Sunday in this way. Very soon, others of greater eminence joined in. There was the national poet of Punjab, Lala Lalchand 'Phalak' as well as Lala Pindidas, Dr Ishwari Prasad and Sufi Amba Prasad, to name a few. Ajit Singh was elected president and Mahant Nandkishore was elected secretary, and their organization was christened hereafter 'Bharat Mata Society'.[2]

If Bhagat Singh carried a heavy burden of his family's rebellious streak, it was not just on account of the activities of his father and his two uncles. His family's mutinous attitude is all too visible if one chooses to look at his distant ancestors. Here it becomes all too clear that if redemption was required for this Sandhu Jat family, Bhagat Singh's family had much to be redeemed for. His great-great grandfather, Fateh Singh, fought in the 1840s for Maharajah Ranjit Singh's kingdom in the Anglo-Sikh Wars. Victory went to the British, and Fateh Singh ended up with half his land being confiscated by them. When he faced the chance to redeem himself, he had the impertinence to decline it. During the 1857 insurrection (during which the Sikhs of Punjab sided with the British), Sir John Lawrence offered to return the confiscated land to those who would join the British against the Great Revolt. Fateh Singh would have none of it. He staunchly refused to lend him his support.[3] The result was that he never saw the return of his lands.

By then Punjab had already been annexed following the fall of the Sikh Empire in 1849. Comprehensive systems of political governance were established in the province thereafter, to finance which the British instigated an efficient land revenue administration, so that from the 1860s onwards Punjab was seen as a 'model agricultural province' in which the loyalty and prosperity of its cultivators became a matter of high colonial priority. For a time, nationalist agitators had the wind taken out of their sails, and the British set out to reconcile political stability with agricultural development. This was easier said than done.[4] So, given its situation as a frontier region, through which invaders had flowed from the time of Alexander the Great, it had to be annexed. This was the political exigency of the day. After 1857, when the rest of India revolted, the rulers were left in little doubt that Punjab had a strategic location. The loyalty of Punjab in the so-called Indian Mutiny of 1857 only strengthened its status for the British. The province provided a stream of Muslim and Sikh soldiers. These helped the British to impose their authority on the rest of India, especially on the Gangetic Plains, where Punjabi soldiers saved British India in 1857. In 1901, five frontier states were annexed to become the North West Frontier Province, further emphasizing the distinctive importance of Punjab to the British. With the Indian Army drawing as much as three-fifths of its recruits from Punjab alone, 'the Punjabization of the Indian Army' was complete even though the Punjabis were only one-tenth of British India's total population.[5] No wonder Punjab was so pivotal to British thinking.

2

1876, Swaraj

In Punjab, the colonial state wanted to develop an expanding commercial society that had a visible presence in the world economy. To succeed, however, it had to locate such activity in an indigenous political base. The result was that while to the public the legal system seemed intent on enforcing modern commercial transactions, privately it shored up age-old traditional structures. In the public realm, the law drew upon commercial and criminal law principles that were inherently British. In the private realm, the indigenous status of landholders still prevailed. This is how the dichotomy between 'modern' public law and 'traditional' private law arose in British India. It linked the state with rural intermediaries. Customary law was given primacy for this reason over religious law. The paternalistic system of imperial rule had already earlier seen the passage of the Punjab Laws Act 1872. Under this, the personal law of an individual was no longer to be found in Islamic law or a Hindu religious framework. It was to be rooted rather in tribal customary law, which differed from religious law in crucial areas of inheritance. Whereas under Islamic sharia law female rights would have been more generous than under customary tribal law, the British preference for the latter was intended to free it from a religious system, which would have excluded Christian claimants as outsiders.[1] The colonial state was in this way able to strengthen its authority, because it could augment the pattern of rural social organization through a rationalization of the applicable laws. As a result, land transfer policy, canal colonization policy and the development of a system of colonial law in Punjab 'triumphed unequivocally' in tying Punjab's agricultural economy into the world market, so that 'a laissez-faire approach to political economy was jettisoned in favour of restrictions on land transfer' and 'customary tribal law was privileged over both western and religious law . . .'.[2] Punjab ended up following a different trajectory to other regions[3] with respect to agrarian relations. This is how, as Talbot observes, 'tradition and transformation served the purposes of the colonial state by justifying the exercise of British power'.[4] All, however, was not as well as it seemed and problems festered underneath the beguiling calm of Punjab's seeming success story.

It was no mean success story. By the 1860s, Punjab's agricultural prices on produce had risen dramatically. Political instability had ended. A canal system of agriculture, based on an improved communications network, had been set up to foster a new prosperity. New cash crops had also been introduced, such as wheat, sugarcane, cotton and even tobacco. By the 1920s, a third of British India's total wheat crop and a tenth of its cotton crop was being produced in Punjab. The problem was that this prosperity was accompanied by increased rural debt. Easy credit meant that farmers borrowed money with abandon. Untrammelled consumption was the order of the day. Lavish sums were expended on weddings. Urban moneylenders used the British legal system to foreclose debts of mortgaged land. This threatened a revolution in landholding. In the backward regions of Punjab, such as Dera Ghazi Khan, moneylenders began appropriating land at a colossal rate. It was to curb this alarming development that the Land Alienation Act 1900 was passed. This prevented the urban commercial castes from permanently acquiring land held by the 'statutory agriculturalist' tribes. In the words of Ian Talbot, '[t]his Magna Carta of the Punjab's peasantry structured political developments in the province for the remainder of the Colonial era.'[5]

This meant that the agriculturalists remained loyal to the British. They abjured communalism in their common interest, which was the defence of their rights and privileges against the Hindu moneylenders in the city. The Congress Party failed to get a strong foothold in Punjab (where the Punjab Unionist Party reigned supreme) against the British because it favoured the urban Hindu moneylenders and was consequently weaker in Punjab than in any other state.

The rural population, and not the townsfolk, were politically predominant. And they were loyal to the British because this loyalty had been secured by new franchise arrangements. These had accompanied the Land Alienation Act 1900, by virtue of cross-community cooperation and coalition politics. The countryside stood as a discrete entity from the towns. The two were siphoned off from each other. The effect of this was that the Jat peasant farmers of East Punjab, together with their Muslim landlords in the west, shared a common bond as power-holders in resistance to the urban commercial castes. Their anti-urban bias began to be collectively reinforced as their debt rose and the price of the produce fell in the inter-war years. Jat farmers and Muslim landlords both joined the Punjab Unionist Party in a cross-communal grouping. They became a formidable force, so much so that in the 1920s and 1930s peasant unrest fuelled by the Kisan Sabha was overcome by the Punjab Unionist Party as it continued to bolster British rule, reaching its apogee in this regard during the Second World War, when it helped in the recruitment effort. Indeed, as Talbot observes, 'communal violence only spread to the Punjab countryside when the Unionist led collaborative mechanism broke down on the very eve of independence'.[6]

So, British paranoia over the continued stability of the Raj was not unjustified. Swami Dayananda Saraswati called for Swaraj just twenty years after the revolt of 1857. He was the first person in India to do so (not Gandhi). Swaraj, a word which derives from the ancient Indian language of Sanskrit, where *sva* means self, or one's own, and *raj* means rule, had worrying forebodings for the British. Swami Dayananda Saraswati invoked the time-honoured Vedic principle in 1876 with his slogan of 'India for Indians'. This enabled him to form a new political organization, in the form of the reformist Hindu crusade of Arya Samaj. Though a family of Sikhs, Bhagat Singh's grandfather Arjan Singh was a steadfast devotee of Swami, so that he prevented his grandson Bhagat Singh from attending the Khalsa High School in Lahore, which was almost *de rigueur* for all Sikh boys in those days, as the school governors were loyal to the British government. Arjan Singh deplored this to such as extent that he had his grandson enlisted instead at the Dayananda Anglo-Vedic High School, which was a far less servile Arya Samajic institution. Arjan Singh joined the Arya Samaj in 1877, which was only a year after Swami Dayananda Saraswati raised the call for Swaraj. He was the first Sikh to do so. Swami Dayananda Saraswati himself initiated (i.e. gave *diksha)* the Sikh into the fold.[7]

Arjan Singh had plenty of reasons to take this step. In the 1890s, after the British Government in Punjab decided to colonize the forest area, they declared that every colonizer would be awarded 25 acres of free land. In 1897, Arjan Singh had left his native ancestral village of Khatkar Kalan, in Jalandhar district, India, to move to Banga village in Lyallpur. This was a tumultuous time, because as Imran Ali explains, '[t]he great agricultural colonisation schemes undertaken in the western Punjab under British rule turned this area into a virtual human laboratory, as castes, clans, and tribes from different parts of the province converged on the new lands'.[8]

In the unfolding melee, Arjan Singh's entire family was politicized. He had an elder brother, Surjan Singh, who appears to have been no less distinguished because he took part as a delegate at the Lahore Session of the Indian National Congress in 1893, when it was presided over by Dadabhai Naoroji. In 1922, Arjan Singh himself set out for Jaranwala Town to boycott the arrival of foreign cloth in India, instigated by the non-cooperation movement, even though upon his arrival there he learnt that Gandhi had decided to call off the picketing. It was, however, in Banga village itself that Arjan Singh made his lasting contribution. It was not just that he built a Sikh temple (i.e., a *gurudwara*) there. He also dug two wells that still exist. He constructed a guesthouse (i.e., *sarai*) for travellers coming from far and wide. His house was a refuge for revolutionaries and activists, many of whom were engaging in banned activities against the British. He performed the duties of a village doctor (i.e., *hakim*) providing free treatment for the poor. His wife Jai Kaur (Bhagat Singh's grandmother) was no less accomplished, mixing the traditional herbal medicines and preparing them for her husband and acquiring the medical skills of bone-setting for the injured and saving the nationalists who took refuge with them from unsuspecting police raids. According to M.M. Juneja, 'she was perhaps the first woman in Punjab who, by virtue of her welfare activities, had the honour of becoming a member of the village *panchayat*'[9] (i.e. village council of elders). So it was not just the men in heritage but also the women who had a formative influence on Bhagat Singh.

3

1887, Chenab Colony

Few people in India today, familiar with Punjab's acclaim as the 'bread-basket' of India, recall the long road to its prosperity taken during those colonial days. Few remember how its modern lineage is traceable to the Canal Colonies of West Punjab during the heady days of the Raj. Fewer still can remember 1887, when the Chenab Colony was created by the Punjab government. This move diverted the waters of the River Chenab into a series of permanent canals and dramatically transformed what was a dry barren wasteland into a spectacularly fertile land, ripe for farming.[1] It is what made the Chenab Colony a model of success as a system of paternalistic administration. It created higher standards of living[2] by implementing carefully crafted methods of sanitation, economic planning and governmental bipartisanship. Yet, the colonial rulers of the Raj were not content to stop there. The model had to be emulated throughout the province. In this way, British colonial policy managed to privilege Punjab's agrarian development over its industrial growth. Security measures after the 1857 rebellion, during which Punjab played a strategic role, were aimed at keeping Punjabi farmers happy. It is worth recalling once again how the waters of the five rivers of the region were harnessed under the Canal Colonies project in an ambitious irrigation development project in such a way that the astonishing transformation of six million acres of desert into one of the richest agricultural regions of the whole of Asia became not just 'a stupendous engineering feat' but also 'the Colonial State's greatest achievement'. In this way, 'nowhere were the ideals of the modern rational state better epitomised than in the neatly laid squares of land in the canal colony villages'.[3] This is also when the eight bazaars of the new market town of Lyallpur, radiating out from the central clock tower, were laid out. And yet, there was a downside that arose from an insuperable contradiction. It was not a minor matter of detail. Where there was order there was also transformation. The two made uncomfortable bed-fellows. Local settlement officers wanted to espouse a modern cultivator in the ordered world of the colony villages. But the Lieutenant-Governor Sir Charles Aitcheson simply wanted 'a manly peasantry capable of self-support and of loyal . . . disposition'.[4]

The Punjab Colonisation of Land Bill was introduced by the government in these circumstances in October 1906 in the local legislative council. Its conditions on issues such as sanitation, tree planting and construction, when imposed on the Chenab Colony, were retroactive however. The penalty for breach of conditions was fines imposed in the same way as the collection of revenue. The farmer could not turn to the courts for relief because under Section 31 the courts were deprived of jurisdiction in the Colony. As if this was not bad enough, the following month in November, the occupier rate, involving a charge on canal water, was raised hugely by the government. The Bari Doab Canal area ran through the districts of Amritsar, Gurdaspur and Lahore, and here the rates had been traditionally lower, because the government had adopted a policy of leniency in revenue to ensure the loyalty of the Sikh Jats who supplied recruits for the Indian Army.[5] When the bill sought to extract the extra legal fees in the Chenab Colony, this was vehemently contested by the yeomen farmers. Corruption and maladministration now stood to be challenged as the entire system of interference and paternalism began to be opposed. James Ker recognizes that the raising of the water rates on the Bari Doab Canal in the Lahore

District 'was resented by the cultivators' and these grievances led to 'an easy transition' of 'anti-British feelings', which even resulted in 'assaults on Europeans in Lahore and Rawalpindi'. However, '[t]he trouble in the Lyallpur district was the most dangerous for two reasons: first because special attention was directed to military pensioners of whom the colony was full, and secondly because it spread naturally from there to districts from which the canal colonists originally came.' It did not stop there, because not only did the agitators approach the pensioners, they also approached the Sikh regiments, and at Ferozepur several hundred sepoys 'attended a most seditious meeting to which they had been specially invited'. The developing situation of 'a campaign of sedition' was viewed so seriously that it 'was described by the Lieutenant-Governor at the end of April, 1907, as exceedingly serious, exceedingly dangerous, and urgently demanding a remedy'.[6] If this is how the lieutenant-governor felt, he had good reason to do so.

A retired postal officer by the name of Sifaj-ud Din Ahmed had in 1903 established a newspaper, appropriately called the *Zamindar*, to vent the frustrations of colonists like Bhagat Singh's grandfather, Sardar Arjan Singh, who had migrated from Khatkar Kalan in Jalandhar District to the canal area where they settled at Banga village, in Lyallpur. If anyone understood the problems of the yeoman farmers, it would be people like Bhagat Singh's uncle, Ajit Singh. His time would come before long. Simmering discontent would not take long to turn into outright political opposition. When the *Zamindar* held a public meeting on 22 and 23 March 1907 to demonstrate against the The Punjab Colonisation of Land Bill of 1906, Ajit Singh made haste to find ways of opposing it. He despatched delegates from the Bharat Mata Society to campaign against the coming into law of the bill. Lala Lajpat Rai was asked by the *Zamindar* to address the yeomanry. As he left for Lyallpur, he sent a communique to Ajit Singh in which he intimated that there should be an expression of gratitude from the podium for the government having agreed to a previous amendment, before a demand was made for the repeal of the bill. Ajit Singh disagreed.

He wanted to prepare the masses for a no-revenue campaign and did not want to have a record of thanks being given. The two differed on tactics. This was reflected in the manner in which they both spoke at the meeting of 22 and 23 March 1907 in Lyallpur, with Lala Lajpat Rai being conciliatory and Ajit Singh being defiant.

This is how the 1907 disturbances in the Canal Colonies occurred, and they shook the colonial state to its roots. Suddenly, the idea of the unshakeable loyalty of the Punjab rural peasantry was broken. Initially, officialdom thought of blaming urban agitators, and that is how blame came to be pinned on Lala Lajpat Rai and Ajit Singh. Both of them were arrested and exiled. But the real cause was the conservative resistance of peasant farmers to an attempt to modernize them. And, there is modern-day equivalence in the passing of the three farm bills by the Modi government in 2020 as explained below. Back then, these farmers harboured a deep-seated resentment to the modern system of imposing fines for their failure to abide by the rules of sanitation, inheritance and resistance. The revolt was successful. Within five years, the Colony Act 1912 had abandoned state-controlled supervision of a system of modern progressive cultivation.

What is vital to note here is that the tumultuous political changes that began in 1907 did not end there and continued apace right through to 1947, and Bhagat Singh himself was not unaware or unaffected by them. The importance of the political changes is clear from Pandit Pearay Mohan's 'Punjab Rebellion' of 1919,[7] where he penned a memorable foreword to his valuable study of the epoch leading up to Indian Independence. He describes how the 1919 rebellion was preceded by such pivotal events in Punjab as 'the unrest of 1907, the historic trial of Arya Samajists in 1909, the prosecutions for sedition of 1909-1910, the conspiracy cases of 1913-1914, and the political trials held during the war'.[8]

It is true that during this time new forms of protest emerged as Gandhi's non-violent movement was beset with violent outbreaks. In the aftermath of these, Gandhi himself withdrew from agitational politics in the early 1920s. In Nagpur in 1925,

Dr Keshav Baliram Hedgewar (also known as 'Doctor Ji') set up the Rashtriya Swayamsevak Sangh, (popularly known today as the 'RSS'), an Indian right-wing Hindu nationalist organization, which organized anti-British activities through the 'Kranti Dal' (the 'Party of Revolution'). But there is no doubt that the most notable of these was the Hindustan Socialist Republic Association, set up in 1929 by Chandrashekar Azad and Bhagat Singh, which forged ahead with a new, non-Gandhian approach in the fight for freedom. Although Chris Moffat is slightly critical of the emphasis historians have placed on Bhagat Singh's family inheritance, being more interested in his critical attitude towards them, there is no doubt that Bhagat Singh adored his uncle Ajit Singh and even corresponded with him in exile and asked after him. Yet, remarkably, the influence on Bhagat Singh's political development of his family, which was itself influenced by provincial developments in Punjab, has not been as well made out as it should have been. Common folklore in Punjab, however, makes no such mistake. This is as true on the Pakistan side as it is on the Indian side of Punjab.

So, the year 1907 set the stage for what was to follow over the following decades, with the emergence of a clear conflict with the government, and it was indeed this conflict within which the history of the Ghadar Party can be mapped as well. Bhagat Singh's own political trajectory needs to be understood against this backdrop. It is the historic failure to do so that has led to the wholesale pre-eminence being given to Gandhi's swadeshi/swaraj philosophy as the force for Independence, even though this had ended by 1911, whereas Bhagat Singh came into his own several years after that.

Sadly, little seems to have been learnt from this past. Modern-day India's Modi government appears to be quite oblivious of Punjab's tortuous history. Why else would it have so blithely passed on 5 June 2020 three ordinances on agricultural marketing which set out to structurally alter its basis?[9] The Indian economy was already in the grips of the maelstrom of the COVID-19 pandemic. As panic set in over the economy's catastrophic disintegration, the government, under cover of an unprecedented public health crisis and over the heads of state governments, forced through a series of highly controversial agricultural reforms, not unlike a hundred years ago, without consultation and without warning. Within three months on 14 September 2020, the three ordinances were passed before Parliament as legislative bills. Following a cursory discussion, they had the full imprimatur of the law by the end of the month, receiving the presidential assent on 27 September 2020, while leaving the public at large mystified about the government's purpose and vision for national agricultural policy. As with a hundred years ago, the government's intention was to 'modernize' farming practice by making it more competitive. As then, this is not how the farmers of Punjab understood it.

The three bills were designed to allow private actors to invest and participate in agri-food supply chains. The farmers would ostensibly benefit from higher output prices. The first bill, accordingly, removed restrictions on the purchase and sale of farm produce, while the second bill removed restrictions on stocking, and the third bill then ushered in new laws to facilitate contract farming underpinned by written agreements. Given the complexities involved, which remained largely unexplained by the government, some lauded the three bills as bringing Indian agriculture into the modern era while others decried them as a final nail in the coffin of already struggling Indian farmers. What is true is that former Indian Prime Minister H.D. Deve Gowda was distinctly unhappy with the way in which the bills were rushed through Parliament. What is equally true is that they presaged a turning-point: an irrevocable and permanent withdrawal of state support for farmers in favour of the rapacious big business. Nothing seems to have been learnt from the British 'reforms' of a hundred years ago, and riots erupted in Punjab, which showed little signs of abating until the Government finally had to give in.[10] In the meantime, the Congress Party promised to reverse the 'reforms'.[11]

All this should have been forseen. It was forseen by Shekhar Gupta, the editor-in-chief of the well-regarded *The Print*, who at the time pointed out how, 'the Modi-Shah BJP does not understand

Punjab, Punjabis, their politics, or even more specifically, the Sikhs.' He reminded everyone how 'Punjab was the outlier that defied the Modi magic in the north', because the BJP there lost the general elections of 2014 and 2019 even when it had 'a formidable ally, Shiromani Akali Dal, the pre-eminent Sikh party'. What he meant by this was that whereas 'on the farm bills, there is hardly a buzz in the other major farming states' such as 'Maharashtra, with massive agricultural population and an established record of farmer politics and protests', which 'is calm', the question that the farm laws was raising was: 'Why's Punjab angry? Because the state is different, as are the Sikhs.' In Punjab, the BJP government's 'politics of polarization' does not work, with the result that, '[t]he few Muslims who live in Punjab, in the tiny enclave of Malerkotla, have enjoyed the Sikhs' affection and protection since the times of the tenth Guru, Guru Gobind Singh', and the reason for this is that 'the nawab here tried to protect the Guru's sons from Aurangzeb. It isn't just revenge that the Sikhs have a long memory for. It is also for gratitude'. Although 'the RSS and the BJP' have both 'seen Sikhs as fellow Hindus', the reality, as Shekhar Gupta explained at the time was that, despite being lauded as 'the sword arm of India', the fact remains that 'Sikhs are not Hindus. They are not impressed by Hindutva. If they were, they would not have rejected Modi at his peak thrice'. As he boldly maintains, '[t]he Sikh peasantry, especially Jatts, also revel in agitation' and that '[t]his goes back to the "*Pagdi Sambhal Jatta*" movement in the early 20th century, launched by Sardar Ajit Singh'.

Shekhar Gupta ended his insightful article by connecting present-day events to the events of a hundred years ago when he reminded us of how '[i]ts slogan also became the anthem of his nephew's incredibly brave revolution' and that '[t]he nephew was Shaheed Bhagat Singh, whom everybody swears by, Left, Right and Centre'. In his view, '[t]he Sikhs love a good fight, and that's what the Modi government has given them. It won't work. You have to reason with the Punjabis'.[12] And, of course, in March 2022, the BJP lost Punjab again, winning only two out of 72 contested seats.[13]

Swearing by the name of Bhagat Singh is indeed everyone's prerogative. The question is why that should be so. As everyone knows, the farm bills were protested. It was Punjab's farmers who took the lead. They instigated the largest labour protest in human history, numbering no less than 1,25,000 protestors on the march. By their fourth week in December 2020, thousands had occupied several kilometres between the Tikri border in Delhi and Haryana's Bahadurgarh. As their ranks were fortified, Punjab and Haryana's new-found cultural unity was even expressed in musical performances, such as that of the Haryanvi Raginis, which was dedicated to the freedom fighter.[14] By February 2021, it was being reported that with the farmers having conceded nothing, the Modi government had lost the farm laws battle and that raising the Sikh separatist bogey 'will be a grave error' because 'this BJP does not understand Punjab or the Sikhs'.[15] On 19 November 2021 the farm bills were withdrawn. It had taken 358 days of protests, with 719 dead, but the announcement only 'emboldened many in the camps who said they would not leave until other significant issues in the agriculture sector had been resolved . . .'.[16] By early 2022, there was widespread acclaim of how 'the farmers persevered through chilly winters, blistering summers, monsoon floods, the pandemic's second wave, and a relentless, ruthless propaganda war unleashed by the government through its lapdog corporate media' and all in order to 'win against the right-wing government of Narendra Modi . . .'.[17] But why did the farmers ever choose the name of Bhagat Singh? Why, when there were so many freedom fighters to find inspiration from? The answer lies in part in Bhagat Singh's family—a family led by his grandfather, Arjan Singh, whose name is now forgotten, but to whom we must now turn.

4

1906, Land Colonisation Bill

Arjan Singh and Jai Kaur had three sons. All doggedly followed in their parents' illustrious footsteps. There was Kishan Singh (1878–1951), who was Bhagat Singh's father, and then there were his two uncles, Ajit Singh (1881–1947) and Swaran Singh (1887–1910). All three of them were born in Khatkar Kalan on the Indian side of Punjab. All three met with an unsung and uncelebrated death. Kishan Singh had originally been named 'Gobind Singh' and was called by the nick-name of 'Gobinda' until he underwent Sikh baptism at the age of eight at a Holi celebration in 1886 and was given the name Kishan Singh. In 1906, as an ardent follower of the Arya Samaj, he formed the Bharat Mata Society ('Hail Mother Country' Society) together with his two brothers. In 1907, the year that Bhagat Singh was born, he opposed the Bari Doab Canal Rates and the Land Colonisation Bill.[1] That is when he was arrested and suffered life-long exile as explained below.

It is often forgotten that India had two freedom movements. One consisted of the demands of urban Indian politicians; the other of indigenous political organizations[2] living off the land (as we have already seen in this chapter so far). The latter group has been much neglected in accounts of India's quest for freedom from foreign rule. Yet, it was a powerful movement, as it was most affected by the

Punjab Alienation of Land Act 1900, as previously noted. This was the first paternal legislation passed by the British. It divested the farming community of zamindars, of their right to sell or mortgage their land unless approved by the district officer. This left them justifiably aggrieved. An approval for land alienation would only be granted by a district officer if the recipient of the land could show that he belonged to a tribe designated in the government gazette as an 'agricultural' tribe.[3] The condition prevented the transfer of land to a person outside the agricultural community.[4] When the Hindu commercial classes who monopolized money-lending in Punjab failed to mobilize the cultivators against the legislation, an emboldened Punjab government went on to pass additional bills. These strengthened the position of a small aristocratic class at the expense of the peasantry. In order to amend the Punjab Colonisation of Land Act 1893, the Punjab Land Colonisation Bill 1906 was introduced in the legislative council on 25 October 1906, and then passed in February 1907, as already recounted. Some twenty years earlier in 1887, the Punjab government had embarked upon the Chenab Canal Colony project. Yet, the problem was that not only were these reforms promulgated very fast, but they were also so far-reaching that the government was able to extend its reach right into the heart of the daily life of the peasant grantees. This is what proved intolerable for the yeomanry. They were told that they had to live on their land, cut wood from specified areas, maintain a clean compound and have arrangements made for sanitary disposal of night soil.

The colonization officer and his subordinate Indian staff supervised all aspects of colony life. They made sure that the colonizer fulfilled all the conditions. The grant of an absolute power made the officer a virtual dictator. His word was final in any dispute. The 'fine system', compulsory tree planting, sanitary rules, transfer of land by will and a higher occupancy fee were included in the contracts after 1902, which took a heavy toll on the peasant farmer. Moreover, only strict primogeniture, as interpreted by the canal officer, would be permitted in the future.[5] And, if a new settler died without gaining occupancy rights (which was generally before five years), the land lapsed to the government, which reserved the right to re-allot the property to lineal heirs or to unrelated tenants.[6] Fines were legalized, and the courts were prevented from interfering with executive orders. What the government of the day failed to realize at the time was that 'the year 1906 was the wrong time to present a measure extending official powers' because there was 'discontent over maladministration in the colony which had been spreading since 1900', when the Punjab Alienation of Land Act of that year first robbed the zamindars of their right to sell or mortgage their land in Punjab's first piece of colonial paternal land legislation. By 1906, it should have been clear to the rulers that 'the colonists hated the extra-legal fine system that had cost them over Rs. 3,00,000 in penalties'. As if this was not enough, the severely oppressed and downtrodden peasant grantees had salt rubbed into their wounds as they came to feel that 'more offensive than fines, however, was the rampant corruption amongst lower officials' who made the greatest possible use of extorting bribes.[7]

In this way, the conditions for an agrarian revolt were ripe. At a livestock show in Lyallpur on 22 and 23 March 1907, approximately 9,000 colonists converged. Their aim was to protest against government despotism. A local editor, Lala Bankay Dyal,[8] opened the programme. He began an inflammatory poem titled '*Pagri Sambhal O Jatta*' ('Protect the honour of your turban, o Jatta!'). The scene was memorably depicted in Manoj Kumar's 1965 film *Shaheed*,[9] the first film that went onto win the Indian government's 'Best Feature Film on National Unity and Emotional Integration Award'[10] in Hindi, and the poem is part of Indian folklore. Lala Bankay Dyal's recital in real life, however, was far more explosive because, 'the Turban was a symbol of self-respect for the war-like Jat Zamindars . . .'.[11] After a number of patriotic songs had been sung, it was Lala Lajpat Rai and Ajit Singh who made the main speeches, but Ajit Singh was by far the fiercest in his criticism. James Ker was not far wrong when he recalled that whilst Lajpat Rai 'was the most prominent of the "intellectuals" associated with the movement' so that 'he was everywhere recognised as the moving spirit of the agitation', when it came to Ajit Singh, 'he was much more prominent as a speaker than Lajpatrai, and his speeches were much more violent . . .'.[12] The crowd was whipped up into a frenzy. Whereas Lala Lajpat Rai was more conciliatory, Ajit Singh 'spoke of the need for bloody sacrifice and demanded a boycott of all government posts'. Colonists, he said, should band together and not pay revenue. After the March meeting, Lala Lajpat Rai went on a lecture tour of the United Provinces, but Ajit Singh and his organization, the *Anjuman-hi-Mohibann-i-Watan* (Society of Lovers of the Homeland) orchestrated demonstrations against the Bari Doab enhancements. Riots then occurred in Amritsar, Lahore and Rawalpindi. Ajit Singh was accused of trying to spread disaffection amongst the troops and students.

The scene is once again portrayed well in one of the early Bollywood films on Bhagat Singh in 1965. A further comment on this is due. The grainy crackling black-and-white film shows how early on Ajit Singh comes to the aid of a peasant farmer prostrating himself before a white English customs officer, begging that he be granted reprieve from his dues. Ajit Singh grabs hold of him, stands him up and lets out the shrill cry with the song of 'Pagri sambhal Jatta', whereupon he is promptly seized by security officers and whisked away into custody. This is why Manoj Kumar's 1965 film *Shaheed* is the definitive film on Bhagat Singh. It narrowly escaped not being made because two films already existed and it had no heroine in it. Yet, it stands today as 'one of the most revered films on patriotism' and launched Manoj Kumar's career, making him 'India's de facto patriotic hero' and paving the way for other films such as *Upkar*, *Purab Aur Paschim* and *Kranti* on Indian patriotism. Although directed by S. Ram Sharma and produced by Kewal Kashyap, 'Manoj Kumar accepts that he actually directed it'. Such was the impact of the film that 'Shaheed became an official document for Bhagat Singh's proud mother and the Government of India'. In an interview in 2014, Manoj Kumar explained how

It took four years of research to prepare for the role. I visited newspaper offices and read old books, magazine, papers, anything that I could lay my hands on regarding the freedom fighters. In Madras (now Chennai), I would go to Hindu Library after completing the shooting of my films that were being shot there and read books. I met Bhagat Singh's lawyer one day and many *krantikaris* (i.e. revolutionaries) who imparted a lot of knowledge about the martyr. It was a gainful insight and helped me during the shooting.

Shooting for the film began in 1963, and after it was released in December 1965, Manoj Kumar became the first actor to win the National Award for Best Writing for *Shaheed*. So popular was the film that it went on to secure the National Award for Best Feature Film in Hindi. No less importantly, it also won the Best Feature Film Award on National Integration. Just twenty years after Indian Independence, not only were memories of pre-Partition India still raw and unblemished, but many associated with the freedom struggle were still alive. One such was Vidyavati, Bhagat Singh's mother. When it was announced that the illustrious awards ceremony in New Delhi would be attended by Indira Gandhi herself, Manoj Kumar's father hastened to Chandigarh in Punjab to collect Vidyavati so that she could attend the esteemed gathering of luminaries in the capital city. Recalling the event in 2014, Manoj Kumar said of Vidyavati that

> When she came on the dais, there was a standing ovation of a full 15 minutes. Madam Gandhi (Indira Gandhi) the then Prime Minister touched her feet to seek her blessings and we gave the entire prize money that came with the award to Vidyavatiji. We got tremendous love and affection from his mother.[13]

Of all the songs which featured in many a subsequent film on Bhagat Singh in the ensuing years, the songs of *Shaheed* are still sung by devotees of Bhagat Singh. Songs such as 'Mera rang de basanti chola' have become a classic, as have 'Aye vatan ay vatan humko teri kasam' and 'Sarfaroshi ki tamanna'. The songs, 'Pagdi sambhal Jatta' and 'Watan pe marne wale zinda rahega tera naam' remain a rallying cry for revolution to this day.

After the Lyallpur incident of 22–23 March 1907, Denzil Ibbetson, the lieutenant-governor of Punjab, concluded that there was a secret plot to overthrow the British Government. His fears were not entirely baseless because 'the Arya Samaj, under the leadership of Ajit Singh and Lala Lajpat Rai, had succeeded in getting the rural population to suspend revenue payments', and if that was so, then 'the next step would be open revolt'. This is when Ibbetson moved to ban public meetings. Printing presses were seized. Individuals inciting zamindars not to pay revenue were to be arrested. Ajit Singh and Lajpat Rai, however, needed to be made examples of. So they were to be deported 'to strike terror into the minds of those concerned'.[14] The deportations were carried out under Regulation III of the 1818 Bengal Regulations, because in the words of James Ker, 'it was considered undesirable to prosecute these men in the ordinary way'.[15] This gave the governor-general in council the right to deport Indians to a place in India or outside on the grounds that they endangered 'peace'. The deportations to Mandalay, we learn from James Ker, 'had an immediate effect in calming the agitation for a time, not only in the Punjab but all over India'.[16] Two decades later, this power would be used against Bhagat Singh, not to deport him but to sentence him to be hanged at the gallows.

The dice had been cast. The Punjab revolt of 1907, though much neglected by Indian historians of Independence, continued in its opposition to British rule right through to 1947, when freedom arrived. With such a background, it is not hard to resist the conclusion that Bhagat Singh's destiny was already being engraved in stone by his elders even as he was growing up.

But it was not just one uncle in the family who would so brazenly take on the British. All three sons of Arjan Singh and Jai Kaur—Kishan Singh, Ajit Singh and Swaran Singh—were members of the Ghadar Party, a fact barely recalled these days in relation to the story of Bhagat Singh. The Ghadar Party was a multi-ethnic revolutionary party founded by Indians in 1913 in San Francisco. Its leaders came from Sikh, Hindu and Muslim religions. Although it is much forgotten these days by Indians, it is the real precursor of the modern-day Congress Party, with its emphasis on secularism and cosmopolitanism. One of its main leaders, Kartar Singh Sarabha, was a student at the University of California in Berkeley. He had a great influence on Kishan Singh, who is reputed to have donated Rs. 1,000 to Kartar Singh Sarabha. Kishan Singh himself, described as a 'Jat of Jullunder and Lahore' by James Ker, 'took an active part in the disturbances in Lahore in 1907' and was as a result 'sentenced to 2-years imprisonment in the Lahore riot case'.[17] But this was not all because when later 'the peace of the Province was again disturbed in 1909 by the issue from Lahore of a flood of seditious literature', he was one of those, who was held responsible according to James Ker.[18] In March 1910, Kishan Singh was convicted 'in respect of seven pamphlets which' he was 'proved to have published or sold' and was sentenced to ten months' imprisonment.[19]

It is impossible for Bhagat Singh not to have been impacted by this. Kishan Singh lived to see the day India became free but not long enough to enjoy this freedom. He died at Khatkar Kalan on 30 May 1951.

Ajit Singh, his younger brother, was no less affected by the aura of Kartar Singh Sarabha. He suffered prolonged political exile, first at the hands of the British in Mandalay Jail in Burma along with Lala Lajpat Rai. He then fled to South America, where he lived for decades.

Swaran Singh died at home in Lahore after his release from prison in 1910. This was just three years after 1907, following the moment of Bhagat Singh's birth. Growing up in such family circumstances, Bhagat Singh himself was not immune to ideas of 'self-rule' and to take the fight for Independence to the British from a very early age. His upbringing was in an environment where the calls for expression of Indian patriotism abounded. This was as true outside the family as it was inside it.

5

Rebel Blood

The evidence, therefore, shows that Bhagat Singh's life in revolution was forged on the anvil of the master workmen in his family. These included his grandfather, father and his two uncles. Without them, his initial sensibilities in relation to a Punjab in turmoil would not have developed so early in life. This perspective on his life is not always understood, as the focus is on his later years when, after his arrest on 8 April 1929, he went into prison until he was put to death on 23 March 1931. During this time he read some 300 books and imbibed the revolutionary fervour of many anarchists and communists from across the world. He was influenced by these books, but the seeds of his resistance were already sown in him through family upbringing. This thesis is not entirely uncontested. In his masterly *India's Revolutionary Inheritance*, the author Chris Moffat is sceptical about Punjabi anecdotes that suggest that Bhagat Singh's pronounced anti-colonial resistance 'was ingrained in his conscience from the very beginning'.[1] After all, Bhagat Singh borrowed widely from other transnational insurgents in the USA, Europe and Russia. For this reason, he takes a jaundiced view of hagiographers' tendency 'to point to Bhagat Singh's "rebel blood"[2]: or, in less sensational terms, to a childhood spent amid a politically active family'. Nevertheless, Moffat's meticulous research does

not blind him to how Bhagat Singh's father Kishan Singh was so
'frequently at odds with the colonial regime'[3] that after the Punjab
agrarian revolt of 1907, he was even mentioned in James Ker's report
for the Criminal Intelligence Department.[4] In that report, Kishan
Singh is held personally responsible for 'flooding the Punjab with
seditious literature'.[5] On this basis, Moffat recognizes how, for
many in Punjab, '[i]t is the particularity of this family environment,
overseen by Bhagat Singh's grandfather Arjun Singh',[6] that is
chiefly responsible for the young man's flowering into a towering
national leader who rivalled Gandhi. Moffat, however, rejects this
implication for three reasons, arguing that if Bhagat Singh grew
up to be great, it was because he defined himself in opposition to
his family.

First, there was his 'his rejection of arrangements made for his
marriage in 1923: a charged decision which led the young man to run
away to Cawnpore'. However, whilst this may have been a rejection
of marriage, what it was not was a repudiation of his family values.
Bhagat Singh was sixteen years old then, and his grandmother,
impatient in seeing her grandson still a bachelor, made haste to
arrange for a match for him. Bhagat Singh tried in vain to dissuade
her from this course of action. Frustrated, he left Lahore for Kanpur,
where he met up with a noted Congress leader, Ganesh Shankar
Vidyarthi, and began to edit the newspaper *Pratap* in Hindi. It
turned out to be a fateful step as it was there that he met three of
the twenty-four named insurgents in the Lahore Conspiracy Case,
namely, B.K. Dutt, Shiv Kumar Verma, and Bejoy Kumar Sinha.
On his way to Kanpur, he left behind a letter for his father humbly
requesting that, 'I hope you will be magnanimous and forgive me'
but that 'my life has been dedicated to the cause of attaining freedom
for Hindustan' and that 'worldly desires and comfort hold no
attraction for me'. His father would hardly have been in a position to
argue. In Hinduism, a rite of passage that starts the period of formal
education for a young boy is when he receives a sacred thread in a
formal ritual, and Bhagat Singh lost no time in reminding his father
when as a child his grandfather 'had announced that by the time of

my *yagyopavit* ceremony that I would be dedicated to the service of my nation'.[7] In so writing, rather than disowning his family, Bhagat connects himself with its very essence.

Second, it is said that he abandoned religion altogether, which was not an insignificant matter given 'his father's Hindu reformist roots in the Arya Samaj and his mother's Sikhism', and he did so to such an extent that he even set his iconoclasm out 'in the 1931 essay *"Why I am an Atheist"'*. While this is true, it must not be forgotten that in that very essay, when Bhagat Singh is a condemned man awaiting the gallows, he is writing about his father's move in 1917 from Banga Village in Lyallpur to Lahore. This was a time when he was ten years old. He was all set to go to high school. Despite all the influences of the big city to which he would have been open, he describes how '[i]t was through my father's teachings that I aspired to devote my life to the cause of freedom'.[8] But perhaps more than anything else, what sets him apart from his family, Moffat proceeds to correctly recount, is 'his stern condemnation' as a prisoner on the brink of execution in 1930 'of the mercy plea submitted to the Viceroy of India by Kishan Singh,[9] demanding his son be saved from the gallows'. Moffat is not wrong to draw attention to how Bhagat Singh upbraided his father 'in a public letter and chastises [him] for weakness'.[10] Indeed, Bhagat Singh has no qualms about telling his father how 'in the political field my views have always differed with those of yours. I have always been acting independently without having cared for your approval or disapproval'.[11]

One cannot, however, overlook the formative influence that Bhagat Singh's family—in particular his uncles and his grandfather—had on his inner development as a young man who took on the British Raj. That influence has been there even if we bear in mind the strong words of the letter Bhagat Singh wrote to his father shortly before his death. It is his last letter to his father. Despite his exasperation at his father, he tells him that 'I know you have devoted your life to the cause of Indian independence . . .'. It is true that Bhagat Singh is 'astounded' and indeed 'quite perplexed' at his father's intervention to save his life. He fights hard to control his outrage, pointing out that 'I fear I might overlook the ordinary principles of etiquette, and my language may become a little harsh'. But this is only because he and his fellow condemned prisoners 'have been pursuing a definite policy in this trial'. Against this background, Bhagat Singh was bound to have chided his father with the words that 'I feel as though I have been stabbed in the back'. He was bound to have described this sort of action to his father as being 'nothing short of treachery'. While the words used are indeed scathing coming from a son to his father, Bhagat Singh recognizes that this is because, 'in your case, let me say that it has been a weakness—a weakness of the worst type'. It is the weakness of the father's utter helplessness, of a father driven to despair as he awaits the inevitable—the hanging to death of his eldest son. Bhagat Singh recognizes this only too well. This is why he tells his father, 'I know you are as sincere a patriot as one can be.'[12]

From this it is clear that Bhagat Singh's unabated anger at his father is motivated by the loss of face with his condemned comrades. They had all determinedly decided to wilfully face the gallows, kissing the noose as they proceeded to joyously place it around their necks. For them there were no half measures. What they wanted was to make the ultimate sacrifice. It is righteous anger that Bhagat Singh now felt for his father, an indignation at his father's attempt to dissuade him from his long-planned course of action—a meeting with death. This is why all three condemned prisoners—Bhagat Singh, Rajguru and Sukhdev—offered no defence. They entered no plea. This is why Bhagat Singh berated his father for a 'weakness of the worst type' as this was a weakness of a father unable to countenance with equanimity his son's determination to extinguish himself.

But that is not to say that his father had no formative influence on him. To obscure or negate his family's critical role in his revolutionary upbringing is to focus on the part and to miss the whole. The decisive influence on his later life may have lain elsewhere. It may have been the case, as Moffat describes, that Bhagat Singh staked out a claim to work 'outside a trajectory determined by bloodlines and instead in the context of twentieth-century revolutionary politics more generally'.[13] It may be that he had 'a peculiarly *para-national* sensibility', grounded in a relationship with nationalism but not circumscribed by it, given how he and his associates had founded the student, Naujawan Bharat Sabha.[14]

Yet, it is clear that his family background was such that he could not have been blissfully unaware of it. Tied to this is the fact that the agrarian revolts of 1907, in which Bhagat Singh's uncle Ajit Singh was involved, had a distinctly 'Punjabi' provenance in the subsequent struggle for Indian Independence, which was eventually realized in 1947. Like many others, it has been overlooked. It is true that outside Punjab there were broader mobilizations taking place across India at this time. These were principally in the name of swadeshi/swaraj, the Gandhian idea of 'self-sufficiency' that was aimed at wresting control of indigenous industries, given that the British relied on them for their economic power.[15] However, these mobilizations should not be allowed to obscure the revolt from indigenous political organizations. Bhagat Singh's family played a major role in these. So much so that by the time that Bhagat Singh was born his family had already laid the foundations for his revolutionary activities, as we shall see in the next chapter.

To separate Bhagat Singh's story from that of his family is to overlook precisely how and why he rose to the national scene as he did. This is all too revealingly shown in the 1917 work of James Campbell Ker. He was the personal assistant to the director of criminal intelligence from 1907 to 1913 and therefore one of the senior officers of the Home Department of the British Indian Government. 'In this capacity', according to Jamna Das Akhtar, 'he had direct access to the highly confidential documents relating to the political activities that had become [a] source of embarrassment to the British rulers'.[16] He puts the role of Bhagat Singh's family so high in the revolutionary moment of Punjab that, when referring to the 'flood of seditious literature in the form of books and pamphlets in the vernacular' in the province, he states 'two agencies were mainly responsible for their production', and of these, 'the second [was] by Ajit Singh, the deportee, his two brothers, Kishen Singh and Sowaran Singh'.[17] Bhagat Singh came from solid stock.

6

1907, Canal Colonies Disturbance

From an early age, Bhagat Singh was deeply affected by the plight of his two uncles. He had seen both Ajit Singh and Swaran Singh having to undergo long bouts of incarceration. Yet, all the time that he was growing up, he longed to have them around him. The loneliness of his two aunts in the family household was a daily reminder to him of the price of being a revolutionary and eventually led him to eschew marriage for himself. He did not want his wife to be subjected to the same tribulations. In the circumstances, he developed a burning hatred for the British.[1] It is not difficult to understand how, as the veteran writer, Malwinder Jit Singh Waraich states that the 'obsession of Bhagat Singh with his *Chacha* [uncle] never left him'.[2] Ajit Singh had it particularly hard, when as a peasant organizer who had founded the Bharat Mata Society, he spent most of his life in exile. For Bhagat Singh, this was on top of having to see his father, Kishan Singh, a Congress worker, not being spared time on scores of occasions. Unsurprisingly, Bhagat Singh too found himself falling under British surveillance from a young age. He was barely out of his teenage years when the police labelled him a 'well-known suspect'. But by then Bhagat Singh was not only immersed in his own activities with the Punjabi youth organization Naujawan Bharat

Sabha, but further afield had also established connections with the HRA in Kanpur.

As early as 1926, the Criminal Intelligence Department (CID) was able to give a tolerably clear description of him as being 'of medium height; thin oval face; fair complexion; slightly pock-pitted; aquiline nose; bright eyes; small beard and moustache; wears Khaddar'.[3] By 1927, he was being unnecessarily subjected to police harassment. This is when he was suspected of complicity in the bombing of a crowd which was celebrating the festival of Dussehra in Lahore. He was quite innocent in this instance. The police, nevertheless, charged him with bomb testing, alleging a protracted plot to free HRA bombers in the Kakori conspiracy case. However, notwithstanding his detention at their hands for a month, the police failed to nail him. He was released after he paid a bond. That left him to continue in his organizational activities. He remained unbowed. He formed the HSRA. The aim was to have an impact on political opinion, and so this party sought openings in the Indian political landscape. The strategic attacks on public official targets, carefully planned and calculated with maximum impact in mind, were suitably called 'Actions'.[4] For all these reasons, it would be remiss not to give a detailed consideration to Bhagat Singh's background. We can start with Ajit Singh, with whom Bhagat Singh was besotted.

Born in Katkar Kalan on 23 February 1881, Ajit Singh, initially worked as a teacher following his graduation from DAV College in Lahore. His incendiary speech, where he denounced the Punjab Colonisation of Land Act for having disposed of the peasantry,[5] was such that some in his audience were moved to revolt. When they set alight government buildings, he was arrested with Lala Lajpat Rai and deported for six months to Mandalay. Ajit Singh's actions were portentous, for in the words of Ian Talbot, 'the contradictions in British policy were laid bare by the 1907 disturbances in the canal colonies' and that 'the protests were shocking for the colonial states as they called into question the much vaunted claim that Punjab's stability rested on the loyalty of the rural population'.[6] Ajit Singh's punishment did not placate him. It had the opposite effect. It fortified his militancy, so that in 1909 upon his release he fled to Iran, and from there on to Europe in 1911. As Professor Tim Murphy recounts, he was part of the 'fresh waves of exiles' who were drawn 'towards new revolutionary centres' in 'the cities of the Middle East' where Ajit was 'one more dangerous man on an unsettled frontier between empires,' and where 'there were already close connection between the anarchists of the Mediterranean and the Americas'.[7] His life of intrigue is again captured by James Ker, who records how 'after a short visit to the Paris group he went onto Lausanne where he tried to maintain himself as a teacher of Oriental Languages; here he posed as a Persian, and adopted the Persian alias Mirza Hassna Khan'.[8] Somewhat risibly, he even notes how '[a]t the beginning of September, 1914, he left Paris very hurriedly, without even informing his landlady – which is considered a low trick by agents of the secret service in any country – and on September 25th he was at Dakar in Senegal'.[9] As the First World War engulfed Europe, he found himself in Brazil. There he was known to be in close contact with the Ghadar Party in San Francisco. After that, he was back in Europe in time for the Second World War, where he met with Subhas Chandra Bose but was arrested and jailed again after the Axis powers were defeated.

It was through the efforts of Jawaharlal Nehru, as the prospects of Independence loomed, that Ajit Singh returned to India in March 1947. He died in Dalhousie, Punjab (now Himachal Pradesh) on the very day freedom was granted on 15 August 1947. It is said that at his funeral, this sleepy summer hill station, which is located on five hills and still has an old-world charm to it, was thronged by 'thousands of people',[10] despite being at an elevation of 1,970 m above sea level; such was the reverence in which Ajit Singh was held. This is remarkable given that his period of exile, from 1909 to 1947, was probably the longest of any freedom fighter at the time, such that he would have been barely even remembered by anyone in India upon his return. Naturally, the period of absence from his family took a heavy toll on them. He was married to Harnam Kaur from Kasur. The two of them lived a life bereft of each other for forty years. During this time, he was unable to come to her aid when she fell ill. It is said that moments before he died, Ajit Singh begged her pardon and told her, 'I am sorry that I could not serve you in illness.' He then bowed in front of her, touching her feet and collapsing.[11] A man of heroic stature and true intrinsic human strength—no wonder Bhagat Singh idolized him.

Swaran Singh's story was equally heart-wrenching. Yet, he is the less well-known of Bhagat Singh's two uncles. This remains a paradox, because of all the three sons of Arjan Singh, Swaran Singh came to resemble Bhagat Singh the most. While participating in the Bharat Mata Society with Ajit Singh, he published anti-government literature. In it, like Arjan Singh, he too protested against the pernicious government land reforms. But it was quite a different incident which led to him being crushed by the authorities. It occurred when an English police superintendent shot a pig for sport. A Muslim orderly was asked to carry its carcass. Not surprisingly, the orderly categorically refused to do so. The police superintendent promptly shot him dead. He faced no retribution for doing so. Given that killings by white officers of Indian servants were not entirely unknown,[12] the atrocity may well have been completely ignored. On 11 April 1906, however, *The Punjabee* reported the story under the heading, 'A Deliberate Murder'. The public were incandescent. An outcry arose. The authorities were stunned and taken aback. But then, instead of issuing a severe reprimand against the police officer, they prosecuted the manager of the publication, Lala Jaswant Rai, and the editor, Mr K.K. Athwale. Both were sentenced to rigorous imprisonment on 15 February 1907.[13]

Anti-British protests now erupted across Punjab. This brought Muslims, Sikhs and Hindus together. The person who led the agitation from Lahore was none other than the young Swaran Singh. For his temerity, he was duly arrested, alongside a number of Hindus, such as Gahseeta Ram, Bahaali Ram and Govardhan Dass. Along with another Sikh, Ram Singh, they were all sentenced on 20 July 1907 to one-and-a-half years' rigorous imprisonment, and one other Hindu, Gandharva Sen, received thirty lashes. The punishment in Lahore Central Jail took its toll on the young Swaran Singh. He was driven like an ox and made to toil mercilessly in unforgiving prison conditions. He contracted tuberculosis and died at the age of just twenty-three years in 1910. James Ker puts it rather euphemistically when he explains that in 1909, when the government became concerned with the spread of seditious materials in Punjab, 'proceedings were taken against Swaran Singh as well as against Kishen Singh and Ajit Singh', but that 'the cases against Sowaran Singh were withdrawn on account of an illness of which he died the following year'.[14] Swaran Singh was the same age in March 1931 as Bhagat Singh when he died.

For this reason, Swaran Singh has been described as 'the "forerunner" of his nephew Bhagat Singh',[15] who was also imprisoned in Lahore Central Jail and also died aged twenty-three. Bhagat Singh would have been just three years old at the time of Swaran Singh's death. What would certainly have been impressed upon his mind indelibly would have been the presence in the family household of Swaran Singh's grieving widowed wife, Hukam Kaur, who went on to live for fifty-six years, alongside Ajit's wife, Harnam Kaur, who was no less destitute of the affections of her exiled husband. Hukam Kaur and Swaran Singh had no children. The only daughter of her parents and the only sister of several brothers, she lost all faith in life. Virendra Sindhu, Bhagat Singh's niece, records her as having bewailed, *'Mujhe kya diya hai Bhagwan ne, jo main uski pooja karoon / Sirr parr patti naheen, gaud mein santaan nahi'*[16] ('What has God given me that I should worship Him / my protection is gone, and my womb is barren'). Bhagat Singh was acutely aware of the painful circumstances of his two aunts and in particular of the widowed Hukam Kaur. His first letter written in his native tongue Gurmukhi sees him, in 1921 at the age of fourteen only, writing from Lahore informing her about a picture of his uncle Swaran Singh that he had been working on, explaining that 'Chachaji's portrait is almost ready. I was supposed to bring it along, but it could not be completed by then; so please forgive me.'[17] Bhagat Singh only wrote two letters in the Gurmukhi language. Both were written to Hukam Kaur.

Another, written the following month in November 1921, refers to her as 'my dearest chachiji' (meaning aunt) and asks for her forgiveness because 'I've got delayed in writing the letter'.[18] Such was the deep obligation he felt towards her, even at such a tender age, while still at school. The women in Bhagat Singh's life could not but leave a lasting impression on him even as he turned into a revolutionary.

7

1917, Lahore

Kishan Singh fared better than either of his two younger brothers. He was the only one of Arjan Singh's sons to have had children— he and his wife, Vidyavati, had nine children. The first of these, Jagat Singh, did not survive infancy. The second, Bhagat Singh, did, only to be hanged, having barely reached adulthood. He was followed by his sister Amar Kaur and then two brothers, Kulbir Singh and Kultur Singh. His second and third sisters were Prakash Kaur and Shakuntla. After them came his youngest two brothers, Ranbir Singh and Rajendra Singh, a total of six sons and three daughters. Arjun Singh's Arya Samajist influence remained with the sons. While all three sisters married into Sikh households, the four surviving brothers all married as Arya Samajists. Bhagat Singh's mother Smitri Vidyavati (1886–1975) helped instil the Arya Samaj influence in Bhagat Singh's life. Though born a Sikh with the name 'Inder Kaur' (through which she assumed the nickname 'Indo'), her marriage to Kishan Singh in 1897 was according to the Arya Samaj tradition. Indeed, after marriage she assumed the name of 'Vidyavati' (the 'literate') although she was entirely uneducated. As a child bride, she did not join Kishan Singh in Banga Village until three years later in 1900, where she quickly became accustomed to running a household that served as a sanctuary and hideout for many a fugitive from British justice.[1] Her first child, Jagat Singh, was born to her four years later in 1904 but died a year later in 1905. With Kishan Singh away from home for long periods of time, and the presence of her two sisters-in-law, Harnam Kaur and Hukam Kaur, who were 'gasping in an emotional vacuum', it is said that she eked out her life in a manner that 'what was a struggle for her husband, was a "crisis" for her'.[2]

Bhagat Singh's grandmother, Jai Kaur, gave him the delightfully endearing name of 'Bhagonwala' (or the 'blessed one') upon his birth. She was delirious with joy. Her grandson was arriving in this world just as Ajit Singh and Swaran Singh were also making their way back home from prison. Who could have blamed her for her ecstatic utterance, 'Yah beta bhagon-wale hai' ('This child is the bearer of good tidings for us'). Nor would it have been subsequently surprising to see him being formally invested with the name 'Bhagat Singh' (the 'devoted one') when the time came. Jai Kaur could not have imagined it, but Bhagat Singh in his short life would live up to both these names. He would do so even as he grew up to be a practising atheist and even as the shadow of the hangman's noose swayed before him. He would do so for his country and for his countrymen. For them, 'Bhagat' the 'Bhagonwala' would sacrifice his life and do so spectacularly.

In 1917, at the age of ten, Bhagat Singh found himself in Lahore. His father had decided to relocate to that great city in search of work. The family left Chak No. 105, Lyallpur Banga. They trekked a distance of some 250 km in a rickety cavalcade before ending up in Nawankot on the outskirts of Lahore. By then, Bhagat Singh had already passed his Class IV examinations at his village school. The value of education had early been ingrained in him. In the first letter, written at the age of eleven to his grandfather Arjan Singh, who was still living in their ancestral village of Khatkar Kalan, Bhagat Singh is seen to be writing joyously in Urdu on 22 July 1918 to say how he has 'passed comfortably' in the subjects of English and Sanskrit in Class VI.[3] The second letter discovered, also written to his grandfather in Urdu, again emphasizes the importance of education in his life. This time he is aged twelve, and he writes that 'I have passed in all the subjects in the half-yearly exams' although 'many students have failed the Maths paper'.[4] Armed with his early school success, Bhagat Singh was able to cheerfully enter DAV School upon his arrival in Lahore. He was the first Sikh boy to do so, because Sikh boys invariably went to the Khalsa schools, their own religious institutions, where they participated in daily Sikh prayers in the morning. In Bhagat Singh's case, it was not the Sikh prayers that Kishan Singh objected to. He objected to the way in which the Khalsa schools stooped in supplication to the British Empire.

The D.A.V. School in Lahore had no such pretensions. Founded in 1885 on Arya Samaji principles under the tutelage of Lala Lajpat Rai, it held no such fears for Kishan Singh, which was just as well, because by the time that Bhagat Singh entered Class IX, he was already joining processions and collecting foreign clothes and setting them alight in a bonfire. He had learnt to support the Gandhian non-cooperation movement slogan of '*Hindu–Muslim Ekta Zindabad / Gandhi Ki Jai*'[5] ('Long Live the Unity of Hindus and Muslims as One / and Long Live Gandhi'). Already, when on 20 February 1921, during the time when Sikhs were struggling to assume democratic control over their historic places of worship (gurudwaras) from government-appointed priests (mahants), hundreds of pilgrims at Nankana Sahib Gurudwara in Sheikhpura District were shot down by them, hacked to pieces and burnt with kerosene. Bhagat Singh went out of his way to visit the site on his way to his village in Banga. He was only fourteen years old then and he even attended a conference there on 5 March 1921. Indeed, as Professor Malwinder Jit Waraich writes, 'his visit to Nankana Sahib in the wake of the gruesome killing was in line with his visit to Jallianwala Bagh on 14 April 1919',[6] a day after the Amritsar Massacre, when he would have been only twelve.

If the decision to send a Sikh boy into the DAV College was historic, Bhagat Singh's entry six years later in 1923 into the National College in Lahore was momentous, because it was affiliated with the Punjab Quami Vidyapith. The 'Vidyapith' schools were based on a new model of education, established in different parts of the country, from as far afield as Calcutta, Patna, Benares, Aligarh and Delhi as well as Lahore. They emphasized curricula that prioritized the learning of history, culture, tradition and philosophy and aimed to inculcate patriotic sentiments in the youth in a way that government-aided institutions did not do. The Lahore 'Vidyapith' school was founded and managed by Lala Lajpat Rai and Bhai Parmanand. It successfully managed to bring into its curriculum the principle of 'swadeshi'. As Lala Lajpat Rai himself explained, he aimed for his college to produce 'self reliant, aggressive (in order to be progressive) men and women that new India wants'.[7] Here it was, as Bhagat Singh writes in 'Why I Am an Atheist' that,

> An incessant desire to study filled my heart. 'Study more and more', said I to myself so that I might be able to face the arguments of my opponents. 'Study' to support your point of view with convincing arguments. And I began to study in a serious manner. My previous beliefs and convictions underwent a radical change.

Bhagat Singh was also now in the heart of a city which had the province's largest number of literate classes according to a 1920 Congress report.[8] Lahore was growing at such a pace that its population of 2,02,964 in 1901 more than doubled to 4,29,747 by the time Bhagat Singh was executed in 1931.[9] Bhagat Singh saw a place which was in fact 'not one place but several'.[10]

In the 1920s, the city was already well acquainted with holding regular processions, beginning or ending at Mochi Bagh. Eminent figures from Lajpat Rai to Allama Iqbal to even Motilal Nehru addressed the rallies. Bradlaugh Hall, which opened with financial support from the Indian National Congress in the west of the old city in 1900, provided a venue that was especially constructed for political meetings.[11] Punjabi interest in the nationalist cause was in this way fully mobilized, and Bhagat Singh could not have failed to note this. In the last available letter written to his grandfather from Lahore on 14 November 1921, there lies buried amongst the felicitations to his elder relatives in Khatkar Kalan a reference to how 'the railway people are planning to go on a strike', about which Bhagat Singh adds, 'one hopes that it would begin immediately after next week'.[12] Today, much of this history lies forgotten in 'a city overwhelmed by nostalgia' even though it was formerly a great regional centre.[13]

Bhagat Singh entered the National College in Lahore aged 14 in 1921. It was the first time that a student without a matriculation degree had been admitted for his undergraduate studies. The college was on the same site as the Tilak School of Politics, founded only the previous year in December 1920. It was to be a watershed moment in Bhagat Singh's life, as he had the kind of exposure at the college that helped mature his intellectual transformation. He was tutored by those who disagreed with Gandhian non-violence and favoured instead a violent revolutionary overthrow of imperialism. This was against the background of mounting anti-government feelings in Punjab. Though his academic prowess was great, Bhagat Singh failed to graduate despite having passed his BA intermediate examinations in 1923. It was not because he spent too much time on sports. In fact, he abjured these. He was good in drama classes. He even played an active part in the college drama club. Indeed, he became an accomplished actor in the National College. His fame spread widely in other colleges as well for his acting skills. He liked singing and was good at that too. Remarkably, he cared little for his appearance. This was remembered decades later by those who knew him at the National College, where he was known to enter the class-room with his unkempt hair loosely tied underneath a crumpled pagri (turban). He is remembered as having worn 'Khaddar' clothes, of home-spun cotton. These were often unclean and ill-fitted. While the custom among young men in those days was to wear a pair of loose trousers tied by a drawstring around the waist, Bhagat Singh instead wore a lungi, which is an even looser garment that is similar to a sarong and which extended all the way down to his ankles.[14]

His fellow revolutionary, Ajoy Ghosh, remembers the sixteen-year-old in 1923 as 'tall and thin, rather shabbily dressed, very quiet', but surprisingly also as someone who 'seemed a typical village-lad, lacking smartness and self-confidence'. Ghosh has no qualms about saying, 'I did not think very highly of him'[15] at the time. Durga Bhabhi, who helped plan the nineteen-year-old Bhagat Singh's escape the night after the Delhi Assembly Bomb in 1928, remembers his clothes as being stained and shredded. She was left to marvel in later years at how he could have risen 'to shake the British Raj by its roots'.[16] Yet, the worn lungi did not dampen his developing political resolve as Bhagat Singh played out his various acting roles at the National College. It was here also that in 1923, the year he passed his intermediate examinations, that Bhagat Singh joined the Hindustan Republican Association (HRA). This too was not the reason why he failed to stay and graduate. The reason was that, faced with family pressure to get married in the middle of 1923, Bhagat Singh fled to Kanpur and left Lahore. Over the next year, he worked for the Hindi journal, *Pratap*, using the name 'Balwant', and came under the influence of a journalist named Ganesh Shankar Vidyarthi, who was a staunch revolutionary. From now on, Bhagat Singh's life would be steeped in the company of fellow revolutionaries, and they would come from all over India.

PART 2

WHOSE BHAGAT SINGH?

Dosti keh sahare mehn bhi tujhse the;
Shayad tum bhul gai;
Hum tere apne the

Once we were friends,
Maybe you have forgotten,
Once we were each other's.

—Zeba Nazreen Siddiqui

8

1929, Jinnah and Bhagat Singh

As Bhagat Singh spent his formative years in Lahore, one would think that he would not be forgotten there. And so it has proved to be the case. This is despite his family having moved back to the Jalandhar district in India after the Partition of 1947 and despite Bhagat Singh's exclusion from official Pakistan narratives as a national icon, given the country's adopted policy of Islamicization in the 1970s. In fact, there is a forgotten link between the nation's founding father and Bhagat Singh which has still to be fully acknowledged by Pakistan's intellectuals. In the words of Shoaib Daniyal, although '[m]uch has been written about the Mohandas Gandhi-Bhagat Singh dynamic', the irony is that far '[l]ess is known, though, of the dynamic between Mahomed Ali Jinnah (as he spelt the name) and Bhagat Singh'. Of course, the two men, in terms of background and upbringing, were poles apart. Yet, they were united in one distinctive respect. Both recognized they were fighting the British for the Independence of their people. As such, neither flinched at standing up for fairness and justice. Daniyal[1] writes that although 'Jinnah in 1931 was a politician who had missed the bus as far as Congress-style mass politics would be concerned', nevertheless, '[h]e was still at the high table of Indian politics . . .' However, the difference between the two men could not have been

47

more stark in that 'Jinnah strongly believed in constitutionalism, reposing faith in the institutions of Empire such as legislatures, courts and even the British Parliament to deliver progress to India', while 'Marxist-Leninist Bhagat Singh was, of course, the polar opposite, believing that violent armed struggle was a legitimate way to overthrow the Raj'.

The link between the two arose after Bhagat Singh's arrest upon throwing the smoke bombs in the Central Legislative Assembly in New Delhi in 1929 'to make the deaf hear' (as he endearingly put it). This is when he was confined to jail and put on trial. There he joined the hunger strike on 24 June 1929 with fellow inmates such as Jatindra Das, who would eventually die from it. Such was their determination to use the device of a hunger strike as the ultimate tool of non-cooperation that they made the ordinary continuation trial processes difficult to conduct. The government, however, was resolute in its objective of getting a conviction of a death sentence while maintaining as far as possible the sham façade of a trial conducted under the rule of law. To this end, therefore, they proceeded to attempt to pass the Hunger Strike Bill which would enable a trial to proceed, even if the accused in question in a death penalty case was not present in court! This was a travesty of justice of the highest order and the very negation of the rule of law. Yet the government ordained that this could be done if the accused 'has voluntarily rendered himself incapable of remaining before the court'. It made nonsense of the idea of a fair trial if an accused could not even be present in court to defend himself against accusations which would result in the death penalty being meted out to him. It was also quite unprecedented.

At the time, Jinnah was representing Bombay in the Legislative Assembly. In a speech in September 1929, which has rung through the chronicles of time for those who have cared to listen, Jinnah vehemently and yet eloquently opposed the bill. He was not, after all, the highest-paid lawyer of his day in India for nothing. Of all the leading protagonists in the struggle for Independence, from Gandhi to Nehru to Sardar Vallabhbhai Patel, he alone held the distinction

of being a highly skilled consummate court-room lawyer. He did
not waste this skill. Rising up defiantly in the legislative chamber
while others looked on, he proceeded to call the trial a 'farce' and a
'travesty of justice' and expressed the only truism that there was in
the government's ill-advised artifice—if the trial continued in the
absence of the accused, he 'stands already condemned'. He did not
stop there. Jinnah recognized that like him, Bhagat Singh too was
fighting for Independence. As such, he made it quite clear that Singh
was nothing short of a political prisoner and that the government
needed to treat him as such and not just as a common criminal. With
devastating effect, Jinnah said,

> Well, you know perfectly well that these men are determined to
> die. It is not a joke. I ask the honourable law member to realise
> that it is not everybody who can go on starving himself to death.
> Try it for a little while and you will see . . . The man who goes on
> hunger strike has a soul. He is moved by that soul and he believes
> in the justice of his cause; he is not an ordinary criminal who is
> guilty of cold-blooded, sordid, wicked crime.[2]

So impressive was Jinnah that, as he continued, oblivious of the time
when the day's session for the assembly came to an abrupt end, a
Hindutva stalwart who had once been a Congress Party president
by the name of Madan Mohan Malaviya begged the speaker of the
assembly saying, 'Sir, cannot we go on for another 15 minutes?' His
earnest request was turned down as the time was up for the day. If
Jinnah wished to continue his entreaties on behalf of Bhagat Singh,
he had to return to the assembly the next day and continue. Jinnah had
no compunction in doing so. The next day, in a withering critique,
Jinnah also denounced the proposed new law by the Government as
quite simply 'an absurd provision' in language that is worth setting
out in full:

> It seems to me, Sir, that the great and fundamental doctrine of
> British jurisprudence, which is incorporated and codified in the

Penal Code and the Criminal Procedure Code has very wisely
not made such an absurd provision in the criminal law of this
country and I am not satisfied that there is a lacuna in our system
of criminal law.[3]

Despite this, Jinnah's contribution in the life of Bhagat Singh is
almost entirely overlooked today. In his book *Jinnah and Tilak*,
A.G. Noorani explains how the effect since Independence of 'state
control of universities' and 'misdirected patriotism'[4] is that today
more than half a century after Independence, '[m]any a myth
deserves to be dispelled', as unlike other Congress leaders in India,
'[n]one of the Liberals criticized the British as trenchantly as he did.
None participated in mass politics. Jinnah's rhetoric reflected fierce
patriotism'.[5] Later in his book, he describes how

> Jinnah was as anti-British as any Congressman. The British hated
> him. Willingdon recommended to his successor as Governor
> of Bombay, Lord Lloyd, Jinnah's deportation to Burma. Lloyd
> 'was not disposed to begin his career by conferring unnecessary
> martyrdom'.[6]

Indeed, it is said that 'two of his best performances stand out', and
of these, '[o]ne was his attack on the order banning Vallabhbhai
Patel from speaking for one month at a public meeting',[7] while '[t]
he other instance was his powerful defence of Bhagat Singh in the
Assembly'.[8] Needless to say, so maligned is Jinnah in India today
that neither events would be remotely accredited to him by the
Government of India, which is why as Noorani states, 'as a person
Jinnah has received less than is his due'.[9] While it is true that in
his monumental 'Jinnah',[10] the political scientist Dr Ishtiaq Ahmed
has meticulously traced Jinnah's journey from Indian nationalist
to Muslim communitarian, it is worth recalling the time when he
stood for communal peace and harmony. One only has to note how
when he gave evidence before the British Parliament Joint Select
Committee on the Government of India Bill Secretary of State Edwin

S. Montagu 'began to question him in an offensive manner'. When he was quizzed whether 'at the earliest moment you wish to do away in political life with any distinction between Mohammedans and Hindoos', he replied: 'Yes. Nothing will please me more than when that day comes.'[11] Noorani has no doubt that 'Jinnah set an example equalled by few'[12] and that 'the final responsibility for partition was not his'.[13] This is because 'a united India implied a sharing of power, which the Congress abhorred. Worse still, it had no role for Jinnah as a partner in a united India. He had "no real place in the country" Nehru maintained repeatedly'. It is for this reason that 'Jinnah was an expellee, not an exile. His dreams lie buried in India as well as in Pakistan'.[14]

It was therefore in no small measure thanks to Jinnah's defence of Bhagat Singh and his castigation of the ill-fated and ill-thought-out government measures that the Hunger Strike Bill failed to pass. The assembly rejected it lock, stock and barrel. The government, however, was determined to press ahead. It was going to have Bhagat Singh convicted and sentenced to death one way or the other, by hook or crook. If legislative action would not deliver to it the legal mechanism it needed to hang Bhagat Singh, then it would resort to ministerial action, and this would be the governor-general's ordinance, which would be as good as a statute. A bare semblance of legality was all that was needed. As the documents of the time make clear, it fooled no one, and not least the lawyers acting for Bhagat Singh. Their dedication and forensic acumen deserve special recognition, especially in legal circles, but have gone completely unrecognized so far. First, however, there needs to be recognition of Bhagat Singh as a freedom fighter central to India's Independence Movement and not marginalized to eke out a shadowy existence on the periphery.

9

1924, *Matwala*

Hope exists that Bhagat Singh may yet assume centre stage in the annals of mainstream political history. This is because some of the most spirited claims on the legacy of Bhagat Singh already come from thoughtful Pakistani writers, even whilst recognizing the constraints to which they are subject. According to Ammara Ahmad, while Bhagat Singh 'is a much loved and adored figure in Pakistan', the problem is that 'this doesn't translate into public acceptance or acknowledgement of his efforts, cause or sacrifice'. As a result, '[h]is absence from the public discourse, memory and history books is as ubiquitous as that of Gandhi's or Pakistani politician Sikandar Hyat Khan's', who, as leader of the Punjab Unionist Party in1921, upheld the interests of Muslims, Sikhs, and Hindus alike, until his untimely death in 1942. This is because although, 'Singh was young, spirited and passionate enough to carry out what he believed in and then die for it', the fact was that 'he was also an atheist'. That being so, 'he is naturally immune to being Islamised' and that can be a problem for many Pakistanis conscious of the basis upon which their state was avowedly founded. For them, '[a]ccepting Singh as a national hero will also mean accepting the idea that one can be great without being a Muslim' but that if this could be done, then it would indeed be possible for everyone to 'realise that the Pakistan Movement was just one segment of the larger freedom struggle in India'.

In this way, 'Singh can indeed exemplify defiance against authority and illustrate why the British were the colonial enemies'. There are two arguments for suggesting that this should be done.

First, it is important today that we 'understand that freedom in 1947 wasn't just a "Muslim effort" but a combined effort of all religious communities'. It is remarkable how, with the passage of time, this singularly vital dimension of the Freedom Movement has all but been forgotten in Pakistan. Second, and just as importantly, 'freedom wasn't from the "conniving Hindus" as is popularly believed but from the British, whom the forefathers of many people in the current Pakistani elite admired and served'. The result is that today '[i]n Pakistan, rarely is the British rule questioned and explained' and '[m]ost Pakistani history books focus on the suffering of Muslims as a minority before partition'. Thus, they inevitably 'highlight the difference between Islam and Hinduism as religions to reinforce the theory that the two communities could not have lived together'. Such is the combined perversion of the two falsities that today, 'Pakistan's narrative does not define the British as colonisers and exploiters who created the civil service, infrastructure, education system and other institutions for its administration', but that '[i]nstead, the narrative defines Hindus as exploiters' to the extent that '[s]ome people in Pakistan are still in awe of the British and voice the idea that had they stayed in India longer, the country would have been even more developed and peaceful'.

There is, however, a third reason why Bhagat Singh could be important for setting the record straight in Pakistan. This is a country in search of suitable icons. One such was 'Zulfikar Ali Bhutto . . . often credited with democratising and empowering Pakistan's poor in the 1970s', and though his life was brutally cut short, '[f]rom his descendants to current Pakistani political leaders such as Imran Khan and Shahbaz Sharif—all have tried to copy Bhutto's public persona and political intrigues' because the fact was that 'Bhutto was a progressive, socialist and a liberal'. Yet, largely because of his folly in trying 'to appease his right-wing opponents' by defining 'what a Muslim is in Pakistan's 1973 Constitution' and 'thus, declaring Ahmedis legally non-Muslim', his name has been tarnished and '[h]ence, his legacy is forever tainted and controversial'. Consequently, for the Lahore-based writer and journalist Ammara Ahmad, '[t]his makes somebody of the stature of Bhagat Singh an even more important historical figure for Pakistan', not least because '[m]ore than half of Pakistani population is ethnically Punjabi, as is the political elite . . .'. This is because what is distinctive about Bhagat Singh is that '[l]ike Bhutto, he was also a socialist, with a soft corner for the poor', and this can have a huge significance in today's Pakistan. She is clear in her view that, 'having space for Bhagat Singh in Pakistan's narrative will lead to a more mature polity', not least because, 'if Bhagat Singh is inducted in Pakistan's history books and made a national icon like Iqbal and Jinnah, then young Pakistanis seeking more freedom and equality will be more empowered', because speaking as a Pakistani herself, 'Singh's presence will force us to question some of the historical suppositions made when teaching the history of Partition and the Pakistan Movement'.[1]

Small wonder then that on 25 April 2016, the Punjab Government in Pakistan announced that it would bear the entire expenditure of the purchase of Shaheed Bhagat Singh's house and its conversion into a world-class memorial at Chak No. 105 GB (now Banga village) in Lyallpur, Pakistan. In April 2018, the chief secretary of Pakistan's Punjab province went on to call Bhagat Singh a 'hero of both India and Pakistan'. He is therefore now unmistakably a shared hero of both India and Pakistan, prompting notable writers on Bhagat Singh to ask, 'What's there in Bhagat Singh that can bring India and Pakistan together? Is it his ultimate martyrdom or something more that recommends him as a common hero?' with a view to inquiring into how the two nations can move away from the 'divisive politics' and 'narrow jingoistic politics' that have plagued both nations since their inception and turned them into sworn enemies despite a common bond of land and ancestry. India's distinguished public intellectual, S. Irfan Habib, has argued that it is 'his distinctive political and social ideals' which mean that today, 'Singh is probably the only one from amongst our freedom struggle heroes who can be celebrated by both India and Pakistan'.

The reason for that is quite simply because 'he stood for a non-sectarian and egalitarian world' and had 'never espoused any divisive idea in his short life'. [2]

In 1924, when he was barely seventeen, Bhagat Singh published his first article in *Matwala*, a Hindi magazine from Calcutta, and wrote on 'universal brotherhood'. He imagined a world in which 'all of us being one and none is the other. It will really be a comforting time when the world will have no strangers'.[3] In hindsight today, this is indeed the very polar opposite of what has come to pass in the post-Partition subcontinent where erstwhile friends are seen as foes. Religion, caste, language and culture have been inducted into a new post-Independence narrative to divide Punjab's unique millenia-long hybridity and cosmopolitan coexistence.

Although little is known of Bhagat Singh as a scribe, he worked as a journalist for popular publications such as *Kirti*, *Arjun* and *Pratap*. In *Kirti*, he wrote two articles in June 1928. The first was called 'On Untouchability' ('Achoot ka Sawaal'). The second was called 'Communal Riots and their Solutions' ('Sampradayik Dange aur unka Ilaj'). As is especially clear from the second article, Bhagat Singh's lure today lies in a telling reminder to the people of how they have once again to 'start believing that we all are born equal and our vocation, as well, need not divide us. If someone is born in a sweeper's family that does not mean that he/she has to continue in the family profession [of] cleaning . . . all his life, with no right to participate in any developmental work'.[4]

In the writings that Bhagat Singh left behind, he emphasized the following: 'As long as the words like black and white, civilized and uncivilized, ruler and the ruled, rich and poor, touchable and untouchable, etc. are in vogue where is the scope for universal brotherhood? This can only be preached by free people. The slave India cannot refer to it.' It was on this basis that he demanded, 'We will have to campaign for equality and equity. Will have to punish those who oppose the creation of such a world.'[5] Amid the failed politics of post-Independence India and Pakistan, these words now resonate with the common man on the street. According to Irfan

Habib, the fact that Bhagat Singh commands such reverence in Pakistan now suggests that 'he surely must be more than a territorial nationalist', and in fact 'a nationalist who stood for the freedom of all oppressed communities across the colonised world'. Bhagat Singh warned against the very divisive politics which now plagues the Indian subcontinent—with its divisive news anchors who have scant regard for the truth—as it does much of the democratic world.

In an excoriating critique of the press from mid-1928, a year before he was arrested, he wrote,

> The real duty of the newspapers is to educate, to cleanse the minds of people, to save them from narrow sectarian divisiveness, and to eradicate communal feelings to promote the idea of common nationalism. Instead their main objective seems to be spreading ignorance, preaching and propagating sectarianism and chauvinism, communalism, people's minds leading to the destruction of our composite culture and shared heritage.[6]

Although it has been suppressed from national memories, either by design or by accident, for close to a century, the story of Bhagat Singh is suddenly now back in the public consciousness as never before, being evident in the media, popular culture and government announcements of both India and Pakistan. The question is, however, what the story should be and who has the right to tell it. To this we must now turn.

10

Punjabiyat

In early 2018, for the first time in its history, the Punjab government in Lahore decided to exhibit the contents of the case file of the trial of Bhagat Singh and others who were hanged to death with him on 23 March 1931. The exhibition was inaugurated at the tomb of Anarkali, which is 'the main storehouse of the Punjab archives department',[1] by Additional Chief Secretary Umar Rasool. The documents displayed included the arrest by the British Indian police of some twenty-five members of the Hindustan Socialist Republican Army and the Naujawan Bharat Sabha from different parts of India. There were also the documents relating to the parties, their manifestos and literature. Also disclosed for the first time were the addresses of places where Bhagat Singh and his comrades used to stay, including a factory on Ravi Road, a rented house in Gowalmandi, another in Mozang and in Kashmir Building on McLeod Road. In fact, the size of the Anarkali repository is clear from the inclusion of the admission register of one of Bhagat Singh's associates studying at DAV College in Lahore (now Islamia College Civil Lines). In addition, Bhagat Singh's reading material, ranging across books, novels and other revolutionary literature, was also displayed. This is referred to in the books named '*Punjab Tragedy, Zakhmi Punjab,*

Ganga Das Dakoo, Sultana Dakoo, The Evolution of Sinn Fein and
History of the Sinn Fein Movement.[2]

Although the Punjabis of East Punjab (India) have long regarded
Bhagat Singh as one of their own, the assertion of the same claim
by the Lahoris of West Punjab (Pakistan) on another Lahori by
the name of Bhagat Singh heralds a new recognition of the shared
culture of the Punjabis, notwithstanding the national border, in the
clear recognition that what unites them is far more significant than
what divides them. This is not illogical, because in her recent work,
Dr Pippa Virdee has shown how Punjab—which had uniquely
achieved a hybridity of communal coexistence between Muslims,
Hindus and Sikhs on the basis of a shared inheritance of *Punjabiyat*
carefully nurtured over centuries past—saw in the Partition of
1947 its ethnic history submerged within respective national and
religious identity(s) like no other state in the subcontinent. She
has persuasively demonstrated how none paid the price of Partition
like the pluralistic, pre-Partition Punjab.[3] This idea of *Punjabiyat*
was moulded by none other than Maharajah Ranjit Singh, who
held sway over Punjab from 1792 until his death in 1839, covering
an area which is roughly the size of modern-day Pakistan. This is
highlighted by the foremost historian Fakir S. Aijazuddin, who has
recently made it clear how, 'Ranjit Singh's uniqueness lay in giving
Punjabiyat a political identity, in welding the Punjab nation into a
sovereign state', in circumstances where Punjab, through a thousand
years of conquest, had actually belonged 'never to itself'[4] but to
others. Punjabis therefore do not recognize the identity politics of
Gujarat in present-day India, as the concept is alien to them.

Bhagat Singh can help resurrect the importance of Punjabiyat in
a collective culture shared by the peoples of both West Punjab (in
Pakistan) and East Punjab (in India) just as Maharajah Ranjit Singh
did in times long since forgotten. Those who remember Ranjit Singh
do so not only with a fondness for what stood as the high-point of
Punjab's multicultural identity, but also as an acknowledgement and
a longing for Punjab's one-time greatness. As Aijazuddin reminds
us, 'Few of the post-Mughal regional courts had the power or the

military might and discipline to take on armies of the East India
Company. But one that did with great success was Ranjit Singh's
Sikh Empire.'[5]

In the same way, those who today recall what Bhagat Singh
stood for do so with no less admiration for the ultimate ideals of
Punjabiyat—namely, the pluralism, diversity, broad-mindedness and
tolerance of its people. It is Punjabiyat that has ultimately become
the basis of the quest for a better and a more just future. A false
dividing border—all too arbitrarily imposed after Independence in
1947 by the departing imperial forces, whom Bhagat Singh and other
revolutionaries such as Ashfaqullah Khan so vehemently opposed
and which many on both sides of the border continue to regret to
this day—often obscures this fact. Yet, the reality is that even before
then, as Aijazuddin makes clear, '[c]enturies of hostility had divided
Sikhs and Muslims until what had been a common approach to
God – a belief in monotheism – had become blurred by blistering
resentment and bloody outbreaks'. In the event, '[t]he fabric of their
communal history bore indelible stains of blood, primarily Punjabi
blood, spilt or shed to defend divergent and ultimately opposing
causes'.[6] It is precisely because of a history of such needless blood-
letting, which arose when the peoples of Punjab misguidedly staked
out for themselves 'divergent and opposing causes', that Bhagat
Singh can help remind them, as Maharajah Ranjit Singh once did,
that they have an ineradicable common culture and deep-rooted ties
with each other. The legacy of Maharajah Ranjit Singh has been
largely lost over time. Only a few men of letters, stalwarts such as
Fakir Aijazuddin, have devoted themselves to keeping it alive in
Pakistan. Otherwise, it is either forgotten or deliberately suppressed.
In Pakistan, this is for reasons both religious and political. In India
too, those who remember Ranjit Singh's true legacy of secularism,
religious tolerance and communal coexistence are few and far
between. He does not figure prominently in school history textbooks.
And Indians are barely able to recall how Ranjit Singh kept the
marauding eye of the foreign invader in check by commanding the
most powerful army in all of Asia.

It is almost entirely unknown that in the day-to-day administration of his kingdom, Ranjit Singh relied on Muslim administrators' impeccable credentials and loyalty. These were the Fakir Brothers (Fakir Azizuddin, Imamuddin and Nuruddin). Yet the contribution that these 'three brothers from a Muslim family . . . had made to enhancing the image of the Sikh Court of Lahore during the rule of Maharajah Ranjit Singh' and 'in the tumultuous period thereafter'[7] is one which is still today so undervalued and largely unrecognized, not least in Lahore itself, that they have failed to become the household names on both sides of the border, which they so richly deserve. If truth be told, they were the backbone to his rule, never once betraying him nor abusing the trust which he so unflinchingly bestowed upon them. Fakir S. Aijazuddin, the direct linear descendant of Fakir Nuruddin, recognizes the paradox even back then in the early 1800s of how it was that '[n]o one at the time could have been unaware of the anomaly of a Sikh ruler reposing so much faith in these young men, all of three belonging to another religion and that too to Islam'.[8] However, Maharajah Ranjit Singh, during whose rule there was not a single public execution of a person, may have been robbed of the sight in his left eye (as he was blinded in the left eye as a child through an affliction of small-pox), but it was said that he used his one remaining unimpaired eye more wisely than most who had two, for he used his one eye 'just so that he could view all religions with an impartial singularity',[9] treating, Hindus, Muslims and Sikhs entirely alike.

By contrast with Maharajah Ranjit Singh, Bhagat Singh's legacy is not lost in the fog of time. There are still people alive in both India and Pakistan who remember his struggle in Punjab against foreign rule. As a result, there are today an ever increasing number of people in both countries, of varying hues and tones, who wish to lay claim to his heritage. This has turned Bhagat Singh into an inscrutable and impenetrable figure in official narratives, but not necessarily so in popular and folk narratives on both sides of the border. Chris Moffat has referred to the enigma of 'Bhagat Singh's brief but eventful life as a revolutionary organizer, Bolshevik sympathizer and critic of Gandhi', but says that his name 'is celebrated from the Hindu nationalist right to the Maoist left, from Sikh militants to environmentalist youth groups, the Army in India to pacifists in Pakistan'.[10] Yet, as Moffat has also most accurately stated, Bhagat Singh is for all intents and purposes 'a figure outside the narrative of Muslim struggle curated by the Pakistan state'.[11] In an important book that has followed more recently, Moffat has argued that anti-colonial histories have a real meaning for politics in contemporary India by enabling us to understand a political terrain that, although appearing to be crowded with the dead and heroic figures from past struggles, enables us to call the living to account and demand action.[12] But the 'problem of inheritance' that he refers to is not one of India alone, but also of Pakistan, if recent evidence is anything to go by.

Perhaps the person who has best encapsulated the significance of Bhagat Singh in today's politics in the Indian subcontinent is the Oxford-based economist Professor Pritam Singh, who wrote a piece in 2007 for Bhagat Singh's 100th birth anniversary. In it, he lamented how little was appreciated about Bhagat Singh even in his own native country despite the fact that '[a]s an icon, Bhagat Singh can be called the Che Guevara of India. Yet, his 100th birth anniversary was the least celebrated of all the anniversaries except the 250th anniversary of the Battle of Plassey'. This is because it 'represents a challenge to almost every tendency in Indian politics', given how the 'Gandhi-inspired Indian nationalists, Hindu nationalists, Sikh nationalists, the parliamentary Left and the pro-armed struggle Naxalite Left compete with each other to appropriate the legacy of Bhagat Singh, and yet each one of them is faced with a contradiction in making a claim to his legacy'. Thus, as he explains,

> Gandhi-inspired Indian nationalists find Bhagat Singh's resort to violence problematic, the Hindu and Sikh nationalists find his atheism troubling, the parliamentary Left finds his ideas and actions as more close to the perspective of the Naxalites and the Naxalites find Bhagat Singh's critique of individual terrorism in his later life an uncomfortable historical fact.

Pritam Singh may just as well have added that across the border from India the people of Pakistan too struggle to lay claim to him as one of their own—not only was he not religious, but he was also not a Muslim. So, the enigma of Bhagat Singh is to do with who can claim him, and as a result what we have are 'the claims of different contestations to the legacy of Bhagat Singh'.

In fact, given how Bhagat Singh's developmental years were lived in what is today Pakistan, the claim on him is no less strong there. This is reflected in the words of Indian writers. Professor Chaman Lal, in his latest book *The Bhagat Singh Reader*, marvels at how it is that, '[l]ooking back, more than eight decades later, one can only wonder that how come no memorial was built to these martyrs in Lahore or in Lyallpur, the birthplace of Bhagat Singh and Sukhdev, which is now called Faisalabad in Pakistan'. The reason why this is so puzzling is, 'Bhagat Singh is the one and perhaps only symbol which evokes respect among both Indian and Pakistani people.' Indeed, in his words, 'Bhagat Singh is the common thread between the now-divided Punjabis – a symbol of resistance against colonialism and imperialism.' His enduring importance today is such that '[h]e can still become a common symbol of resistance against the new colonial corporate regime as well'.[13] Whether this will ever come to pass must remain an open question even if it is a pressing one.

11

2019, Shadman Chowk

Everyone in India and Pakistan today will remember the Pulwama bomb attack, the enormous casualties of young men returning to work after a short spell at home, and the Indian Air Force attack in Balakot that followed in response. The facts are worth recounting. On 14 February 2019, a convoy of seventy-eight vehicles carrying young cadets of the Central Reserve Police Force (CRPF) was ambushed in India when it was slowly making its way along the Srinagar–Jammu highway to Pulwama. The convoy was trudging along in the clear daylight of the mid-afternoon sun. There had been no movement on the highway for the last two to three days. The weather had been exceptionally bad that year. A lone suicide bomber, belonging to the Pakistan-based militant group Jaish-e-Mohammad, emerged suddenly, violently crashing his SUV, with its 300 kg of explosives, into the convoy. The resulting carnage saw no less than some forty-four personnel of the CRPF killed. It was a dastardly and cowardly assault in the contested north-western Indian province of Jammu and Kashmir, and the deadliest and most horrific terror attack on India's state security personnel in Kashmir since 1989. So bad it was that '[t]he site of the Pulwama attack', it was said, 'resembled a war zone with body parts and vehicle debris strewn about'.[1] The Indian government promptly blamed Pakistan.

Pakistan condemned the attack and denied any connection to it. Prime Minister Modi's Indian government retaliated swiftly. Half-way through the cold dead of night, on 26 February 2019, the Indian air force stealthily crossed the Line of Control at the border of the two countries. It was the first time they had done so since the Indo–Pakistan War of 1971. They launched a thunderous airstrike by despatching twelve Mirage 2000 fighter aircraft. They entered deep into Pakistani territory, dropping bombs in Khyber Pakhtunkhwa, which was in the vicinity of the town of Balakot.

The airstrike was immediately confirmed by the Pakistani military, but with the proviso the Indian planes had only managed to drop their payload in an uninhabited wooded hilltop area. India nevertheless declared it as a pre-emptive strike against a terrorist training camp and controversially maintained that of its bombs, 'four penetrated the rooftops of the building in which the terrorists were sleeping'.[2] In the days and weeks that followed, relations between the two countries plummeted to an all-time low in what had once been described by US President Bill Clinton as 'the most dangerous place on earth'.[3] Soon it was lamented that '[t]he "all or nothing" policy that the Narendra Modi government has followed towards Pakistan has failed. Bilateral relations have deteriorated and violence in Kashmir is at a new high'.[4] Within a month, the bad blood between the two countries had reached such a crescendo that the Indian government even boycotted the Pakistan National Day and stopped Indians from attending a programme at the Pakistan High Commission on 23 March 2019.[5]

On the same day in Pakistan, however, something quite different was stirring. Given that it was amid the febrile atmosphere of two nuclear powers now poised to go to war with each other, it was all the more unexpected. And, it was taking place in the very heart of Lahore, in what was once the citadel of cosmopolitanism, memorialized in a slogan which every Lahori has on his lips when he meets a non-Lahori. The origins of this slogan have all but now been forgotten—'*jeneh Lahore nahin dekhya oh jamiyan nahin*', which translates into, 'He who has not seen Lahore has not enjoyed being born.' That day was the 88th Martyrdom Day of Bhagat Singh, Rajguru and Sukhdev, who had been hastily executed by the colonial government for the murder of a British police officer, J.P. Saunders.[6] Amid the prospect of a looming cross-border war, Lahoris on this day refused to be cowed and were determined to celebrate the Lahore that once was—the Lahore of many cities, of many cultures, of many diverse faiths. They thronged its streets, unperturbed and with not a care in the world. Rising above deep-seated divisions of distrust and disharmony between the two countries, a chorus of voices cried out in a shrill slogan of, 'Long live the memory of Bhagat Singh!' on that Saturday evening. They had resolved against all adversity to commemorate the hanging to death on 23 March 1931 of these three iconic figures in Lahore Central Jail. Indeed, some years ago, oblivious to the importance of its preservation, a traffic roundabout christened Shadman Chowk was said to have sprung up at this very spot. Now, however, a motley of people young and old, in surprisingly large numbers, excitedly descended upon this very spot. They rushed to pay tributes to the hanged three, heedless of the impending wrath of the hard-line religious zealots objecting to the deification of individuals who were not Muslims. Nearly 200 km away too, in Banga village, near Faisalabad, where Bhagat Singh was born, there was reverence shown in remembrance of the ultimate sacrifices he made for the cause of freedom in what was then pre-Partition India.

The day of commemoration had been long planned and organized by the chairman of the Lahore-based Bhagat Singh Memorial Foundation, Imtiaz Rashid Qureshi, and his father Abdul Rashid Qureshi, both supreme court lawyers. At Shadman Chowk, bright white candles were lit as the sun set in the distant and the grey light of dusk fell upon the city and gave it its distinctive colour. Established and aspiring artists rose up to sing traditional Punjabi folk songs and verses in memory of the revolutionaries. Bhagat Singh was designated not only a martyr of India but of the whole subcontinent. In a telephone interview given to the *Times of India*, Imtiaz Qureshi explained, 'We too have every right over

the memory of Bhagat Singh as the freedom fighter was not only
born in Pakistan, but had spent most of the time of his short but
meaningful life at Lahore. We see him as an icon of struggle.' He
said about his objective, 'We want Bhagat Singh to be treated as a
freedom fighter in Pakistan and Shadman Chowk should be named
after him.' He saw nothing incongruous in the fact that Bhagat was
not a Muslim because, the 'Founder of Pakistan, Muhammad Ali
Jinnah, had paid tributes to Bhagat Singh in Delhi assembly on
September 4, 1929, and Bhagat Singh is a hero to many Pakistanis.'
Imtiaz Qureshi was not content with just paying homage to
Bhagat Singh. What he and his followers have been demanding
for some years now, consistent with a claim raised a year earlier, is
that Bhagat Singh be given the accolade of 'Nishan-e-Haider',[7] so
that he is declared a 'national' martyr by the Pakistan government;
that it issue a postage stamp in his name; that it put up a statue
at Shadman Chowk which should be re-named as 'Bhagat Singh
Chowk' and that there be an apology from the British queen for the
hanging of Bhagat Singh and his comrades.[8]

Thus it is that, almost a hundred years after the death of Bhagat
Singh, two groups in Pakistan now want him declared a 'national
hero'. These are the Bhagat Singh Memorial Foundation (BSMF)
and the Bhagat Singh Foundation Pakistan (BSFP). On the eighty-
seventh death anniversary of the freedom fighter on 23 March 2018,
each group held separate functions at Shadman Chowk, where
Bhagat Singh and his two comrades were allegedly hanged, under
strict security arrangements. Each had participants pay glowing
tributes to those they considered martyred by the state, as they had
done in years past. In fact, there was even a telephone address from
some relatives of Bhagat Singh from across the border in India
that was arranged by the organizers, such was their desire to rise
above communal interests and support the cause of a non-sectarian,
pluralistic and egalitarian society, which they believed had been
denied them as their birthright ever since they gained Independence.
The leaders of both organizations spoke similarly. Imtiaz Rashid, the
chairman of BSMF, 'presented a resolution demanding the British

Queen to tender an apology for hanging the three freedom fighters and compensate their families'. He also demanded naming a road after Bhagat Singh and revising the Pakistani school curriculum to include a chapter on Bhagat Singh. For his part, Abdullah Malik, the president of BSFP, reminded the audience of how 'Bhagat Singh raised his voice against imperialism' and that it was high time that the governments of both India and of Pakistan declare Bhagat Singh and his comrades 'national heroes'.

All this despite the fact that these proposals are strenuously opposed by the Hurmat-e-Rasool, a sister organization of Jamaat-u-Dawah, led by the mastermind of the Mumbai terror attack, Hafiz Saeed.[9] When plans to rename Shadman Chowk as 'Bhagat Singh Chowk' were aborted in 2012, Britain's *Daily Mail* reported that 'Shadman Chowk stands on the spot that marks the execution ground of the Lahore Central Jail . . .'.[10] This is not quite true. Shadman Chowk is strictly speaking part of the Shadman area and was indeed previously more accurately known as Fawara Chowk. This is located today in the area known as Government Officer Residence ('GOR'), on an old site where the 'Female Penitentiary' once existed, but where the Fatima Memorial Hospital today stands. It is about a kilometre's distance from where an old lunatic asylum stood, though it has now been replaced by the Institute of Mental Health. In front of the entire GOP area is an old watercourse some 70 m wide, which can be traversed by a bridge. That is where the vast complex of the Lahore Central Jail once stood, in an area of about a square kilometre, close to Shadman Gardens. This is where the Shadman Market is presently located, some 300 km from Fawara Chowk, more recently called Shadman Chowk. Thus, whereas Shadman Market is north of the water channel Shadman Chowk is to the south of it.

12

Colonialism's Racial Cast

In this way, the pre-Independence past continues to assert itself. So much so that courts of law are even now involved in remedying colonialism's worst excesses. On 3 February 2016, some three-quarters of a century after Bhagat Singh and his comrades were hanged, the Lahore High Court in Pakistan was presented with a petition. Its purpose was to prove the innocence of this much-neglected freedom fighter, whose shadow lurked in the faded memories of all those who lived during the pre-Independence years and even immediately thereafter. The monumental news was excitedly reported on the Indian side of the border a week before the event on 31 January 2016, by NDTV, the Indian news channel. It explained how Chief Justice Ijazul Ahsan had constituted a bench headed by Khalid Mahmood Khan. In fact, unknown to the public at large on both sides of the Indo–Pak border, interest in Bhagat Singh appears to have been long-standing in Pakistan because in May 2013 the petition had been heard by Shujaat Ali Khan, and it was he who had then referred the matter to the chief justice so that it could be heard by a larger bench.

Thereafter, Advocate Imtiaz Rashid Qureshi, as chairman of the Bhagat Singh Memorial Foundation, filed a plea for the matter to be expedited in November 2013. It was shortly after the filing of this petition that the Lahore Police in 2014 provided the copy of the first information report (FIR)[1] on the killing of Saunders in 1928 to the petitioner on the court's order,[2] which showed that when the FIR was registered at the Anarkali Police Station in Lahore on 17 December 1928 at 4.30 p.m., it referred to only two 'unknown gunmen' and made no reference to Bhagat Singh by name, for which a case against them was registered under Sections 302, 1201 and 109 of the Indian Penal Code. However, this is not to say that Bhagat did not commit the atrocity together with his accomplices. Such is the commitment to the cause of Bhagat Singh and what he stood for that in Pakistan the advocate Imtiaz Rashid Qureshi has latched on to the fact that given that the initial FIR, by which prosecutions are first initiated in the Indian subcontinent, did not mention the three accused, Bhagat Singh, Rajguru and Sukhdev, cannot be shown to have committed the murder of Saunders and should be exonerated.

When Qureshi procured a copy of the FIR in mid-2019, it was widely reported that it could form the basis of proof that Bhagat Singh, Rajguru and Sukhdev were innocent of the murder of Saunders.[3] Yet, nothing can be more misconceived. Bhagat Singh was not innocent of the crime of killing Saunders. He and his colleagues admitted they shot and killed Saunders. It was the trial that was contrary to every cannon of natural justice and due process and begs questions with its material irregularities. These included trying the accused without ensuring his attendance in court while he remained confined in detention. It included doing so in the absence of proper legal representation. It involved removing two of the three panel judges within a month of a special tribunal being established so that only one judge heard all of the evidence from beginning to end. And it involved the passing of a sentence of death without cross-examination of the 450 state witnesses arraigned by the state. Bhagat Singh and Dutt had both been identified by Sir Sobha Singh, then a member of the Legislative Assembly and the grandfather of the noted Indian writer and journalist, Khushwant Singh, as the pair who had thrown the smoke bombs in the legislative chamber in Delhi.

So the real issue is not that the initial FIR referred to two 'unknown gunmen' and not to Bhagat Singh and his two companions, but the rampant coercive colonial violence of his trial.

This was structural violence because it was based on the Lahore Ordinance III of 1930, passed by the governor-general and viceroy of the time, Lord Irwin. The fact that the special tribunal set up for the trial disappeared into thin air suggested that it was an execution court. Its only purpose was to ensure that Bhagat Singh and his two colleagues, Sukhdev and Rajguru, were not spared. The rule of law, the much-vaunted edifice of the English common law eulogized so heavily by its judges down the ages, was a chimera. It was a charade.

The violence of the special tribunal was not just structural. It was also actual. If there was any doubt left that the trial was taking place outside the established canons of the rule of law, it was dispelled by the vicious bouts and acts of actual violence meted out to the accused by police officers both in the courtroom and outside it. It is an illustration of what Radhika Singha has described as the 'racially structured legal jurisdiction' in colonial India.[4] As she points out, from the time of the East India Company, 'courts in India were conspicuously lacking in any of the forms which dignified the proceedings of English courts'. In the circumstances, 'race shaped the way in which judicial and magisterial authority were communicated'. The result was that '[t]he British magistrate or judge occupied his office as a white ruler'.[5] The 'racial cast of magisterial authority'[6] permeated all legal proceedings. And Bhagat Singh fell victim to such a system.

The irony for Bhagat Singh is that he could have lived. After the assassination of J.P. Saunders on 17 December 1928, Bhagat Singh had successfully escaped the scene of the crime. The police had no leads on him. He would not have been identified. However, he invited arrest by himself plastering notices of the killing across the city of Lahore, signed off in his own handwriting, and claiming that by this act the death of Lala Lajpat Rai had been avenged. He would not have been caught had it not been for the fact that, not only did he then go on to take part in the Delhi Assembly Bomb

Case on 8 April 1929, but he also willingly chose to give himself up so that at the trial he could denounce the government by making an open speech before the judge. The trial over the Delhi Assembly Bomb Case began before Magistrate R.B. Pool on 7 May 1929, but it was on 6 June 1929 that he made his historic courtroom statement. Although the statement was suppressed, it leaked into the public domain quite quickly, so that when on 12 June 1929 the Delhi sessions judge, Justice Leonard Middleton, gave his judgment sentencing both Bhagat Singh and B.K. Dutt, his statement intended 'to make the deaf hear' and call for revolution because 'revolution is an alienable right of mankind' was well-known to all.

In hindsight, this is hardly surprising, given that even as Bhagat Singh hurled down the smoke bombs from the balcony, he had shouted out, together with B.K. Dutt, who accompanied him, the slogan *Inquilab zindabad*. The phrase means 'Long live the Revolution'. *Inquilab zindabad* was a slogan coined by the Urdu poet and Indian freedom fighter Maulana Hasrat, who was a founder of the Indian Communist Party in 1921. The adage was popularized, however, by Bhagat Singh through its repeated invocation in his speeches and writings. The Hindustan Socialist Republican Association (HSRA) adopted it as its official mantra, as did the All India Azad Muslim Conference. Thereafter, it served as a motto for the Indian Independence Movement. Today, it is even used in India as a catchphrase in the fight against bigotry and injustice. The crack of the explosion from the smoke bombs split the air, sending those nearby screaming and scrambling for cover. It was the desired effect the two revolutionaries had aimed for. Fear and panic flooded the chamber. What flooded India was the light of humanity. It is this light which the rest of this book must now explore.

PART 3

A LIFE IN REVOLUTION

Tum se pehle jo aik shakhs yahan takht nasheen tha
Uss ko bhi apne khuda hone pe itna hi yaqeen tha

Before you also, there were others
who sat on the seat of governance
and who thought they would rule forever,
and whose vanity brought them down.

—Habib Jalib

13

1919, The Lahore File

In the Lahore Archives, there lies a large file stamped as 'Secret'. It was written in the immediate aftermath of the Amritsar Massacre 1919 and followed the unrest in Punjab at the time.[1] On 28 May 1919, Chief Secretary to the Government of Punjab J.P. Thompson wrote on behalf of the lieutenant-governor of Punjab to all the commissioners and deputy commissioners of Punjab, asking them to report on 'the immediate causes of the outbreak in the districts where outbreaks . . . actually occurred'.[2] This was particularly because '[t]he introduction of Martial Law was a novel experiment in this country, and in examining the method in which it has been administered, there should be no hesitation in drawing attention to what actual experience has shown to be unnecessary or undesirable'. After all, 'prompt' action 'of the military authorities checked the spread of disorder and in all probability saved the province from a state of temporary anarchy'.[3] On this basis, what the lieutenant-governor of Punjab now desired was that the commissioners of Jullunder, Ambala and Lahore Divisions, together with the political agents of the Phulkian States and the Bahawalpur Agency, 'submit brief reports on the recent disturbances so far as they have affected the States in the Agencies'.[4]

The most striking report sent to the lieutenant-governor in this file is by the Lahore commissioner. What he wishes to point out is 'a very necessary result of the lesson that India is not different from the India of 1857 but the same'. This is quite a remarkable statement to make in 1919. More than half-a-century had gone by since the East India Company was replaced after the so-called 'Indian Mutiny of 1857' by direct rule from London. In its aftermath, an iron-clad system of control and administration had been imposed. Yet, what the Lahore report now seemed to suggest was that this had been to no avail because, after the unrest of 1919, 'there is one effect which every Englishman feels in his bones, and that is that there is a change in his feeling towards the native of India'. So much so that, '[h]e now realizes that East is East and West is West'. The conviction of this belief arose from the fact that both '[t]he educated classes and the townsfolk have shown their hands. They have at once shown to the Englishman that he is in a land of an inferior civilisation, among a people which has not yet advanced beyond medievalism'. This alleged realization by the Englishman was significant because '[a]t anytime he may have to treat them as enemies' and that '[i]t is idle to refuse to look facts in the face and to pretend that the situation remains unaltered'. The inference that the commissioner in Lahore drew from this assessment was that '[t]hese reflections will inevitably weaken the English official's enthusiasm, and will incline him to leave the country at the earliest opportunity'.[5] What is manifestly plain from this report is a clear recognition by the British administration that the 1919 insurgency was no different from the first war of Indian Independence in 1857. This was despite the fact that in 1919 they still had 'the loyal attitude of the troops; and the fact that the disaffected elements were not those from which the recruits were drawn'.[6] In fact, it was openly accepted that '[i]t is curious that fire-arms were never used by the rebels'.[7]

The secret report from the 'Amritsar District' on the disturbances in Amritsar in 1919 was no different from the one on Lahore when it recognized that although the 'plots against the British Government in India' had been 'detected and suppressed', what they successfully managed to do was that they 'made men's minds familiar with the possibility of that Government being overthrown'. It was almost as if a red line had been passed, and the Rubicon had been crossed, to the point of no return. The view from Amritsar was that 'the great herd of the people had, so to speak, their heads up and when they have their heads up it is not far to a stampede'.[8] Four clear sources could be identified in the reports for this concern.

First, there was the First World War from 1914 to 1918, which culminated with the Armistice in November 1918. The Amritsar report acknowledged that '[d]uring these years the confidence of the people in the established order of things had been shaken' so that '[t]hey were daily assailed with rumours pointing to the defeat of the British Arms, and no rumour was too wild to be believed'.[9] Second, there was the concern of 'the Musalman of India' for the plight of the Sultan, Mehmed VI of Turkey, who feared he would be deposed after the First World War, so that what the Government of India faced at home were the 'religious troubles' arising from the fact that '[f]or four years the British Empire has been fighting the Commander of the Faithful, and for the most loyal Musalman that is an uncomfortable and distressing position'. Moreover, 'this feeling was aggravated by the general belief that the British Government had instigated a puppet in the shape of the King of the Hedjaz to rise against the lawful authority of the Khalifa'.[10] There were therefore strong religious undercurrents which risked lighting the fuse of fire, which is why the report records that '[t]he penultimate stage of the agitation may be said to date from January 31st, when a meeting was held to protest about the future of Constantinople'.[11] Third, there was the economic hardship that the ordinary person was having to endure which raised the very real spectre of an insurrection. At the end of the Great War, 'the common people, and above all the lower middle class, were being hard hit by the rise in prices' and 'a large part of the urban population was suffering want and there is nothing which better prepares the ground for revolution'.[12] In fact, it was not just the ordinary person because '[t]he commercial classes were irritated by taxation which they were not used to . . .'.[13] Fourth, it was said that '[t]o all this must be added the reaction after the armistice' and what was meant by this was that '[s]o long as the War went on, people could and did accept their discomforts as a natural consequence, and hope for the end. But when the end came and the victory had been celebrated nothing seemed to happen'. So now, '[p]rices and taxes were as high as ever, and it is no wonder that discontent grew into an angry bewilderment as to whether after all the people were not being tricked and Government was not for some obscure motive at the bottom of all their troubles'.[14]

All in all, therefore, the cumulative effect of these four different sources of discontent was that 'a soil was thus prepared to receive the seed by agitation which was focussed round the Rowlatt Act [and] the future of Turkey'.[15] The Rowlatt Act was significant because it 'recommended the continuation of repressive measures such as limiting the right to a jury trial in the case of certain political offenses and the suspension of *habeas corpus* through a provision that suspects might be detained because they were suspected of sedition'.[16] It was as a consequence of such measures that the nationalist Lala Lajpat Rai was assaulted during a protest March in October 1928. When he died in hospital, 'his death at the hands of the Punjab police gave rise to a new round political violence',[17] in which Bhagat Singh set out to avenge his death by wrongly firing upon J.P. Saunders in December 1928.

There is, however, a fifth reason which the 1919 secret report does not expressly cite. It is readily discernible from a closer analysis of the text. The increased repression and accompanying economic hardships of the time were bringing people of different faiths together in Punjab in a way that threatened to upset British rule in the province and which they wished to prevent. The British viewed their coming together with foreboding. As the meetings began to take place, '[t]he speeches at these gatherings were couched in a higher and higher key. No opportunity was lost of blaming Government for economic conditions and of alarming the people with the terms of the Rowlatt Bill, and there is no doubt that these inflammatory utterances began to influence the minds of the masses, imbuing them with the feeling that their sufferings were the direct result of the British Raj'.[18] Amid such turmoil, what actually gave the authorities a real cause for concern was that '[a]t the same time there may be seen a quiet and persistent attempt to bring Muhammadans into line with an agitation that was in its source Hindu. We find Hindus attending Muhammadan meetings and Muhammadans given the places of prominence in the general meetings, the chief link between the two *being always found* in the person of Dr. Saif-ud-din Kitchlew'.[19]

Against this background, one should not forget that the local Congress Party Committee was founded in Amritsar only two years earlier in October 1917, expressly 'with the object of uniting Hindus and Musalmans in political action', so that it was not too difficult to see how '[t]he fact that the next meeting of the All India Congress [that] was to be held in Amritsar' thereafter became 'undoubtedly a contributory cause' to the agitation in 1919.[20] Remarkably, there was still no risk of impending mob violence. What was threatened was civil disobedience. It was for this reason that the government of the day had to find more insidious ways of dealing with what it saw as a threat to its authority. All along there was no risk of violence nor was any one threatened. What it was having to deal with was passive resistance. For the government, '[t]he situation had however begun to take a threatening aspect. It was not that any immediate violence was apprehended. On the contrary the policy of the brains behind the movement appeared to be directed in the opposite direction. It seemed their intention [was] to avoid any collision with authority which would justify armed intervention and to train the crowd with a view to some collective form of passive disobedience to authority . . . '.[21]

To their horror, the Muslims and Hindus of Punjab did come together when, '[o]n the evening of April 9th the festival of Ram Naumi was observed. An important feature of this was the fact that although it is a purely Hindu festival it was celebrated by Muhammadans and Hindus alike. Water was provided by Muhammadans and drunk from their hands by Hindus, although, it is true, in silver vessels. And as the procession passed, the cries raised were, in place of those giving honour to the Hindu deities, the political shouts of "*Hindu Musalman Ki Jai*".[22] What is surprising but fully acknowledged by the authorities is that '[a]t the same time there was little sign of active hostility to Government and none of the hostility to Europeans as such. The Deputy Commissioner by accident was caught in the crowd and witnessed the procession unguarded from the verandah of the Allahabad Bank'.[23] There was accordingly no threat to public security or a risk of public disorder. The Muslims and Hindus of Punjab planned to make common cause in their shared concern over the plight of their respective people. Despite this, '[o]n his return from the procession at about 7.30 p.m. the Deputy Commissioner received the order of Government that Drs. Kitchlew and Satyapal were to be escorted quietly to Dharmsala'.[24] This was an unnecessary act of deliberate government provocation. It risked the situation immediately deteriorating. The government authorities would have known that the deportation out of Punjab of these two leaders could goad an entirely peaceful gathering of people into agitation. Even then, however, '[t]he situation as it presented itself did not seem to argue any serious results as likely to arise from the arrests' because '[t]here had been no signs of enmity to Europeans as such; during the *hartal* [. . .] of the preceding Sunday Europeans had been walking about among the crowd quite unmolested'.

So remote was the risk of impending violence that the authorities' settled view was that '[w]hat was considered a more likely occurrence was that an attempt might be made to rescue the deportees on the way, and to meet this danger the Deputy Commissioner asked Mr. Rehill, the Superintendent of Police, the only responsible officer who knew the way, to accompany the escort'.[25] The authorities did not stop there. The colonial authorities continued to push their luck. Not content to let matters rest there, '[a]s regards Amritsar, it was decided that no crowd should be allowed to cross the railway line, and three European Magistrates were detailed to the three main crossings, and on the following morning received written orders to the effect that any crowd attempting to cross the line was to be dealt with as an unlawful assembly'. So the ordinary people of Punjab were criminalized at the stroke of a pen as participating in an unlawful assembly even if they only wished to go to the railway line while Drs Kitchlew and Satyapal were escorted to Dharamshala some 200 km way. Therefore, it is plain to see from this how the law was inducted, and the courts used, in the installation and execution of a framework of coercive colonial legalism.

If these 1919 'secret' reports are anything to go by, it is clear that as early as the Jallianwala Bagh Massacre, British officials in Lahore believed that their time in India was up. They were aware that the uneasy hold on India of the four years of the First World War was slipping out of their hands. They were also aware that the Muslims and Hindus of Punjab were coming together to protest against the economic and political hardships of the time that continued unabated well after the Great War. The response of the Raj was to pass the Rowlatt Act in February 1919, through the legislature of the Imperial Legislative Council, which made it possible for the courts to try political cases in the absence of a jury and allowed the internment of suspects without trial, in much the same way as the Guantanamo Bay has functioned today in Cuba under American control in the ill-fated 'War on Terror'. Whether the Hindus and Muslims of India can still come together, in spite of the divisive policies of the British colonizers, at a time when they are all but being emulated by governmental policy in a free India remains to be seen.

14

1919, Rowlatt Act

The wider political background during the unfolding decade of the 1920s is yet to be fully grasped by those studying India's revolutionary movements. As Durba Ghosh makes clear, 'The year 1919 marked the formal end of the First World War and provided an opportunity to the British government in India to defuse radical and militant Indian nationalists who had challenged colonial rule through acts of political violence.'[1] But the fact is this opportunity was squandered. The British government passed the Government of India Act 1919 immediately after the war 'to privilege Indian elites who were politically moderate by creating a road map to allow Indians the ability to eventually govern themselves, but with British supervision', and this ran in tandem with 'the continuation of repressive legislation through the recommendations of the Rowlatt Commission',[2] which in turn led to the so-called 'Rowlatt Act'. This was the chillingly worded Anarchical and Revolutionary Crimes Act, designed to curb the impact of radicals and militants by restricting, in respect of political crimes, the right to trial by jury and the abeyance, for seditious offences, of habeas corpus. The combined effect of these provisions was to ensure the incarceration and eventual trial by a judge alone of an accused.

The impetus to this lay in the habits developed during the First World War, which proved difficult to relinquish. Just four days after the Great War broke out, on 8 August 1914, the British government passed the Defence of the Realm Act 1914[3] (DORA). It allowed the government to acquire wide-ranging emergency powers, from being able to requisition buildings for the war effort to creating new criminal offences by passing regulations. DORA paved the way for the most draconian censorship, as the government embarked on a concerted programme of authoritarian social control. This is clear from the words in the regulation that, 'No person shall by way of mouth or in writing spread reports likely to cause disaffection or alarm among any of His Majesty's forces or among the civilian population',[4] causing well-known figures such as Bertrand Russell and John William Muir to be incarcerated with impunity. To mirror these developments in India, the Defence of India Act 1915 was passed in the first year of the Great War to introduce measures under which all those who posed a threat to the security of the state could be detained while it was engaged in war. Yet, when the Great War ended, all these powers were retained in the United Kingdom.

In India, the Rowlatt Commission recommended that these measures be carried forward into peacetime by the Anarchical and Revolutionary Crimes Act, even though the 1915 Act was decidedly a temporary measure designed specifically for the exigency of war, when the state had to resort to emergency powers in order to preserve and safeguard itself. As a preventative piece of legislation, it allowed the arbitrary internment and detention of a range of actors from members of opposition political parties to revolutionaries, and from Germans to terrorists. Like the UK act, for which the extension was repeatedly renewed, the Indian act met with the same fate. In India, however, it was the unabated threat of revolutionary terrorism that was used as the justification for the extension of temporary executive powers with an eye to put them on a more permanent footing.

In December 1917, the colonial government authorized the formation of a commission, headed by Sir Sidney Rowlatt, to 'investigate and report on the nature of the criminal conspiracies connected with the revolutionary movement in India' and to 'advise as to the legislations, if any, necessary to enable the Government to deal effectively with them'.[5] Less than six months later in April 1918, the Rowlatt Report was published, despite the fact that the formal cessation of hostilities in Europe was still to occur and the Defence of India Act 1915 was still extant. Durba Ghosh remarks that at '[t]his peculiar timing and logic – producing the language and rationale for a permanent executive order' was something which 'was fueled by the anxiety of what might happen to the colonial government if it lost its executive privileges to detain suspects on suspicion of sedition as it did in a time of emergency'. Yet, as she is careful to point out,[6] 'there was no immediate threat of emergency except by the circular reasoning that the lack of repressive measures might potentially cause the government to face a political emergency'.[7] Nevertheless, there is no escaping the fact that 'it is demonstrable that the presence of the revolutionaries on the political landscape during these crucial inter-war years strengthened the anticolonial front, even as they tested and ultimately redefined the policy of nonviolence'.[8]

By 1925, just five years after the anti-Rowlatt protest, the colonial government enacted a series of emergency ordinances and legislative acts that authorized police and intelligence officials in India to arrest and detain suspected terrorists, revolutionaries and violent dissidents and try them in special courts. Yet, the Repressive Laws Committee had strongly recommended in 1921 the repeal of all regulations authorizing executive detention. It was headed by the political moderate, Tej Bahadur Sapru, and it was obviously perfectly aware of the risks of not doing so at the time of the anti-Rowlatt protests taking place in Punjab. The decision to doggedly proceed nonetheless with draconian coercive legal measures where, as Durba Ghosh puts it, 'the language and logic of this new legislation drew substantially from the terms of the Defence of India Act of 1915 and the Rowlatt Act',[9] was nothing short of an incitement to violence by the colonial government. This is clear from the death of Lala Lajpat Rai, who was protesting against the Simon Commission in Lahore in 1928.

In 1919, the Montagu-Chelmsford Reforms led to the passing of the Government of India Act 1919. This introduced governance by diarchy in India, which consisted of double government. This was done by dividing the executive branch of each provincial government into two tiers. The first consisted of executive councillors appointed by the Crown. This was just as it had always been before. It was the undemocratic tier of governance. The second consisted of ministers chosen by the governor from the elected members of the provincial legislature. This second tier had some semblance of democratic legitimacy. This system of diarchy was opposed by Indian nationalist leaders. The act, however, contained a provision for the appointment of a commission after ten years to investigate, and report upon, the progress of constitutional reforms, with a view to making further reforms, but such a review was not due until 1929. However, at home in the United Kingdom, the Conservative government of Stanley Baldwin was about to lose the upcoming elections to the Labour Party. This was headed by Clement Attlee. It therefore acted early in 1927 to appoint 'The Indian Statutory Commission', more popularly known as the 'Simon Commission', headed by the distinguished liberal lawyer, Sir John Allsebrook Simon. Its purpose was to delay and forestall further constitutional reform. Consisting of seven British MPs, one of whom was Clement Attlee, it arrived in British India in 1928. It was almost immediately met by stormy opposition by Indian nationalist leaders when it arrived in Bombay on 3 February 1928.

The Simon Commission did not contain a single Indian member, though it was to determine the future of India. The Indian National Congress boycotted it and Muhammed Ali Jinnah led a faction of the Muslim League against it. On 30 October 1928, when the commission arrived in Lahore, it was met by a demonstration led by the Indian nationalist leader, Lala Lajpat Rai, waving black flags, who had already in February 1928 moved a resolution in the Punjab Legislative Assembly against the commission. The local police, in an effort to make way for the commission, began beating the protesters. Lala Lajpat Rai suffered head injuries and died two weeks later, and it was his death that Bhagat Singh set out to avenge when he mistakenly assassinated J.P. Saunders instead of his superior,

J.A. Scott, the superintendent of police in charge of controlling the crowd in Lahore at the time of the arrival of the Simon Commission.

The Simon Commission went on to publish a two-volume report in May 1930 proposing provincial autonomy for India but rejecting central parliamentary responsibility in Delhi, through a federated arrangement, whereby the British Crown would retain direct contact with the Indian states. In fact, it sowed the seeds for the eventual partition of India. This is why when the Government of India Act 1935 was passed, its call for 'responsible' government was directed to the provinces and not to the centre. It is noteworthy that by 1934 Attlee himself had become committed to the cause of Indian Independence. He did not think Britain could provide India with the constitutional reforms it needed. It should have, he believed, dominion status within the British Empire. As Prime Minister he eventually saw India gain Independence, but at a grave cost to India itself. The painful legacy of how India gained its independence—achieved not through a fight for independence but given as a departing gift by the colonial invader—continues to this day.

15

Colonialism's Civilising Mission

In the background unnoticed by many, the British government was continuing with its civilising mission all along. It is how the imperial masters understood its colonized peoples. The trial and execution of Bhagat Singh in 1931 is an example of legal historiography of colonial violence which arises from this so-called civilising mission. Kim Wagner, a scholar of the history of colonial India and the British Empire, has recently described how 'a growing body of scholarship has explored the role of colonial violence, both epistemic and physical, as an intrinsic aspect of British and European imperialism'. However, Wagner maintains, '[t]he insights provided by such studies have yet to make much of an inroad in conventional historiography of the Empire.' His work thus sets out to examine 'the violence at the heart of British colonial counterinsurgency during the high-point of Empire'[1] instead of merely 'settler violence' on which much has been written. Yet if this shortcoming is true of 'conventional historiography', it is doubly true of the 'legal historiography' of the British Empire in India. The Lahore Conspiracy Case and the trial of Bhagat Singh are cases in point. In fact, the backdrop to Wagner's valuable study is precisely that '[w]ithin the last few years the subject of colonial violence has come to the fore in debates on the legacies of the British Empire, with a range of lawsuits and calls for formal apologies and reparation . . .'.[2] The purpose of this discussion is to demonstrate that the execution of Bhagat Singh falls squarely within this milieu. Indeed, there can scarcely be a more deserving case.

Thus, Wagner has explained how, 'British knowledge and understanding of the people they fought throughout the Empire was invariably shaped by the colonial ideologies and racial hierarchies impact in the "civilising mission" and central to the imperial experience'.[3] It is worth observing here, however, that what was instrumental in this 'civilising mission' and 'colonial experience' was an elaborate artifice of the law and judicial administration. It is this which, I would suggest here, is the source of the development of law as a form of coercive colonial legalism. He goes on to explain that the '[c]onstruction of the enemy as "un-civilised", "savage", or "fanatic" had severe implications for the conduct of what became known as savage warfare; it dictated and justified techniques of violence that were by the same token considered unacceptable in conflicts between so-called "civilised" nations'. By this standard, a trial that would have been deemed utterly unacceptable and repugnant in Britain was considered to be justified in the execution of Bhagat Singh and was in fact so endorsed by the UK Privy Council in 1931,[4] despite there being no right of appeal in India for a man who was condemned to death by hanging on the gallows.

To justify this differential treatment, colonial imperial doctrine and practice relied on 'cultural knowledge'. But as Wagner explains, 'Cultural knowledge was not simply a facet of imperialism; it was an organizing principle underwriting the rule of colonial difference according to which "un-civilised" people had to be treated by different standards.' It was in this way that 'the rule of colonial difference informed savage warfare at every level during the high-point of Empire'. Bhagat Singh's trial took place at a time when that high-point was under sustained challenge in India and was in fact very much beginning to creak. This is why colonial people had to be treated differently, such that '[f]rom the sordid everyday beatings or rape of labourers and servants, to the exemplary execution and spectacular massacres of rebels – whether routine or exceptional –

colonial violence relied on the same logic of difference, insisting that brute force was the only language "natives" understood'.[5] Mark Condos too has recently explained how colonial power in British India was consolidated through 'colonial terror' and that the Amritsar Massacre of 1919 'could be read as the ultimate expression of colonial power' because 'what could be more evocative of the brute strength of colonial domination than the ability to inflict such devastating and indiscriminate slaughter upon its own subjects?'.[6]

It was the construction of a rule of colonial difference, with its concomitant reliance on ferocious violence, which also informed colonial penal policy. This is clear from a distinguished historian of the British Indian Empire, Taylor Sherman, who has analysed the study of colonial penal practices across the world.[7] She observes that the first generation of research focussed narrowly on imprisonment.[8] A second generation of such studies, emerging only since around 2004, focussed on capital and corporal punishment as well as policing and the courts. Interestingly, this also included research on the way indigenous people also experienced and interpreted their punishments. A third generation of scholarly study is now needed, however, to develop 'a new focus for the study of colonial punishment', she argues, and one 'which views colonial coercive techniques' as part of imperial 'coercive networks'.[9] This book hopes to be part of that endeavour, focussing as it does on the imperial technique of 'coercive colonial laws' which led to the improper hanging of Bhagat Singh. The coercive colonial legalism arose because, as Taylor Sherman explained in an earlier work, of the changed political circumstances of the 1930s. This meant that '[w]hile the 1920s witnessed a short period of moderate political liberalization, the early 1930s saw a reversal of this trend as the colonial regime cracked down on both a second nationalist civil disobedience campaign and violent revolutionary activities. With the revival of the activities of small groups of revolutionaries in colonial India, these groups were called terrorists in the 1930s . . .'.[10] Many could disagree.

16

1920, 'Lal Bal Pal'

Long before Gandhi had made a political impact on the Indian liberation struggle, it was Bal Gangadhar Tilak, Bipin Chandra Pal and Lala Lajpat Rai who, having laid the bedrock for muscular and uncompromising nationalism, propelled themselves into the national consciousness as the triad of 'Bal Pal Lal' within the Congress Party, thus establishing the roots of its radicalization. Today the names of 'Bal Pal Lal' are all but forgotten, even in the Indian subcontinent. Yet in their time, these three were a force to contend with. It was they who turned the Congress Party from a pro-government to an anti-government force. Although Gandhi had assumed leadership of the Congress Party in 1920, from where he would call for non-cooperation with the British even after the Jallianwala Bagh Massacre in Amritsar in 1919, Lajpat Rai in Lahore would have none of it. He was much more popular than Gandhi in Punjab. Thereafter, although he grudgingly went along with Mahatma Gandhi's non-cooperation programme for the two years that it lasted, he was convinced that as an ideology it would fail. In February 1922, after policemen shot down twenty-five protesters in Chauri Chaura in Uttar Pradesh, he demanded that Gandhi renounce this strategy altogether. Not unnaturally, given the stance that these three militant nationalists adopted, they were regarded within the Congress Party as extremists.

The epithet was not inaccurate for, unlike the rest of the Congress Party who believed in sharing power with the British, these three stood for complete autonomy for India within the Empire. Such was their transformative impact that prior to their arrival on the scene the Indian National Congress was widely known to be a pro-Empire party with an abiding belief in benign colonialism.

So great was Lala Lajpat Rai's influence in his demand for dignity from the colonial government that he inspired two generations of Indians. He was content to fight on without the assurance of a seat in government, which is not what one could say of many of the others in the Congress Party of 1905. This emboldened him to speak truth to power. The government, he declared, lacked credibility in its claim of preparing Indians for self-rule, if it was also at the same time passing repressive measures like the Rowlatt Act to stifle dissent. This reeked of humbug. In his calling out the government in this manner, which many in the Congress Party regarded to be intemperate, he was joined by Bipin Chandra Pal from Bengal and Bal Gangadhar Tilak from Maharashtra. All three chided the Congress Party for lacking any dignity.

When he was struck in the lathi charge by Superintendent Scott in Lahore, he was sixty-three years old. He recovered despite his injuries and even held some public meetings, in which he scorned the colonial government's intransigence in opposing the will of the Indian people. However, a fortnight later he fell ill again. Two days later he was dead. Whether it was death due to natural causes or whether he had a heart attack or whether he was still suffering from the long-drawn effects of the lathi blow is not known. Nor did it matter. It was enough that he had been so brutally assaulted that he died. Lajpat Rai's death at the hands of the police helped to shatter the fallacy of benign colonialism once and for all. Bhagat Singh, who saw him as his mentor, moved to take revenge.

Alongside the nationwide non-cooperation movement and Khilafat movement between 1920 and 1922, the continued existence of the revolutionary terrorist movement, from the middle of the 1920s onwards, showed that anti-colonial sentiment was widespread in India. Moreover, perhaps more alarmingly for British officials, revolutionary terrorists were drawing on global trends and were connected to international radical movements. In 1922, the Interdepartmental Committee on Eastern Unrest had already been convened in London to survey the threats the British Empire faced from Indian, Turkish and Egyptian nationalists, the pan-Islamic movement, Bolshevik activities and Indian revolutionaries in Europe, America and Asia. The committee brought together the Foreign Office, the War Office, the Colonial Office and the India Office to coordinate a response to transnational anti-colonial movements that connected different regions, such as the Indian revolutionary movements, which had a following in Bengal, Punjab, the United Provinces, Central Provinces and further afield in London, Berlin, Paris and Moscow.[1]

Daniel Elam remarks on how Bhagat Singh [himself] borrowed from the writings of the Russian-born anarchist, Emma Goldman, which she discovered in his possession when she visited him in Lahore Jail cell at the end of March 1931. 'Bhagat Singh's writings on anarchism reflect a direct engagement with Emma Goldman's writing,' writes Elam. This engagement is so direct that 'in a serial essay on anarchism, published in Lahore in 1928, he uses Goldman's definition of anarchism verbatim: "Anarchism – the philosophy of a new social order based on liberty unrestricted by man-made Law; the theory that all forms of Government rest on violence, and are therefore wrong and harmful, as well as unnecessary"'.[2] There is in fact a strong link between the triumph of the Russian Revolution and the early revolutionary fervour of the 1920s. It is often overlooked in India, but it had a dramatic effect on the young armed freedom fighters there, just as it did pretty much everywhere else. What the success of the Russian Revolution did was to infuse the young revolutionaries with an unshakeable confidence that they too could overcome imperialism and throw off the foreign yoke; that there was a new social and economic vision to embrace which could be the foundation of an independent India and that the adoption of Marxist and communist principles was the way to achieve it. Indeed, it was all too easily overlooked by many in the West that October 2017 was in fact the centenary of the October Revolution in 1917, which ushered in the era of communism. Back then, it had been shocking to see how quickly the storming of the Winter Palace led to the seizure of power and the world's first worker's state.

It is easy to forget today how quickly it transformed a country of oppressed peasantry into an industrial giant, eliminating poverty, establishing free healthcare, free education, subsidized housing and a commitment to guaranteeing employment, such that almost every third world country had intellectuals rushing to embrace it in the rise to an international movement for socialism. Bhagat Singh was one such person. In fact, in just under half a century, over a third of humanity fell under socialist rule. The Great Depression of the 1930s left it largely unaffected, even though the Soviet Union was still less than two decades old, as it raced forward in industrial production at astronomic speed while also ensuring that agricultural production was not left behind. Hunger became a thing of the past. A universal right to education was established even at secondary level. Healthcare was available to all. In fact, Russia became the first country to send a man into outer space. Soviet athletes easily competed with the best from the advanced capitalist economies of the West with distinctive success. We have forgotten today how it was that by the 1960s the Soviet Union was doing better by most human development indices than their Western capitalist counterparts. Today, we know only of Putin's Russia. A Russia that wages war with the intensity of ferocious medieval barbarity in the Ukraine. A Russia which makes it possible in March 2022 for the *Washington Post* to write of how, 'Russia's invasion of Ukraine is a seismic event, perhaps the most significant one in international life since the fall of the Berlin Wall . . . This war marks the end of an age.'[3] But it is as well to remember that there was another Russian age. One that inspired the developing world.

Those who lived through that earlier period, however, only remember too well that in those heady days long before the fall of the Iron Curtain in 1991, it had indeed seemed that a wide-ranging

European Revolution would follow hot on the heels of the October Revolution. It was for this reason that in the 1920s and 1930s, as Kama Maclean notes, '[t]he revolutionaries of the HSRA were motivated by socialist ideologies and methodologies of dissent in Russia and Ireland; they aspired to free India from foreign domination as the first step towards the larger goal of creating an equitable society. As such they were deeply engaged in the nationalist enterprise even as they embraced different strategies while having their eyes on a larger goal'.[4] If this is right then Indian revolutionaries could hardly have been regarded as 'terrorists', as that term is conventionally understood.

17

1922, Chauri Chaura

Indian revolutionaries got their chance to show their mettle with the violent Chauri Chaura incident in what is now Uttar Pradesh (previously United Provinces). It began on 2 February 1922. Large numbers of volunteers were participating in a protest against high food prices. Although led by a retired Army soldier, Bhagwan Ahir, it was part of Gandhi's non-cooperation movement. When this happened, the police not only beat them back but also arrested several of their leaders and locked them up at the Chauri Chaura police station. On 4 February, two days later, protestors set out to demonstrate against police brutality at the local marketplace. They ended up clashing with the police, who fired at them. Angry rioters soon attacked the police station and set fire to it. Not only were three civilians killed, but twenty-three policemen were also burnt alive in the police station. Ever the one to appease British sentiments, Mahatma Gandhi called off the non-cooperation movement a week later on 12 February 1922. In doing so, he consulted no one in the executive committee of the Congress Party and he ascertained no facts as to what exactly happened. Many in the Congress Party felt deceived and abandoned. To call off the non-cooperation movement just as it was beginning to bear fruit was unwarranted. As Professor Tim Murphy points out in his recent magnum opus '[t]o many nationalists this was precisely the problem: that the means might stifle the end,' and for some like the Bengal Congress leader, C.R. Das, 'this was a rejection of politics itself.'[1] In fact, the *Times of India* recently recounted of the Chauri Chaura incident that, '[t]he atrocity might have remained one unsavoury event in the freedom struggle, had Gandhi not unilaterally called off the struggle' because in doing so he had 'disavowed the peasants who rose up in his name'. Indeed, '[i]t remained a terrible cautionary tale for him ever after'. And yet, '[f]ew shared this stand' because although 'Jawaharlal Nehru, Sardar Patel and Rajendra Prasad reluctantly went along, others like Chittaranjan Das and Motilal Nehru dissented' because 'they felt let down'. Perhaps, the magnitude of the betrayal felt was expressed most poetically by Lala Lajpat Rai in his lament, 'Our defeat is in proportion to the greatness of our leader.'[2] Subhas Chandra Bose caustically observed how '[n]o one could understand why Mahatma should have used the isolated incident at Chauri Chaura for strangling the movement all over the country.'[3] In the words of Tim Murphy 'for the moderates, Chauri Chaura showed how quickly open defiance of the Raj could collapse, and they were antagonised by Gandhi's failure to negotiate with its offers of reform.'[4] Yet the shame of the Chauri Chaura incident lies forgotten in India today, even in relation to Gandhi himself.

Gandhi's rescission of his campaign had another effect. It created a political vacuum. Many in the non-violent resistance were so stunned and left so deeply aggrieved that they abandoned the non-violent struggle altogether. New radical revolutionary movements moved in to fill the vacuum. These aimed to overthrow British rule by violent means. A paradox arose—the very leaders who were participants in the non-cooperation movement felt failed by it. They moved on to become leaders of a new revolutionary 'terror' politics, when previously they had been ardent participants in Gandhi's non-cooperation movement. This not only demonstrates the extent of their disenchantment with non-violent resistance but also emphasizes the importance of their kind of politics in India's freedom movement after the 1920s. Gandhian non-violence is accredited with the march towards India's freedom when this is just half the story. The other half remains unpalatable and unspoken of even today. It is that it was not just Sukhdev, Shiv Verma, Bhagwati Charan Vohra and Jaidev Kapoor, who had previously been passionate adherents of Gandhi's peaceful non-cooperation movement, who now rejected it. It was also others like Jogesh Chandra Chatterjee, Surya Sen, Jatin Das and Chandrashekhar Azad. All left the Congress Party.

Such was the speed with which India's revolutionary movements mushroomed that different organizations rose up across India. In the words of Kama Maclean, 'By the late 1920s, the small but powerful canon of martial heroes and nationalist models had been established, which provided a framework within which dissidents could aspire to challenge the Raj.'[5] The most notable of these were in Punjab, Uttar Pradesh, Bihar and Bengal. The febrile atmosphere of the time is evocatively described by Moffat. He explains how 'across North India in the 1920s appeared a constellation of temporary safe houses, mobile bomb factories and shifting weapon holds, perpetually under threat of detection'.[6] Elsewhere he writes how 'the 1920s are filled with incitement to rupture'.[7]

Bhagat Singh has come to epitomize that remembrance. This was not because he was hanged in Lahore Jail (now in Pakistan) on 23 March 1931, together with Rajguru and Sukhdev, when the schedule for his hanging was moved forward by eleven hours, much to everyone's shock. It is because his execution was not the first for the crime of conspiracy against the King, because '[t]hroughout the early 1920s, the government of India prosecuted a number of inter-provincial conspiracy cases against a range of insurgent groups who used political violence; many of these cases involved revolutionary terrorists from Bengal, who had made links with their counterparts in other provinces.' We forget today how truly young some of these people were. Many were barely out of their teens. There was the nineteen-year-old Khudiram Bose, who was hanged 112 years ago by the British government for his attack on the British magistrate Charles Kingsford, an attack in which two British ladies were accidentally killed. His defence counsel argued that his

compatriot Prafulla Chaki threw the bomb. Prafulla, who was older
and much stronger, had immediately committed suicide. Khudiram
was still sentenced to death. According to the *Amrita Bazar Patrika*,
'he walked to the gallows firmly and cheerfully and even smiled
when the cap was drawn over his head'. Pitambar Das wrote a song
'*Ekbar biday de Ma ghure ashi*', which describes Khudiram saying
goodbye to his mother before going to the gallows, a song almost
every Bengali child has grown up listening. He was hanged in
Muzaffarpur in Bihar. A jail still stands there named after him as
'Khudiram Bose Central Jail'. If only the Lahore Central Jail had
not been demolished in the mid 1960s, it would have been possible
to do the same today. It would certainly have avoided all the legal
wrangles that currently engulf 'Bhagat Singh Chowk' at Shadman
Chowk in Lahore.

It is in this way that Bengali revolutionaries such as Jogesh
Chandra Chatterjee, Sachindra Nath Sanyal, Jatin Das and
members of the Anushilan Samiti came to be affiliated with the
Hindustan Socialist Republican Army,[8] an organization between
underground groups in the United Provinces, Punjab and Bengal
to coordinate robberies, bombings and assassinations that alarmed
government officials.

Yet, the narrative of India's freedom struggle is skewed. To
find a reason for this, one needs to go to the origins of the Indian
Independence struggle. This is when, as Kama Maclean makes
clear, the '[n]arratives of the Indian freedom struggle had been
predominantly framed as a triumph for the Gandhian ideology of
non- violence', and yet, as she points out, 'there is much evidence to
suggest that the interwar years were marked by urgent discussions
questioning its viability'.[9] In fact, by the early 1920s, 'it was not clear
whether Gandhi would continue to command nationalist action,
or even be in a position to continue to steer the Indian National
Congress within non-violent parameters'.[10] Following 1909, after
he had written *Hind Swaraj*, 'much of Gandhi's thinking about
nonviolence was framed as a dialogue with activists who favoured
violence as a means of political redress for the oppression of

colonialism'. There was no reason to believe, however, that his non-cooperation strategy would trump the creed of those who favoured an armed revolt against the British Raj. The result was that, 'by the early 1920s, Gandhi had withdrawn from agitational politics, dismayed and disillusioned by the violent outbreaks that attended the Non-Cooperation Movement'.[11] Indeed by February 1922, he had called off his non-cooperation movement completely. This is why, referring to Judith Brown, Kama Maclean emphasizes, '[t]he degree to which Gandhi struggled to gain acceptance of nonviolence as Congress policy'.[12] And yet, it remains the case to this day that '[h]istorians have generally accounted for the centrality of nonviolence in the anticolonial movement', and this is all because of 'the influence and determination of one extraordinary individual: Mohandas Karamchand Gandhi'.[13]

What this overlooks is that Gandhi's philosophy of non-violence was indicative of a political frailty on his part. In *The Impossible Indian*, Faisal Devji explains that 'Gandhi confessed many times during this period to his realisation that the non-violence adopted by the Congress in the past had been born of weakness not strength . . .'. In fact, it was utterly ineffectual because 'it was merely passive resistance and had no transformative effect'. Worse, it was counter-productive. In an interview to Reuters on 5 May 1947, Gandhi himself admitted that 'the lack of an armed struggle against the British had prevented the development of a single nationality among Indians'. Was Bhagat Singh not then truer to the cause of Indian Independence than Gandhi? Was it not better to jointly fight the invader than fight each other? The question needs posing because as Devji goes on to say of Gandhi, 'He held that passive resistance was merely the preparation for an armed struggle.' But if this is so then he was surely far behind Bhagat Singh, who was already advocating armed resistance and was doing so from a position of moral strength of the kind that Gandhi had abandoned after the Chauri Chaura incident. Devji himself in his masterly study is no less sparing of Gandhi when he considers the legacy left behind by Gandhism because 'it was perhaps due to their consciousness of this cowardly and perverted exercise of nonviolence that so many Indians now turned with redoubled violence against their neighbors, since they had after all failed to engage the colonial state by force of arms'.

In the end, the tragedy of India was that 'though the British could be met with what Gandhi called the nonviolence of the weak; this was not possible in the far more intimate relations subsisting between Hindus and Muslims, where only the non-violence of the strong was possible'.[14] In a sense, therefore, Gandhism hurt not only the Independence struggle but hurt the very people of India itself, pitching Muslims against Hindus and Sikhs and making communal life impossible. By contrast, Bhagat Singh offered armed national resistance that Gandhi stubbornly opposed and a belief in '*sarfaroshī kī tamannā*'. His path would not have allowed Partition and would not have sowed the seeds of ethno-nationalism that we see on both sides of the border today.

18

1924, *'Sarfaroshi Ki Tamanna'*

It was in this maelstrom that the Hindustan Republican Association (HRA) was formed in an East Bengal village in 1924. Its goal was to organize armed resistance against British rule. One of its founding members was the poet Ram Prasad Bismil, who immortalized the 1921 revolutionary song *'sarfaroshī kī tamannā ab hamāre dil meñ hai / dekhnā hai zor kitnā bāzū-e-qātil meñ hai'*[1], written by Bismil Azimabadi, (which translated means, 'The desire for revolution is in our hearts / Let us see what strength there is in the arms of our executioner'[2]). The original version of the song is held at the Khuda Bakhsh Oriental Library in Patna, Bihar. This idea of the revolutionaries' self-conception, in living out a vision of revolution, as found in their conversations, banter, and anecdotes, has been neatly captured in Dr Aparna Vaidik's, *Waiting for Swaraj*[3], providing a valuable insight into their thinking. The other founding member was Sachindra Nath Sanyal, under whose influence Bhagat Singh was to come while a student at National College in Lahore in 1924 so as to become his protégé. Sanyal had penned the revolutionary tract *Bandi Jiwani*, which was to become the Bible of a new revolutionary politics. The clear objective of the HRA was the formation of a Federated Republic of the United States of India, which would be based on universal adult suffrage and which would have avoided the partition of India in 1947 had it come to fruition.

An armed struggle could not be waged without money. The recruitment and training of men, the procurement of arms and the organization of a nation-wide propaganda machine had to be financed. North Indian revolutionaries were the first to emerge as an organized group when in 1924 the Hindustan Republican Association (or Army) was formed by Ram Prasad Bismil, Sachindra Nath Sanyal, Sachindra Nath Bakshi and Jogesh Chandra Chatterjee. They met at Kanpur in October 1924 and vowed to overthrow colonial rule and establish a federated democratic India. On 9 August 1925 in a nondescript village by the name of Kakori near Lucknow, ten men set upon the Number 8 Down Train and ransacked the official treasury of the railway. They were all quickly arrested. Government retribution was swift and harsh—five of them were hanged, including Ashfaqullah Khan, Ram Prasad Bismil, Roshan Singh and Rajendra Lahiri. Four were destined for life in the gruelling conditions of the Andaman Islands. One such was Mahavir Singh, who was to emerge again later. Long years of imprisonment awaited seventeen others. Remarkably, Chandrashekhar Azad escaped. With strategic acumen, Bhagat Singh saw an opportunity to revitalize the revolutionary movement. So in 1926 came into prominence the Naujawan Bharat Sabha to bring the youth under one socialist non-religious banner with its 'proselytising thrust against communal politics . . .'.[4]

Bhagat Singh had to take such drastic action because the defeat of the plotters in the Kakori Conspiracy Case of 1925 had decapitated India's insurrectionary forces. Ram Prasad Bismil and Ashfaqullah Khan, the trailblazers in the vanguard of that short-lived movement, were no more. At a stroke the leadership of India's revolutionary movement had been destroyed, calling for a new breed of rebel leaders. Leaders who would resurrect the revolutionary movement from its ashes and give it renewed life and sustenance. Bhagat Singh had imbibed from the Arya Samajist and Ghadarite traditions of his staunchly militant family. As a boy aged twelve, he had recoiled in revulsion at the cold-blooded killing of hundreds of innocents by General Dyer in the Jallianwala Bagh Massacre of 1919 in Amritsar. Alongside many others at the time, he had joined Mahatma Gandhi's non-cooperation struggle. But the Mahatma had soon abandoned this campaign. Like many others, Bhagat Singh had become disillusioned with the Mahatma. His establishment in 1926 of the Naujawan Bharat Sabha became an eerie prologue to the later formation of the Hindustan Socialist Republican Association in 1928 on the dead bones of the Hindustan Republican Association, whose derisory record had been such that it had been 'scarcely able to move beyond the stage of fundraising'.[5] On the other hand, the Naujawan Bharat Sabha's 'events brought together individuals across caste and creed in an attempt to encourage a sort of transgressive sociality'.[6]

The Kakori Conspiracy Case of 1925 is therefore a pivotal event in the freedom movement. Though it is much overlooked, it is of great historical significance because, with many of the HRA's young leaders now dead, Bhagat Singh found himself in the burning furnace of the revolutionary freedom struggle. This struggle was markedly different from the struggle of Gandhi. It had set its face against communalism. There was no more urgent a task than to forge a strong national unity regardless of race, class or creed. Colonialism had undermined the unity of India's diverse nation by setting one Indian against another. It was now the priority if the country was to successfully move towards the kind of Independence India deserved. Nothing demonstrates this better than how in 1927, just three days before he was hanged, Ashfaqullah Khan wrote an open letter to his countrymen expressing concern over rising communalism in India. He condemned the Tabligh and Shuddhi movements. Hindus and Muslims had to learn to live together, or they would fail to shake off the bondage of servitude. If they failed in this, it would negatively impact the fight for Independence. His words were unequivocally harsh: 'It is impossible to purify seven crore Muslims and similarly it is absurd to think that twenty five crore Hindus can be converted to Islam. But yes, it is easy that we all put the chains of slavery around our necks.'[7]

Mahavir Singh too wrote in similar terms to his father as he faced life imprisonment in the Andaman Islands:

By *Samaj* (Society) I do not mean *Arya Samaj* or any other narrow *Samaj* but a society of common people. This is because these religious societies mean nothing to me due to their myopia. Moreover, I want to keep away from all the religions because they are narrow, self centred and based on injustice and want others also to do the same. What I believe to be of greatest benefit to man and society is the following principle: the human relations should not be based on any distinction of caste, colour, religion or money.[8]

Ashfaqullah Khan made it quite clear that India should not substitute one form of oppressive rule with another by gaining Independence:

I consider alien rule an evil, and at the same time I hate any democratic Indian rule where the weak are denied rights, [if] it is the creation of the rich and the landed, or if there is no equal participation of farmers and workers, or if government laws are based on inequality and unequal treatment . . .[9]

The recognition of this alternative tradition of the revolutionaries is more important today than it ever was given the politics of the entire subcontinent. We have forgotten that precisely at the time when the RSS was being organized in 1925 in Nagpur, Bhagat Singh and his comrades were founding the Naujawan Bharat Sabha in Lahore in 1926. One stood for division and the other for unity. One was based on religion and the other on secularism. We should therefore not forget this period when 'Bhagat Singh was acutely conscious of the growing menace of communalism in the 1920s', because this was after all 'the decade which saw the emergence of the *Hindu Mahasabah* and the *Rashtriya Swayamsevak Sangh* (RSS)' but where there were also 'specific movements of the Muslims like *Tablighi Jamaat*'. 'Bhagat Singh questioned the policy of encouraging competing communalisms, which ultimately led to the partition of the country in 1947.'[10] Such was the significance of this alternative approach to India's freedom struggle which eschewed Gandhian non-violence, that among the cases, the government prosecuted not only the Kakori Train Dacoity Case, but also other cases like the Deoghar Conspiracy Case, Cawnpore Conspiracy Case, Meerut Conspiracy Trials and the Lahore Conspiracy Case.[11] Of these it was the latter which was the most significant.

It was colonialism's 'civilising mission' that gave rise to this alternative tradition, and this is another reason why the revolutionary tradition needs to be memorialized. This is the tradition of 'sarfaroshi' and of self-sacrifice. It came about in Bhagat Singh's life because he was a witness to a number of violent colonial events. He was only eight years old when the executions in the First Lahore Conspiracy Case took place. These consisted of no less than nine cases, which arose after the failed Ghadar Conspiracy from 26 April to 13 September 1915. Once again, it was a trial by special tribunal, this time constituted under the Defence of India Act 1925. Forty-two of the 291 convicted conspirators were executed. A majority of 114 got life sentences, and ninety-three were given terms of imprisonment of varying lengths. Only forty-two defendants in the trial were acquitted. One of the hanged was Kartar Singh Sarabha. It is said that Bhagat Singh used to carry a photo of Kartar Singh Sarabha on his person in a locket. If he did do so, it is no surprise, for Bhagat Singh's life was to be not dissimilar to that of Sarabha's.

Sarabha too appeared suddenly on the national stage to leave a tear-drop on the destiny of India. In 1912, Sarabha left Ludhiana in Punjab for San Francisco, where he was radicalized. Entering Berkeley University as an engineering student, he founded the Ghadar Party with other Indians there. When the First World War broke out, the Ghadar Party too declared its *Ailan-i-Jang* on Britain in the form of a declaration of war, following which Sarabha hastened to return to India, where unfortunately he was betrayed, just as Bhagat Singh was by his comrades, by an accomplice in 1915.

After Sarabha was captured, a tribunal was specially convened to sentence him to death in the First Lahore Conspiracy Case.[12]

Barely an adult at 19, he was executed on conspiracy charges, much like Bhagat Singh. He was hanged in November 1915. It is often forgotten that he too, like Bhagat Singh, faced death extra-judicially under emergency procedures, and his impact on Bhagat Singh was deep and long-lasting.

Bhagat Singh wrote an article titled 'Bhai Kartar Singh Sarabha' in *Kirti* in its April/May 1927 issue describing him as 'this heroic devotee of the deity of battle' who 'was not even 20 years old when he sacrificed his life' after 'he appeared from nowhere like a whirlwind'. Sarabha, like Bhagat Singh, made the ultimate sacrifice, because 'it was impossible for him to remain unaffected by the events around him'. Bhagat Singh continues, '[h]e was constantly tormented by the question of how the country would attain freedom if the path of non-violence failed.'[13] In April 1927, Bhagat Singh wrote another sketch on Sarabha, where he explains how 'when Kartar Singhji went to America, he went here from slavery' and that 'when he saw the movements of free men there, he remembered his home', which was a 'home, where his countrymen were rotting and from which he had just left'.[14] After he was hauled up before the courts for trial, 'he gave two great statements in the court' and 'in those, he very bravely and courageously admitted to everything' because Kartar Singh was a brave man and he did not know how to die like a coward'.[15] This was, of course, exactly the manner in which Bhagat Singh too went to his death.

Another formative event in Bhagat Singh's life was the Amritsar Massacre of 1919, which stands as the leading example of colonial coercive technique in India. Its memories were brought alive again most vividly when in 2019 the tercentenary was commemorated. A flurry of books, articles and programmes were devoted to its remembrance, with world leaders adding their voice of regret to its occurrence a hundred years ago. The name of Udham Singh appeared in Western literature for the first time. He was the man who plotted over a number of years to kill Michael O'Dwyer, the lieutenant-governor of Punjab, held chiefly responsible for the massacre. What few would have come to realize is the importance of another Indian hero, one by the name of Bhagat Singh, in the influence he had on Udham Singh, who had avenged the Jallianwala Bagh Massacre. His fame has been such that he has been popularly known as 'Shaheed-i-Azam Sardar Udham Singh'. It was he who, as Anita Anand has memorably described in her recent book, shot O'Dwyer in London in March 1940, twenty years after the 1919 massacre, holding him responsible for the repressive measures which culminated in the Amritsar Massacre. Udham Singh insisted on describing himself as 'Mohammad Singh Azad' while in custody awaiting the hangman's noose, because when he shot to kill O'Dwyer as he moved to the Speaking Platform in Caxton Hall, where a joint meeting of the East India Association and the Central Asian Society had been convened, he did so on behalf of those who had died as Hindus, Muslims and Sikhs on that balmy April evening in 1919 in Amritsar. Udham Singh was tried for the murder at the Central Criminal Court on 4 and 5 June 1940 before Justice Atkinson.

Unfortunately, Udham Singh had a farcical defence. It was bungled by the rank opportunism and incompetence of Krishna Menon, himself widely seen as an early Indian hero of the pre-Independence freedom struggle. Described as 'calculating',[16] Krishna Menon was a forceful and highly abrasive man, driven always by an ambition to prove himself. He was a close friend of Nehru and destined in the views of many to be the second most powerful man in India after Nehru became prime minister. He 'had initially wanted to dissociate himself from Udham's actions' and had 'repudiated the shootings within hours of the event'.[17] What then appeared to change his mind was that 'Gandhi and Nehru had been locked in delicate negotiations with the British and wanted desperately to promote a counternarrative to that of Sir Michael O'Dwyer', which suggested that 'Indians were not violent barbarians'.[18] However, 'when it became clear how much publicity Udham's case was getting and how much support he had within British Indian circles, Krishna Menon appeared to rethink his own position. If there was to be a trial, it would be a very high-profile affair, and Krishna Menon wanted in'.[19] Then, 'with no legal standing in the case, Krishna Menon' informed everyone that 'he was now running Udham's defence'.[20] In the event, 'Krishna Menon did not care about Udham's motivations or state of mind'[21] and his involvement 'would allow him to steer proceedings in a direction that best helped his friends Nehru and Gandhi in India. If it did not serve their interest to have Udham's nationalism dragged into court, he could keep it out'.[22] When Udham Singh was sentenced to death by hanging, and others clamoured to have his sentence commuted to life imprisonment, 'Krishna Menon did nothing at all'.[23] Upon Independence in 1947, Menon was appointed by the Congress Party as India's first high commissioner to the United Kingdom.

Documents from the Public and Judicial Department of New Scotland Yard confirm that after two hours of deliberation, the jury returned a verdict of 'Guilty of Murder'. It is said that 'Singh then started to read some sort of statement written on paper but soon gave up and addressed the court in very stilted phrases which were difficult to follow'. Nevertheless, 'he was heard to say, however, that he was not afraid to die and that when he had gone, thousands of his countrymen would drive "Your dirty dogs out of my country"' and that '[a]fter the death sentence had been passed upon him, Singh raised his right arm and shouted "Imrah" ["rebel"] three times. He also spat upon the table below the Judge'.[24] In Udham Singh's trial it is said that the words used by Udham Singh when he addressed the court and which were interrupted by the Judge included a 'few lines [which] consist of a poem in Urdu, which is signed "Bawa", this being the name by which he was commonly known to his associates'. However, there then 'followed a stanza of a Gurmukhi [Punjabi script used by Sikhs] poem on Indian martyrs. The words "Bhagat Singh", "Dutt", "Tilak" and "Lajpat", all well known figures in the national struggle, appear in this poem'.[25] In this document, which is dated 20 June 1940, and stamped in bold capital letters with the word 'SECRET' in the top left-hand corner,[26] it is said, 'I am sending you herewith a copy of a note prepared in this office, giving the substance of the papers which UDHAM SINGH brought into court with him on the day when he was sentenced to death. These papers consisted of four sheets in the English, Gurmukhi and Urdu hand-writing of the accused. *I do not think that there is anything in them which indicates outside influence:* the sentiments expressed are *typical of the half-educated Ghadr revolutionary,* and the writing appears to have covered a period of several weeks'.[27] Half-educated or not, it is clear that Bhagat Singh, together with other revolutionaries of the day, was a major influence on Udham Singh.

In his majestic *Amritsar 1919,* Kim Wagner ends with the observation that, along with Udham Singh who avenged the Jallianwala Bagh Massacre, Bhagat Singh 'is Punjab's most celebrated hero' today. Much folklore has grown around these two men. Fact and fiction merge into one. He observes how '[i]t is said that Udham Singh had himself been present at the Jallianwalla Bagh and was wounded in the arm, although there is little evidence of this'.[28] What is not in doubt is that Udham Singh himself 'was deeply influenced by the activities of Bhagat Singh' and that 'in 1935, when he was on a visit to Kashmir, he was found carrying Bhagat Singh's portrait' and that 'he invariably referred to him as his guru . . .'.[29] In fact, there exist notes where he refers to Bhagat Singh and others who fought for Indian Independence.[30] Malwinder Jit Singh Waraich, who had in earlier years interviewed the surviving members of Bhagat Singh's family, including his mother at her home, had in relation to the blood soaked bottle of sand written, 'The massacre of Jallianwala is a watershed in our struggle for freedom. It is also a turning point in the life of young Bhagat Singh.'[31]

Yet another event of colonial violence that left a deep imprint on Bhagat Singh's mind was the Babbar Akali Agitation of 1926. Bhagat Singh got to learn about this after he had fled from the National College, Lahore, when confronted with the prospect of marriage in 1923, as he had headed for Kanpur. There he joined the editorial board of the weekly *Pratap,* and began publishing. It was there that he also formed close relationships with leading revolutionaries who retained life-long attachments with him: Shiv Verma, Jaidev Kapoor, Batukeshwar Dutt, Bejoy Kumar Sinha, to name but a few. He became fully immersed in life there and also helped with the flood relief

operations in Kanpur at the time. He was even appointed headmaster
of National School at Shadipur village in Aligarh District after the
owner of *Pratap*, Ganesh Shankar Vidyarthi, sent Bhagat Singh there
to keep him away from the prying eyes of the police. However, when
six activists[32] of the Babbar Akalis were hanged in Lahore Central Jail
on 27 February 1926 for launching an armed revolt against the British
Empire, on the festival of Holi, Bhagat Singh wrote an essay titled
'Drops of Blood on the Day of Holi' ('Holi ke din khoon ke chhinte')
on 15 March 1926 for *Pratap*. Bhagat Singh was then eighteen years
old and was deeply affected.

Once again, however, he learnt from their example which in the
fullness of time he would himself emulate. Thus, he refers to how 'the
contempt and lightheartedness that these people had demonstrated
for nearly two years during their trial proved how earnestly [they]
had been waiting for just such a day'. In fact, when 'the Honourable
Judge pronounced his verdict after months' one could see how
'the brave defendants thundered' and 'the sky reverberated with
their enthusiastic victory cries'.[33] Initially, five had been sentenced
to death and the sixth to exile in the Andaman Islands. Such was
the unremitting ferocity of colonial violence that on appeal, rather
than reduce the sentence of the five, all six were sentenced to the
gallows. This is how it came to be that when 'the city was filled with
festivities' and 'people were throwing colour on the passers-by as
usual', 'suddenly we saw a small group of people accompanying the
dead bodies to the cremation ground on Holi' so that 'quietly, their
last rites were conducted'. And yet, lest we forget, 'they were fearless
patriots' and 'whatever they did was for this unfortunate country'
because 'they could not endure injustice' and 'they could not see
the country in this fallen state'. The result was that 'the oppression
inflicted upon the weak became intolerable for them'. In the end,
'they were visionaries'.[34] And no doubt, Bhagat Singh would learn
from them too.

PART 4

THE ASSASSINATION

Rah-e-dur-e-ishq men rota hai kya
aage aage dekhiye hota hai kya

In the long road of love, do not despair.
Just wait and see what destiny unfolds for you next.

—Meer Taqi Meer

19

1923, National College

From Kartar Singh Sarabha in the First Lahore Conspiracy Case in 1915 to the Amritsar Massacre in 1919, and then from Ashfaqullah Khan in the Kakori Conspiracy Case of 1925 to the Babbar Akali Agitation of 1926, Bhagat Singh had been so deeply touched by martyrs and martyrdom that he had written about their sacrifices in endearing terms. But alongside these influences, which left a lasting impression on his young mind from the age of eight in 1915 until the age of nineteen in 1926, there was also the influence on him of the National College, into which he gained admission at the age of fourteen years.

Here there were two further influences that made his transformation complete as a revolutionary freedom fighter. These in particular shaped Bhagat Singh's life in his later years. First, there were the students with whom Bhagat Singh got to rub shoulders. These included names like Sukhdev, Bhagwati Charan Vohra, Yash Pal, Jaidev Gupta and Ram Krishen, all of whom participated in the Lahore Conspiracy Case 1931. Bhagat Singh's association with them remained steadfast, and although he left the National College a year later, he continued to visit it right up to 1926, the year when he was first arrested as a nineteen-year-old by the Lahore Police for being associated with the Kakori case. Second, there were the teachers of the National College in Lahore who left a lasting impression on him. Firebrands such as Acharya Jugal Kishore and Uday Shankar Bhatt were radical, free-thinking and irreverent.

Such teachers were openly contemptuous of the supine weakness of the non-violent non-cooperation satyagraha movement of Mahatma Gandhi, which they believed was singularly ineffective in delivering the kind of freedom that India deserved. Together, these teachers helped transform the minds of a generation of young men—students who had abandoned their studies at government-sponsored schools and colleges in order to flock to an institution which encouraged discussion and dissent. Here the study of history, economics and politics enabled them to learn about the liberation movements of other countries. It was not just that 'debates had been made a regular feature from the beginning' of the teaching curriculum, in the words of a former chief secretary of the Delhi Administration, but that here although teaching was in Hindi, 'students were also taught English' because many 'books were only available in English'. History in particular 'gripped the atmosphere of the college and was the main subject of discussion'.[1] The National College could not escape but be 'a nursery of revolutionary nationalists'. When undeniably five student members of the Hindustan Socialist Republican Association turned out to have betrayed Bhagat Singh in the Lahore Conspiracy Case by becoming 'Approvers' for the government, it was a matter of pride for Durga Bhabhi—the rare woman revolutionary in India's armed freedom struggle, who had helped Bhagat Singh escape in the thick of night by disguising herself as his wife after the shooting of J.P. Saunders—that 'none of the five had ever been a student of the National College.'[2]

Three teachers in particular stood out at Lahore's National Law College. There was Bhai Parmanand. Born in 1874, he lived till 1947. He was an Arya Samajist, who had studied history abroad at King's College London. Tim Murphy reminds us how '[l]ike many exiles of all nations, he found sanctuary in the reading room of the British Library' where he wrote a master's thesis on 'The Rise of British Power in India', but which '[h]is examiners did not take to'.

In the event, it mattered little to Parmanand who, 'in any case, . . .had come to the view that English education was introduced to "destroy our national consciousness."'[3] Parmanand had met with Ghadarites when he was sent abroad in 1912 to preach its doctrines. He was such a thorn in the side of the British that his book on the history of India had been proscribed by the British. James Campbell Ker, who was the personal assistant to the director of criminal intelligence from 1907 to 1913 and had access to secretly held information in highly confidential documents, describes him as 'an itinerant lecturer of the Arya Samaj'. However, in the proceedings against Kishen and Ajit Singh, during a search conducted in November 1909, 'a box belonging to Professor Parmanand was examined, and in it was found a copy of the celebrated manual of explosives with some manuscripts relating to seditious and revolutionary schemes'.[4] It did not end there. Such was the obsession of the authorities with socialist literature regarded as subversive that James Ker also explains how in that search '[t] here were also a few old letters written by Lajpatrai to Parmanand in 1907, when the latter was in London studying history at King's College, in which Lajpatrai asked him to procure certain books on socialistic and revolutionary subjects'.[5] In that febrile atmosphere, 'a good deal of doubtful literature was consigned to the flames at this time in the colleges of Lahore and other cities of the Punjab'.[6] It was hardly surprising therefore that when the incriminating documents were discovered in Bhai Parmanand's possession he was suspended from DAV College, and when the case was finally decided against him, he was dismissed.

He retired for a time to his own village, but in October 1910 he sailed from Bombay for Europe, 'giving out that he was going to study medicine'.[7] He travelled to Paris and then to British Guiana, where in March 1911 'he was trying to make the Hindus in the Colony start a school, partly in order to prevent the Hindu children from being converted to Christianity (one of the main objects of the Arya Samaj)'.[8] But by September 1911 he found himself in California, and upon meeting the noted Ghadarite Har Dayal, 'became one of his associates'. That too was short-lived, because in 1913 he left for

England, but then in September of that year he was in Paris again. In this way, '[h]aving completed his tour of the revolutionary centres he arrived back in India in December, 1913, and returned to Lahore, and when the Ghadar movement started in the Punjab it was found that his house was a place of call for dangerous members of the party'. When one of the accused in the first Lahore Conspiracy Case of 1915 was traced back to Bhai Parmanand, his fate was sealed. The tribunal reached the unanimous conclusion that 'this accused was not only one of the persons concerned in the present conspiracy, but was one of the most important revolutionists'. Where the tribunal was not unanimous was on the matter of whether he should be put to death. Two of the three members of the tribunal sentenced him to death, but the third member 'did not think a capital sentence called for, and the sentence was eventually commuted by the Viceroy to transportation for life'.[9] Spared from the hangman's noose, like the Russian novelist Fyodor Dostoevsky, Bhai Parmanand was instead given deportation for life in the Andaman Islands. From there his luck only improved. He was released after just five years in 1920. Upon his return to the mainland, he was in 1921 astonishingly appointed chancellor when National College joined the Punjab Quami Vidyapeeth. With his background in history from King's College London, he was the one who taught history to the students at National College. Using his firebrand style, he relished expostulating the role of revolutions in the democratic development of Europe. [10]

Then there was Principal Chhabil Das. He was born in 1900 and went on to live to a ripe old age until 1988. Initially a member of Lala Lajpat Rai's Lok Sewak Mandal (the 'Servants Of The People Society'), a non-profit organization dedicated to the service of the people, he started teaching English at the National College in 1924. He too was responsible for a number of seditious publications. These included works bearing such provocative names as *Bharat Mata Keh Darshan* ('Let us meet our Motherland') and *Nauzawanon se do do baten* ('A Conversation with the Youth'), not to mention *Chingarian* ('Fireworks'), which was by far his most popular with the young men in his college right up until Independence.

These were incendiary writings, but they did him no harm, as a year later in 1925 he was appointed principal. Bhagat Singh held him in high esteem and often spoke to him privately. Chhabil Das himself recalls how 'I had good relations with him'. These were to such an extent that 'when Bhagat Singh heard that I was going to be married, he insisted that I should not marry'.[11] It was not because Bhagat Singh himself was free from fleeting desires, but he considered that such attachments were possible only when freedom was possible.[12]

It was, however, Professor Jaichandra Vidyalankar who had the biggest impact on Bhagat Singh. A teacher of the history of India, he was particularly concerned with the effect of the Rowlatt Committee Report, which paved the way to the extension of the powers of the viceroy's government in dealing with sedition through the censorship of the press and the detention of political activists without trial, as well as in the effectiveness of the non-cooperation movement in the struggle for freedom. This would have surprised no one, as not only was he an author of two history books himself but he also acted as a conduit between the students of National College and leading revolutionaries outside. He had the credentials to do so. Bhagat Singh had met his fellow revolutionary, Sachindra Nath Sanyal, at his house in 1922 for the first time. Juneja describes Sanyal as 'the political guru of Bhagat Singh'.[13] Others in rival revolutionary outfits, such as the Ghadar Party, were only too aware of this. This is why attempts were made to wean Bhagat Singh away from Sanyal. They were singularly unsuccessful. One person who tried to do so was the stalwart Sikh Ghadri Baba, Gurmukh Singh. In 1914, he had boarded the Komagata Maru to head off to Canada only to be prevented from landing because of Canada's all-white policy. Over 300 passengers met with the same fate. The forlorn ship had no option but to return to India. Upon arrival at Budge Budge Ghat in Calcutta, the police attacked the defenceless passengers, firing upon them without provocation. Gurmukh Singh managed to escape. He was on the run for three days, only to be arrested and imprisoned in Lahore Central Jail before being tried with others in the First Lahore

Conspiracy Case in 1915. He was sentenced to imprisonment in the Andamans but managed to escape yet again after jumping from a moving train as it was taking the prisoners to their destination. He eventually found sanctuary in Kabul.

With such a strong pedigree, one would have thought that Gurmukh Singh was entitled to warn Bhagat Singh that unless he escaped from the clutches of the Bengali insurgents he would end up with a noose around his neck and achieve nothing in the process (*'Tum Bengalion ke pher mein mut paro, inke pher mein paroge to "Phansi" par lataq jayonge / Aur qaam kuch bhi nahin kar payoge'*). But Bhagat Singh paid no heed. Sachindra Nath Sanyal was a Bengali, as was his close associate Rash Behari Bose, who was later to flee to Japan, but as Sanyal proudly recalled many years later, 'In spite of the best efforts of Gurmukh Singh, Bhagat Singh never dissociated himself from us.'[14] If Sanyal had been found sitting in Professor Jaichandra Vidyalankar's house for the purposes of affecting an introduction with Bhagat Singh, this too was not to be unexpected. Born in 1893, Vidyalankar was a veteran of revolutionary activities, having participated in the Kakori train robbery, and had not once but twice suffered deportation to the Andaman Islands from 1915 to 1919. He died before Independence in 1943. In his autobiography, he explains how in meetings with the students of the Tilak School of Politics, he 'had long talks with these young men separately'. He added, 'I particularly emphasised before them that India could not become independent except through armed struggle' and that is why 'I initiated them in the revolutionary path'.[15]

20

1926, Dussehra Bomb Blast

Pandit Pearay Mohan's seminal work on the Punjab Rebellion of 1919[1] shows the year 1919 to be a pivotal one, not just because of the Amritsar Massacre, but the fact that it was preceded by the Anarchical and Revolutionary Crimes Act of 1919. This is popularly known as the 'Rowlatt Act', and in being passed by the Imperial Legislative Council, the legislature of British India, it allowed political trials to be conducted in the absence of a jury and even the internment of suspects without trial. Gandhi set out to oppose this legislation by mobilizing a non-violent civil resistance (satyagraha) against its oppressive use. The act, passed in February, came into effect in March with many of Punjab's leaders being immediately arrested, and by April 1919 there was the Jallianwala Bagh shooting in Amritsar, when General Dyer took exception to an impromptu satyagraha meeting taking place there in the face of the ban on gatherings at the time that had come into effect under the Rowlatt Act. Bhagat Singh at the time was just twelve. He was studying at the DAV College. It is rumoured that incensed at the barbarity, Bhagat Singh tiptoed out of his house in Banga and travelled all the way to Amritsar the day after the massacre in order to collect the blood-soaked soil of the martyrs in a glass jar. The story is apocryphal and cannot have been true because Jallianwala Bagh was cordoned off by the police and barely accessible to a 12-year old, even if he could have got there from Banga on foot.[2] Common folklore in fact has it that, following his visit there, Bhagat Singh himself kept a bottle of the blood-soaked soil from the ground at Jallianwala Bagh.[3] That bottle is said to be housed in the Shaheed-e-Azam Sardar Bhagat Singh Museum in his ancestral village at Khatkar Kalan in Punjab, where it is said there lie, 'three glass jars with sand and pebbles "soaked in the blood of martyrs".'[4] On the other hand, Bhagat Singh did very likely go to Nankana Sahib Gurdwara, Sheikhpura District, in March 1921 after scores of pilgrims were murdered in cold blood by government appointed priests for demanding democratic control of their places of worship when he was just 14-years old. Two months later the National College was to be established in Lahore in May 1921 at which Bhagat Singh would enrol. What is not in doubt is that by the time he had come into his own, Bhagat Singh wanted to become like his uncle, Ajit Singh, 'and to give hell to the British'.[5]

Unsurprisingly, by 1926, when just nineteen, Bhagat Singh was already falling under the watchful eye of the authorities. His letters were being intercepted by the police. He realized this when he noticed how 'all the letters addressed to me were stamped and then stamped again' as they were 'cut exactly at the same place' and that 'this of course did arouse suspicion in my mind'.[6] When on 17 November 1926 Bhagat Singh asked whether his letters were being detained 'under orders of the Punjab Government' and 'are there any letters that were intercepted and never delivered to me?',[7] he was initially met with no reply. Bhagat Singh was among thirty-five persons being shadowed by the CID in Punjab and whose mail was being intercepted in 1926. He was listed under Serial No. 16, and his report read, 'Bhagat Singh, originally of Jullunder District, now of Khawasarian, P.S. Mopzang, Lahore'. When he wrote again a week later protesting how, 'naturally, I was very anxious to know what led the Punjab Government to issue such orders', making it clear that 'as an honest person I have a right to enquire such a question . . .',[8] it was the chief secretary of Punjab himself who confirmed the next day on 27 November 1926 that no less a person than the governor of Punjab had ordered the interception of Bhagat Singh's letters. Within six months, Bhagat Singh was wrongly arrested. This was on 29 May 1927 in relation to the Dussehra bomb blast, which had occurred in Lahore in October 1926.

What happened was that Bhagat Singh was apprehended by the police in Lahore when blissfully passing through a garden and then detained in a cell by the Railway Police, where he languished for a month. This was on suspicion of his involvement in the Kakori train robbery case. Given that he was innocent of the charge the Kakori case had a big impact on Bhagat Singh's life. It haunted him. It was alleged that while that trial was going on in Lucknow he had gone there and that in an effort to secure the release of the accused, 'had procured some bombs, that by way of test one of the bombs was thrown in the crowd on the occasion of Dussehra 1926'. We know this because Bhagat Singh gives an account of this in his essay, 'Why I Am an Atheist'. Here he describes how,

In May 1927, I was arrested in Lahore. This arrest came as a big surprise for me. I had not the slightest idea that I was wanted by the police. I was passing through a garden and all of a sudden the police surrounded me . . . I was taken into police custody. The next day I was taken to the Railway Police lockup where I spent a whole month. After many days' conversation with police personnel, I guessed that they had some information about my connection with the Kakori Party . . . They told me that I was in Lucknow during the Kakori Party Trial so that I might devise a scheme to rescue the culprits. They also said that after the plan had been approved, we procured some bombs and by way of test, one of those bombs was thrown into a crowd on the occasion of Dussehra in 1926. They offered to release me on condition that I gave a statement on the activities on of the Revolutionary Party. In this way I would be set free and even rewarded . . . I could not help laughing at their proposals. It was all humbug. People who have ideas like ours do not throw bombs at their own innocent people . . . I was completely innocent. [9]

They further informed me, in my interest, that if I could give any Statement throwing some light on the activities of the revolutionary party, I was not to be imprisoned but on the contrary set free and rewarded, even without being produced as an approver in court. I laughed at the proposal. It was all humbug.[10]

He was detained for five long weeks and only released on bail on the payment of an exorbitant Rs 60,000, offered by Dunichand, a fervent nationalist himself, and Daulat Ram, a philanthropist, leading to Bhagat Singh's release on 4 July 1927. It was perhaps the biggest bail amount set in Indian legal history up to that time. After Dr Gopichand Bhargava raised the matter in the Punjab Assembly, an inquiry was expedited, leading to the conclusion that there was no case against Bhagat Singh, and it was then that he was freed from bail altogether. But the damage had been done.

21

1929, Love Is Never Bestial

It now became clear to Bhagat Singh that he would not be left alone by the police. He thought it better to leave the country. In a rare letter to his friend Amar Chand written in 1927, he referred to the police harassment and how 'I have been in quite a state' and 'have constantly been facing a lot of problems'. He explains how 'finally, the case has been withdrawn' and refers to his 'desire to go abroad to pursue my studies'. He is worried about his uncle in exile in America, Ajit Singh, inquiring of Amar Chand that 'perhaps you may hear something about Sardarji from San Francisco' and enjoins him, 'please make an effort to find out about him. At least we will be reassured that he is alive'. What is most revealing about his position at this time of his life, when barely out of his teenage years at twenty, is the feeling of being needlessly harassed and persecuted. Any chance of Bhagat Singh turning away from the path of a revolutionary freedom-fighter would have been lost at this stage. On the contrary, these facts suggest that he was being driven into it by the actions of a repressive state itself. He ends his letter to his friend exasperated and forlorn:

What else should I write about myself; that I've been a target of suspicion needlessly? My mail is being checked. Letters are opened. I wonder why they have begun to regard me with so much suspicion. Anyway, Brother, finally, the truth will surface and prevail.[1]

Such is his harassment that by 19 June 1928 Bhagat Singh is still found to be requesting the superintendent of the CID that he 'return all my clothes and papers that were taken from my body at the time of my arrest on May 29 1927, and the clothes and books that were sent by my father while I was in police custody'. He even demands, but to no avail, 'will you kindly let me know by return when and where I can get the same?'.[2]

After that incident Bhagat Singh did turn to revolutionary activism but given that he was just twenty-three years old at the time of his execution, the period of his activism was just seven years, from 1924 to 1931. Clearly, a lot had to be done in these years and marriage would get in the way, so he became determined not to marry. But this was not the only reason for his not marrying. As his letters show, even as a youngster he carried the anguished memories of two forlorn aunts, Harnam Kaur and Hukam Kaur, living in the family household, but without their husbands, bereft of their love, pining for them in their abandoned state, and yet known as the wives of Ajit Singh and Sarwan Singh. Bhagat Singh decided early on that he would not cause the same despair to another young woman, who would have the poisoned chalice of marrying him. This was despite the fact that he had been betrothed from a very young age, by his grandmother, Jai Kaur, and his father, Kishan Singh, to be married to another young girl. With his older brother, Jagat Singh, having died, Bhagat Singh was now the eldest child in a family of eight children. The pressure to marry was intense. But Bhagat Singh also knew that if he married, he would not be able to participate at the highest levels of the revolutionary movement, which his involvement in the Hindustan Socialist Republican Association demanded of him as he would have to spend long periods away from home, working secretly and remotely. He was also influenced by his mentor, Sachindra Nath Sanyal, in this decision. When the pressure came, Bhagat

Singh was sixteen and studying at National College in Lahore in 1923 and had just passed his intermediate exams. That is when, to escape marriage, he fled to Kanpur in Uttar Pradesh, where he stayed with Mani Lal Avasthi.[3]

So convinced was Bhagat Singh about the incompatibility of marriage with the life of a revolutionary that he even set out to persuade his teacher, Principal Chhabil Das of National College, that Das should not do so, despite Das' protestations that eminent revolutionaries such as Sun Yat-Sen, Lenin and Karl Marx were all married.[4] However, this was not because Bhagat Singh himself frowned upon marriage as an institution. It was because a truly fulfilling marriage for him was only attainable in a climate of full personal freedom which at the time was a chimera for most Indians. As he explained to his friend, Raja Ram Shastri, he too was in the prime of his life with desires and longings which he wished to make known to someone.[5] But not without freedom. Bhagat Singh's determination not to get married is also confirmed by his niece, Virendra Sindhu.[6] Bejoy Kumar Sinha too confirms how on 1 April 1929, which was only a week before the Assembly bomb attack took place on 7 April 1929, the two of them were watching a group of young boys and girls playing in a Delhi park, when Bhagat Singh sorrowfully remarked on the tragedy of their lives, where amidst the beauty of life before them, they had to choose to die for their beliefs rather than to live.[7] When, therefore, in the face of unabating family pressure to marry, Bhagat Singh had left home in August 1923, he had done so leaving behind a letter in his father's office drawer reminding him that 'at the time of my sacred thread ceremony, when I was quite young, Bapu Ji (i.e. his grandfather) pledged me for the service of my country', a pledge which he would now honour.[8]

In fact, the Assembly bomb attack of 8 April 1929 is revealing in one very important respect which has been entirely overlooked. This is to do with his attitude to love. If he had been able to love, Bhagat Singh would have loved passionately. And, it would have been the love of a revolutionary. Initially, when the HSRA decided to have bombs thrown in the Delhi Assembly,

Bhagat Singh was not in the frame, even though he had pleaded
to go, given two other comrades in the organization who were
presented to go. Sukhdev, who had not been present at the meeting
where the decision was made, however, accused Bhagat Singh of
ducking out because Sukhdev alleged he wanted to spend more
time with a certain woman who held a 'fascination' for him. Hurt
by this baseless allegation by one so close to him as Sukhdev,
Bhagat Singh insisted that a meeting be immediately reconvened
where he could be authorized to go on such an expedition. Had
he not done so he would not have been arrested after the Delhi
bomb blast and hanged as he was. After this meeting was done,
he had a letter sent to Sukhdev on 5 April 1929 through Shiv
Verma. In this he explained that although he was now on his way
to the Delhi Assembly and had 'travelled far away towards my
destination', the fact was that 'one thing has continued to prick
my heart', and 'this is that my own brother misunderstood me
and levelled a very serious charge of weakness towards me'. He
makes it clear to him that he is committed to 'sacrifice in the true
sense of the word'.

It is interesting that he does not deny that he is not partial to
love. On the contrary, he extols the virtues of love and disabuses
Sukhdev of the notion that it is a source of weakness. He begins
with the observation that 'in the context of discussing someone's
character, one thing that is worth thinking about is if love has ever
proved to be helpful to any person. Let me answer this today – yes
it did, for Mazzini'. He gives the example of Mazzini because of
his 'first unsuccessful rebellion', which had left him with 'the grief
of heart-wrenching failure, and the memory of martyred comrades'.
Bhagat Singh explains of Mazzini how, in the circumstances,
'he could have either gone mad or committed suicide, but with a
letter from his beloved, he became not only as strong as others, but
stronger than everybody else'. Against this backdrop, Bhagat Singh
proceeds to speak of love as 'a very sweet human emotion. Love is
never a bestial passion'. In fact, 'the character of a person is always
elevated by love . . .'. Of girls who fall in love, he states 'you cannot

call these girls mad' before proclaiming that 'true love can never be created. It wells up by itself when no one can predict'.[9] There is then an extraordinary statement where he clearly endorses the falling in love by revolutionaries, in terms that 'it is not bad in modern times; rather, it is good and beneficial for man'. Indeed, despite his own strict religious family background, he finds himself reprimanding Sukhdev for his straight-laced, prudish and rather spartan outlook on love. As he explains, 'we cannot adopt the Arya Samaj model of puritan morality' and asks him 'to temper the extreme idealism that you have'. One may wonder here whether Bhagat Singh makes an admission here of his own love when he admonishes Sukhdev with the words, 'Don't be cold to those who lag behind and *fall prey to a disease like mine*; don't heighten their pain by scolding them, because they need your sympathy.' Such an inference is certainly possible. It appears that Bhagat Singh knows something that Sukhdev doesn't. It is arguable that this is why he tells Sukhdev, 'But you cannot understand these things till you have yourself fallen prey to this.' Fallen prey to what?[10] Surely, it must mean the 'very sweet human emotion' where 'the character of a person is always elevated by love . . .'. Bhagat Singh, in short, was not oblivious to the finer feelings of the human condition. On the contrary, he had a high opinion of romantic love, which he proclaimed as particularly good for revolutionaries. Bhagat Singh believed not only in real emotional relationships between people but also in the role of love in the making of political networks and movements. Few have understood this.

22

1928, J.P. Saunders' Murder

It was the assassination of a police officer by Bhagat Singh and his comrades that, in the end, sent him to the gallows. This was in turn a consequence of the killing by the Lahore police of Lala Lajpat Rai, who had decided to mobilize support against the Simon Commission. But well before the arrival of the Simon Commission in Lahore on 30 October 1928, Indian organizations, from the Congress Party, the Naujawan Bharat Sabha, the Students' Union and the Hindustani Sewa Daal had decided to boycott this delegation. Some 5,000 protesters had gathered at the Lahore Railway Station to oppose the seven-man commission spearheaded by Sir John Allsebrook Simon. When the Simon Commission arrived in Lahore on 30 October 1928, it was greeted by an angry procession chanting, '*Hindustani hain hum, Hindustan hamara / Mur Jao Simon jahan hai desh tumhara*' ('Hindustani we are, Hindustan is ours/ Go and die Simon, in that country which is yours'). The authorities were all too aware of the mood on the street. This is why as Kuldip Nayar observes, the police superintendent of Lahore, J.A. Scott, ordered a lathi charge. When Lala Lajpat Rai enjoined them to hold on to their positions as satyagrahis, (true warriors) many turned back upon hearing his exhortations. It was then that 'Scott spotted Lajpat Rai from a distance and went for him' and 'the policeman used his baton to beat the Indian leader mercilessly and did not stop even when blood began spurting from Lajpat Rai's chest'. In fact, 'Scott did not stop till Lalaji fell down' and 'it looked as if Scott was releasing his pent-up anger against all those who defied the British'. If this was so, then it was all too reminiscent of how 'only nine years earlier, General R.E.H. Dyer, an Irishman born in Shimla, had wreaked his vengeance upon the people at Jallianwala Bagh of Amritsar for heckling a British woman in one of the City's bazaars'.[1] With the attack on Lajpat Rai 'a wave of horror and indignation swept through the crowd' and soon 'anger gripped the country'.[2] Lala Lajpat Rai died ten days later on 17 November 1928. There was massive public mourning. At a condolence meeting in Calcutta on 29 November 1928, Basanti Devi, the widow of the Bengali Congressman C.R. Das, a renowned nationalist, summed up the mood at large when she raged at her countrymen's inaction with the inflammatory words, 'I quake with shame and disgrace.' She demanded to know whether 'the youth and manhood of the country still exist'.[3] This is when Bhagat Singh 'swore to avenge the insult'.[4] The HSRA began to plot revenge for Lala Lajpat Rai's death. It was to be the first of the strategic attacks on public officials which the revolutionaries described as 'Actions'.[5]

And so it was, that two days before the planned assassination in revenge of the killing of Lajpat Rai, four men from the HSRA met up on 15 December 1928 to plan the assassination of a state official. Bhagat Singh, Chandrashekhar Azad, Rajguru and Jai Gopal were to have a dry run of their individual assignments in the planned plot. It was futile. J.A. Scott was to go out of town to Kasur on official police business on the day of his planned assassination on 17 December 1928. An ill-fated twenty-one-year-old probationary officer, J.P. Saunders, was the assistant superintendent of police who found himself leaving work at the Anarkali Police Station on a cool breezy afternoon at 4.20 p.m. With his motor cycle he was gently making his way towards the gate which would open out onto the road. Before he got to the gate, he heard someone cry out from behind him. It was the head constable, Chanan Singh. The young J.P. Saunders had forgotten to take his keys with him. Running out towards him, Chanan Singh thrust the keys into his hands. Saunders took them, put them in his pocket and sped out of the front gate onto the road. Suddenly, shots rang out. Jai Gopal, wearing a turban and a warm coat over a pair of loose trousers tied with a drawstring around the waist, had given the signal to Rajguru, who was wearing a felt cap and a cotton coat. Rajguru fired the first shot. Saunders was hit and fell off his motorcycle. As he lay there groaning, Bhagat Singh, in a coloured felt cap and warm coat over his khaki shorts and in a black pair of shoes, ran towards him and fired another seven bullets into him.[6]

The two assassins were then seen to make off. They headed in the opposite direction of the police station into DAV College through its gate. The head constable gave chase. A traffic inspector, Mr Fearn, also joined in. Without warning, one of the men, Chandrashekhar Azad, in an almond-coloured turban, a loose salwar and wearing a pair of running shoes, turned around and fired. His bullet hit Chanan Singh, who fell mortally wounded.[7] The next day, on 18 December 1928, the assassins having already realized that Saunders was not Scott altered their pre-prepared posters to substitute the name of Scott with Saunders', and posted them all over Lahore, with the heading, 'Saunders is dead. Lalaji is avenged'. Interestingly, while the text of the posters explained why the assassination had to be carried out they also added, 'Sorry for the death of the man. But in this man had died the representative of an institution which is so cruel, lowly and so base that it must be abolished.'[8] They also declared that, 'We are sorry to admit that we who attach so great a sanctity to human life, who dream of a glorious future, when man will be enjoying perfect peace and full liberty, have been forced to shed human blood.' These are astonishing words that would rarely have been uttered before in the annals of revolutionary movement and especially in the very heat of the moment of performing the revolutionary act in question. Yet, they are illuminating in every way. They are a resounding rejection of violence in every form.

It was then time to make oneself scarce. Bhagat Singh had already cut his hair in September 1928 at Ferozpur after a meeting at the fort of Ferozeshah Kotla in Delhi, and so all he needed to do now was to don a hat.[9] Disguising himself as a wealthy sahib or an Anglo-Indian and accompanied by Durga Bhabhi[10] (one of the few women revolutionaries who actually participated in armed revolution against the British), he made haste in the middle of the night to escape for Lahore Railway Station, from where he took a train for Calcutta. The HSRA dispersed, only to regroup in Agra. There they set up a bomb factory. Plans were made on how to take further 'Actions'. New plots were hatched. One of these, which never materialized, even set out to target the Simon Commission in Delhi, so daring and determined was the HSRA.

The murder created an instant stir. It won the admiration of members of the Congress Party. Although the latter had previously disapproved of the tactics of the HSRA revolutionaries, they now began to provide them with financial assistance.[11] Ajoy Ghosh, who had stood trial with Bhagat Singh in the Lahore Conspiracy Case but had been acquitted, said of the murder, 'well-timed and daringly executed, it was an action that was acclaimed by the public with joy'.[12] And yet, it seems that Bhagat Singh himself remained not altogether untroubled by the deed. Shiv Verma, another accomplice of his, claimed that 'Bhagat Singh remained upset for some days',[13] given the bloodshed. Nevertheless, what was ultimately acknowledged even at the highest levels was, as Jawaharlal Nehru put it, that 'Bhagat Singh did not become popular because of his act of terrorism, but because he seemed to vindicate, for the moment, the honour of Lala Lajpat Rai; and through him the nation'. So much so that, 'within a few months, each town and village of the Punjab . . . resounded with Bhagat Singh's name' and very soon 'innumerable songs grew up about him'.[14]

For a man who met with such a high-profile death at the gallows, the bitterest irony for those who revered him is that both he and his comrades were initially destined to cleanly get away with this gruesome murder. The murder had taken place in broad daylight at 4.30 p.m. It was executed in the immediate vicinity of the police station on College Road. Rajguru had fired the first shot. But no attempt was then made for the assailants to get away. Instead, Bhagat Singh had moved in to fire a further seven shots himself afterwards. The killers had then fled in the opposite direction through the gates of the DAV College. As they fled, there had been one other unnecessary fatality. Chandrashekhar Azad had chased and shot at Constable Chanan Singh, who later died at Mayo Hospital. And yet, the authorities did not have the slightest clue about the assailants or where even to begin with their inquiries. On 10 January 1929, a telegram from the viceroy in India to the secretary of state for India recorded how the 'first phase of investigation has ended in the release on bail of all the persons arrested'. They were not even sure why the murder happened and worked on the 'accepted theory, which is probably correct, . . . that the murder was a direct act of revenge for death of Lajpat Rai'. All they could say was that, 'against some of those arrested there was secret information of complicity, while a number of others have been indulging in inflammatory speeches ever since his death'. Remarkably, this was being maintained while the authorities were clear that, 'in no case, however, was there anything material enough to justify further detention'. All that they could say was that the 'Punjab Government are meantime sparing no effort'.

Although optimism was expressed in the statement that 'there are several eye-witnesses who profess ability to identify one or more of the murderers', the blunt truth was that at that stage no eyewitness could identify anyone. All that they could say with reasonable confidence was that, 'it is also reasonably certain that carefully chosen line of retreat through D.A.V College compound required intimate local knowledge in the part of one or more of the culprits', but they were speculating when they declared that they 'were probably seen by large number of students'. In fact, it was even more speculative for the viceroy to assert that 'fired cartridge cases are also thought to bear sufficiently distinctive marks to lead to the identification of firearms used if they are recovered', because almost a month after the assassination the authorities still had no recovered cartridges. Such was the extent of pure conjecture as to who the assailants were and how they worked that the viceroy even wondered out loud in his telegram, that the 'possibility of outside persons having been imported is being carefully examined, and every other likely line of enquiry is being actively followed up'.[15]

23

1929, Delhi Assembly Bombs

The only reason that Bhagat Singh and his fellow conspirators were caught was because four months later the HSRA decided to throw two harmless smoke bombs in the Delhi legislature to make an impact. The irony is that Bhagat Singh may still not have been caught because originally it was B.K Sinha who was chosen to throw the bombs with B.K Dutt, but Sukhdev was unhappy with this decision and so Bhagat Singh replaced B.K. Sinha when Sukhdev goaded him into taking part.[1] Bhagat Singh, together with B.K. Dutt, was now set for the next escapade of the HSRA. The task at hand involved throwing two harmless smoke bombs in what is now the Indian Lok Sabha (i.e. Parliament), but was then the Central Legislative Assembly in New Delhi. This took place on 8 April 1929. The timing was propitious. The closing years of the tumultuous 1920s had climaxed with a series of nation-wide workers' strikes from 1927–1928, which had rocked the country. The government was determined to quash all dissent. It planned to pass two bills in Parliament, the Trades Dispute Bill and the Public Safety Bill. Public opposition to the bills was palpable. Ordinary people were all too aware of their needless oppression by the state. The government planned to play out a democratic charade of passing 'laws' which would oppress the workers even more. The restriction on the rights of ordinary citizens to protest would be passed as bills into law before their own representatives. For this reason, the HSRA was determined to prevent the passing of these two laws. The HSRA agreed that it would be Bhagat Singh and B.K. Dutt who would undertake the task. They would throw two home-made smoke bombs, accompanied by the showering of pamphlets making clear their objection to the new laws, just as they were being passed. They would then hand themselves over to the police. This was a remarkable design. Had Bhagat Singh and B.K. Dutt decided that they would flee, Bhagat Singh could still have escaped the gallows, if such a stratagem had been successful. Yet, they had deliberately chosen not to do so. The reason is that Bhagat Singh wanted an opportunity to make a speech to the court highlighting their political grievances and thereby giving the HSRA the publicity it needed at this point. Just throwing printed leaflets, with statements inscribed on them, in a smoke-filled legislative chamber was not enough. The insurgents also wanted the opportunity to make an oral statement, which would be widely reported, in open court before a judge tried them.

For this reason, Bhagat Singh and his co-conspirator, B.K. Dutt, deliberately chose to throw the smoke bombs, from the vantage point of the visitors' gallery, on the right side of the speaker, because they knew that they could cause no casualties. They wished only to frighten. And, so they did. The smoke bombs were followed by the firing of two shots from a small pistol in the air. This calculated act had the desired effect of Bhagat Singh and B.K Dutt drawing immediate and prompt attention to themselves from the men on the floor of the assembly below, as they looked up in shock and disbelief. The two of them then pointedly showered their home-made HSRA leaflets upon the panic-stricken assembly members below. It was a frightening spectacle for all involved. At about 12.30 p.m., a bluish smoke arose from the centre of the chamber of the Legislative Assembly. The traffic inspector immediately gave the order that visitors should be prevented from leaving the gallery. Just then another explosion took place. This time smoke appeared from the chamber below the ladies' gallery. Two pistol shots were fired in quick succession soon afterwards. People rushed frantically to the exit door. Some, pointing to the central door, exclaimed, 'There they are.' But Bhagat Singh and B.K. Dutt were not there. They were in the public gallery midway between the central door and the ladies' gallery. They were heard shouting, 'Down with imperialism.' When arrested, neither offered any resistance whatsoever, even though Bhagat Singh was allegedly seen 'gesticulating with a pistol in his right hand'. When searched, Bhagat Singh had some newspapers and pamphlets on his person. Sergeant McCready and Paxto, together with Sub-Inspectors Hans Raj and Prem Chand, then took the men away, who offered no resistance.[2]

It had worked exactly as Bhagat Singh and B.K. Dutt had intended. And, their timing was particularly apt. Two bills were being debated on the floor of the house. Both had raised considerable concern in the popular press. Both were widely castigated as needless repressive measures by a paranoid oppressive government determined to suppress basic freedoms of the people of India. One was designed to quell and subjugate labour unrest. The other, introduced in the interests of 'public safety', was to do with banning the entry of those Communist Party members who came to India from abroad. Once again the fear of a communist revolution in India on the crest of a thunderously successful Bolshevik revolution in Russia during the past decade had unnerved the British government to its foundations and made them deeply wary of such movements. Both labour rights and the right to engage with the leading socialist thinkers had been the subject of considerable discussion in the nationalist press for some days. For Bhagat Singh and B.K. Dutt, their purpose, in creating such a calamitous spectacle in the Delhi Assembly, was to 'make the deaf hear'. Their leaflets could not have made this any more abundantly clear. They were 'to make a loud noise'. And they succeeded. The news spread instantly.

With it, just as instantly, followed fame. Bhagat Singh was fond of drinking milk. He relished buffalo milk in particular. Heavier and richer than cow's milk, it is renowned for its creaminess. Kiron Das, the younger brother of Jatin Das who was to die in Lahore Jail on 13 September 1929 after sixty-three days on hunger strike, recalls the time when Bhagat Singh spent a night with Jatin Das in his Hazara Road Mess, with the aim of learning from him how to make the bombs. At dawn, Bhagat Singh had upon awakening glimpsed from his bedroom window a man milking his buffalo on the other side of the road. Springing out of his bed, he had rushed out to the milkman, grabbed 'the full bucket of milk without caring to boil the same and paid him one rupee as price for the milk consumed' and gulped the contents of the bucket right down. Having paid the milkman, Bhagat Singh may have thought that to be the end of the matter. This it may indeed have been for him. It was not for the milkman. The morning after the Legislative Assembly bomb blast, with the news having been reported in the press, the milkman sought out Jatin Das at his Hazara Road Mess and insisted on returning the rupee back to him so that it could be returned to Bhagat Singh, 'as he felt honoured and proud to have served such a distinguished patriot'.[3]

A trial followed. It is important to remember that Bhagat Singh actually underwent three trials, and not one, and this is often not fully appreciated. Yet, it is necessary to keep these three trials distinct if one is to understand properly the steps leading up to his hanging in 1931. The first trial he faced was the Delhi Assembly Bomb Case trial, which began on 7 May 1929, and at the conclusion of which Bhagat Singh was not sentenced to death but faced transportation to the Andaman Islands for life. The second trial is the one he is most known for, and this is the Lahore Conspiracy Case, when together with Sukhdev Thapar and Shivram Rajguru, he was tried for the murder of J.P. Saunders, and when he was sentenced to death. This trial began initially before a regular magistrate by the name of Rai Sahib Pandit Sri Kishen on 10 July 1929. It ran for ten months. Over 200 witnesses were called for the prosecution. Then suddenly the trial was brought to an abrupt end and deferred to a special tribunal. This was set up under the governor-general's Lahore Ordinance No. III of 1930 which was signed off on 1 May 1930 and which was to sit in Poonch House where the Lahore Civil Secretariat is presently located. Five days later it began to hear the rest of the case against the

Lahore conspirators, beginning on 5 May 1930, rushing through the evidence and allowing no right of cross-examination to the defence counsel. At the end of this trial, Bhagat Singh was sentenced to death together with Sukhdev Thapar and Shivram Rajguru, on 7 October 1930. There was no right of appeal against the sentence of death from the special tribunal to the high court in Lahore, as there would have been from the magistrate's court had it been allowed to complete the trial, and so the only appeal that could be exercised lay before the judicial committee of the Privy Council in London. This was the third trial and the least known and least commented upon.[4] It was argued only on a single day by the redoubtable left-wing British lawyer, D.N. Pritt, on 11 February 1931, on an application for 'permission to appeal' before five judges, who gave him short shrift and did not even accede to allowing the matter to go for a full hearing before it. This meant that the government lawyer on the day, A.M. Dunne, was not even called upon to put forward the government's case. At the end of it, only one judge, Lord Dunedin, gave one short one-and-half page judgment on 27 February 1931, in the case of *Bhagat Singh v. The King Emperor*. He dismissed the appeal with the legally wrong statement that 'although the Governor-General thought it fit to expound the reasons which induced him to promulgate this Ordinance, this was not in their Lordships' opinion in any way incumbent on him as a matter of law,'[5] when clearly reasons had to be given to show why a state of emergency existed justifying the passing of an ordinance to try the Lahore Conspiracy accused. Almost exactly a month later, on 23 March 1931, Bhagat Singh and his two accomplices were hanged to death in Lahore Central Jail. The jail and the gallows remained intact until they were finally dismantled in the 1960s to build a residential colony. With its dismantling, the details of Bhagat Singh's life also vanished like ether into thin air with the passage of time.

The first case, Delhi Assembly Bomb Case, arose soon after the arrest of Bhagat Singh and B.K. Dutt, when they were accused of throwing bombs 'to kill or cause injuries to the King Majesty's subjects'.[6] And they decided that they wished to be treated as 'political prisoners' and not as common criminals. This was important to them because their action had been castigated as an 'outrage' and the pair described as 'lunatics'. Soon afterwards, the two prisoners found themselves in the sessions court before the magistrate, F.B. Pool, on 7 May 1929. A sessions court is a court of law which exists in a number of Commonwealth countries. It is the highest criminal court in a district and it is the court of first instance for trying serious offences, that is to say, those which carry a punishment of imprisonment of seven years or more, life imprisonment or death. It is called a sessions court because it was designed to sit in consecutive sessions, hearing one case after another and giving instantaneous rulings and thus disposing of cases quickly. Ironically, the practice of this jurisdiction in India today is the opposite, with innumerable adjournments and consequent delays in the disposal of cases by sessions court judges. Kishan Singh had asked the lawyer, Asaf Ali, to represent his son, Bhagat Singh. At 9.50 a.m., F.B. Pool dawdled into the court-room. He saw Bhagat Singh's grandmother, Jai Kaur, and Ajit Singh's wife, Harnam Kaur, seated at a distance from him. The public prosecutor was Rai Bahadur Suryanarayan and the court-room was full of people attending in support of the accused. At the outset, Bhagat Singh made clear that he would answer none of his questions unless first recognized as a political prisoner. To prove that this was his proper designation, he wished to give a long speech setting out the manifesto of his party. What he said then provides us with the most penetrating insights into the thinking of this young revolutionary. It is hardly recalled these days by anyone anywhere. It is, however, a statement to which we will return later.

PART 5

1928, THE NAUJAWAN BHARAT SABHA

Main sochta huun bahut zindagi ke baare mein
Ye zindagi bhi mujhe soch kar na rah jaae

Much time I spend thinking of this life
lest it mock me for having no purpose in life.

—Abhishek Shukla

24

1928, Ferozeshah Kotla

On a cold dank night on 8 September 1928, under cover of darkness, some townsfolk, having wrapped themselves in finely woven homespun woollen shawls, gathered around the ramparts of an old medieval fort, in earnest, to listen to the evening's classical musical performance. A sarangi twanged in the distance as its custodian applied the bow to the metal wires, its piercing sound echoing in the still of the night. A tabla player tendentiously checked the tone of his tabla, readying himself to spring into action. The singer cleared his throat and opened with a *bada khayal* in an evening raga in Yaman Kalyan. Unbeknownst to them, a tall young man dressed in *khaddar* in a lungi stretching down to his ankles, but with chiselled good looks, had also stolen in amid the haunting red sandstone ruins of the Qutub complex. Over two days, he would welcome other young men and preside over a meeting of various insurgent groups that had sprung up in India in the early 1920s. Delhi in those days lacked auditoriums. This is where the fort of Ferozeshah Kotla, with its awe-inspiring architectural ruins, provided a perfect backdrop for gatherings and assemblies of disaffected youth who could meet in secret, away from the prying eyes of the security services. Here they found just the safety and seclusion that they craved to hatch their seditious plans.

For all these reasons, the significance of the meeting at the fort of Ferozeshah Kotla ought not to be lost on independent India. A single lonely plaque is displayed today on the site. It does not do it justice, and nor does the fact that it remains off the beaten track, hardly visited today by anyone. By calling that meeting, what Bhagat Singh had managed to do was to unify the various revolutionary groups from different parts of the country. These ranged from the Anushilan and Yogantar groups in Bengal to the Ghadar Party in Punjab. He did that at a meeting which extended over 8 and 9 September 1928. It was at the Ferozeshah Kotla Fort that he brought all these groups together under the banner of the Hindustan Republican Association (HRA). It remains significant that revolutionaries came to this meeting from as far afield as Uttar Pradesh, Bihar, Rajasthan and Punjab. What Bhagat Singh now did was both to add the word 'socialism' to turn it into the 'HSRA' and to propose that a central committee of seven members run it. At that meeting, Chandrashekhar Azad was elected the commander-in-chief of the HSRA. Not only was it agreed to boycott the Simon Commission, but a further 'action' was also agreed upon, namely, to throw a bomb at the train that carried its members. It was also agreed that bomb factories should be set up in Saharanpur, Agra and in Lahore.[1]

It is time therefore to openly acknowledge that in the build-up to Indian Independence, there were two rival traditions vying for recognition: one was the Gandhian tradition of 'non-violence', and the other was the revolutionary tradition of a 'violent struggle for freedom'. An alternative to Gandhian non-violence is once again being given attention because of the path that Indian democracy is currently eking out for itself. As retired Indian Supreme Court Justice Katju has recently lamented, 'The path of Gandhi and his associates like Nehru, Patel, etc. resulted in parliamentary democracy, which in India really means appeasing and appealing to caste and communal vote banks.' For him, '[c]asteism and communalism are feudal forces which must be destroyed if India is to progress, but parliamentary democracy further entrenches them'. It is in this way that 'the path of Gandhi and his associates continues to divide India on caste and communal lines, whereas if we had adopted the path of Bhagat Singh and Surya Sen we would have become united in our struggle against poverty, unemployment and other evils, and like China emerged as an industrialised and powerful nation, with our people enjoying decent lives'.[2] This, therefore, acknowledges the possibility of a rival tradition, and one adopted by neighbouring China, which has been vanquished but which would have made all the difference, had it been allowed to flourish.

The loss of this alternative road to freedom has been much lamented, although it remains little comprehended in modern India today, but as Irfan Habib has stated, in the hanging of Bhagat Singh and his comrades, 'we did not lose merely individuals' but that 'we lost rather an alternative framework of governance for post-independent India'.[3] When most revolutionaries had agreed to suspend action in support of Mahatma Gandhi's non-cooperation movement, the disappointment that arose from the failings of 'the national Bourgeois leadership' after 1922 led to the widespread feeling that 'it had betrayed the workers, the peasants and the youth' and this is when the HRA was formed with its manifesto 'The Revolutionary'.[4]

The Ferozeshah Kotla meeting of 1928 itself arose against the backdrop of the decimation of the previous revolutionary leadership, following the Kakori train robbery Case in 1925, when so many of them were promptly caught and hanged. Bhagat Singh took the opportunity to build on the foundations of the 'Naujawan Bharat Sabha' (Youth Society of India) but precisely when that body was formed is unclear. We learn from the account of Comrade Ram Chandra, who was a close associate of Bhagat Singh in his earlier years, that 'there is no record of the Sabha available' but that 'from my memory . . . I say that it was formed towards the end of 1924'. In fact, he had 'come across a file in the All India National Archives' which 'is Home Political File No. 27/5 of 1931,' which lends support to this.[5] Ram Chandra played a key role in the formation of the Sabha notwithstanding his inability to precisely remember when it was founded. What he recalled fifty years later was that, 'I was first to propose that the name of the [new] organisation should be "Naujawan Bharat Sabha".[6] His account remains the best of the Sabha from a witness of the events of that time and we are lucky to have it. It only came about because in 1975 when he was busily involved in making arrangements for holding 'a freedom fighters conference in Delhi,' Kulbir Singh, the younger brother of Bhagat Singh, came over to him and told him that a 'greater duty' rested on his shoulders than arranging a conference, and that was to write an account of the Sabha in the way that only he could. After five years of holding personal interviews with old comrades, and setting out 'to collect old material from government files'[7] Comrade Ram Chandra finally published his indispensable account, covering everything from early days at the National College in Lahore with Bhagat Singh, right down to his execution, and beyond to when Subhas Chandra Bose sided himself with the Axis countries against the British in the Second World War. Others, however, take the view that whatever the genesis of the Sabha, Bhagat Singh was instrumental in actually turning it into the force that it eventually became and that it was a young Bhagat Singh aged nineteen who actually started the Naujawan Bharat Sabha (Youth Society of India) in 1926 and that it was his creation in the way in which we have come to understand it. In the words of Simona Sawhney, he had been, '[i]nspired, like many of his contemporaries, by Giuseppe Mazzini's Young Italy Movement (1831)'[8] in doing so. The purpose of the Naujawan Bharat Sabha was to bring the youth of Punjab together under the umbrella of a new socialist non-religious organization. Socialism and humanism were thus amalgamated with nationalism. It is this which Bhagat Singh championed. It is this syncretism that made him so distinct from other leaders of the revolutionary movement. Others such as Mittal and Habib have explained how '[t]he *Naujawan Bharat Sabha* was formed to channelize the militant nationalist movement on ideological lines in March 1926 by Bhagat Singh', with a 'wider perspective' so that whilst 'it believed in the freedom of other enslaved nations also',[9] the fact was that '[t]he Sabha also stood for secularism'.[10]

25

1929, The HSRA

After the Naujawan Bharat Sabha, it was an easy step two years later for Bhagat Singh to inaugurate the mutinous HSRA, which was set up in 1929, principally by Chandrashekhar Azad and Bhagat Singh. He was 21 years old then. Though on the site of the fort of Ferozeshah Kotla, a plaque today commemorates the establishment of the HSRA with the names of Bhagat Singh, Sukhdev and Rajguru, few realize that it was the establishment on that cold night in September 1928, on the outskirts of Delhi in the dilapidated ruins of a medieval fort, of the Hindustan Socialist Republican Association ('HRSA') that completed the transformation that Bhagat Singh was seeking in the nature of the revolutionary struggle that had to be waged against colonial rule.

The HRA was henceforth to be the HSRA, with 'socialism' being given an added emphasis. The central committee of the HSRA comprised such stalwarts as Sukhdev, an ardent adherent of communist philosophy. It also included the journalist Vijay Kumar Sinha (also known as 'Bejoy'). Since the genesis of the movement was traceable to India's three provinces of Punjab, the United Provinces (now Uttar Pradesh) and Bihar, there were to be two representatives from each of these provinces in the central committee. The HSRA itself was to comprise two parts. These were to be the ideological and the military wings. Bhagat Singh took charge of the ideological wing. The task of managing the HSRA's 'military' operations was handed over to such hardened activists as Shiv Verma and Chandrashekhar Azad (who had participated in the Kakori train robbery a year earlier in 1925). The fact that Bhagat Singh later participated in the killing of the policeman J.P. Saunders shows that he took part in the military faction as well as being in charge of the ideological wing.

The youthfulness of these revolutionaries was not without significance. The young were devoid of all hope for the future of India. This is clear from a manifesto produced in 1928 for the All-Punjab Naujawan Bharat Sabha in Amritsar. It was produced by Bhagwant Charan Vohra, the propagandist secretary of the HSRA. In it he proclaimed how 'the young bear the most inhuman tortures smilingly and face death without hesitation'.[1] After that, an emboldened HSRA published its manifesto in the following year in 1929. This contained the proclamation, 'Revolution is Law, Revolution is Order and Revolution is the Truth.' It continued, 'The youths of our nation have realised this truth'[2]—a commitment best encapsulated in the declaration Inquilab Zindabad[3] ('Long live the revolution'). The call for 'revolution' was not, however, to be misunderstood. It was not a single event. Nor was it necessarily violent. What it represented was an eternal, everlasting and permanent search for renewal and revitalization of the present. This is because, as Subhas Chandra Bose stated at the meeting of the All India Youth Congress in Calcutta in 1929, the youth were 'no longer content with handing over all responsibility to older leaders' and to be content 'following like dumb, driven cattle'.[4]

And so it came to be that it was in the person of Bhagat Singh that these popular dissidents acquired a form which could be venerated and passed down through oral narratives of the road to freedom in India. Whatever may have been the officially endorsed narrative of the 'centrality of nonviolence' in the anti-colonial movement before Independence, it is the centrality of Bhagat Singh to the lives and basic aspirations of the ordinary man in the Indian subcontinent that is significant today. They are the ones who are still struggling to make ends meet. This is why Chris Moffat has observed that when it comes to Bhagat Singh, it is '[t]he contours of this militant life – partisan commitment, unflinching action, heroic self-sacrifice – [that] continue to shape Bhagat Singh's ghost; acknowledging the weight of this legacy allows us to approach the enduring appeal to the revolutionary and the implications of his invocation today'.[5] In the words of Bipan Chandra, Bhagat Singh was not 'only one of India's greatest freedom fighters and revolutionary socialists, but also one of its early Marxist thinkers and ideologues'.[6] This explains why, as Christopher Pinney has noted, in the period up to Independence in 1947, 'images of Bhagat Singh were more prevalent than those of Mahatma Gandhi, in both contemporary India and in chromolithographs of the pre-independence era'. Small wonder then that he describes this as 'a stunning anomaly, given the dominance of the Mahatma in narratives of the nationalist movement'.[7] Ironically, however, the predominant narrative today is that it is Gandhian non-violence that secured India's Independence. The young revolutionaries are at best marginalized and at worst forgotten. It remains a paradox how the non-violent creed paved the way to the violence of Partition, something to which the revolutionaries would never have agreed, with a million dead and fifteen million uprooted from their homes. Yet, the 'violence' of the revolutionaries is derided and disparaged. The real violence of how India came to gain its freedom is bizarrely accepted as an inevitable part of the story of how the country achieved its freedom.

This is why an Indian scholar recently felt it necessary to declare that 'Even though India did not have a revolution, it has a large number of revolutionaries.'[8] R.C. Majumdar is described by Durba Ghosh as 'perhaps the most eminent Bengali historian to claim, against an official nationalist consensus, that Bengal's history of militant nationalism had been central to forging the necessary politics for an anti-colonial movement'.[9] In the foreword to Uma Mukherjee's *Two Great Indian Revolutionaries: Rash Behari and Jyotindra Nath Banerjee*, he has explained how, '[i]n spite of the attempts in some quarters to minimize the role of the revolutionaries in the history

of the freedom movement in India, their countrymen are now
becoming gradually conscious of the deep debt of gratitude they
owe to these heroes for the achievement of Indian independence'.[10]
Indeed, as Aparna Vaidik has more recently pointed out, even 'the
role of the anti-hero' such as 'Hans Raj Vohra (1909–1985), who
testified against his *HSRA* comrades in the Lahore Conspiracy Case'
needs to be understood in the context of 'a non-celebratory history
of nationalism, which is sensitive to the instances when nationalist
solidarity is fractured and betrayed'. In this way, we can see such
figures 'as integral to the history of nationalism and martyrdom'.[11]

In fact, in the words of Durba Ghosh, 'Among participants
of the underground groups, there were widespread concerns
throughout the 1950s and well into the 1960s that the history of
revolutionary terrorism would be forgotten.'[12] Indeed, so it has
proved today because barely anyone is familiar with the names of
these great revolutionaries outside India today, and even within
India hardly anyone knows about their contribution to the cause of
Independence. She refers to 'participants among the underground
groups', but even in the mainstream now, no one knows. And few
even care. Yet, it is a salutary reminder of how freedom is won. In
fact, one reason for this is how postcolonial India has extended
the shibboleth of Gandhian non-violence beyond Independence.
As Ghosh explains, 'Between 1947 and 1952, the early years of
independent India, as the government of India began a project of
national consolidation, it resorted to classifying opposing political
movements such as communism, trade union organization, battles
for land redistribution as threats to national security.'[13]

One reason why the revolutionaries' political inclinations gave
the colonial government much concern was because of the impact it
had on liberal opinion at home. This is vividly demonstrated by the
Meerut Conspiracy Case which arose in March 1929 when a railway
strike was organized by several trade unionists. Three of them were
Englishmen. The British Government convicted thirty-three of
them in 1933 in proceedings which were widely regarded as being
falsely contrived against them. This was one of the detrimental

effects of colonization. And it was immediately seized upon by the Manchester Street theatre troupe, which ran a play by the name of *Meerut* in 1932. The play laid bare the savage prison sentences of the leaders of the Indian rail-strike.[14] The sentences were all the more harsh for fear of communist influence on them. As Durba Ghosh explains, 'Much of the concern in left and liberal circles about political prisoners in India focused on those arrested in the Meerut Conspiracy Case – who had been under detention without charge for a number of years because of their suspected attachments to communism.'[15]

Despite some similarities, Bhagat Singh's case, however, stands in many ways in stark contrast to the Meerut Conspiracy Case, which began in camera on 15 March 1929. The district magistrate of Meerut issued warrants for the arrest of the accused. Langford James, the special prosecutor, opened the case before the magistrate on 12 June 1929. The accused were committed to trial by the sessions court on 13 January 1930. The trial was scheduled to be heard before a judge, accompanied by five assessors. At that stage, on 31 January 1930, the applications for a trial by jury had already been rejected by the chief justice of the Allahabad High Court. But it then took until 17 January 1933 for the judgment to be delivered.

Thereafter, the appeal was determined by the high court in a judgment some six months later on 13 August 1933. Importantly, the charge in that case was also 'conspiracy to deprive the King Emperor of his sovereignty of British India'. The government fielded 320 prosecution witnesses in the magistrate's court. In the sessions court, there were 281 prosecution witnesses. There was a mountain of documents to get through. The charge was that the accused had entered into a conspiracy to further the objectives of the Communist International in Moscow. However, in that case the accused consisted of some of the most eminent leaders of the communist and trade union movement in India, such as S.A. Dange, Muzaffar Ahmad, S.V. Ghate, S.S. Mirajkar, Sohan Singh Josh, M.A. Majid and P.C. Joshi. They also included three Englishmen: Philip Spratt, Benjamin Bradley and Lester Hutchinson. But the difference with the Lahore Conspiracy Case lay in the fact that the Meerut Prisoners' Defence Committee was formed largely through the efforts of Jawaharlal Nehru. His father Motilal Nehru was the chairman of the Meerut Prisoners' Defence Committee. Bizarrely, there was no such person or counsel of national eminence involved in the Lahore Conspiracy Case. The Lahore High Court Bar protested vigorously and the accused themselves were contemptuous of the maverick way in which the legal procedures were used against them. Unlike Bhagat Singh, those in the Meerut Conspiracy Case were relatively isolated from the political mainstream. Nevertheless, this very fact helped raise their popularity in public and they got off relatively leniently. This was not to be the case with Bhagat Singh. He ended up paying the ultimate price.

26

1930, 'Peace, Order and Good Government'

The Lahore Conspiracy Case began in court after Bhagat Singh was arrested on 8 April 1929 with B.K. Dutt for throwing smoke bombs in the central Legislative Assembly in New Delhi, 'to make the deaf hear'.[1] B.K. Dutt was a Bengali. A number of Bengalis had been involved in Lahore,[2] and the HSRA had been recruiting followers of Anushilan Samiti.[3] The action by Bhagat Singh and B.K. Dutt was designed to demonstrate their opposition to the continued British occupation of India.

Police investigations showed that members of the HSRA were behind the December 1928 assassination of a British official J.P. Saunders, who had been mistaken for his boss, J.A. Scott, the superintendent of police. Scott had been in charge when the nationalist figure, Lala Lajpat Rai, who had lived in Lahore since 1880 and had studied law at its Government College, was assaulted by police batons while marching against the Simon Commission in October 1928, whereas one writer said 'the public will have apparently none of the play'.[4] When Lajpat Rai died in the hospital on 17 November 1928, his death at the hands of the Punjab police gave rise to a new round of political violence. It was in fact the event that transformed the political landscape of India. Bhagat Singh set out to avenge the death of Lala Lajpat Rai. This is how J.P. Saunders came to be shot on 17 December 1928. Bhagat Singh became immensely popular. In her recent work on the Lahore Conspiracy Case,[5] Taylor Sherman considers Bhagat Singh's trial in the context of India's nationalist revolutionary movements of the time, the hunger strike undertaken, and then followed by his hasty execution. She observes how when the Punjab police put together the Lahore Conspiracy Case in 1929 'to charge twenty-five members of the HSRA, [Hindustan Socialist Republican Association] including Bhagat Singh and B.K. Dutt, with conspiracy against the government,'[6] from that time onwards '[t]he popularity of the accused in the Lahore Conspiracy Case, including Bhagat Singh and Jatindranath Das, has been a controversy to many scholars'.[7] However, she argues that it was actually 'the hunger strike which the accused undertook during their trial [which] was instrumental in establishing these men in the nationalist pantheon'.[8] There were three reasons for this.

First, she states, the hunger strike and the trial provided the HSRA 'with a stage from which they could display their charismatic defiance of British authority to a larger public'. Second, the case was prosecuted 'at a time when the Indian National Congress was preparing for another nation-wide anti-British campaign' so that 'many Congressmen were drawn to support the hunger strike'. Third, that 'when Jatin Dass succumbed during the strike, and Bhagat Singh, Shivram Rajguru and Sukh Dev were executed after the trial, they provided the nationalist with martyrs to Mother India'. This was of huge significance because, '[i]n nationalist movements in which few prominent figures gave their lives, the symbolic value of the martyrdom of these four men was incalculable'. She argues that '[a]s a result, the hunger strike was woven into the larger political choreography of the nationalist movement'.[9]

However, as is clear from Taylor Sherman's own valuable analysis, it was not just the 'hunger strike' which was woven into the larger political choreography of the times, but the execution by hanging of Bhagat Singh and his two comrades. In fact, it was the execution which was the more dramatic of the two. The execution, precisely because of its coercive legal machinations, imprinted itself indelibly on the consciousness of the people of the subcontinent, and it did so for generations to come. As Taylor Sherman puts it only too well, 'The trial thus became a showcase for the defiance and bravery of the accused.' She continues, 'Newspapers conveyed the many ways in which the revolutionaries, though weakened by their fast, were able to undermine the authority of the magistrate.'[10] Chris Moffat refers to Bhagat Singh's 'uncommon passion' and explains that rather than the hunger strike alone, it was 'the bomb, the bullet, the chant, the hunger strike, the kissing of the hangman's noose that did the demonstrative work'[11] for him and his comrades. The HSRA, he argues, was instrumental in this because of its 'conception of a militant life' so that 'the HSRA in their actions sought to signal an existing wrong of an emergent possibility, whatever the risk to themselves'.[12]

The trial of the accused, however, was by the governor-general's own legislative enactment in the form of an ordinance and that too is noteworthy because it is all too often overlooked. The significance of government by ordinance continues in India to this day. In his path-breaking study, Shubhankar Dam ruefully observes how 'Although constitutionally limited to circumstances when it is necessary to take immediate action, ordinances, in practice, have an expansive presence in India's parliamentary annals.' So much so that far from being a constitutional exception they are a constitutional norm of governance, so that, '[a]fter six decades, they are neither exceptional nor limited. Rather, they are a convenient and – distressingly at times – the *preferred* legislative method'.[13] Ordinances are now passed in India to circumvent parliamentary scrutiny. As such they can have no equivalence with legislative enactments which have the Parliament's democratic imprimatur. 'Ordinances' were used during colonial times. Under the Indian Councils Act 1861, the power of making laws and regulations was vested in the 'Governor General in Council'[14] and although 'the Council became British India's primary legislative body', in certain circumstances the 1861 Act 'vested original legislative power on the governor-general, independent of the Council', in the words of Shubhankar Dam.[15]

This is because the 1861 act also contained a provision to the effect that, 'Notwithstanding anything in this Act contained, it shall be lawful for the Governor-General, in cases of emergency, to make and promulgate, from time to time, ordinance for the peace and good government of the said territories . . .'. When this is done, then 'every such ordinance shall have life force of law or regulation made by the Governor-General in Council'. However, this is to be 'for the space of not more than six months from its promulgation, unless the disallowance of such ordinance by Her Majesty . . . Or unless such ordinance shall be controlled or superseded by some law made by the Governor-General in Council'.[16] It is this provision, confined as it was to situations of emergency only which related to 'peace and good government' limited to a six-month period, that found its way into Article 123 of the Indian Constitution.

Ordinances became ubiquitous in three ways in the regulatory scheme of everyday governance following the Government of India Act 1935, which replaced that of the act of 1915 of the same name. First, ordinances were to be the usual method of governance, rather than being unusual, because they were to be the preferred mechanism of legislative choice.[17] Second, a single ordinance for a particular matter under consideration was not enough, as there had to be a sequence or succession of ordinances, on the same matter for good effect. Third, ordinances began to be used side-by-side and in tandem with conventional legislative arrangements. A prime example of this is the Public Safety Ordinance. This, as Dam reminds us, was introduced in the Legislative Assembly in September 1928. What it did was to authorize, 'the removal from British India . . . of certain persons engaged in subversive propaganda',[18] only for the Assembly to reject it.[19]

Lord Irwin, however, was convinced of the necessity of such legislation in the interests of 'good government' and pressed ahead and 'promulgated the ordinance that incorporated the provisions earlier rejected by the assembly. The law set a new precedent, making ordinances an executive alternative to parliamentary legislation. Clearly aware of his extraordinary innovation, the governor-general invoked the support of the 'vast majority of India's people' in promulgating it. In a statement attached to the ordinance, he explained the 'serious character of [his] personal decision', claiming that he had no doubt that his action would command 'the approval of that vast majority of India's people who have faith in India's future and whose first desire is to see their country prosperous, contended and secure'.[20] But if this is right then the much-vaunted 'good government' had to be in the interests of the people being governed and there is much evidence that it was not shown to be so. The meaning of 'emergency' was now to be more fluid and less exacting. It would cover administrative inconvenience. This is what got Bhagat Singh, Sukhdev, and Rajguru in the end. Their trial for the killing of the assistant superintendent of police, John Saunders, and that of head constable, Chanan Singh, began in Lahore on 11th July 1929. Since Bhagat Singh and his co-defendants promptly resorted to hunger strikes the progress of the trial was slow and leisurely. In addition, there was what Dam refers to as the "'disorderly conduct' in the courtroom and demonstrations by the public outside" which also "led to some more adjournments" so that "By March 1930, only 234 of the 600 potential witnesses had been produced in the court." There was the fear now of "the trial likely to drag on indefinitely," and this is when Lord Irwin had little compunction exercising his own personal legislative powers. By his own edict he announced the Lahore Ordinance III of 1930, "arguing that 'disorderly conduct and revolutionary demonstrations, [had] to bring the administration of justice into contempt, [making] it impossible to count upon obtaining a conclusion by the normal methods of procedure within any calculable period.'"[21] A hunger strike is not, however, a 'disorderly conduct' by any stretch of imagination. But for Lord Irwin, as Dam explains, "public policy, as he understood it, required that the grave charges be 'thoroughly scrutinised and finally adjudicated upon with the least possible delay,'" and this is why he decreed that there be a three-judge tribunal instead of a regular court of law "investing them 'with powers to deal with wilful obstruction'" to try the accused in what was to become the second Lahore Conspiracy Case.

But even if this is so, was legislating by executive ordinance, so as to alter normal due process trial, the right way to go about it? As Dam himself continues to explain, 'The administrative character of the events mentioned here . . . involved nothing more than challenges in enforcing ordinary law and procedure. But in describing them as an "emergency" requiring special legislation, Lord Irwin brought the power to promulgate the ordinances ever closer to the legislature's power to enact primary legislation.' It may be more accurate to say that he in fact did, and did so illicitly! 'When contested, the Privy Council returned a verdict inscribing the governor-general's view into law.' In *Bhagat Singh and Others v. The Kings-Emperor*,[22] Viscount Dunedin concluded that a state of emergency 'is something that [did] not permit of any exact definition', but the fact that this may be so is not the same as saying that no case need be made out at all by the governor-general when invoking such an awesome power. As a state of matter calling for drastic action, 'emergency' had to be judged by someone. That someone, he wrote, could be 'the Governor-General, and he alone'.[23] In other words, emergency was whatever the governor-general felt it was; nothing else mattered.'[24]

We know from the general history of the common law during war-time that this approach was not just confined to the territories of the Empire but was used in none other a place than England itself. In the war-time case of *Liversidge v. Anderson* the same was done, except that in that case there was a thundering dissent by Lord Atkin. In the colonial territories, however, the impact of such an approach was to have profound and long-lasting effects. As Dam points out, 'Taken together, these developments made ordinances the new normal in India, both in numbers and in status. Numerically, they were vastly common – much more than in the earlier period. It was "normal" in its status too. By 1935, there were effectively two legislative authorities.' This was along with 'The Imperial Legislature [which] obviously had legislative powers'.[25]

The issue is timely and important. Pre-Independence India had competing rival approaches to the quest for freedom, which as Neeti Nair makes clear 'are seen to exemplify absolutely contrasting strategies of resistance'[26]—one based on the creed of non-violent Gandhism, the other a Marxist revolutionary call-to-arms movement championed by Bhagat Singh, who at the time of his death was more popular than Gandhi, so that had he lived the history of the Indian subcontinent would have been very different. Moreover, as S. Irfan Habib has written, with a special tribunal set up under the fiat of the governor-general specifically to hand down a judgment of death on Bhagat Singh after rag-tag judicial proceedings in which the judicial bench twice changed its judges, 'we lost an alternative framework of governance for post-independent India'.[27]

If 'jurisdiction' was wrongly created to hang Bhagat Singh, then might there be a case for an official pardon today? In truth, as early as 4 May 1930 Bhagat Singh's lawyers objected that the special tribunal 'had no jurisdiction to try the case'. Such protestations fell on stony ground. In her *Despotism of Law*, Radhika Singha explains how penal law from the time of early East India Company rule was used to have an impact on 'the range of social transactions which shaped the process of colonial state-formation',[28] whereby it became acceptable in some cases 'that the judge should use a different and lesser standard to hang a man . . .'.[29] Even if Bhagat Singh's trial concerned, what a modern case analysing the application of the formula, 'peace, order and good government', has said involved the affairs of 'incontestably the colony' can it be argued that 'it is capable of being rendered invalid by jurisdictional error or malpractice'?[30] The question is important because it is only in recent years that there has been an awareness of how in many Commonwealth jurisdictions, the phrase 'peace, order and good government' was traditionally used to express the legitimate objects of legislative powers conferred by statute. This has helped raise the possibility of comparative legal insights into how this power was to be exercised. Historically, the phrase has appeared in Imperial Acts of Parliament and Letters Patent. Today, it is to be seen in the constitutions of

Canada[31] and the Commonwealth of Australia.[32] It used to be evident in the constitutions of New Zealand and of South Africa. In the years before the Independence of India, the use of a legislative power to make an ordinance on the basis of 'peace, order and good government' was regularly used to try, convict and hang those who stood up to the government.

The historian Mark Condos has shown recently how 'the British in India regularly abandoned their high-minded notions about the "civilising mission", and reverted to much more brutal and pragmatic measures in order to ensure the stability and security of the colonial regime',[33] so that although 'peace, order and good government' may ordinarily be treated as epitomes of high virtue, they were not infrequently subverted by the colonial state through the medium of the law to maintain control. This is how Bhagat Singh came to be executed. Bhagat Singh and his comrades went on to become national heroes because of 'their practice of hunger strikes and non-violence civil disobedience within the walls of Lahore's prisons in 1929-30', as Neeti Nair has explained, and 'the quality of anti-colonial nationalism represented by Bhagat Singh was central to the resolution of many of the divisions that racked pre-partition Punjab'.[34] Yet, today we have a situation in India and Pakistan where, if anything, those divisions are even more pronounced, and '[t]he revolutionaries of the HSRA have long been marginalised in the academic history or geography of nationalism,' as Kama Maclean tells us. This is 'despite their extraordinary popularity in popular culture' and 'in colonial India, this was most evident in prescribed literature and posters, and in contemporary India, in film, posters, comics and bazaar histories'.[35] Today's India foments division and distrust.

PART 6

THE ASSEMBLY BOMB SPEECHES

Khird-mandon se kya puchhun ki meri ibtida kya hai
Ki main is fikr men rahta huun meri intiha kya hai

What could I ask a mystic about my origin
when I am worried that I do not know my own limits?

—Allama Iqbal

27

6 June 1929 Statement

If Bhagat Singh's anti-colonialism eschewed communal divisions, it is because he fused myriad sources of inspiration, sometimes Marxist and sometimes anarchist. This is why he is an enigma. The freedom movement of the 1920s of pre-Partition India was plagued by communal divisions. Post-Partition too, the tensions between Hindus and Muslims or Indians and Pakistanis have shown no signs of subsiding. In many ways, they are exacerbated today. So, Bhagat Singh is a puzzle, a paradox of the Indian subcontinent, and different from leaders who represented specific vote banks and communal interests. Bhagat Singh did not represent any sectional interests. For this reason he places these leaders in a quandary because it was not communities he championed but causes. Pre-eminent amongst these were the causes of the poor, the dispossessed and the marginalized. His throwing of two bombs in the Central Legislative Assembly was intended to disrupt the passage of the Public Safety and Trade Disputes Bill, so that assembly members would not be able to vote on a bill designed to circumscribe the rights of Indian workers. It was not accordingly an act of anarchism pure and simple. But there was a second purpose which made the act even further removed from anarchism. It was to expose what purported to be an Indian Parliament, in the form of the Central Legislative Assembly, as nothing more than a vassal of the Imperial Parliament in London.

The bomb throwing was an act of censure. As such, both acts were more aligned to the socialist cause that Bhagat Singh and the HSRA espoused than to anarchism. The pamphlets thrown into the assembly made it only too clear that Bhagat Singh's political philosophy did not allow him to endorse violence because of 'our love for humanity' bearing 'no personal grudge' against anyone. This is why Bhagat Singh and B.K. Dutt appeared before the trial judges afterwards and explained how they had deliberately thrown the two bombs at the unoccupied rows where no assembly members were seated. In the words of Bhagat Singh, 'The two bombs exploded in vacant spaces within the wooden barriers of the desks and benches.'[1] This was to scrupulously avoid people being injured. Had they chosen to, they could have used lethal and highly destructive devices to obliterate the chamber. They chose not to do so.

On 6 June 1929, Bhagat Singh and B.K. Dutt presented a statement before the sessions court.[2] It was a truly significant moment because although Bhagat Singh went through two further trials after this, in no other trial did he get to put out a statement for public consumption in this way. No other statement encapsulates his thoughts on revolution or, indeed, on anarchism. None other defines what he means by revolution. Nor does anything else set out his objectives in the same way. The day of the statement was the most important day of the trial. There were in fact two statements. The second statement was made on 12 June 1929 in the appeal against conviction and sentence of transportation for life, and this was made before the high court in the same case. The two statements are the only court-room statements made by Bhagat Singh, and of these the first one of 6 June is by far the more important. In this statement, Bhagat Singh made it clear, through his lawyer Asaf Ali, that Governor-General Lord Irwin was quite wrong to describe the Delhi Legislative Assembly bomb as 'an attack directed against no individual but an institution itself'. On the contrary, the purpose of the assembly bomb was 'to emphasise the historical lesson' of the changes sweeping the world over that the imperial government neglected at its peril. This is why, '[w]e wanted to emphasise that *lettres de cachet* and Bastilles could not crush the revolutionary movement in France', and why the, '[g]allows and Siberian mines could not extinguish the Russian Revolution'. Even within Great Britain, 'Bloody Sunday and Black and Tans failed to strangle the movement of Irish freedom'. Therefore, when the government now sets out to curb the unrest that was brewing before its very nose, he asks rhetorically, '[c]an Ordinances and Safety Bills snuff out the flames of freedom in India?'.[3] He is clear that laws such as the Public Safety and Trade Disputes Bill, which was presented before the Central Legislative Assembly, cannot achieve this aim. He is clear that fraudulent and fabricated charges against the young who are hauled up before the courts in their ever-expanding numbers will not vanquish them. The truth is that when it comes to it, 'conspiracy cases, trumped up or discovered and the incarceration of all young men, who cherish the vision of a great ideal, cannot check the march of revolution'. With a thundering and prophetic claim he asserts how in these circumstances, 'we took it upon ourselves to provide this warning and our duty is done'.[4]

Bhagat Singh and B.K. Dutt do not just chide 'the heedless' to give them 'a timely warning' that underneath 'the seeming stillness of the sea of Indian humanity' there is about to be 'a veritable storm', which is why they have 'to warn those who are speeding along without heeding the grave dangers ahead'. They also make it clear that if India's present predicament is left unaddressed, it is 'bound to lead to chaos'. They have no doubt that 'this state of affairs cannot last long' given that 'the present order of society in merry-making is on the brink of a volcano'.[5] To ensure that their warning was heeded, Bhagat Singh and B.K. Dutt now wanted 'to make the deaf hear'. In fact, these actions were not just those of Bhagat Singh and B.K. Dutt alone. They were an emulation of the actions of the French anarchist, Auguste Vaillant, who had launched a similar bomb attack on the French Chamber of Deputies on 9

December 1893. Like Bhagat Singh, he had also thrown a home-made device from the public gallery. And like Bhagat Singh, he too was immediately arrested. Indeed, Vaillant's device was also a weak one. It also only caused slight injuries in the chamber. He also had said that his aim was to 'make the deaf hear', but not to kill anyone, in revenge for the state execution the previous year of a fellow anarchist, Ravachol. Vaillant was put to death and faced the guillotine on 5 February 1894.[6] His actions inspired a number of anarchists after him, one of whom was Bhagat Singh. Like Vaillant, whose last words were 'Death to the Bourgeoisie! Long live Anarchy!', Bhagat Singh used the slogan 'Inquilab Zindabad' on a regular basis, right up to the time of his own death by hanging. The imitation of Auguste Vaillant was not in vain. The statement on behalf of Bhagat Singh and B.K Dutt by Asaf Ali declared that 'revolution is an inalienable right of mankind' and that 'freedom is an imperishable birth-right of all'. It was immediately reported on by the leading national newspapers of the day.

This was despite the fact that the magistrate had put in place rigid censorship controls that would curtail the making of manifesto speeches. The authorities viewed the trial in the context of the growth of communism in the 1920s. Left-wing radical groups were gaining strength in Europe and in America. Their activities had to be rigorously controlled and restricted. The authorities' fear was not allayed by the accused defiantly entering the courtroom with shouts of 'Inquilab Zindabad', making Bhagat Singh's name synonymous with this slogan. To this day, from student protests to farmer's revolts, 'Long live the revolution' is the one slogan that is associated with the name of Bhagat Singh.

So, on 9 June 1929, F.B. Pool ruled that, provided that sections of Bhagat Singh's speech could be 'expunged' from the record, he would allow it as the magistrate in charge. He reasoned that, given that the words in question had no impact on the case he had to decide, the offending words in Bhagat Singh's statement 'cannot be referred to here, nor, being irrelevant, could they affect the case'. The magistrate's entreaties, however, were in vain. No sooner had the trial started than Bhagat Singh's written testimony was in the public domain. It was widely available to all as it had been leaked to the press. Copies were even translated into Bengali and Gujarati and then circulated in revolutionary circles. It is not difficult to see why. When Bhagat Singh and B.K. Dutt called for revolution, in one of the expunged passages from their speech, what they were calling for was not a revolution of blood-letting but a revolution of ideas. If India forgets this today, it does so at its cost, for in doing so, it loses the chance to renew, revitalize, and replenish itself in a way that brings all its peoples together, and not just the few.

28

6 June 1929 and the Rejection of 'Utopian Non-violence'

Although large portions of the statement that the two of them made were redacted from the record on 9 June 1929, the text that is preserved in the National Archives of India[1] in New Delhi contains the complete version. The statement was originally in eight paragraphs. However, less than half of it was allowed to be put before the Sessions Court and paragraphs 6, 7 and 8 towards the end were almost entirely eliminated. In the expunged paragraph 6, they state that 'the Imperialist Exploiters cannot succeed' because 'by crushing individuals they cannot kill ideas'.[2] After setting out their aims and objectives, they make it clear that '[f]or these ideals, and for this faith, we shall welcome any suffering to which we may be condemned'.[3] What were these ideals? And what was this faith?

First, they wished to make it known that '[w]e are next to none in our love for humanity and so far as having any malice against any individual we hold human life sacred beyond words'. This being so, '[w]e are neither perpetrators of dastardly outrages and therefore to the country, nor are we "lunatics"'. They continue, 'We humbly claim to be no more than serious students of this history and conditions of our country and human aspirations, and we despise hypocrisy.'[4]

These words demonstrate how Bhagat Singh was operating from deep-seated philosophical convictions that informed the nature of his rebellion against the British Raj. In fact, far from Bhagat Singh being a young hot-headed malcontent, it is manifestly plain from this that he stood on par with Frantz Fanon, who was to come much later in the twentieth century. He writes, 'We dropped the bombs on the floor of the house Assembly Chamber to register our protest on behalf of those who had no other means left to give expression to their heart-rending agony. Our sole purpose was "to make the deaf hear".'

The attack on the Delhi Assembly killed no one, and nor was it intended to, but it did cause minor injuries. Bhagat Singh and B.K. Dutt had to give an explanation, namely, that it was 'to give the heedless a timely warning',[5] given that members of the assembly on that day included Motilal Nehru (the father of Jawaharlal Nehru), Sardar Vallabhbhai Patel, Muhammad Ali Jinnah, Madan Mohan Malaviya and John Simon (of the Simon Commission). However, '[w]e bore no personal grudge or malice against any one of those who received slight injuries or against any other person in the Assembly' and this is why 'the two bombs exploded in vacant spaces within wooden barriers of desks and benches' and why 'even those who were within two-feet of the explosion were either not hurt or only slightly scratched'.[6]

Second, the redacted portions of the statement reveal why these two members of the HSRA chose to target the Delhi legislature itself. As they state,

Our practical protest was against the institution which since its birth has eminently helped to display not only its worthlessness but its far-reaching power for mischief. The more we have pondered the more deeply we have been convinced that it exists only to demonstrate to the world India's humiliation and helplessness and it symbolises the overriding domination of an irresponsible and autocratic rule. Time and again the national demand has been pressed by the people's representatives only to find the waste-paper basket as its final destination.[7]

It is small wonder that this incendiary denunciation of the assembly was expunged from the record. But it did not end there. As the two of them continued, 'In spite of earnest endeavour we have utterly failed to find any justification for the existence of an institution which despite all the pomp and splendour organised with the hard-earned money of the sweating millions of India is only a hollow show and a mischievous make-believe.' Their excoriating damnation ended with a reference to 'the public leaders who help to squander public time and money on such a manifestly stage-managed an exhibition of India's helpless subjection'. In subsequent parts of the statement which are not redacted, there is a reference to the 'starving and struggling millions' of their countrymen who 'were deprived of their primary right and the sole means of improving their economic welfare' so that 'none who has felt like us for the dumb-driven drudges of labourers could possibly witness this spectacle with equanimity' and 'none whose heart bleeds for those who have given their life-blood in silence to the building up of the economic structure of the Exploiters, of whom the Government happens to be the biggest in this country, could repress the cry of soul-agonising anguish which so ruthless a blow wrung out of our hearts'.[8]

Third, it is against this background that Bhagat Singh and B.K. Dutt reject the notion of Gandhian 'utopian non-violence' in preference to the use of legitimate revolutionary force against the oppressor and the idea of revolution. Unfortunately, this was redacted from the statement presented before the sessions court, but what they wished to do here was to draw attention to 'the end of utopian non-violence of whose futility the rising generation has been convinced beyond the shadow of doubt'. What the sessions court did get to learn of, however, was their justification for the use of force, in a way which showed them to have been far more sophisticated than Mahatma Gandhi's passive non-cooperation, in that, 'Force when aggressively applied is "violence" and is therefore morally unjustifiable; but when it is used in the furtherance of a legitimate cause it has its moral justification,' a suggestion that Frantz Fanon forty years later would not have resiled from. The authorities apparently then, however, considered what was to follow from these words to be objectionable, because the following context of the use of force is expunged, and yet it is deeply revealing:

> The elimination of force at all costs is utopian and the new movement which has arisen in the country, and of which we have given the warning, is inspired by the ideals which guided Guru Gobind Singh and Shivaji, Kamal Pasha & Riza Khan, Washington & Garibaldi, Lafayette & Lenin.[9]

Unfortunately, as they continue with barely concealed exasperation, 'both the alien Government and the Indian public leaders appeared to have shut their eyes and closed their ears against the existence and the voice of this movement . . .'. The very fact that this statement, even when made, was deliberately erased from the record in 1929, shows the determined effort of both the authorities and other Indian leaders to suppress and to eventually wipe out any trace of what is referred to as the 'new movement'.

Fourth, there is to be a 'revolution'. In a vitally important part of the same statement that was expunged by the sessions court, the two of them explain how when, 'Bhagat Singh was asked in the Lower Court as to what we meant by the word, "Revolution"' that '[i]n answer to the question, I would say that Revolution does not necessarily involve sanguinary strife, nor is there any place in it for individual vendetta', because '[i]t is not the cult of the bomb and the pistol'. So what is it then, one might ask? The answer Bhagat Singh gave was, 'By Revolution we mean that the present order of things which is based on manifest injustice must change.' It was against this background, where Bhagat Singh had defined the term 'revolution' as the elimination of 'manifest injustice', that the obliterated portion of the statement went to prophesy that '[t]he whole edifice of this civilisation, if not saved in time, shall crumble'. This is why, 'A radical change, therefore, is necessary; and it is the duty of those who realise this to reorganise society on the socialistic basis.' One look at this and one straight away realizes how dramatically different this vision was from that of Mahatma Gandhi, who subsequently became such an icon of the Indian Independence struggle. And yet, it was Bhagat Singh who epitomized the plight of the Indian masses with the excoriating words that:

> Unless this thing is done and the exploitation of man by man and nations by nations, which goes masquerading as Imperialism, is brought to an end, the sufferings and carnage with which humanity is threatened today cannot be prevented and all talks of ending war and ushering in an era of universal peace is undisguised hypocrisy. By Revolution we mean the ultimate establishment of an order of society which may not be threatened by such a break-down, and in which the sovereignty of the proletariat should be recognised, and as the result of which a world-federation should redeem humanity from the bondage of capitalism and the misery of imperial wars.[10]

The above then was the whole of paragraph 7 of the statement that was meant to be formally presented before the sessions court. Not only was this removed from the rest of the statement, but paragraph 8 was too. 'This is our ideal,' Bhagat Singh had here said and continued with the declaration, 'Revolution is the inalienable right of mankind. Freedom is the imprescriptible birth-right of all. The labourer is the real sustainer of society. The Sovereignty of the people is the ultimate destiny of the workers.'[11] With thunderous effect Bhagat Singh and B.K. Dutt then ended their statement with the acclaim, 'To the altar of this revolution we have brought our youth as incense, for no sacrifice is too great for so magnificent a cause.'[12] These words shed light on why it is that Bhagat Singh is described by the Indians of his homeland as a 'shaheed' (a martyr) because he was prepared to die for his beliefs. But ultimately, however, his aim as a revolutionary was to spread the idea of revolution amongst the masses. This is also clear from forty typed leaflets that both he and B.K. Dutt threw into the Delhi Central Assembly after the bombs had exploded. These had been written by Bhagat Singh himself according to Shiv Verma, who was another one of his comrades, in their Sitaram Bazaar hideout, and they were subsequently published in full by the *Hindustan Times*, on the same day of 8 April 1929.[13] In these he explains, 'We want to emphasise the lesson often repeated by history that it is easy to kill the individuals, but you cannot kill the ideas.' He continues, 'Great empires crumbled but the ideas survived. Bourbons and Czars fell while the revolution marched ahead triumphantly.'

How clear, however, was Bhagat Singh about the ideas he was fighting for? He was strikingly clear. Few leaders of India who succeeded the Raj after Independence were as clear. In his homeland, 'producers or the labourers, in spite of being the most necessary element of society are robbed by the exploiters of the fruits of their labour and deprived of their elementary rights'. These words were not going to be music to the government's ears. On the other hand, they were milk and honey for the oppressed poor and went straight to the heart of the common man. In both India and Pakistan, they still do. The expunged statement spoke of how 'the peasant who grows corn for all starves with this family; the weaver who supplies the world market with textile fabrics cannot find enough to cover his own and his children's bodies; the masons, smiths and carpenters who rear magnificent palaces, live and perish in slums'. No ruling government could have sat idly by to hear of 'the capitalist exploiters, the parasites of Society squander millions on their whims' that such utterances railed against. Bhagat Singh and B.K. Dutt took them to task as they directly questioned '[t]hese terrible inequalities, and forced disparity of chances' which they believed was inevitably 'heading towards chaos'.

With these words, these young students challenged the British Raj, in a way in which Gandhi and the Congress Party refused to do. This is what made them so dangerous to the Raj. Faced with this, the response of the authorities was not to engage with them, but to dismiss them as lunatics and fanatics. This allowed them to delete the ideological basis of the couple's attack on the Delhi Legislative Assembly. This is why to this day these statements by Bhagat Singh and B.K. Dutt, which espoused the very essence of their revolutionary philosophy, lie forgotten in India. It served the interests of the imperial government to dismiss these two disparagingly as deranged with the result that they 'were being wrongly ascribed the status of madmen and fanatics'.[14] Yet, this was an old colonial habit, one of maligning insurgents as 'lunatics', and it is one which still exists in the political culture of the region today, but which back then was deliberately designed to camouflage the exercise of unsparing, unadorned and unvarnished oppressive state power under the ruse of the rule of law.

This is why, as long ago as 1867, the Government of India had passed what Mark Condos describes as 'one of the most brutal-minded and draconian laws ever created in colonial India', and this was the Murderous Outrages Act. Although it was originally designed to deal with 'fanatics' in the North-West Frontier, it was far from peripheral in its impact, and Condos has shown how 'this law both drew upon and enabled a wider legal culture that pervaded India in the wake of 1857' and in the end worked 'to mask the brute power of executive authority through legalistic terms'.[15] This is why, in the words of Neeti Nair, as soon as the trial started, the government proceeded with 'labelling these revolutionaries "murderers" and "terrorists"', and in this way, 'the British sought to dismiss their non-violent demands for rights as "political prisoners"'.[16] At the end of the trial, both men were sentenced to transportation for life when the Delhi sessions judge, Leonard Middleton, gave his forty-one-page judgment a week later on 12 June 1929. There was then an appeal to the Punjab High Court in Lahore. This was heard before Justices Sir Cecil Forde and James Addison. Here both men redeemed themselves spectacularly.

12 June 1929, We Could Have Easily Escaped

It was before the Punjab High Court in Lahore that Bhagat Singh had his second courtroom statement made on 12 June 1929. He argued that he and B.K. Dutt could not have been properly convicted before the sessions court because 'the point is as to what were our intentions'. What he meant by this was that '[a]ccording to the famous jurist Solomon, one should not be punished for this criminal offence if his aim is not against the law'.[1] Pressing his point further, he explained, 'The point to be considered is that the two bombs we threw in the Assembly did not harm anybody physically or economically. As such the punishment awarded to us is not only very harsh but revengeful also.' He was, of course, entirely right in making this claim both as a matter of logic and of law. And convinced of this he gave an example. It was one which the two high court judges, Justices Sir Cecil Forde and James Addison, would have found unnerving. He said, 'The question of motive is of special importance. Take the example of General Dyer. He resorted to firing and killing hundreds of innocent and unarmed people. But the military court did not order him to be shot. It gave him lakhs of rupees as award.'[2] Then came the defiance. It was clear. And it was uncompromising. This was to say that 'under these circumstances, please permit us to assert that a government which seeks shelter behind such methods has no right to exist. If it exists, it is for the time being only, and that too with the blood of thousands of people on its head. If the law does not see the motive there can be no justice, nor can there be stable peace'.[3] So pure were the motives of Bhagat Singh and B.K. Dutt that '[t]he Sessions Judge admitted that we could have very easily escaped, had we any intention like that. We accepted our offence and gave a Statement explaining our position. We are not afraid of punishment. But we do not want that we should be wrongly understood'.[4]

What was it that they did not want misunderstood? The explanation is startling. The statement went on, 'According to us, our country is passing through a delicate phase. We saw the coming catastrophe and thought it proper to give a timely warning with a loud voice, and we gave the warning in the manner we thought proper.'[5] It is clear from this that far from being purveyors of mindless violence, the actions of Bhagat Singh and B.K. Dutt arose from deep political and philosophical convictions. They were masters of strategic defiance. Then came the reference to 'revolution'. With meticulous care and leaving no room for any doubt, they adumbrated how '[i]n our Statement we explained in detail what we mean by "Long Live Revolution"' and that this 'formed the crux of our ideas'. Aggrieved, they pointed out how '[t]hat portion was removed from our statement'. This meant that 'a wrong meaning is attributed to the word revolution' but '[t]hat is not our understanding', because '[b]ombs and pistols do not make a revolution' but rather that '[t] he sword of revolution is sharpened on the whetting-stone of ideas'. They continued, 'This is what we wanted to emphasise. By revolution, we mean the end of the miseries of capitalist wars. It was not proper to pronounce judgment without understanding our aims and objects and the process of achieving them. To associate wrong ideas with our names is out and out injustice.'[6]

If the sessions court statement of 6 June 1929 was important, then the high court statement of 12 June 1929 was only marginally less so. Both emphasized that when Bhagat Singh and his colleagues in the HSRA spoke of 'revolution', it was not a revolution of bombs and pistols, but a revolution of ideas. It is significant, however, that this portion was removed from their statement. It was not by accident. What these young men were up against was a state system of unmatched coercion and brutality that was intent on treating them as murderers, fanatics and lunatics. Such refined distinctions were lost on those now judging them as were such sophisticated motives. Small wonder then that the justices would have none of it. They ruled 'motive' to be irrelevant to the sentence even though this was not correct as a matter of law. The fact that Justice Forde went on to accept nevertheless that 'Bhagat Singh is a sincere revolutionary' after hearing his arguments in his defence only goes to show that deep down he knew that Bhagat Singh was on to something.

On 15 June 1929, both Bhagat Singh and B.K. Dutt were taken to their respective jails. Bhagat Singh was whisked off to Mianwali Jail. B.K. Dutt was sent to Lahore Jail. On the way, the two of them had an opportunity to sit together in the train carriage. This is when they decided that, if the state continued to refuse to treat them as political prisoners, they would go on hunger strike. They had ample reason to feel so aggrieved. Though they ended up in jail, neither Bhagat Singh nor B.K. Dutt, however, were subject to transportation. But this was not because the high court subsequently decided to show them leniency. It was because both were now linked to the Lahore Conspiracy Case. There was to be a new trial, one that would lead to Bhagat Singh's execution. This was the second of the three trials which Bhagat Singh had to face. This second trial began in the sessions court on 10 July 1929 before Judge Rai Sahib Pandit Sri Kishen, an Indian judge.

The trial of the Delhi Assembly Bomb Case had been long, excruciating and painfully drawn-out. The unforgiving glare of media publicity monitored and attested to everything that happened in the courtroom. By the end, Bhagat Singh, ever a consummate believer in the justness of his cause, had turned public opinion in his favour. In the process, however, and indeed soon after his arrest, he had also been linked to the Saunders murder. This was unsurprising. Bhagat Singh had left signed copies, in his own handwriting, splattered across the city of Lahore, making it easy for the authorities to link him to the murder. By 16 April 1929, most of the core members of the HSRA had been arrested and sent to trial. What followed in the Lahore Conspiracy Case drew the public's sympathy in his favour because, as Maclean states, 'Bhagat Singh conducted the court case with considerable *nous,* inviting extraordinary suffering, undertaking several hunger strikes and withstanding police abuse in the courtroom. In the 23 months it took for the imperial justice system to take him to the gallows, Bhagat Singh became a household name.'[7] At the height of his ordeal at the hands of colonial justice, a handcuffed Bhagat Singh, still on hunger strike, had to be brought to court on a stretcher. His weight had fallen by 14 lbs from 133 to 119 lbs. His trial had originally started off in Borstal Jail in Lahore on 10 July 1929. Kiron Das, the younger brother of Jatin Das recalls how, as the trial opened at 7 a.m., 'all approaches to the jail as far as Lawrence Gardens were strictly guarded by the police'.[8] After all, he and his younger colleagues were charged with murder, conspiracy and waging war against the King.

From there the case was transferred to the stately Poonch House, where it commenced on 5 May 1930. The composition of the judicial bench originally consisted of Justice Coldstream (President), Justice G.C. Hilton and Justice Agha Haider. So inept, back-handed and injudicious was the conduct of the proceedings, however, that just two weeks later two of the judges were removed by Chief Justice Shadhi Lal of the Lahore High Court: Justice Coldstream for presiding over the physical mistreatment of the accused and Justice Agha Haider for refusing to support such abuse.

The composition of the tribunal then changed on 20 June 1930 to comprise Justice G.C. Hilton (President), Justice Tapp and Justice Sir Abdul Qadir, the latter being a more compliant judge. None of this would have inspired confidence in proceedings that led to Bhagat Singh's eventual death at the hands of the state. Such was the conspicuous vulgarity of his abuse that it extended into the courtroom. Bhagat Singh and his fellow prisoners were mercilessly beaten in front of the magistrate. The violence of colonialism is well known in its physical beatings, imprisonment and routine hangings. What is not so well known is how such violence also entered the courtroom in circumstances where the essence of the courtroom proceedings was to provide a veneer of legality to what was otherwise nothing short of state oppression, and yet here was a case where the mask not just slipped but fell right down, to expose the reality of colonial coercion even in a court of law. It deserves therefore to be recognized as coercive colonial legalism pure and simple. Yet, the violence of the courtroom, both real and symbolic, has thus far escaped the attention it deserves.

In part, this is because as Maclean has observed, although there is now at long last a discernible body of Bhagat Singh scholarship, this 'curiously has had little impact in the Western academy'.[9] Indeed, 'it is only relatively recently that scholarship has begun to position Bhagat Singh and the HSRA within a larger historical framework'. Even so, there has been remarkably little written on the trial itself with a few notable exceptions such as the path-breaking account of A.G. Noorani,[10] more than twenty years ago now, and more recently this writer's own work on *The Trial of Bhagat Singh: Heresies of the Raj*, which has set out to redress that imbalance.[11] In fact, Christopher Pinney, describes it as 'one of the puzzles of 20th-century Indian history that academics don't seem to have engaged with'.[12] Bhagat Singh has truly been much neglected by historians.[13] For Pinney, it is extraordinary that the 'official history has diverted so fundamentally from the popular narrative'. But it is precisely this neglect which has then so enhanced the popular image of Bhagat Singh as a heroic and chivalrous figure in the struggle for independent India like no other.

30

1929, The Enigma

Rajmohan Gandhi, a grandson of Mahatma Gandhi, has recently observed that 'the romance of many in the twenty-first century India with the Bhagat Singh legend is not necessarily an accurate indication of the political realities of the Punjab of the heroes own time'. The view is an uncharitable one. For him, 'Punjab's Muslims were generally not drawn to the agenda of the revolutionaries, and Sikh involvement too was minimal.' As he explains, 'The list of the eighteen men accused in May 1930 in the Lahore Conspiracy Case, as it was called, contains no Muslim name and one Sikh name, that of Bhagat Singh. Five others who had absconded and five who had turned approver were also, it seems, Hindus. Moreover, many of the twenty-eight charged were from outside Punjab.'[1] However, it is surely remiss of him to overlook the fact that whereas five of them were from Kanpur, some of the leading figures were from Punjab. Bhagat Singh, Bhagwati Charan and Yashpal were from Lahore. Sukhdev was from Lyallpur. Kishori Rattan Lal was from Hoshiarpur. And both Des Raj and Agya Ram were from Sialkot. That is a significant Punjabi presence in the conspiracy. HSRA was a nation-wide movement in any event and drew its recruits from across the country. Punjabis do not exaggerate their role in the revolutionary movement if their overall involvement in

India's freedom movement is considered, which is by no stretch of imagination insignificant. Bhagat Singh himself belonged to a family of revolutionaries. Moreover, as Kuldip Nayyar[2] explains, the government lawyer Carden Noad, at the beginning of the trial had said that there were twenty-eight accused in all. Of these, five had absconded and five had turned witness for the prosecution (known as 'approvers') so that eighteen were present in court. Carden Noad read their names out in court in the following order:

1. *Sukhdev*, alias Dayal, alias Swami, alias villager;
2. *Kishori Lal Rattan*, alias Dee Dutt Rattan, alias Mast Ram Shastri;
3. *Des Raj*;
4. *Prem Dutt*, alias Master, alias Amrit Lal;
5. *Jai Dev*, alias Harish Chander;
6. *Sheo Verma*, alias Parbhat, alias Hamarain, alias Ram Narain Kapur;
7. *Gya Prashad*, alias Dr. B.S. Nigham, alias Ram Lal, alias Ram Nath, alias Desh Bhagat;
8. *Mahabir Singh*, alias Partab;
9. *Bhagat Singh*; who had the most aliases, including 'Balraj' as 'Chief of the Hindustan Republican Army'.
10. *Ajoy Kumar Ghosh*, alias Negro General;
11. *Jatin Sanyal* (Jatinder Nath Sanyal);
12. *Bejoy Kumar Sinha*, alias Bachu;
13. *Shivram Rajguru*, alias 'M';
14. *Kundan Lal*, alias Partap, alias No. 1;
15. *Kanwalk Nath Trivedi*, alias Kanwal Nath Tewari.

Notwithstanding Rajmohan Gandhi's views, the fact remains that, as the *Hindustan Times* recorded, 'Bhagat Singh remains the most iconic – and beloved – martyr in the collective consciousness of India.'[3] There is surely a reason for this. After the Jallianwala Bagh Massacre, the non-cooperation movement started in 1920 spearheaded by Mahatma Gandhi. Bhagat Singh left the DAV

School in Lahore. He joined the National College. It was there
that he met with his fellow revolutionary friends, Bhagwati Charan
Vohra, Sukhdev and Yashpal, becoming an avid reader, with a keen
interest in the history of revolutions, but having to abandon college
at the age of seventeen in 1924. He gave up his undergraduate
studies, left Lahore and made haste for Kanpur. His grandmother
and father had decided it was time for him to marry. Bhagat Singh
was not one for marrying, however. His nuptials were with India's
freedom struggle. That is how he would live. And that is how he
would perish.

What has also added to the enigma and mystique of Bhagat
Singh is that his earlier years are difficult to fathom with any degree
of certainty. This is largely due to his own actions. He had decided
to remain secretive and elusive before his arrest. This was consistent
with the policy of the HSRA. Its members were required to be
informed of 'actions' purely on a need-to-know basis. Party plans
were communicated only to members of the inner circle. In so
conducting itself, the HSRA had learned much from the experience
of the Kakori Conspiracy Case, which involved the trial of members
of the Hindustan Republication Association ('HRA'), an armed
revolutionary organization of India established in 1924, which had
the aim of establishing a 'Federated Republic of the United States
of India'. In that case, it had been the evidence of three former
members that had led directly to the capture and conviction of
members of key importance. The HSRA was determined not to
make the same mistake.

Indeed, after his first arrest in May 1927, following the
Dussehra Bomb Case, Bhagat Singh had come under pressure to
betray his comrades and to become a government witness, which is
described in the judgment itself as an 'approver'. He had fallen under
suspicion for two reasons. First, he was 'the nephew of the notorious
Ajit Singh'.[4] Second, he had known connections with a number
of left-wing youth movements. These included, in particular, the
Naujawan Bharat Sabha. The Bureau of Intelligence described
this organization as having 'adopted as the ideal the inculcation of

revolutionary sentiments and of disloyalty to the government'.[5] Once again, therefore, a fear of disloyalty, spurred on by an attraction of violent communist revolution amongst the youth, was officialdom's impending and ever present nightmare from which it could not break free.

But the authorities were wasting their time. They could not induce Bhagat Singh into becoming a turncoat. 'Bhagat Singh,' as Kama Maclean observes, 'was contemptuous of the offer of freedom and reward in return for a statement.'[6] This early political precocity is significant. So committed was he in the defence of his ideals that it remained with him throughout, from his trial through to his ultimate execution. His steadfastness was consistent with the ethos of the HSRA. As an organization, the HSRA had learnt how the pressure brought to bear upon suspects and under-trial prisoners, by the application of various forms of maltreatment, inducements, and undue pressure, risked breaking them and turning them into 'approvers' as witnesses on behalf of the state in long drawn-out conspiracy trials. For this reason, the HSRA conducted itself with its cards held close to its chest, disclosing only such information amongst its foot-soldiers as was absolutely necessary. This enabled its members to plausibly deny knowledge of what was actually going on within the HSRA. Nothing demonstrates this better than the testimony of Jai Gopal, who turned 'approver' and gave evidence, which eventually convicted Bhagat Singh and his comrades in the Lahore Conspiracy Case. Yet, in his evidence, he could repeatedly do no more than demonstrate his stark ignorance of events when describing how Sukhdev 'used to keep all the facts concealed' from him. In fact, as he explained, he was even barred from 'divulging any secret of the society to Pandit Yashpal', who ironically as it happened, was himself a prominent member of the HSRA.[7]

The intense secrecy which the HSRA demanded of its members when conducting themselves meant that Bhagat Singh himself also had to adopt many identities, adding further mystery to his persona. In the late 1920s, when he first came into public view following the Dussehra Bomb Case, he was known as 'Balwant'. Even then, he used several adjectival pen-names when he wrote for newspapers and periodicals, such as '*Vidrohi*' (rebel), '*Agyat*' (unknown) and '*Sainik*' (soldier). So effective was he in camouflaging himself that the director of intelligence in Delhi, who had previously served as senior superintendent of Lahore and who was later on to become the director-general of MI5, had with the most unshakeable conviction been bold enough to declare that there was 'incontrovertible' evidence that Bhagat Singh was one by the name of 'Balraj', chief of the Hindustan Republican Army. Yet, he was flatly contradicted many decades later by Shiv Verma, a member of the inner circle of the HSRA, who quietly divulged the fact that 'Balraj' was actually none other than Chandrashekhar Azad.[8] Such misapprehensions on the part of even the intelligence services were not surprising, though all the more telling for that.

The HSRA even used coded language among party members to hide the meaning of party communications, which were never meant to be taken literally. So elaborate were the devices adopted to outwit the government authorities that, as Sohan Singh 'Josh' explained in an interview with Max Harcourt in the 1960s, when an invitation to observe a *shraddha* ceremony (a ceremony in Hinduism performed in honour of a dead ancestor) was sent to a recipient, this was in fact nothing more than a more mundane invitation to attend a provincial HSRA council meeting.[9] This explains why the popular folklore narrative surrounding Bhagat Singh of an enigmatic and baffling figure has gained such widespread currency over the years. The nebulous and surreptitious movements of shadowy HSRA members travelling through the night, taking care to escape all recognition by using indecipherable language of perplexing codes and ciphers on false pretexts, all led to popular speculation and conjecture about them. The different disguises adopted by HSRA members meant that they were able to move through various towns with relative ease and operate as they wished undetected.

This is where Bhagat Singh excelled. He was a master at the art of camouflage. At one point he slung off his traditional Punjabi kurta-pyjama and adopted the appearance of the Gujarati businessman, wearing a dhoti and coat. On another occasion, he styled himself as a Delhi-walla. Despite this, according to Shiv Verma, 'Bhagat Singh was the hardest of all party members to disguise, because by the late 1920s he was well known to police, and besides, he "was a handsome figure amongst hundreds of people, obviously, he would be spotted".'[10] When Bhagat Singh attended the Calcutta Congress in December 1928 it was in disguise. When in early January 1929 he fled Lahore following J.P. Saunder's murder, he was in disguise as well. Intrigue, fantasy and legend followed his Houdini-style movements like a latter day Scarlet Pimpernel. No less a person than Bhagat Singh's former teacher in Lahore, Chhabil Das, appears to have been mistaken, when he claimed to have caught fleeting glimpses of him in the Calcutta home of a Punjabi merchant by the name of Chhaju Ram. Yet, this was wholly contradicted by Durga Devi Vohra (known in Indian revolutionary circles as 'Durga Bhabhi') in an interview she gave in 1972. She was one of the few women in the HSRA and the one who accompanied Bhagat Singh on the train when he made his itinerant escape in disguise after the shooting J.P. Saunders. So she would probably have known better than Chhabil Das, who ended up being deceived in this way.

What also made such trickery possible was that Bhagat Singh, who had an interest in Congress politics, also attended earlier Congress sessions. On the face of it, this is not altogether unusual, because back in the 1920s there was a degree of shared communion between the Congress Party and the Naujawan Sabha. Indeed, the CID itself had confirmed how it was the 'consistent practice of revolutionaries from various parts of India to take advantage of the annual sessions of the Congress in order to discuss their plans in secret, and to interchange their views', and as MacLean makes clear, 'this almost certainly accounts for Bhagat Singh's activities in Calcutta'.[11] This is how, as surviving revolutionaries have since confirmed, Bhagat Singh managed during this period to establish contacts with Bengali organizations, such as the Anushilan Samiti (Bodybuilding Society) in Calcutta. This arose from an amalgamation of local youths and bodybuilding gyms (Akhara) in 1902. Anushilan Samiti was dedicated to the use of revolutionary violence to end British rule in India. As the HSRA began to orient its focus to bomb-making, it became more attractive to other organizations devoted to the use of revolutionary violence in the cause of gaining national freedom. With its headquarters in Agra, the HSRA went on to extend its activities in the United Provinces with satellite operations elsewhere.

Bhagat Singh was known to be active in Allahabad in January 1929 because the testimony of Lalit Kumar Mukherji, who turned 'approver', was that he had met a sardar, by the name of 'Ranjit', which was another name that Bhagat Singh was known by, at a secret meeting where the assassination of CID officers was discussed between them.[12] Such was the extent to which he was by now nationally known that the intelligence bureau had confirmed that Bhagat Singh was 'wandering about India in the most suspicious manner the past few months', although they did not seem to able to capture him nor did they have enough information to be able to apprehend him. Bhagat Singh had managed to foil them, staying always one step ahead, under cover of concealment, deception and fakery, all of which he combined with great effect to frustrate the authorities as they set out to detect and capture him, until he was finally taken into custody on 8 April 1929. Along the way, he left behind a long fabled narrative of his revolutionary life. Today, it has entered the common folklore of both India and Pakistan. And it has made Bhagat Singh immortal.

PART 7

JUDICIAL REPRISALS

Yuun na qatil ko jab yaqin aaya
Ham ne dil khol kar dikhai chot

When my tormentor refused to believe,
I opened up my heart and displayed the wounds

–Fani Badayuni

31

5 May 1930, Inalienable Rights

Once Bhagat Singh was arrested and taken into custody on 8 April 1929, his pursuit of the techniques of camouflage, disinformation, and imitation to avoid detection by the colonial authorities was quickly vindicated. For justice was a scarce commodity in the court of the 30th viceroy and governor-general of India, Lord Irwin, who had been appointed two years earlier on 3 April 1926, during the most tempestuous time in the politics of India. And it was Lord Irwin's court. It was he who had passed an ordinance and created an impromptu makeshift tribunal to try Bhagat Singh and his co-accused when they were already subject to legal proceedings in a regular court before a special magistrate and for close to a year. Given the deliberate setting up of a system of trial outside the regular judicial structure, neither the accused nor their lawyers were in any doubt that justice was the last thing Lord Irwin intended to deliver through flagrant institutional innovation. Due process and natural justice would be sacrificed to the political expediency of seeing these men hang. Which is why, since the trial before the special tribunal did not comply with the essential requirements of the rule of law, from the outset there was a challenge to its jurisdiction that it could not try the accused.

This is why in their letter to the commissioners dated 5 May 1930, the lawyers for five of the young men under trial wrote, 'We do not propose to take any part in the proceedings of this case because we do not recognize this Govt to be based on justice as established by law.' Further, they wrote, 'Since this Govt is an utter negation of these principles its very existence is not justifiable.' Their attack was not just on the tribunal but on the government which enabled such a tribunal to be set up to subvert the ordinary processes of the law. For them, 'such Govts as are organized to exploit the oppressed nations have no right to exist except by the right of the sword (i.e. brute force) with which they try to curb all the ideas of liberty and freedom and the legitimate aspirations of the people'. What the accused were facing, it was being contended, was nothing but a sham. So the letter of 5 May 1930 excoriated the government with the remarks, 'We believe all such Govts. and particularly this British Government thrust upon the helpless but unwilling Indian nation to be no better than an organized gang of robbers and a pack of exploiters equipped with all the means of carnage and devastations.' This is why they were less than enamoured by the government setting up this special tribunal, because '[i]In the name of "law and order" they crush all those who dare to expose or oppose them'. The letter to the commissioners did not end there. It went on to attack the entire imperialist project of the Raj, describing imperialism as 'nothing but a vast conspiracy organized with predatory motives' in which the British Government, 'by their designs not only commits judicial murders through their law-courts but also organize general crimes like war'. This was the reason why they would not participate in the tribunal proceedings, even though they had participated in the court proceedings which had not been irregular.

By boycotting the proceedings, the accused would stand by their 'inalienable rights', which they must have known was a concept itself borrowed from the English common law, but now deployed with great effect against the Crown itself. They had little hesitation in pointing out that the government was such that 'they feel no hesitation in shooting down innocent and unarmed people who refuse to yield to their depredatory (sic) demands or to acquiesce in their ruinous and abominable designs'. And yet, they use the language of law and order to commit the gravest injustices, being so clever that 'under the garb of custodians of "law and order" they break peace, create disorder, kill people and commit all conceivable designs'. They had every right to protest because their right in freedom provided them with a basis for a revolt against a government which did not respect the 'inalienable' rights of humanity. They believed in these inalienable rights because '[w]e believe that freedom is the undeniable birthright of all people, that every man has the inalienable right to enjoying the fruits of his labour and that every nation is indisputably the master of his resources'. For this reason, '[i]f any Govt. deprives them of those primary rights it is the right of people – nay it is their duty to destroy that Govt'.[1] With impeccable logic, they provided a moral justification for their actions, in that, '[s]ince the British govt. is a negation of these principles for which we stand it is our firm conviction that every effort made, every method adopted to bring about a Revolution and to destroy this Govt. is morally justified'. The revolutionaries were not idle talkers but believed in transforming their living conditions, which was why, '[w]e stand for a change, a radical change in the existing order of affairs in racial, political and economic spheres and the complete replacement of the existing order by a new era rendering the exploitation of man by man impossible and thus guaranteeing full liberty to all the people in all the spheres'. It was not just the elimination of racial and political injustice that they were after but that '[w]e feel that unless the whole social order is changed and socialistic society is established the whole world is in danger of a disastrous catastrophe'.

To the question of whether this meant that the young revolutionaries would resort to violence to achieve such far-reaching ends, they had a ready answer. It was as clear as it could be. If Gandhi disapproved of their errant ways that is because he failed to understand them. Nor did he make any attempt to do so. For him, it was enough that they deviated from his chosen path of 'non-violence'. He had turned this into a fetish, wielding it uncompromisingly in all situations no matter the circumstances. For their temerity in taking a different course of action from him, he would refuse to align himself with these young men at all costs.

The letter of 5 May 1930 was written on the first day of the tribunal's sitting and is crystal clear in its rejection of violence. Violence was not a central plank of revolutionary socialism. In a careful and sophisticated analysis, this letter explains that, 'As regards the methods – peaceful or otherwise – to be adopted for the consummation of the revolutionary ideal, let us declaim that the choice rests with those who hold power.' The choice is not with the revolutionaries who would rather not use any violence because, '[r] *evolutionaries by virtue of their altruistic principles are lovers of peace – a genuine and permanent peace based on justice and equity*, not the illusory peace resulting from cowardice and maintained at the point of bayonets' (emphasis added). What they object to is being forced into servility and quietude at the tip of a bayonet. This is why '[i] f *the revolutionaries take to bombs and pistols it is only as a measure of terrible necessity as a last recourse*' (emphasis added). They themselves were not against law and order that was genuinely intended to serve such ends. They were against it if it was a sham. The charges levelled against the young men were preposterous if they implied that they were against 'Law and Order.' This is because 'as the supreme juris counsil (sic) of Revolutionary France has well expressed', when the law is properly deployed it brings freedom for its people so that 'the end of law is not to abolish or restrain but to preserve and enlarge freedom'. The present colonial government was not acting in the interests of the common welfare of the Indian people. It had no legal basis to act as it did because 'legitimate power is required to govern by promulgated laws *established for the common good alone* and resting alone *on the consent and the authority of the people, from which law, no one is exempt – not even the legislature*' (emphases added). In fact, this exact position was affirmed in the English Court of Appeal in 2007 in the Chagos Islands case where the importance of a colonial law, being 'directed to the wellbeing of a dependent territory and its population', was firmly emphasized in terms of 'what is best for a colony . . .'. The function of a judicial tribunal is that 'it is their constitutional function to decide whether what has been enacted . . . is rationally and legally capable of providing for a colony's wellbeing. If it is not, then it falls outside the prerogative power' and '[t]hat territory's interests will not necessarily be the interests of the United Kingdom or of its allies'.[2]

The young revolutionaries were ahead of their time when they declared that the governors and the governed were subject to law. In this way, they could question the very authority under which they were being tried. And no answer was ever given to them in response! The special tribunal, they maintained, was not founded on law. An unjust law, they argued, cannot be a basis of peace and stability in society. This was not the same as rejecting the law itself. To say so is to misunderstand what the revolutionaries stood for. It is why they have never really been fully rehabilitated in the Indian consciousness. They have always stood outside it. The best they could achieve was to be seen as a romanticized, impractical and ill-fated group of young men awkwardly attempting to secure India's Independence but sacrificing all for little or no gain to themselves. Yet, the revolutionaries did believe in law but only with the proviso that '[t]he sanctity of law can be maintained only so long as it is the expression of the will of the people' but not otherwise, because '[w]hen it becomes a mere instrument in the hands of an oppressing class it loses sanctity and significance for the fundamental preliminary for the administration of justice is the elimination of every interest'.[3]

These words display remarkable foresight. They show these young men to be ahead of their time. It was to be almost another half a century before the call for equal rights and equality of treatment were to arise in the USA. The admonishment that 'as soon as the law ceases to correspond to the popular racial needs, it becomes the means for perpetration of injustice and tyranny' may just as well be one taken from a decision of a constitutional court of a Western democracy today. It was so modern. The demand for the 'elimination of every interest' was a demand for the elimination of 'special' interests in society because these were an obstacle to equal treatment for all under the law. The revolutionaries, therefore, believed that 'the maintaining of such a law is nothing but a hypocritical assertion of a special interest against the common interest'. This is why they did not appear before the special tribunal choosing instead to boycott its proceedings. In hearing the case under the Lahore Ordinance III, the special tribunal could dispense with the attendance of the accused when it wanted. It could even dispense with any of its judges, and two of the three were actually removed at the drop of a hat. Not surprisingly, in a pulverizing statement which allowed for no quarter, the letter of 5 May 1930 thundered, 'The laws of the present Govt. exist for the interest of the alien rulers against the interest of our people, and as such, they have no moral binding whatsoever.' So the tribunal had no jurisdiction over the accused and in turn the accused had no duty to appear before the tribunal. They had no hesitation in declaring that 'for this reason, we decline to be a party to this farcical show and henceforth we shall not take part in the proceedings of this case'.[4] This boycott of legal proceedings in the Lahore Conspiracy Case, on the very first day of the tribunal proceedings, was a shrewd move. Those who instigated it would be proven right that this was a political trial. These trials always ended badly for those charged. The dice was always loaded against them. They started off with all the semblance and appearance of purporting to be fair, but the emerging reality would declare a different truth. So it was also in the Lahore Conspiracy Case.

This is nowhere more clear than in the modern epitome of a military court which is located today in Guantánamo. Its long chronicle began in November 2001. This is when President Bush announced plans to employ military commissions to prosecute people captured in what was described as a 'War on Terror'. The Bush administration followed this with a declaration that such prisoners would be both held at the US Naval Base at Guantánamo, in Cuba, and tried in a court there. This was not US territory, but it was held by the US on a lease. In January 2002, the first prisoners arrived at this base. Within a year, the prison at Guantánamo was holding 780 prisoners. The position of the US Government was that once the prisoners had disembarked in Cuba there was no jurisdiction in any court to determine the lawfulness or otherwise of their detention, and nor could any court consider whether or not the prisoners were being treated humanely. The first lawsuit was filed in February 2002 under the name of *Rasul et al. v. Bush*. This was on behalf of the imprisoned detainees in the United States District Court for the District of Columbia. It included three prisoners, two of whom were from Britain and a third from Australia, although a fourth one, another Australian, was also added two months later to the claim.

Initially, the litigation against the Bush administration was conceived of as a challenge to the military commission system, but once it became clear that if the government could detain prisoners indefinitely without 'due process' then it would not hold any trials at all either, the litigation in *Rasul* turned into a challenge to the lawfulness of indefinite detention without legal process. The US Supreme Court gave its decision in June 2004 and declared that the Guantánamo prisoners could seek a writ of habeas corpus. They could do so to challenge both the factual and legal basis of their detention in the federal district court. However, Congress then immediately responded by amending the habeas corpus statute and removed statutory jurisdiction. When this too was challenged, the US Supreme Court in 2018 held that the prisoners at the base had a constitutional right to habeas corpus. In what was known as the *Boumediene Case*, the supreme court left no doubt that a statute could not arbitrarily remove such a basic right in the constitution. The intent of the supreme court, however, was to only declare the general principle that applied. It was still up to the lower courts to give it effect. When the matter returned before the District of Columbia Court of Appeals, new procedural rules were developed in that court, together with the creation of a further substantive standard, which impeded the right of an imprisoned detainee at Guantánamo to secure habeas corpus. In short, there was a right to apply for habeas corpus by filing a writ. There was no right to acquire habeas corpus. The court had successfully stymied the individual's right to habeas corpus against the state by crafting further rules which disfavoured the individual. In this way, the right to habeas corpus was rendered totally illusory and artificial behind a shabby curtain of legal artifice. It was not a real and effective enunciation of legal principle. The manner and method of the trial of 'political prisoners' in this way is in fact traceable to the manner and method of such trials during the time of empire in Britain, and in particular the Bhagat Singh case. The aim was to create the chimera of a process according to law. The reality was a mirage. The closer the lawyers got to it the further it moved away from them. Today, the Julian Assange trial in the United Kingdom smacks of the same.[5]

32

1 May 1930, Lahore Ordinance

The Lahore Conspiracy Case has been described as 'one of the most controversial trials to take place in India under the Raj'.[1] It is not just because Bhagat Singh and his accomplice, Rajguru, of the revolutionary Hindustan Socialist Republican Association (HSRA) had so dramatically on 17 December 1928 shot and killed in cold blood a twenty-one-year old probationary police officer. This was John P. Saunders, coming out of a police station in Lahore, with an unsuspecting air of nonchalance. Political assassinations were not unusual at this time. It was not also because the wrong man had been shot. Nor that the killers cared little of this fact when Saunders had been mistaken for James Scott, the police superintendent who the alleged conspirators in the murder blamed for the callous beating to death of the self-made man Lala Lajpat Rai on 17 November 1928. Nor was it the fact that the latter was the radical firebrand leader who had broken away from Congress and had led a bold protest march against the Simon Commission in Lahore barely three weeks earlier on 30 October 1928 mocking and berating them. The Lahore Conspiracy Case 1931 was controversial because although initially tried under normal criminal law procedures, Bhagat Singh was then tried under a specially created law passed just for him and his two dozen co-accused, specifically for the purpose of hanging him. Some would say (and did say at the time) that he was not being tried under a 'law' at all. They would say that he was tried and executed under a regime created well outside the law and deliberately so in a way that he and his comrades would remain well beyond the reach of the law. They would point to the irony that both he and his co-accused were already being tried in regular committal proceedings before a regular and well-respected magistrate by the name of Rai Sahib Pandit Sri Kishen for some ten months from 10 April 1929 until 1 May 1930, by which time over 200 witnesses had already been examined and the remaining number would have been too without any significant delay if only he had been allowed to carry on. And, they would say that it is therefore astonishing that ongoing proceedings, from which a right of appeal created by the Imperial Parliament in London would have lain to the Lahore High Court, was aborted by a governor-general acting on his own volition in India. It is the manner of his trial, leading up to his eventual execution which is so blatantly wrong, that we must now consider. It is important to remember, however, that there was more than one trial. As Binda Preet Sahni has confirmed, 'The Bhagat Singh Litigation covered three trials known as the *Delhi Assembly Bomb Case, Second Lahore Conspiracy Case, and the Bhagat Singh v. Emperor* on 2 February 1931.'[2] Of these, the first was the least controversial, whereas the other two were more so, in ascending order, which is why this chapter focuses on these two trials.

The FIR, which is written in Urdu, was procured by Pakistani lawyer Imtiaz Qureshi in 2019 after eight decades, following a trawl through the Anarkali Police Station files. It makes the following clear. First, the Delhi Bomb Case started on 7 May 1929 in Delhi before the sessions judge, under Section 307 of the Indian Penal Code.[3] Here Bhagat Singh defended himself with the help of a legal adviser, Mr Asaf Ali. In less than one week, both Bhagat Singh and B.K. Dutt were convicted and transported for life on 12 June 1929. On 14 June 1929, Bhagat Singh was transferred to Mianwali and B.K. Dutt was sent to Lahore Jail. The next day, on 15 June 1929, Bhagat Singh went on a hunger strike, asking to be given political prisoner status. It was then that he was moved to Lahore Jail. In the meantime, there, on 13 September 1929, Jatindra Nath Das died on hunger strike. Bhagat Singh and others ended their hunger strike on 4 October 1929, even though they were still not being granted political prisoner status, despite the fact that the Punjab High Court recognized Bhagat Singh as a 'sincere revolutionary'. Second, there was the Lahore Conspiracy Case trial, which was conducted by Special Magistrate Rai Sahib Pandit Kishen Chand.

However, while this trial was in progress, Viceroy Irwin suddenly issued the Lahore Conspiracy Ordinance on 1 May 1930, the effect of which was that: (i) a three-judge special tribunal was mandated to complete the hearing within a fixed period; (ii) the special tribunal's judgment could not be challenged on appeal and (iii) only the Privy Council in London could hear the appeal. We know the legal and constitutional difficulties that this manner of a criminal trial posed. These difficulties have never been resolved. There were the stark facts that the ordinance was never approved by the Central Assembly or the British Parliament; it lapsed without any legal or constitutional support and it is clear that its only purpose was to try and hang Bhagat Singh in the shortest time possible. This resulted in Bhagat Singh, Rajguru and Sukhdev being sentenced to death on 7 October 1930. This particular method of trial and conviction has been ruled subsequently unlawful in Bhagat Singh's land of origin. So the question now is whether there ought to be an atonement, a reckoning, or even a recision of the verdict. Fortunately, we have some clear-cut examples to choose from.

In recent years, a key piece of terrorism-related legislation in Pakistan has been the Anti-Terrorism Act. It came into force in 1997 after being passed by the National Assembly and Senate under the government of Nawaz Sharif.[4] It had propitious timing, following as it did an attack in Lahore in January of that same year. Mehram Ali, member of the Shia extremist group Sipah-e-Muhammad Pakistan (later labelled a terrorist organization), set off a bomb near a courthouse. It killed twenty-three people, including two Sunni leaders of Sipah-e-Sahaba Pakistan, an anti-Shia organization, who were on trial at the time, as well as a journalist and police officers. Ali was tried and sentenced to death by the newly created Anti-Terrorism Court and appealed to the Anti-Terror Appellate Tribunal. His appeal eventually made its way to the Supreme Court of Pakistan on issues of constitutional compatibility with the new legislation, but judges upheld the conviction and Mehram Ali was executed not too long afterwards on 11 August 1998.[5] What is interesting, however, is that despite upholding the sentence of death, the judges of the supreme court found that sections of the Anti-Terrorism Act flew in the face of Pakistan's constitution, in that the newly created courts were not subject to the same rules as the other courts in the nation's judicial system. This concerned such fundamental questions of due process as the tenure of judges and the rules of evidence. As a direct result of the ruling in *Mehram Ali v Federation of Pakistan*, the government issued the Anti-Terrorism (Amendment) Ordinance in October 1998, which disbanded the anti-terror appellate tribunals, with the effect that all appeals hereafter would be handled by the existing regular high courts.[6] This shows that as a matter of due process, Bhagat Singh was not given a fair trial, with the result that he was wrongly convicted. It was in violation of fair trial norms even back then and it was quite deliberate.

Back then the Raj governed, as Sherman has pointed out, through a 'coercive network of the colonial state' rather than the 'rule of law'.[7] The rule of law was deliberately suspended. In its place was what Anderson has described as the infamous 'Bloody Code', so that 'the scale of judicial reprisals seen in Empire . . . had no parallel in nineteenth-century Britain', and the death penalty was used to 'consolidate imperial rule and to eradicate resistance'.[8] In Bhagat Singh's case, these judicial reprisals went one step further. He was tried under a made-up law constructed on the hoof with no institutional backing. He was tried under what his Privy Council lawyer, D.N. Pritt, called a 'privilegium', namely, a law made for just one person. This was a concept of Roman law, from which English law was derived, whereby the Roman emperor bestowed on a single person either a right or a punishment which was anomalous and irregular. The Lahore conspirators were tried under a privilegium because they were subject to a single piece of the governor-general's legislation, namely, the Lahore Ordinance III of 1930, which named the twenty-four specific defendants to be tried, with no offences stipulated, before a specially constituted three-member tribunal, whose sole purpose was to only try these particular individuals, after which it would be functus officio. This was on evidence which was not known to any person beforehand and with no right of appeal thereafter to any court. His conviction was illegal and contrary to law. Should there, accordingly, be an apology from the British Government, as Imtiaz Rashid Qureshi of the Bhagat Singh Memorial Foundation in Lahore has argued, for Bhagat Singh's execution in violation of the rules of natural justice and fairness?

33

1930, The Special Tribunal

In one sense, an atonement is called for. The Lahore Ordinance III of 1 May 1930 was passed by Lord Irwin without being ratified by either the Central Legislative Assembly or by the Council of State. It was not an act of the Indian legislature. It was an edict passed by a single man. That man was the governor-general. It was done at a time when the Lahore conspirators were already being tried before a regular magistrate in a regular court. Their trial had been going on for ten months. Over 200 witnesses had been heard. The power of setting up a special tribunal, by virtue of the governor-general's ordinance, was a very special power to be exercised in rare circumstances only. The Imperial Parliament in London had made it subject to two specific legal restraints. First, the ordinance would be subject to a strict time-limit of six months' validity only as it was a special edict exercisable by the single person, the governor-general, with no legislative oversight. Second, the ordinance could only be invoked 'in cases of emergency' where the 'peace and good government of British India or any part thereof' was at stake. Both these conditions had to be satisfied. Otherwise, the governor-general had to act in the normal way through normal parliamentary legislation. The power was permissive. It was not mandatory. The governor-general 'may' act by way of an ordinance. Nothing directed that he had to. There was nothing in the legislation justifying the use of an ordinance procedure for the purposes of executing anyone. Such a use of power was arguably irrational because the ordinance procedure was an administrative one for 'peace and good government' and not for inflicting the death penalty. It was an 'emergency' power only. This is why Section 72 of the Government of India Act 1919 stated,

> The governor general of India may, *in cases of emergency*, make and promulgate ordinances *for the peace and good government of British India or any part thereof,* and any ordinance so made shall, for the space of not more than six months from its promulgation, have the like *for the space of not more than six months from its promulgation,* have the like force of law as an Act passed by the Indian legislature . . . (emphases added).

The British government in London could 'disallow' an ordinance on grounds that the governor-general had exceeded his authority by passing it. It could do so in the same way that it could disallow a statute passed by the Indian legislature and assented to by the governor-general.[1] The governor-general had to give reasons for issuing his ordinance. So in the Preamble, Governor-General Irwin declared, '. . . an emergency has arisen which makes it necessary to provide specially for the trial of the accused in the cases known as the Lahore Conspiracy case.' But he did not say that this was in the interests of maintaining 'peace and good government' in India. So the reasons were not good.[2] It was not enough for Irwin to claim that the offences were of an 'unusually serious character' because they arose from 'revolutionary activities'. Nor was it enough to say that 'it would be necessary to produce about 600 witnesses'. Nor that there has been an earlier 'hunger strike before the commencement of the enquiry', which had caused the magistrate Rai Sahib Pandit Sri Kishen to adjourn proceedings for two months from 26 July to 24 September 1930. None of these are reasons which have anything to do with 'peace and good government' in India, nor do they amount to an emergency.

In fact, some of the 'reasons' he gave were positively bad reasons which could not stand up in court if challenged. To say of the magistrate's trial that 'it was then resumed, but there were numerous interruptions owing to defiant and disorderly conduct by some of the accused or demonstrations by members of the public' does not justify a trial by ordinance. The maintenance of order and courtroom decorum is the task of every judge in a criminal trial. In fact, the accused were not 'disorderly', there were no demonstrations by members of the public before judge Rai Sahib Pandit Sri Kishen, and some 230 witnesses had already been called. So, the suggestion that he would not be able 'to count upon obtaining a conclusion by the normal methods of procedure within any calculable period' was plainly against the weight of the evidence before him. He, the governor-general, then wished to call 600 witnesses in any event, but then chose to not call anywhere near that number, whilst still expressing worry that the proceedings were going 'to drag out to a length which cannot at present be foreseen' and wanting the charges to be 'finally adjudicated upon with the least possible delay'. None of these are reasons for an ordinance. One person who saw through all this was none other than Mohammed Ali Jinnah. On 12 September 1929, Jinnah castigated the Governor-General in the Delhi Central Assembly with his excoriating denunciation of his actions: 'Can you imagine that 600 witnesses are necessary to prove the case against each one of the accused?' he demanded with incredulity. 'Well, Sir, it may seem a joke and it may seem that I am making fun of the statement made to this effect', he continued, 'but the first impression that one gets is that, when a case cannot be proved without the testimony of 600 witnesses, that is a very bad case.'[3]

Yet, at a stroke the edict decided that 'all cases pending in the Court of *Rai Sahib Pandit Sri Kishen*, Magistrate of the First Class, Lahore, against any or all of the accused named . . . shall be tried by the Tribunal to be constituted . . .'[4] and 'consisting of three persons who at the time of the constitution are Judges'.[5] And yet, adding farce to irony, he decided not only that 'it shall not be incumbent on the Tribunal to re-call or re-hear any witness who has already given evidence . . .' and that 'it may act on any evidence already recorded by or produced before it',[6] but also that 'where any accused . . . in any way wilfully conducts himself to the serious prejudice of the trial, *the Tribunal may, at any stage of the trial, dispense with the attendance of such accused* for such period as it may think fit and proceed with the trial in his absence'[7] (emphases added). On this basis, 'the jurisdiction of the aforesaid Magistrate shall cease'.[8] Even more bizarrely, the special tribunal 'shall be deemed to be a Court of Session'.[9] But if it was a court of session, one would expect there to be a right of appeal from it to a higher court. Not so. This was after all a trial by 'privilegium'. However, '[t]he Tribunal may pass upon any person convicted by it any sentence authorized by law . . .'. Nevertheless, 'the judgment of the Tribunal shall be final and conclusive' and remarkably 'there shall be no appeal from any order or sentence of the Court'.[10]

Once the trial before the special tribunal began, the ramshackle proceedings soon ran into difficulties. Within two weeks, two of the three judges had to be replaced. This meant only one judge had heard all the evidence before pronouncing the sentence of death. Of the evidence eventually called, the 457 prosecution witnesses were not allowed to be cross-examined. The government relied on the evidence of former conspirators now turned turncoats. But the accused were allowed to cross-examine only one of the five approvers. In the circumstances, the accused refused to attend proceedings. The proceedings ran for five months, from 5 May 1930. On 7 October 1930 a sentence of death was announced on Bhagat Singh, Sukhdev and Rajguru. The ordinance lapsed. The trial was over. It never had any legal or constitutional support in the first place. The passing of a sentence of death was its only purpose.

34

A 'Striking Power'

Four months after the sentence of death by the special tribunal on 7 October 1930, an English lawyer in London, D.N. Pritt KC, took a taxi to Downing Street. It was a cold wet morning on 11 February 1931. He had arrived to argue the case of Bhagat Singh and his two comrades before the judicial committee of the Privy Council, before five judges. They were headed by Viscount Dunedin with his enormous walrus moustache. If that gave the impression of geniality it was a mistaken impression, for these judges were not favourably disposed towards Pritt. They harangued him, taunted him and ridiculed him at every juncture. But the suave debonair Winchester College-educated lawyer had little choice but to appear before them as the court of last resort in the British Empire because there was no right of appeal against the sentence of death from the special tribunal to the Lahore High Court in India. Pritt began by explaining that Section 72 of the Government of India Act was unique in that 'it creates a somewhat striking power, and . . . which any court will construe with care', and was exercisable only 'when the conditions are fulfilled'. This is because 'the power it creates is a limited power of delegated legislation', which was contingent on certain conditions being fulfilled. These were that 'there must be a case of emergency, whatever "emergency" may mean', but also 'that the ordinance must be an Ordinance falling within the description that it is an Ordinance for the peace and good government of British India, or some part thereof'.[1]

In short, as D.N. Pritt KC submitted, 'something must happen before the power comes into force at all', and that 'when it has come into force, that is to say when there is an emergency and the Governor-General must do something, there are two limits'. These two limits were as follows. First, that 'it is necessary to establish affirmatively that there is a case of emergency'. But second, and even more importantly, 'it is not for the executive, if I may so describe the Governor-General, to say there is an emergency; it must be proved; like any other question of fact lying at the root of the jurisdiction, it has to be established before the courts, in my humble submission'. This was not a novel plea. It happens all the time when 'facts' have to be established because, 'the courts in British countries are places where facts are decided' and '[a]t the root of the Governor General's right to make an Ordinance lies in every case the question of fact: "Was there an emergency?". If it becomes material to know whether there was an emergency or not, that is a matter which has to be proved before the court.' When Viscount Dunedin feigned incredulity and retorted with the question: 'What do you mean by "the Courts?"', Pritt tried to explain that the governor-general did not have an absolute power under Section 72 because, 'when it is looked at, there must be some limits to the word "emergency", and that he can only act within those limits'. Indeed, '[o]ne or two courts in India . . . have laid down expressly that is for the court to make up its mind and investigate the questions of fact whether there is an emergency or not . . .'.

Pritt asked for an opportunity to be granted a full hearing, 'if leave to appeal was granted', in which he could explain in detail what he meant by this, but this right was denied to him by a haughty, imperious and disdainful court. Eventually, he returned to the nature of the 'power' in question and reminded the board that 'it must be for the peace and good government of British India' but that 'this particular ordinance is a privilegium of a very terrible description' and that 'whether it could possibly conduce to peace is a matter of some difficulty . . .'. This is because, 'on the true construction of section 72 it is plainly intended to empower the governor general in cases of *general emergency* or cases of a *particular emergency* area', and neither was shown to have existed in this case. Pritt rounded off with a reminder to the judges that they should be in no doubt about the nature of the power in question here because it was one which 'in every Roman law country any jurisprudent would indignantly deny to be legislation at all'. It was a submission that was to be of no avail. Not only did Viscount Dunedin dismiss the appeal in a single short judgment of under two pages, without giving Pritt leave to appeal to argue the matter in a full hearing before the Board of the Privy Council but he did so on grounds that were manifestly wrong. He decided that, 'although the Governor-General thought it fit to expound the reasons which induced him to promulgate this Ordinance, this was not in their Lordships opinion in any way incumbent on him as a matter of law'.[2] This is simply wrong as a matter of law. Not only did the governor-general have to give reasons—and did in fact attempt to do so—he had to give good reasons upon which he was calling out an 'emergency'. The Privy Council's decision is a striking example of coercive colonial legalism being used to undermine the rule of law and to administer a judicial reprisal on individuals before it.

Unbeknownst to Pritt, he was to be vindicated when a hundred years after he was born a British court in 2007 in a case called *Bancoult*[3] held that the phrase 'peace, order and good government' is one which 'has a long legislative pedigree' and 'has become a term of art in the sense that it is regularly used without further explanation to denote the delegation of large but undefined powers to a nominated rule-maker'. It remained, nevertheless, 'a power of the greatest importance carrying commensurate responsibilities' with its usage. This means that 'it has limits, even if these are self-imposed'. Emphasizing the principle of territoriality, which distinguished between the United Kingdom and its colonial territories, the judge Sedley LJ, explained how these limits are 'directed to the wellbeing of a dependent territory and its population' as a way of deciding 'what is best for a colony and to affirm that, like every discretion, it is limited by and to its own expressed objects'. The courts could not just rubber-stamp a decision but had to bear in mind that 'it is their constitutional function to decide whether what has been enacted (or what it is proposed to enact) is rationally and legally capable of providing for a colony's wellbeing. If it is not, then it falls outside the prerogative power'. In this way, '[t]he governance of each colonial territory is in constitutional principle a discrete function of the Crown' and '[t]hat territory's interests will not necessarily be the interests of the United Kingdom or of its allies'.[4]

Yet, in Bhagat Singh's case, the interests of Her Majesty's government in London were assumed to be the only interests at stake. They were of paramount importance. The interests of the colonial territory, namely of India, were subsumed into those of the Crown in England. That was a betrayal of the constitutional function of the courts. In the end, even if the law in question is dealing with affairs of 'incontestably the colony', nevertheless 'it is capable of being rendered invalid by jurisdictional error or malpractice'.[5] The following year Lord Bingham confirmed in the House of Lords that a wrongly promulgated colonial law could not be enacted,[6] and Lord Mance said that only the proper governance of the territory could be countenanced as a consideration in a colonial law.[7] This clearly shows Bhagat Singh's conviction to have been unlawfully orchestrated. No wonder the high court in Lahore is seized of an application to set aside the decision. Should a decision from a Pakistani court ever come, it will reverberate across the Indian sub-continent and beyond.

35

The 'Approvers'

Bhagat Singh was convicted on the evidence of 'approvers'. This is the most significant aspect of the trial of the Lahore Conspiracy Case of 1930. An 'approver' is a participant in or accomplice to a crime that is being tried, who then gives evidence for the prosecution. He is a 'turncoat'. He is one who has turned approver in the case because he has confessed himself guilty of the crime in question, but is now approving others of the same crime to save himself. In the Lahore Conspiracy Case, the approvers were given inducements to become 'turncoats'. This, therefore, again begs the question as to whether the trial was fairly conducted. Given that the approvers were erstwhile colleagues of the conspirators, with whom they had exchanged vows, rubbed shoulders and stood side by side in the face of immense adversity until only very recently, if their evidence was now going to be called upon by the prosecution, it was necessary for the defence to have the opportunity to challenge such uncorroborated evidence. Justice demanded nothing less as a minimum requirement. Astonishingly, such evidence was not subject to cross-examination in the Lahore Conspiracy Case. It is not difficult to understand why. Before the special tribunal, two of the approvers said they gave their statements to the police under pressure from them. Indeed, they even wished now to have their statements retracted. It was Ajoy Ghosh, one of those who was eventually acquitted, who a decade later said that, '[d]ue to the tremendous popular enthusiasm that the case had evoked, a number of key witnesses had turned hostile, more were likely to follow suit, and two of the approvers had retracted their confessions'. It was unsurprising then that 'the whole case was in danger of ending in fiasco', which would not have been the case 'if ordinary legal procedure was followed and ordinary legal facilities allowed us'.[1]

This is indeed the crux of the matter. Ordinary legal procedures were not followed. Legal facilities for the defence were not made available. One is bound to ask how this came about in a tribunal that was hand-picked by the governor-general. The answer lies in the fact that by appointing a special tribunal, outside the rules of ordinary trial procedure, the governor-general had only succeeded in creating the most politically charged court hearings of the day. Within two weeks of the special tribunal beginning its sitting on 5 March 1930, two of the three judges had vacated their seats. Justices Coldstream (the President) and Justice Agha Haider, it was alleged in a notification given on 20 June 1930 by Chief Justice Sir Shadi Lal of the Lahore High Court, were 'for reasons of health . . . unable to discharge their duties as members of the Tribunal'.[2] The suggestion that two judges can be struck down with ill-health at the same time is risible. The truth is that Coldstream presided over the beatings of the accused in the courtroom before his very eyes. The accused objected to him continuing to preside over the hearings. So he had to go. Agha Haider, on the other hand, objected to the mistreatment of the accused in court. This made his position untenable and he too now had to go. The judges were replaced by Justices Tapp and Abdul Qadir. Justice Hilton was now to become the president of the special tribunal in place of Justice Coldstream.

In fact, the flaws in the trial procedures go back to the beginning, to the time of magistrate's court hearings on 7 May 1929. On remand, the accused were not even produced in court. The magistrates were instead taken to selected places. These places were where the accused were being held, such as the Borstal Jail in Lahore. The accused had no access to their families. They had no access to legal advice. On top of this, the 'approvers' were not in judicial custody away from the police. Instead, they were being held in police custody throughout the proceedings where the police could interfere with them. The accused objected strongly. It was to no avail. Their applications were thrown out with contempt. In police custody, they were regularly primed to give the kind of evidence which the police demanded of them. This is why, as Ajoy Ghosh wrote, a number of their key witnesses were now turning hostile. In the end, the accused threw in the towel. They boycotted the proceedings. They decided they would not participate in the hearings at all. They were not wrong to do so. One is reminded here of Jinnah's 12 September 1929 speech in the Delhi Central Assembly yet again: 'I appeal to you with all the emphasis I can command, do not be vindicative. Show that you are fair, generous, that you are willing to treat these men decently. At any rate, before they are released or sentenced, given them proper treatment.'[3] And yet, proper treatment was one thing that the accused did not have, and the authorities remained vindicative to the end.

The judicial authorities also were not impartial at all. This is clear from an application before Rai Sahib Pandit Sri Kishen, which was made on 4 October 1929. The application asked for the removal of the approvers to judicial custody. Not only did the magistrate reject the application, but he did so in terms which clearly showed his bias. He employed language which was injudicious and unbecoming of a judge. He reprimanded counsel for the accused saying, 'The Learned defence counsel does not hold a brief on behalf of the Approvers to be in a position to plead for them quite uninvited . . . .' That may be so, but learned counsel did hold a brief for the accused whom he was representing, and it was in their defence that he was making an application for the removal of the approvers into judicial custody where they could not be tampered with. The magistrate then added that 'the proper time for him to elicit details of the nature alluded to by him in his application would be when the Approvers would come into the witness box, and the accused shall have a right to cross examine them'. But learned counsel here was not raising an issue relating to cross-examination, but one relating to fairness of procedures and due process, where the approvers, being in police custody, were in a position to be groomed by the authorities by being told what to say in the witness box.

To crown it all, the magistrate admonished counsel for the accused with the reprimand that, *'there's no jurisdiction of the accused to dictate to the court* as *to how and where the Approvers should be kept* and to enquire as to their whereabouts . . .'.[4] This, however, is not right at all. The Defence Counsel is well within their rights in raising concerns about the fairness of proceedings and the tampering of witnesses who appear for the prosecution. This is a jurisdictional question for the tribunal. Approvers kept in police custody, rather than in judicial custody, risk being pressured in exactly the manner in which the two approvers were, who were to appear for the prosecution, when they decided to retract their statements. The magistrate had living proof before him. Still he chose not to place the approvers in judicial custody. Still he persistently and consistently rejected applications from the accused to do so. The fact that counsel for the defence was then chastised for wanting to assume 'jurisdiction' so as 'to dictate to the court' shows the magistrate was mangling up important legal concepts in a wholly inappropriate manner to refuse an application, which was unanswerable. The refusal of this application through the use of such extravagantly inapt language only served to create the impression which the magistrate would wish to have avoided, namely, that the approvers were indeed being interfered with.

Such an impression was difficult to dispel because, not only were the proceedings before the magistrate's hearing then abruptly stopped after ten months and transferred to the special tribunal, but in those proceedings Mr Justice Hilton alone served throughout the time that the case was being heard. He did not intervene to ensure that the trial proceedings were conducted fairly at any stage. He was the only judge to have first-hand knowledge of how key witnesses for the prosecution retracted their statements. The other judges on the panel were in no position to discuss the frailties of the evidence. They had not been privy to all that had transpired during the hearings. What were the frailties of this evidence? One does not have to look far to see them. The government was represented by C.H. Carden Noad in the tribunal, just as was the case in the magistrate's court. He was accompanied by Khan Saheb Kalandar Ali Khan, the public prosecutor, and L. Gopal Lal.

There was no defence counsel in place for Bhagat Singh because he had chosen to represent himself. However, according to the record of proceedings, he had decided to 'put in an application stating that he wanted *a legal adviser* to watch the proceedings of the tribunal and *to give him advice on lines of cross examination*'. The person he wanted in that capacity was the lawyer Mr Duni Chand. He, however, would neither cross-examine the government witnesses nor address the court. Provided that seating accommodation was available in court, Mr Noad, the public prosecutor, took the view that there could be no reason to disagree with this application by Bhagat Singh. This being so, 'the tribunal sanctioned the arrangement proposed.'5

The case for the prosecution opened. Carden Noad called his first witness. It was G.T. Hamilton. When his statement was looked at it was disarming for what it disclosed: 'I do not know the facts of the case nor did I make the statements made in the complaint. I am acting only as a formal complainant under the instructions of the government.' This shows that the evidence of a British official was doctored in a way that he disclaimed all knowledge even of the statement that was being tendered by the prosecution on his behalf. Indeed, he claimed not to have any knowledge of the facts of the case! By the time we get to the approvers, two of the five withdraw their statements and only one is allowed to be cross-examined. Yet, the accused in the Lahore Conspiracy Case of 1930 were all convicted through the mouths of turncoats in circumstances where the government had no better evidence than that of the 'approvers'. Of the judges, none of them except Mr Justice Agha Haider, deigned to question the approvers closely, much to his eventual cost leading to his prompt removal within two weeks of the special tribunal starting to sit. There was no jury to assess the credibility of the witnesses or their demeanour. How could a tribunal of three judges, two of whom were recent replacements, ensure that the basic demands of fairness and justice were safeguarded? They could not because the special tribunal had not been constituted to serve a noble end. It had one purpose, and one purpose alone, which was to hand down punishment of death. And, in that design, it worked very well.

36

Police Beatings

On two occasions, Bhagat Singh and his fellow accused were mercilessly beaten up in court. On 10 April 1929, the magistrate, Rai Sahib Pandit Sri Kishen, began proceedings in Borstal Jail.[1] Six months later on 21 October 1929 the accused were subjected to extreme brutality.[2] He continued with the hearings for the next ten months until 1 May 1930, after which the proceedings were transferred to Poonch House, Lahore. That is where the second instance of police ill-treatment in the courtroom occurred. This is when the special tribunal took over the case pursuant to Lord Irwin's ordinance from 5 May 1930. However, just a week into that trial, on 12 May 1930, the true nature of colonial legal coercion was exposed when the accused were beaten up even more viciously under the judges' very noses on their express instructions. Both instances bear testimony to how prisoner mistreatment was an integral and inherent part of colonial trials held outside the normal discipline of the law.

The first occasion arose before Magistrate Rai Sahib Pandit Sri Kishen when one of the accused, a juvenile by the name of Prem Dutt Verma, threw a slipper at one of the approvers, Jai Gopal, as he entered the witness box to give evidence, on 21 October 1929. He was immediately seized and sent into solitary confinement for three months by the jail superintendent.[3] The next day, the courtroom management of the rest of the accused coming into court changed. Bhagat Singh and B.K. Dutt were in detention in Central Jail in Lahore. They were used to coming into court without any handcuffs. Those in Borstal Jail, who were juveniles, used to come to court with a handcuff on one hand only. Once they entered the dock these handcuffs were removed. The next day, on 22 October 1929, both Bhagat Singh and B.K. Dutt were required to be shackled on both hands at the gate of the jail as they came out of their cells on their way to the courtroom, which was opposite the jail. It was not clear whether there was an order from the magistrate Rai Sahib Pandit Sri Kishen or whether this was at the behest of the jail superintendent. They resisted. They had every reason to. All the accused had openly dissociated themselves from the unsavoury actions of the juvenile Prem Dutt Verma. They saw it as an impulsive action on his part and they expressed regret at what he had been driven to do upon sight of Jai Gopal.

Those in Borstal Jail were now required to be handcuffed on both hands before coming to court. They too resisted. When they were brought to the porch of Borstal Institute, handcuffs were forcibly put on them, and six of them were then thrown in the back of the lorry, which then sped off to drop them off at the gates of the central jail. Upon arrival there, the accused refused to disembark from the lorry. The press was present at the gate of the jail. The accused told them that they had been beaten, caned and physically mistreated. Many had sustained injuries. The proceedings could not continue, so they were adjourned. When they resumed there was now a lot of bad blood between the authorities and the accused.

All the accused had to return to the courtroom with handcuffs on both hands. As they were resisting, they had to be dragged into the courtroom and flung into the dock. Shiv Verma and Ajoy Ghosh were both rendered unconscious. Bhagat Singh and B.K. Dutt remained lucid, but in great pain. As they entered the courtroom, they were disoriented[4] and they spluttered and choked. Their shrill cries of 'Long live the revolution', 'Long live the Proletariat' and

'Down with imperialism', nevertheless, rang out. Bhagat Singh immediately demanded of the magistrate whether it was he who had ordered that the accused be kicked by the police. He wanted to know why the police were not under his control. Others shouted 'Shame! Shame!' to the magistrate after Bhagat Singh demanded answers. The magistrate feebly ventured to ask who it was that had kicked them. Bhagat pointed them out at once with the words that several officers had sat on them and kicked them on various parts of their body. B.K. Dutt pointed out that he received severe blows to his chest and Prem Dutt gave the magistrate graphic details of how the day before the police had inserted their fingers into their rectum and kicked them in the testicles. They asked the magistrate whether this was 'civilization' and warned him that the time would come when they would turn into 'revolutionaries'.[5] A concerned government lawyer, Carden Noad, asked the magistrate to make a note of this threat. Bhagat Singh wanted to know of Rai Sahib Pandit Sri Kishen whether the police were acting on his orders. He did not answer. Bhagat Singh asked to have his manacles removed in court as he wanted to make a statement. The magistrate denied him this request. Only when the accused were taken to lunch was one handcuff removed from one hand. On 24 October 1929, it was agreed that the accused would now all come to court with handcuffs on only one hand.

The second occasion when the accused were subject to a brutal assault was even more serious. It happened before the special tribunal on 12 May 1930 after Bhagat Singh and the accused had walked into the courtroom. As the three tribunal judges prepared to commence the proceedings and the accused had their handcuffs removed, they began to sing their revolutionary song. This was not unusual. It was a standard feature of political trials in India. The practice was followed as a mark of defiance at the start of the trial. Judges had learnt to accommodate this because these songs were always before the proceedings began in revolutionary trials. The prisoners sang their songs to boost their morale. On this occasion, however, before they raised the cry of 'Inquilab

Zindabad', a disgruntled Justice Coldstream (President) stamped his foot to their great surprise and announced that he would have none of this. The accused, he ordered, should have their handcuffs put on them again and that they be despatched back to their prison cells. Bhagat Singh objected. He refused to be manacled again. He insisted on his right to sing his song before the business of the day commenced. In this, he was only asking for what had already been accorded to him and his fellow prisoners, because from the very first day of the special tribunal hearings on 5 May 1930, they had all been allowed to sing their song. Their handcuffs were still on them. The court was not in session yet. There was no interference with proceedings. On each of the previous days over the last week, they had been allowed to start and finish their song. Justice Coldstream, however, now regarded this as an affront. As president of the tribunal, he instructed the police to physically remove the accused from the courtroom.

It was then that a bevy of 'more than 15 constables sprang on each accused and handcuffed them one by one, by force'.[6] It did not stop there. Prem Dutt and Ajoy Ghosh found themselves flying in the air and crashing over the metal barrier into the prisoners' dock. They blacked out as they were rendered wholly insensate. There were screams of pain from all the accused in the courtroom. Bhagat Singh remonstrated again. He told the judges that they were nothing more than 'cowards and mercenaries'. The other accused asked the Indian judge, Justice Agha Haider, how he could in all conscience continue to serve on the tribunal and asked him to resign. Amid the cacophony, the hearing was adjourned by Justice Coldstream as he brushed his judicial gown, rose up from the bench and walked out.[7] The disorder, however, touched a raw nerve in the Indian judge. His conscience was pricked. The next day he had to sign off the proceedings of the previous day. But Justice Agha Haider refused to do so. Instead, he took it upon himself to take the unprecedented bold step of writing a statement to the effect, saying, 'I was not a party to the order of the removal of the accused from the court to the jail and I was not responsible for it in anyway. I disassociate myself from all that took place . . . today in consequence of that order_ AGHA HAIDAR.'[8]

This must have come as a complete shock to the Tribunal President Justice Coldstream. Yet, Justice Agha Haider was right. Paragraph 9(1) of the ordinance of 1930, containing a reference to the 'Special Powers' of the tribunal to enable it to deal with an accused who behaved in a 'persistently disorderly manner', did not authorize the tribunal to have prisoners beaten up by the police in open court. In this case, the accused were not behaving in 'persistently disorderly conduct'. Their conduct of singing a revolutionary song was not taking place 'at any stage of the trial', as the trial was yet to begin. The long-standing practice had always been to allow the singing to take place, after which the handcuffs would be removed and the visitors would be allowed to proceed to enter and to take their seats in the gallery. The accused saw themselves as 'political prisoners'. This status mattered to them. It went to the very heart of who they were and what they lived for. Beaten up in court, manacled and flung back into their jail cells on the orders of the president of the tribunal without being allowed to sing their revolutionary song, the accused boycotted the tribunal proceedings after 12 May 1930. Sukhdev turned up on 13 May 1930 to have a look but did not return to court after that. On 21 June 1930, Agha Haider was removed from the special tribunal.

On 25 June 1930, orders were passed by the tribunal to dispense with the attendance of the accused. This was under powers conferred by the ordinance. It was something Jinnah had fought hard to avoid. In the Hunger Strike Bill, there was a clause allowing dispensation of the accused. In his speech on 12 September 1929 in the Delhi Central Assembly, Jinnah had lambasted the Governor-General with the words, 'Does it come to this, that you want to carry this Bill, you want to have this Bill placed on the Statute-book, and then you want to give notice to the prisoners that, unless they cease their hunger-strike within a certain period, you are going to proceed *ex parte*? Under that threat you think the prisoners will cease their hunger-strike?'[9] Jinnah had stopped that bill from passing with his stellar oratory in the Central Legislative Assembly. The ordinance, now passed by Governor-General Irwin, secured for the government by executive edict that which it could not have achieved by normal legislative means. With the accused now moved from the dock back into jail, a cold uncanny spectre descended upon the empty courtroom in Poonch House. The defence counsel were there, but without their clients to defend they did not know what to do. The new Indian judge, Sir Abdul Qadir, who had replaced the formidable Agha Haider, recognizing the absurdity of their situation nervously suggested to the defence counsel that although they were now without instructions from their clients, they could still attempt to cross-examine the crown witnesses and then interview their clients the next day and take instructions in that way, little realizing how this only added farce to an untenable situation, which had been created entirely through the actions of Justice Coldstream. No defence counsel would know precisely what question to ask in cross-examination, nor at what point of the evidence of a crown witness, without first having instructions from their client. The defence lawyers were not to be duped, hoodwinked and bamboozled in this way by the urbane self-possessed Sir Abdul Qadir. What they wanted was an interview with their clients before cross-examining the approvers in their evidence for the prosecution. Not the next day. They promptly took themselves off the courtroom to have an interview with their clients in Borstal Jail right then and not the next day as was being suggested. They returned to say that they were under strict instructions not to represent their clients unless the order of 25 June 1930 dispensing with their attendance in court was revoked by the special tribunal so as to allow their attendance in court as was their right. The lawyers for the defence found themselves in an untenable situation. There was nothing more left for them to do. Among the lawyers, Amolak Ram, Baljit Singh and Amar Dass too left the courtroom.

With neither the accused nor their redoubtable lawyers in court, all the prosecution now had to do was to hurtle through the evidence of the prosecution witnesses. With all the advantages before it, the prosecution still failed to redeem itself. Some two weeks later, on 8 July 1930, it called the traffic inspector of police in Lahore, W.J.G. Fearn, to give his evidence-in-chief, because he had been present at the murder scene. Fearn had been present from the time of Saunders stumbling out of the gate of the Anarkali Police Station with his motorbike, to the time when after giving chase to the assailants, Head Police Constable Chanan Singh had collapsed with a bullet wound in his chest. In every way, he was the prosecution's star witness of the killing. He failed, however, to identify either Bhagat Singh or Rajguru. This was despite there being 'several' identification parades held specifically for him. When asked by Carden Noad, his nonchalant response was, 'I attended several identification parades but failed to pick up the two assailants of Mr Saunders.' This is quite remarkable, given that one of them had actually fired directly at Fearn just as he was himself giving chase to them. The absurdities did not end there. When on 10 July 1930, copies of the charge sheets were served by the tribunal on the fifteen accused who were still incarcerated, they were accompanied with an order that the pleas of the fifteen accused should be recorded the next day, but on 11 July 1930 even the pleas of the accused were dispensed with. So now not only was the attendance of the accused dispensed with, but so were their pleas. They had no lawyer in court either fighting their corner for them. The extent of coercive legal control from the courtroom in this judicial reprisal only helps show how draconian the Lahore Ordinance III of 1930 was.

After a month's incarceration in solitary confinement, in the scorching heat of a Lahore jail,[10] one detainee, Kanwal Nath Tiwari, had even gone quite mad. But it was still deemed appropriate to dispense with both his plea and his attendance in court, such was the complete disregard with the elementary principles of criminal justice, as the special tribunal scurried towards ending the proceedings and handing down a sentence of death on three of the accused. No person in such a situation could have the ordinance invoked against them, unless achieving a conviction of the accused was all that the tribunal had in mind, in the six months allocated to it before it became defunct. The tribunal soldiered on remorselessly. A stream of witnesses was called by the prosecution in quick succession as they whirled into the witness box to confirm the events of 17 December 1928 to the prosecution's blatant delight. Confident students, like Som Nath, Abnash Chand and Aftab Ahmad, meandered in and out, to confirm how as witnesses to the day in question they had been residing in the hostel at DAV College. The apprehensive Ajmer Singh ambled in to explain how he had tenaciously hung on to his bicycle when the accused attempted to wrestle it off him, as they hurriedly scuttled off into hiding after entering the precincts of DAV College. All went unchallenged as witnesses, their evidence indisputable and undisputed.

All gave their evidence in the glaring absence of the accused. The accused were not there because some of the accused could not attend as they were medically unfit to do so, while others were on hunger strike in prison and others simply dispensed with in their attendance. On 7 October 1930, with the parody of the trial complete, the special tribunal announced its verdict. Des Raj, Jatinder Nath Sanyal and Ajoy Kumar Ghosh were the only ones who would be released. Kundan Lal and Prem Dutt were handed down terms of imprisonment of seven years and five years respectively. Mahavir, Shiv Verma, Jaidev Kapoor and Vijay Kumar Sinha were sentenced to transportation for life. That left Bhagat Singh, Sukhdev and Rajguru. They were to be hanged by the neck until dead. On 23 March 1931, they were sent to the gallows, which they faced with unmatched valour and chutzpah. Be that as it may, Professor Chaman Lal's memorable lament, 'Rajguru, Sukhdev and Bhagat Singh's hanging was nothing but judicial murder—and that too performed in a hurry, with the colonial state clearly in a state of panic,'[11] reminds us of Mirza Ghalib's immortal incantation: '*Hui muddat ke Ghalib mar gaya par yaad aata hai / Vo har ek baar par kehna ki yoon hota tou kya hota*' ('Long years have passed since Ghalib died, but still his memory torments / Because it was he who always asked: "If it had been different, how different would it have been?"'). If Bhagat Singh had lived, what difference would his life have made? We will never know.

PART 8

'DELUDED PATRIOTS'

Apne saarey dard bhula kar auron ke dukh sehta tha
Hum jub ghazlain kehtey thay wo aksar jail main rehta tha

Oblivious of his own sorrows, he took on those of others.
Whilst we sang ghazals, he languished alone in jail.

—Qateel Shifai

37

1931, I Was Never a Terrorist

It is often said that Bhagat Singh transitioned from a terrorist to a revolutionary in his short life.[1] This claim is based on his last piece of writing, which was drafted in February 1931 just a month before he was sent to the gallows and in which he describes his early espousal of violence as follows:

> Apparently I have acted as a terrorist. *But I am not a terrorist.* I am a revolutionary who has got such definite ideas of a lengthy programme (. . .) Let me announce with all the strength at my command, that I am not a terrorist and never was, *(except) perhaps at the beginning of my revolutionary career* (emphases added).

Was Bhagat Singh then a 'terrorist'? It is said that near the end of his life he had dramatically changed his outlook and that earlier in his life he was a terrorist. The accolade of a 'terrorist', however, ill befits him. It is a claim which he does not himself make. He states, 'I was never a terrorist.' He then adds that perhaps if he was then this was only in his earlier years. But the claim bears scrutiny. Bhagat Singh only took one life. And that was in revenge. His bombing for the Legislative Assembly was not a bombing as we would normally understand it. It consisted of hurling two decidedly harmless smoke bombs in order 'to make the deaf hear' and not to hurt anyone. It was in the form of a political protest. His statement of February 1931 above is at best ambiguous. On the one hand, he asserts, 'I am not a terrorist *and never was . . .*'. On the other hand, he allows for the possibility '(except) perhaps at the beginning of my revolutionary career'. The latter is expressed in rather non-committal terms. So what is the truth?

Perhaps the best explanation was given some forty years ago, when the distinguished Indian historian Bipin Chandra described Bhagat Singh and his fellow revolutionaries as 'men of ideas and ideologies' in a 1972 essay, in which he said that Bhagat Singh's life 'cannot be studied except in motion'.[2] Had Bhagat Singh survived the tumultuous years of the 1920s and 1930s, which led to Independence, today 'he would have become a Marxist Gandhian'.[3] Subsequently, when Moffat, interviewed him in 2012, Chandra confirmed that he saw Bhagat Singh as 'a terrorist in the unmaking' and a 'Marxist in the making'.[4] Yet, as Moffat points out, 'we cannot know what Bhagat Singh would have become had he lived'[5] and that this is so even when it is borne in mind 'that HSRA members like Ghosh and Varma – not to mention Kishori Lal, B.K. Sinha and Jaidev Kapur – all joined the CPI',[6] referring to how they all flocked to the Communist Party of India ('CPI') as their natural home after Independence.

Moffat uses the 'metaphor of a *journey*' and the idea of 'Bhagat Singh *in motion*' to describe how at first Bhagat Singh steadily moves in a way that 'tracks a departure from violence, liberating the revolutionary from the stigma of "terrorist" action',[7] but then secondly in so doing manages an 'arrival at something refined, comprehensive, stable' so that 'for some it is most certainly Marxist, for others anarchist' while for some others 'it is simply a more perfect patriotism'.[8] Instances of the former, according to Moffat, are his sessions court statement in Delhi, where initially in 1929 he doggedly maintains how revolution 'does not necessarily involve a sanguinary strife, nor is there any place in it for individual vendetta' since 'it is not the cult of the bomb or the pistol'. From this, it is said that he journeys by 1931 to a position whereby in his letter 'To Young Political Workers' in that year, he is able to say, 'I am not a terrorist and I never was, except perhaps in the beginning of my revolutionary career.'[9] It is possible to argue, however, that the two statements are not inconsistent. Bhagat Singh does after all declaim to ever having had any pretence to being a 'terrorist', and comments as to how he was such a person even at the very beginning, is adorned with a *caveat* that should not be overlooked. Indeed, his statement in 1931 ends with the declaration that 'mere bomb-throwing is not only useless but sometimes harmful'.[10] This is not so far apart from what he had said at the beginning of his revolutionary journey in 1929 before the sessions court in Delhi, namely that when we think of a revolution 'it is not the cult of the bomb and the pistol'.

The question whether Bhagat Singh was a terrorist is significant for two reasons. First, it is important that we know what Bhagat Singh stood for. Otherwise, we fail to understand him properly. Bhagat Singh himself was always at pains to ensure that he was never misunderstood, whether in terms of his words or his actions. Second, at a time today when issues of terrorism, public safety and national security are so inextricably intertwined all over the world, it is important to be clear what his espousal of violence or revolution meant. Political action can sometimes involve violence. Violence is regrettably part of that normal historical process. When this happens, political and military discourse sometimes wrongly envisions this as a conflagration of impending apocalyptic wars. In the early years of the twentieth century, the unstable world of Empire in India after the First World War led to a perception of a nebulous threat to peace and order waiting to engulf everyone. More recently, we are reminded by the Australian judge in the case of *Singh*[11] of how there is no antithesis between violent retribution and political action when a policeman is killed as an act of revenge.

An Indian citizen, a Mr Singh, of Sikh ethnicity, had in India been involved with the Khalistan Liberation Force (the KLF), an organization that sought the creation of an independent Sikh state and that used violence to achieve this objective. His role in the

KLF was to collect information on their behalf. The KLF used this information when it decided to kill people. Indeed, Mr Singh had assisted in the provision of weapons that were used by the KLF to carry out acts of violence. Mr Singh then murdered a police officer which was described by the Australian High Court judge as 'the most violent of crimes', and not least because the 'crime was committed out of a strong, if not exclusively retributive motivation'.[12] In relation to the killing of the police officer in Ludhiana, Mr Singh had a significant political purpose. Such a purpose was not negatived by the element of revenge because revenge is likely to be an aspect of many political crimes. It was not negatived, moreover, by looking simply at the main political objective of the KLF, which was the establishment of an independent state. The achieving of one of the other KLF objectives was the protection of Sikh people from violence or torture. In the words of the Australian judge, 'There is no bright line between crimes that are political and those that are non-political.'[13] This is because '[i]t may be doubted that the image of the clinical assassin, with a narrow focus upon an oppressive dictator, taking care to avoid what would now be called collateral damage, ever bore much relation to reality'. More strikingly still, he observed how '[w]hile homicide is foreign to our experience of political conflict, that is because we have been favoured with a relatively peaceful history. At other times, and in other places, the taking of life has been, and is, an incident of political action.'[14] The judge even went onto say, 'It is difficult to imagine serious conflict of any kind without the possibility that parties to the conflict will seek retribution for past wrongs, real or imagined. Revenge is not the antithesis of political struggle; it is one of its most common features.'[15]

In fact, Frantz Fanon, the political philosopher from the French colony of Martinique, had something to say about this. His work today is hugely influential in the disciplines of postcolonial studies and critical theory. He wrote from experience having suffered racism as a French West Indian psychiatrist. In his 1961 book *The Wretched of the Earth*, he has a long[16] chapter titled 'Concerning Violence'. Here he writes that '[n]ational liberation, national renaissance, the restoration of nationhood to the people' or 'whatever may be the headings used' meant that 'decolonisation is always a violent phenomenon'. This is because 'decolonisation is quite simply the replacing of a certain "species" of men by another "species" of men. Without any period of transition, there is a total, complete and absolute substitution' and 'the proof of success lies in a whole social structure being changed from the bottom up'.[17] Like Bhagat Singh who emphasized the occurrence of earthly tremors, he also wrote that '[d]ecolonisation, which sets out to change the order of the world, is obviously a programme of complete disorder' and this is because '[d]ecolonisation is the meeting of two forces, opposed to each other by their very nature . . .'.[18]

And yet, for Mahatma Gandhi, the young revolutionaries of the HSRA were 'deluded patriots'.[19] This was not altogether surprising. Bhagat Singh and Gandhi were poles apart. Bhagat Singh was following in the tradition of the three militant nationalists, Lala Lajpat Rai, Bal Gangadhar Tilak, and Bipin Chandra Pal, whom the mainstream in the Congress Party regarded as extremists. Gandhi, with the Congress Party, wanted to share power with the British. Bhagat Singh, like the trio, would have none of it and wanted complete autonomy for India. The Congress was a pro-Empire party.[20] Bhagat Singh's Naujawan Party was not, and neither was the HSRA. Deluded or not, the fact remains that Bhagat Singh forged a new ideological pathway as never before. Indian revolutionaries had hitherto only rejected the twin evils of capitalism and colonialism. Bhagat Singh wanted to do more. He rejected religion as it alienated the masses. This was not all. The rejection of religion for Bhagat Singh also had instrumentalist objectives. It served his socialist agenda of denouncing another towering edifice of oppression, namely, casteism.

This is confirmed by Chaman Lal in his latest book, *The Bhagat Singh Reader*, where he explains how amongst India's freedom fighters against colonial rule, 'Bhagat Singh went beyond the tradition of the early revolutionaries and gave an ideological direction to the whole movement, which had been missing earlier'.[21] This was unique to his brand of revolutionary politics in India. He points out how '[b]efore Bhagat Singh, the revolutionary movement was the study of the bravery, fearlessness, and patriotism of the revolutionaries' but that '[w]ith Bhagat Singh, it took an entirely different turn and became a study of the ideas of the revolutionaries, and not just about their brave actions'.[22] What enabled Bhagat Singh to perform this role was the following:

> He joined the revolutionary movement at the age of sixteen in 1923 and had less than seven years to achieve his goals of the revolution. During this time, he not only carried out political revolutionary acts . . . but also wrote prolifically. He travelled a lot all over India and spent a lot of time reading the best books from all over the world, be it history, economics, or literature. Bhagat Singh wrote in four languages – Urdu, Hindi, Punjabi, and English. He had a good command over Sanskrit, as he had studied it in School, all the more encouraged by his grandfather, Arjun Singh. He understood Bengali very well, and could recite verses by poets such as Nazrul Islam and Tagore fluently in Bengali. At one time, he was learning Persian as well.[23]

With such a background, his written output appears to have been prodigious, notwithstanding the fact that what he has come down in history to be known for are his revolutionary activities rather than what he wrote during that period. What he wrote, however, opens for us a critically important window into all the formative years of his life as a revolutionary, leading right up the time of his hanging on 23 March 1931. Chaman Lal refers to how '[h]e wrote more than 130 documents in seven years, covering nearly 400 pages' and that '[h]e wrote more than fifty letters, apart from numerous court statements, pamphlets, essays and sketches'. In fact, 'it is believed by many, on the basis of the accounts of one of his comrades in jail, that Bhagat Singh wrote four more books in jail – these manuscripts were smuggled out but are yet to be found'.[24] In the circumstances, any other revolutionary writer would not have failed to have got himself noticed in the West. After all, he pitched himself against Gandhi. He too, like Gandhi, was in search for the soul of India. Yet, Bhagat Singh's writings lie entirely forgotten. His name is barely known, not just in the West, but also in India. It is as if there has been a deliberate act of amnesia amongst the opinion-formers and the intelligentsia. In the Cuban Revolution, the Argentine Marxist revolutionary guerrilla leader Che Guevara, with whom Bhagat Singh is often likened in India, did not meet with the same fate, although he too like Bhagat Singh was an author and military theorist and became for many a countercultural symbol of rebellion and revolt.

The social theorist Professor Vivek Chibber of New York University describes how 'a good case can be made for connection between the anticolonial writings of Cabral and Nkrumah, even those of Fanon, and the socialism of Lenin or Marx'.[25] However, he makes no reference to how the writings of Bhagat Singh did exactly the same, even as Slavoj Zizek refers to Vivek Chibber's book on the back cover as 'the book we were all waiting for . . . .'. When Chibber describes how '[f]or much of the twentieth century, trade union and peasant-farmer groups did in fact figure in struggles for democratisation',[26] there is no mention of Bhagat Singh's thinking, even though he regarded precisely these groups as being in the vanguard of a transformative Indian revolution against colonial rule. Indeed, while Chibber's excellent work goes on to refer to 'virtually every important leader in the anticolonial tradition through the twentieth century, from Sun Yat-Sen and Hon-Chi Minh to Franz Fanon and Che Guevara',[27] there is strangely no mention at all of Bhagat Singh or of his forebears. Bhagat Singh had well developed revolutionary ideas, ranging from education to health care to jail reform and universal suffrage amongst others, which were as extensive as any other long before people like Hon-Chi Minh, Franz Fanon and Che Guevara came onto the scene with their ideas in the middle of the twentieth century. They should be remembered.

38

1929, Jail Readings

According to Simona Sawhney, '[t]he revolutionaries have often been judged as romantic, immature, or misguided' but that does less than full justice to how Bhagat Singh himself ultimately justified his actions. There is a moment when he 'outgrew romance'[1] because, as he explains in relation to the mass arrests after the Kakori incident in 1925, 'Till that time I was only a romantic revolutionary, just a follower of our leaders. Then came the time to shoulder the whole responsibility.'[2] But the way Bhagat Singh did this was through 'study'. As he explains, 'Enthusiastic comrades – nay, leader – began to jeer at us. For some time I was afraid that some day I also might not be convinced of the utility of our programme. That was the turning point in my revolutionary career: "Study" was the cry that reverberated in the corridors of my mind.' This is what brought about the ultimate transformation in his life. Hence, 'Study to enable yourself to face the arguments advanced by [the] opposition' but also 'study to arm yourself with arguments in favour of your cult (*sic*). I began to study'.[3] So complete was his transformation that Ajoy Ghosh attests to how when he first met Bhagat Singh in 1923 aged sixteen, having been introduced to him by B.K. Dutt in Cawnpore, what he saw was a 'tall and thin rather shabbily dressed, very quiet' young man who seemed nothing more than 'a typical village lad lacking smartness and self confidence', such that 'I did not think very highly of him and told Dutt so when he was alone'. And yet, five years later 'one day in 1928, I was surprised when a young man walked into my room and greeted me . . . but it was not the Bhagat Singh that I had met . . . before'. For this twenty-one-year old was 'tall and magnificently proportioned, with a keen, intelligent face and gleaming eyes' and 'he looked a different man altogether'. The change was so great that 'all those who met Bhagat Singh then and afterwards have testified to his remarkable intelligence and to the powerful impression he made when talking'. Now 'he spoke with force, passion and earnestness' and 'we talked the whole night' and 'it seemed to me that a new era was dawning for our party'.[4]

How did this happen? The veteran distinguished lawyer and writer A.G. Noorani notes how 'in a real sense, Bhagat Singh's intellectual life properly began only when he entered prison' because although 'he had, of course, read avidly before', the reality was that 'the activist had little time for intellectual pursuits'.[5] This suggests that the date of Bhagat Singh's arrest on 8 April 1929 is the watershed moment in his life. It is what intellectualizes him as a new revolutionary force in India. This is confirmed by Shiv Verma, who was in Lahore Central Jail with him and attests to how 'we had easy access to books in jail since day one and the atmosphere was quite congenial for study and exchange of ideas'. Further, 'we used to discuss ideological and social issues earlier too, but Bhagat Singh's arrival made this much more lively'. As a result, 'seldom a day would pass without having thrashed out an issue threadbare'. He continues, 'The books which had been read during the week, were on diverse topics as Marxism, progress in Soviet Russia, upsurge in Afghanistan, Sino-Japanese strife, League of Nations' fiasco, the Meerut Conspiracy Case, Labour struggle, role of Indian capitalist class, policy of the Congress and possibility of a change in political goal in Lahore Congress session.' One cannot help wonder at this how different India would have been today if, instead of being annihilated as a political force, this emerging class of self-taught intellectuals had been allowed to take their rightful place at the heart of government. For it is a mistake to think that Bhagat

Singh alone was interested in honing his intellectual and political
acumen. Others were too. But as Shiv Verma explained, 'though we
all had a passion for reading, but (*sic*) Bhagat Singh was a class by
himself'.[6] Another inmate, incarcerated with Bhagat Singh, Jatinder
Nath Sanyal, also vouched for his being an 'extremely well-read man'
but 'the economic experiment in Russia under the Bolshevik regime
greatly interested him'. This is reflected in his taking to the reading
in jail of such tracts as '*Ten Days That Shook the World* by Reed;
What Never Happened by Ropshin; *Mother* by Maxim Gorky; *Career
of a Nihilist* by Stepnik; *Nihilists* by Oscar Wilde; etc.'. Moreover,
'besides, Kropotkin's *Memoirs* and Michael Bakunin's *God and the
State* had great influence on Bhagat Singh'.[7]

How did Bhagat Singh get his hands on such books? The answer
seems to a large extent to be the Dwarka Das Library, founded by
Lala Lajpat Rai, as the sister institution of the National College.
M.M. Juneja describes it as 'promoting the noble cause of freedom,
especially the Revolutionary Movement', because it contained 'a rich
repository of books for radical-minded young men in Lahore' where
'its reading room was always crowded with students'. The library
was fortunate in having been gifted with the services of 'its librarian,
Raja Ram Shastri, just 21-years old then, who took over the charge
of the Library in 1926'.[8] Yashpal, who was also closely associated
with Bhagat Singh, wrote in 1951 that Raja Ram Shastri was 'a
well known socialist of Kanpur' and that 'Shastriji often informed
us about those who used to take a keen interest in revolutionary
literature'.[9] When much later, Raja Ram Shastri published his own
memoirs in 1981, aptly titled *Amar Shahidon Ke Sansmaran*, he
confirmed how when he first arrived at the Dwarka Das Library 'it
then contained all the books of Lala Lajpat Rai's personal library,
which was a huge collection of world literature', but that 'I started
collecting books, especially on Socialism, from different book-sellers
of Lahore' including one in Anarkali Bazaar which 'was expert in
smuggling the banned books from England'. Thereafter, 'since the
library was visited by a large number of young readers, I always tried
to supply them Socialist literature' and when Bhagat Singh 'started

visiting my residence, . . . I got him enrolled as a regular member of the Library'. He continues, 'One day I saw him with a book, First War of Indian Independence by Veer Damodar Savarkar. It was a proscribed book.' Even Raja Ram Shastri did 'not know how it was procured by him' but it was clear to him that 'he was greatly impressed by him'.

Bhagat Singh went onto get Veer Savarkar's book published secretly in two volumes 'each volume costing 8 annas' and 'its marketing, which was indeed a difficult task, was mainly done by Sukhdev'.[10] Thereafter it was Shastri who supplied Bhagat Singh with Vaillant's book, *Anarchism and Other Essays*, where 'one of its chapters was "Psychology of Violence" which contained the historic statement of the French anarchist . . . "It takes a loud voice to make the deaf hear." Having read the book, especially the statement of Vaillant, Bhagat Singh embraced me and said, "Dear Friend, you have given me an excellent piece of literature."'[11] Of course, as we now know, it was that statement which Bhagat Singh and B.K. Dutt used when they hurled their smoke bombs on the Delhi Assembly on 8 April 1929. But this was not all.

Bhagat Singh's voracious reading reshaped his mind. Yet, remarkably he is entirely unknown for it as far as the common man is concerned. He is known for his valour. He is not known for his immense learning. This is despite his comrades being fully aware of the influence of books on him. Shiv Verma memorably records how 'Bhagat Singh always moved with a small portable library. I don't remember even a single occasion when Bhagat Singh was not carrying some books. He had always two things with him – *Pistaul* ("pistol") and *Pustak* ("literary book"). I have seen him ill-clad and almost in rags, but even then he carried some book in his pocket'.[12] His mother, Smt. Vidyavati, in her 'Message to the Youth' on 1 November 1966 recalls how 'whenever Bhagat Singh came home, he always had his pocket full of books'. When she would 'pull him up for spoiling his pockets with these books', an unapologetic Bhagat Singh 'often explained with a smile that the books were about martyrs and patriots'.[13] In short, as Raja Ram Shastri explained, 'Bhagat Singh

literally used to devour books' and 'his thirst for knowledge was
ever unquenched'. There was, however, a method in his madness
because 'he would read books, make notes, discuss with his friends
and critically examine his own understanding in the light of new
knowledge'.[14] At the end of this long road, such was the sea change
in Bhagat Singh's intellectual reconstruction that he is himself seen
to be describing this remodelling in 'Why I Am an Atheist' in the
following terms:

> My previous faith and convictions underwent a remarkable
> modification. The romance of violent methods alone, which
> was so prominent amongst our predecessors, was replaced by
> serious ideas. No more mysticism, no more blind faith. Realism
> became our cult. *Use of force justifiable when resorted to as matter
> of terrible necessity, and non-violence as policy indispensable for all
> mass movements.* So much about methods. The most important
> thing was the clear conception of ideal for which we were
> to fight.[15]

Yet, more remarkable than this is how Bhagat Singh kept up with his
reading even in the face of impending death. This is so surreal as to
be unreal. And yet, it is well documented. When Pran Nath Mehta,
Bhagat Singh's lawyer, went to meet him one last time a few hours
before the time of his hanging on 23 March 1931, he was asked by
the condemned man whether the urbane lawyer had brought him
his book, *The Revolutionary Lenin*, and when Mr Mehta gave him
the book, he set about reading it at once. He knew he had little time
left in this world as a mortal man. The time of his hanging had been
brought forward by eleven hours. As the fateful hour descended upon
him in the twilight of the cool breezy evening, a fellow comrade of
his, Manmathnath Gupta, recalls:

> When called upon to mount the scaffold, Bhagat Singh was reading
> a book by Lenin or on Lenin. He continued his reading and said,
> *'Wait a while. A revolutionary is talking to another revolutionary.'*

There was something in his voice which made the executioners pause. Bhagat Singh continued to read. After a few moments, he flung the book towards [the] ceiling and said, '*Let's go.*'[16]

Small wonder that Ms Virendra Sindhu, Bhagat Singh's niece, has pointed out that another reason for Bhagat Singh's greatness lies in how '*Phansi par jhoolne se pahale, Bhagat Singh samaj ko ek naee vyavastha ka pura chitra pradaan kurna chahte the*'[17] ('Bhagat Singh succeeded in showing the world a new way of dying before mounting the gallows'). In fact, Juneja points out how, '[t]he supply of books by the Dwarka Das Library (Lahore) could not keep pace with his speed of reading. He requisitioned books so frequently that it was a problem for the jail authorities to scrutinize them'.[18] It is not implausible therefore that many of Bhagat Singh's friends should have thought that had he lived he would have become a university professor. Some have even argued that were a statue to be raised in his name, it should show him holding a 'pustak' in his hand and not a 'pistaul'. The librarian, Raja Ram Sashtri, perhaps put it best. A few days before his death, he spoke to Bhagat Singh. His words to the martyred shaheed were: '*Jo sahitya tumne para tha, usko Jeevan mein utaarkar, Bhagat Singh tumne saarthak kar diya.*' ('Whatsoever you read, Bhagat Singh, you brought to Life').[19] Bhagat Singh's legacy lies distorted and only partially realized. Is it any wonder?

39

1928, The Awakening

There is a widespread belief that unlike mainstream politicians like Gandhi, 'these daring young men had no social ideology, no thought to guide their actions'[1] as Bipin Chandra has reminded us. Nothing could be further from the truth. The reality was that the 'major commitment' of the revolutionary movement 'was to liberate India from foreign rule and to transform Indian society through a revolution.'[2] In fact, 'the greatest advance' that they made 'was in the definition and development of their aims and objectives'. So that 'the questions that they sought to answer' were 'What were the aims of their struggle against the foreigners?' and 'What sort of changes in society and polity were they aiming at.' They asked the sort of questions that Gandhi never did, such as 'What sort of social order and state structure would replace the present ones?' And what is remarkable, but remains equally much forgotten to this day, is that 'at the purely intellectual level, they succeeded . . .'[3] because they alone brought about a social awareness about the plight of the Indian people.

As an eighteen-year-old in 1928, when writing in Amritsar's *Kirti* in his native Punjabi, Bhagat Singh was already aware that 'when awareness spreads in the countries, the countries don't sleep' and that 'after a few days, they rise with great enthusiasm and launch an attack', which was why 'today, Hindustan is energised once again. Hindustan is gaining strength again. India is awakening again'.[4] This is why, by the time of his first trial in 1929 before the Delhi Sessions Court, he is able to hail 'the end of an era of Utopian non-violence, of whose futility the rising generation has been convinced beyond the shadow of doubt'.[5] From this, Moffat is led to observe how 'there is a genuine sense in HSRA writings that the revolutionaries find themselves at the moment of *beginning*, a new state in history'.[6] The reason for this is that 'the precedent set by Lenin and his professional revolutionaries is enabling: the Bolshevik stands as the signal of a "New Age" and an emergent world-historical moment'.[7] One reason for this was that,

> Bhagat Singh lived in a decade and in a country where he knew mobilization was possible; Gandhi had demonstrated that much. This precedent, buttressed by assumptions about the inexorability of class war; the example of worker strikes in 1928 Bombay, Calcutta and Madras; and evidence of the state's anxiety to curtail labour mobilisation converge to impress a historical moment which cannot be denied.[8]

Moffat's estimation of the HSRA is that 'they fight for the present and all its possibility: as a volcano on the brink, seething toward a future not yet determined but one which will demand equally that revolutionary spirit'.[9] In fact, he could hardly have put it any better when he insightfully observes that ultimately, 'Bhagat Singh is constituted in popular opinion as *the subject of a discourse of truth*: courageous in his conviction, responsive to singularity, rejecting mysticism and blind faith'.[10] Yet, the question may be asked: what was this 'fight for the present'? And what was this 'possibility' that Moffat was alluding to? They were extraordinarily wide-ranging, extending from free education to an end to war based on 'imperialist designs'; from the rehabilitation of criminals to the replacement of the League of Nations with a world federation and from universal suffrage to a democratic unicameral legislature and the removal of state governors. Not Gandhi, and not anyone else in India's leadership at the time, was advocating such a root and branch reform. And yet, here was a twenty-three-year-old former student doing just that.

When Lala Ram Saran Das, who was sentenced after the first Lahore Conspiracy Case in 1915 to life imprisonment, asked Bhagat Singh to write an introduction to his *The Dreamland*, it gave Bhagat Singh the opportunity to expound upon the nature of society that Bhagat Singh wished to create after his socialist revolution. Saran Das had written the book while detained in Salem Central Prison in the Madras Presidency. After his release from prison in the mid-1920s, he contacted Bhagat Singh and then himself started participating in HSRA politics. In that introduction, Bhagat Singh explained, 'Revolution necessarily implies the programme of systematic reconstruction of society on new and better adopted basis, after complete destruction of the existing state of affairs . . .'.[11] He suggested, 'We revolutionaries are striving to capture power in our hands and to organise a revolutionary government which should employ all its resources for mass education, as is being done in Russia today. After capturing power, peaceful methods shall be employed for constructive work, force shall be employed to crush the obstacles.'[12] Noting that Lala Ram Saran Das had highlighted in his book the 'giving of alms to those in need', Bhagat Singh tersely added the corrective, 'In the future society, i.e. the communist society that we want to build, we are not going to establish charitable institutions, and no alms-giving and alms-taking.' Instead, there will be available for all of India's children a 'free education' and this is because 'the socialist government has adopted somewhat the same course in Russia'.

What Bhagat Singh and his comrades had awakened to, therefore, was a world of limitless possibilities where a new world would be carved out of the present, a world transformed. He advocated a complete political reformation, pointing out how '[c]rime is the most serious social problem which needs a very tactful treatment' so that, 'instead of retribution, i.e. retaliation, the reformative theory should form the basis of punishment. Not to punish but to reclaim should be the guiding principle of the administration of justice. Jails should be reformatories and not veritable hells'. How revolutionary this must have sounded in a colonized land where jails were the lynchpin of a system of oppression by the state. And yet, Bhagat Singh did not hesitate to make the call. As for war, he believed it would become redundant 'because in that society there shall be no conflicting or diverse interests that cause war'. If necessary, 'war shall have to be retained as an institution for the transitional period' only. This is because

[i]mperialist designs shall no more actuate our dreamland people to wage wars. There shall be no more war trophies. The revolutionary armies shall march to other lands not to rule or loot the people, but to pull parasitic rulers down from their thrones and stop their blood seeking exploitation and thus to liberate the toiling masses. But, there shall not be the primitive national or racial hatred to goad our men to fight.[13]

That is not to say that war is essential at all because, as Bhagat Singh points out, '[t]he revolutionaries know better than anybody else that the socialist society cannot be brought about by violent means, but that it should grow and evolve from within'. This is why, while criticising 'the so-called League of Nations', he suggests that a 'world-federation is the most popular and immediate object of all the free thinking people . . .'.[14] As for constitutional reform, only a month before his execution, and while cognizant of the fact that he was going to die, Bhagat Singh wrote to young political workers on 2 February 1931 and described 'the scope of franchise' and recommended that '[t]he property qualifications making a man eligible to vote should be altogether abolished and universal suffrage be introduced instead. Every adult, both male and female, should have the right to vote'.[15] He did not stop there. Bhagat Singh wanted urgent democratic reform, which still eludes India today. He noted how 'we have the bicameral government. In my opinion the upper house is much a *bourgeois* superstition or trap. According to me unicameral government is the only best we can expect'. He then addresses 'provincial autonomy' and declares that 'I can only say that the Governor imposed from above, equipped with extraordinary powers, higher and above the legislative, shall prove to be no less than a despot' and suggests, '[l]et us better call it the "provincial tyranny" instead of "autonomy"' because it was 'a strange type of democratisation of the state institution'.[16] For all these reasons, he is impatient for complete freedom from British rule.

After Bhagat Singh's execution, fragments of a document came to light which had all the references to the Soviet Union, Marx, Lenin and the Communist Party expunged from it and published in a secret report in 1936 by the Government of India. The full report, in the form of a photostat copy, lies today preserved in Lucknow at the Martyrs' Memorial and Freedom Struggle Research Centre[17] and is most revealing, as it is Bhagat Singh's detailed address to the young political workers on 2 February 1931. Here he leaves no doubt that '[t]he present movement is bound to end in some sort of compromise. The compromise may be effected sooner or later. And, compromise is not such an ignoble and deplorable a thing as we generally think. It is rather an indispensable factor in the political strategy. Any nation that rises against the oppressor is bound to fail in the beginning' so that 'it is only at the last stage . . . that it can possibly strike the final blow'. However, as he explains, 'even then it might fail, which makes some sort of compromise inevitable'. He gives the example of how after 1917 'the Bolsheviks were not in a position to face the German onslaught and they preferred the [Brest Litovsk] Treaty to the complete annihilation of the Bolshevik Government'. After giving this as an example, Bhagat Singh is clear he is not accepting defeat in compromise because 'for us, compromise never means surrender, but a step forward and some rest,' thus exhibiting acute strategic acumen.

This suggests that had Lord Irwin only been willing to bend a little, Bhagat Singh may well have compromised and negotiated with him. For Bhagat Singh, compromise is an essential weapon which has to be wielded every now and then as the struggle develops. But the thing that we must keep always before us is the idea of the movement. We must always maintain a clear notion as to the aim for the achievement of which we are fighting. That helps us to verify the success and failures of our movements . . .[18]

Moffat expressed the opinion here that 'even if Bhagat Singh would, in a later essay written in prison, accept the possibility of compromise as part of the "medieval period" of a struggle, what was crucial to the revolutionaries' early actions and public performance was their emphasis on courage and conviction as the conditions for an effective politics'.[19]

It is this courage and conviction that impels Bhagat Singh to oppose so vehemently 'the Minto-Morley Reforms . . . which formed the Viceroy's council with consultation rights only'. He complains of how, 'during the Great war, when the Indian help was needed the most, promises about self-government were made' (and where Gandhi played a pivotal role in recruiting Indian soldiers for the war effort) but that '[u]p till now, the executive was never made responsible to the Legislative Assembly and the Viceroy had the veto power, which rendered all the efforts of the elected members futile'.[20] It is also why Bhagat Singh wrote to young political workers on 2 February 1931 about how '[d]uring the last two years the British politicians have been trying to undo Montagu's promise for another dole of reforms to be bestowed every ten years' and that '[w]e can see what they have decided about the future' and about how they had 'to form a clear idea about our situation, so that we may enlighten the masses and prepare them for a further struggle'.[21] Bhagat Singh is impatient for freedom, but not so naïve as to not recognise the need for compromise. Ultimately, his belief in the masses would see India through, and in this commitment, he enjoins the youth everywhere to take up Marxism. The road ahead would not be easy, as he explains in his address to the young political workers. He proceeds with caution, pointing out, 'let me warn the sincere young workers who seriously mean a revolution, that harder times are coming' because of his enduring distrust of the upper classes of India:

> revolution means the complete overthrow of the existing social order and its replacement with the socialist order. For that purpose our immediate aim is the achievement of power. As a matter of fact, the state, the government machinery is just a weapon in the hands of the ruling class to further and safeguard its interest. We want to snatch and handle it to utilise it for the consummation of our ideal, i.e. the social reconstruction on new, i.e. Marxist, basis. [22]

The weaknesses of Bhagat Singh, as Bipin Chandra has pointed out while recognizing his undoubted qualities as a leader of outstanding abilities, are that his movement failed to become an urban phenomenon.[23] Bhagwan Josh, in his magisterial three-volume chronicle of Indian communism, remarked that Bhagat Singh committed the cardinal strategic error of equating the Indian colonial state with the Russian Czarist state when the two were so different.[24] Grewal has argued that the 'most striking weakness' of Bhagat Singh lay in his failure to account for the structure of feudal landlords in India.[25] And yet, when in our own times in the March 2020 election, the fledgling *Aam Aadmi Party* swept the Punjab polls, its triumphant party leader, 'Kejriwal quoted legendary freedom fighter Bhagat Singh as saying that without a change in the system, nothing could change.'[26] Change remains a distant hope.

40

The Legacy

Fears that Bhagat Singh's legacy risked being consigned to oblivion arose soon after Independence. The fears were not without foundation. The Congress politician Asaf Ali, who represented Bhagat Singh in the Assembly Bomb Case 1929, in a newspaper article in Pune 1949 expressed his deep concern that Bhagat Singh, who had only until a few years earlier been a 'household name', stood now to just become 'a page of history which has grown dim' and nothing more than an 'obsolescent page' in India's history.[1] Thirty years later, when G.S. Deol came to write his biography in 1978, he was afraid that the essence of Bhagat Singh risked being entirely diluted if he was being seen 'only as freedom fighter' because this was 'to do injustice to the work of this great son of India'.[2] In order to do 'full honour to his work', what was needed, argued Hooja, was detailed research into Bhagat Singh's life and ideas.[3] Ashok Dhawale observes that Bhagat Singh's thought can be compartmentalized into four aspects of revolutionary struggle. These were his 'struggle against imperialism', his 'resistance to communalism and caste oppression', his 'opposition to bourgeois landlord rule', and his belief in 'Marxism and socialism'.[4] And yet, Bhagat Singh is survived today only by his handwritten manifestoes, letters, essays, notes and pamphlets, and much of this, as Moffat points out, which 'as a prisoner between 1929 and 1931 remains contested'.[5]

Bhagat Singh's nephew Jagmohan Singh, the son of his sister Bibi Amar Kaur, has produced the most well-known compilation of Bhagat Singh's writings, statements and letters in a 1982 Punjabi publication by the name of *Bhagat Singh Ate Uhna De Saathian Diyan Likhtaan*[6] ('Bhagat Singh and his Comrades' Collected Writings'). This is a welcome development. As much as sixty years after Independence. What Bhagat Singh is alleged to have said is still being contested. This is why K.C. Yadav has made a plea for scholars of Bhagat Singh 'to go to the original sources'.[7] Jagmohan Singh declared in an interview that 'it is our duty to liberate Bhagat Singh from current misinterpretations'. In a rebuke to emerging ethnonationalistic political movements, he added, 'Bhagat Singh cannot be frozen in a cheap emotional and nationalistic frame.'[8] The failure to do so risks misappropriation by right-wing ideologues, which will be the cause of 'Bhagat Singh's Second Hanging'.[9] So important is the task of remaining true to the real Bhagat Singh that in 2019, even some seventy years after Independence, in the memorable words of the noted western scholar, Dr Chris Moffat, 'To know what Bhagat Singh died for is to know why the living should also fight.'[10] He writes, 'If Bhagat Singh has been neglected – if he has been sidelined or sentimentalised – then to reconsider the revolutionary is a critical action, challenging the certainties otherwise attached to dominant Gandhian nationalist or socialist stories of postcolonial becoming.'[11] This indeed seems to be the reason for what Krishna Pratap Singh has described as 'the fate of the many revolutionaries whose memories have been cast into the abyss of oblivion'.[12]

In 1986, one of the three released Lahore conspirators, Shiv Verma, published a collection of Bhagat Singh's writings, where he castigated the attempt 'to distort the ideological side of the revolutionary movement' by portraying them as 'blood-thirsty demons' and with 'no aim, no set purpose in life' because, as he explained, '[t]hat Bhagat Singh was an intellectual of high calibre is not known to many'. This is why he had now 'strived to put all available writings of Bhagat Singh at one place and to leave it to the reader to form his own opinion . . .'.[13] In the same way, P.C. Joshi, a leading light of the Indian communist movement, referred during the rise of the Naxalite rebellion in 1969 to what distinguished Bhagat Singh as, 'his undying thirst for knowledge', while still recognizing him as 'the emblem of death-defying determination'.[14] Chaman Lal writes of him that while he was 'fond of films, especially Charlie Chaplin films' and was even renowned as 'a good singer and actor' who took part in college plays, nonetheless also, 'he was a voracious reader – as the Jail Notebook testifies, and had a fine understanding of literature'.[15]

One reason for this reckoning is, as Chris Moffat has argued, that 'Bhagat Singh is often left to speak for himself in histories written'.[16] This is because most books written on him have relied heavily on the citation of large tracts from his writings and speeches, leaving it to the reader to gauge the depth and nuance of the stance that he took during his short life. The result is that, invariably, 'over one-third' of a book may consist of 'appended documents'[17] and in other cases 'the author may reproduce documents in their entirety allowing the protagonist to interject at critical moments',[18] not to mention those books where 'scanned version of newspaper articles and written notes are provided . . .'.[19] They are intended to be, according to Moffat, 'more than simple riches' because 'these writings are wielded as though they will – through the very power of their contents – *change* or *incite* the reader'.[20] In this way, there developed a relationship between the writer and the now-gone Bhagat Singh of 'perfect necromancy' that is ultimately 'a more genuine communication with the dead' that is 'for the sake of the present and the future'.[21]

For his part, Moffat sets out on a different course as he searches for a 'corrective' which is 'not a routine matter of historical excavation but an interventionist act of historical emendation'. The task at hand, he argues, must be 'to challenge certainties' and to 'transform expectations'. This being so, the 'impulse' must be 'to question the form that this pantheon has taken'. The questions to grapple with are, 'How can a figure as impressive as Bhagat Singh be relegated to the periphery? What has been lost in these years of distortion and simplification? And what can be gained by finally "knowing", by arriving at his "true" form at long last?'[22] This indeed is the question for us today. There is no claim here to finding a definitive answer. Rather, the claim is to a continuing endeavour or, as Moffat proclaims, 'to identify obscured alternatives'.[23] If we could identify some key statements and writings of Bhagat Singh and his accomplices, can we truly acquire an understanding of what he stood for? Some answers are readily available for those who care to look.

Bhagat Singh's slogan of 'Long live the Revolution' was drawn from other world revolutionaries before him. In a riposte to Ramanand Chatterji, the editor of *Modern Review*, that the phrase was pointless as it perpetuated the notion of endless agitation, Bhagat Singh and B.K. Dutt gave an explanation which was published in the *Tribune* on 24 December 1929, saying, 'We are not the originators of this cry.' This was because 'the same cry had been used in Russian Revolutionary movements'. However, Bhagat Singh had a far better sense of the development of the term, pointing out that '[t]he sense in which the word Revolution is used in that phrase, is the spirit, the longing for a change for the better'. This is because '[t]he people generally get accustomed to the established order of things and begin to tremble at the very idea of change', but that '[i]t is this lethargical spirit that needs to be replaced by the revolutionary spirit'. It is in this sense that '[t]he spirit of Revolution should always permeate the soul of humanity, so that the reactionary forces may not accumulate strength to check its eternal onward march'. In this way, the '[o]ld order should change, always and ever, yielding place to new, so that one "good" order may not corrupt the world'. This confirms what was said two months earlier on 19 October 1929, when Subhas Chandra Bose opened the Second Punjab Students' Conference in Lahore. He opened it with a signed statement from Bhagat Singh and B.K. Dutt, which he read out in the opening session. This proclaimed, 'Today, we cannot ask the youth to take pistols and bombs.' It clearly demonstrated Bhagat Singh's opposition to violence for its own sake.

He reposed his faith rather in the fact that '[t]he youth will have to spread this revolutionary message to the far corners of the country. They have to awaken crores of slum-dwellers of the industrial areas and villagers living in worn-out cottages, so that we will be independent and the exploitation of man by man will become an impossibility'. Not surprisingly, Shiv Verma, who was at the meeting, noted how the opening address was met with 'a thunderous applause' accompanied by 'slogans of Bhagat Singh Zindabad'.[24]

41

Interpreting Bhagat Singh

How then should we interpret Bhagat Singh? While it is absolutely important to take Bhagat Singh's ideas and writings seriously, there is not much to be gained in calling him the 'Indian Frantz Fanon'. Bhagat Singh was after all writing so many years earlier in a very different global conjuncture, and there are themes that are so vital to Fanon—race, consciousness, psychology—that do not appear in Bhagat Singh's writings in any real sense. Moreover, although Bhagat Singh is associated with violence, his position changes, and there is no explicit meditation on the redemptive power of 'killing the colonizer' as we see articulated in Fanon's *Wretched of the Earth*. It is enough to note the continuities, and indeed the differences, between Bhagat Singh and the later Fanon, but Bhagat Singh should be analysed on his own grounds and in his own context, without the need to attach him to another, such as the 'Indian Che' or the 'Indian Lenin'. That does not explain why he is unknown in the West, and nor is it to excuse it, but it is to emphasize how it is all the more important that this lacuna be rectified. One way to do this is to capture the essence of Bhagat Singh in his scattered and fragmented writings, in an attempt at intellectual reconstruction, so that alternative ways of thinking about his importance can be brought out.

Is this an exercise worth conducting? Yes, it is. Why? Because this mass heedlessness, absent-mindedness and inattention to the facts have obscured the full story of how Independence was achieved in India. Some Indian historians have recognized this, which is why Navtej Singh has referred to it as one of the 'myths' that are 'widespread in bourgeois historiography', that 'Gandhi and the Indian National Congress, with the methods of non-violence and peaceful non-cooperation and civil disobedience, were instrumental in achieving India's independence from the much-hated British Raj'.[1] In his recent book on Har Dayal, who set up the Ghadar Party (i.e. 'rebellion' party) in San Francisco on 1 November 1913, in what he describes as 'the largest international anti-colonial resistance movement',[2] Bhuvan Lall says of Bhagat Singh that he of all people had through his actions 'redeemed and somewhat exceeded the anticolonial objectives of the Ghadr of 1857 and the Ghadr movement in California'.[3] How did Bhagat Singh manage to do that?

First, Bhagat Singh drew from a far wider and deeper source of influences for his convictions than Gandhi ever did when he refers to actions of men such as Washington and Garibaldi, Lafayette and Lenin. This is how Bhagat Singh became the ultimate rationalist in the Indian revolutionary struggle. What distinguished him from other revolutionaries of the time was how, having started off life in the burning embers of insurgent Lyallpur and Lahore, his political development was ultimately refashioned, remoulded and refined by the vast array of international radical literature into which he immersed himself and imbibed right until the very moment of his hanging. He read not only Marx, Engels and Trotsky but also Thomas Paine, Upton Sinclair, Morris Hillquit and Jack London. He went on to read Victor Hugo, Dostoevsky, Spinoza and Bertrand Russell. Classical works were not overlooked so he also read John Stuart Mill, Thomas Jefferson, Kautsky, Bukharin, Burke, Lenin, Thomas Aquinas, Danton, Omar Khayyam, Tagore, N.A. Morozov, Herbert Spencer, Henry Maine and Rousseau. There is also his famous *Jail Book*, which came to light in 1974, of which Moffat writes that it 'includes fragments copied from the work of some seventy different authors and which can be read in a myriad of ways, emphasising the passages on Marx rather than those on Rousseau . . .' and where one can see 'Bhagat Singh's appreciation of Byron and Tennyson or his interest in natural law'.[4]

Second, he believed in personal sacrifice for the attainment of his ideals, including having to give up his life if necessary. Prison gave him the opportunity to read voraciously. So much so that it is said that he wrote four books in prison which were lost after they were smuggled out. A letter written from Lahore Central Jail on 24 July 1930 to Jaidev Gupta, who was a close school friend from boyhood days, implores the latter to 'take the following books in my name from Dwarkadas Library' and have them sent to him through his younger brother, Kulvir, by the following Sunday.[5] The range of the books asked for is astonishing:

'*Militarism* (Karl Liebknecht) *Why Men Fight* (B. Russell)
Soviets at Work   *Collapse of the Second International*
Left-Wing Communism   *Mutual Aid* (Prince Kropotkin)
Fields. Factories and Workshops *Civil War in France* (Marx)
Land Revolution in Russia   *Spy* (Upton Sinclair)'

To this list, Bhagat Singh added 'one more book from Punjab Public Library: Historical Materialism (Bukharin)' and asked 'if some books have been sent to Borstal Jail' because '[t]hey are facing a terrible famine of books' as '[t]hey have not received any book till now'. He rounded off by demanding, 'Also send *Punjab Peasants in Prosperity and Debt* by Malcolm Lyall Darling'.[6]

Bhagat Singh's comrade Shiv Verma said of him, 'No other revolutionary struck such deep rapport with the awakening people, no other became so endeared to the common people and youth as Bhagat Singh did.' One reason for this was that '[a]s an intellectual Bhagat Singh was far superior to any of us'. For this reason, Navtej Singh writes that 'he saw further than his comrades' so that 'it was at his suggestion and insistence that the word socialist was added to the name of the HRA, and the ideas of socialism, formulated in greater depth . . .'.[7]

Nevertheless, the extent of what Bhagat Singh wrote, from the time that he was taken prisoner on 8 April 1929 to the time that he was executed on 23 March 1931, remains contested. Indeed, it has entered into the realms of a make-believe world, populated by conjecture, supposition and even fantasy, to such an extent that it has today acquired a fabled and mythological life, all of its own. There is a reason for this. Take his four legendary books. They have never been found. But Shiv Verma, who was in jail with Bhagat Singh, confirmed later as an editor of Bhagat Singh's selected writings that four books were written by the revolutionary. Chaman Lal, who has written most extensively about this matter, is circumspect, observing, 'It is not clear if Verma actually read or saw these manuscripts or simply heard Bhagat Singh saying that he is working on them.'[8] Nevertheless, what is undoubtedly maintained by Chaman Lal is that 'clearly Bhagat Singh did write something, and what he wrote was smuggled out of the jail by Kumari Lajjawati of Jalandhar'.[9] So the well-settled view appears to be that, after he toiled away to complete his writings, some of them were secretly whisked out of prison into the trusting hands of Kumari Lajjawati, who was after all the secretary of the Lahore Conspiracy Case Defence Committee as well as a renowned Congress activist. She had been visiting the Central Jail in Lahore frequently to ensure that the Lahore conspirators were given such legal assistance in their defence as was possible. She is even said to have tied a 'rakhee' (a talisman that celebrates brotherhood and love) on Bhagat Singh's wrist. The bundle of documents that had been handed over were shown by Lajjawati to the editor of *The People*, Lala Feroz Chand, this being the newspaper founded by Lala Lajpat Rai.

At any rate, this is what Lajjawati appears to have said when she was interviewed for the oral history archive of the Nehru Memorial Museum & Library.[10] The disclosure to Lala Feroz Chand of the bundle of documents enabled the publication of one of the writings of Bhagat Singh, namely, his celebrated, 'Why I Am an Atheist', on

27 September 1931. This was designed to coincide with what would have been Bhagat Singh's twenty-fourth birthday. Indeed, further extracts were also published and these included Bhagat Singh's 'Letter to Young Political Workers'. However, the bundle of documents has never been found. The reason for this is that Lajjawati herself passed them over to Bejoy Kumar Sinha in 1938, after he had served his sentence of transportation for life in the dreaded Andaman Islands following his trial with Bhagat Singh in the Lahore Conspiracy Case. He passed them over to another friend, who wasted little time in destroying them as he feared being raided by the police. In the words of Chaman Lal, 'The loss of these invaluable documents must surely rank as one of the great tragedies of the period.' That a bundle of documents existed appears to be the considered view of Chaman Lal for as he explains,

> Bhagat Singh's father was keen to acquire the papers, or at least to see them. Lajjawati refused to give them to him, purportedly on Bhagat Singh's own instructions. We must consider ourselves fortunate that some member of his family, probably Kulbir Singh, managed to retrieve Jail Notebook . . .[11]

This throws up a couple of questions. First, if the bundle of documents, smuggled out of prison by Kumari Lajjawati was eventually destroyed by an unnamed friend of Bejoy Kumar Sinha, with only 'Why I Am an Atheist' and 'Letter to Young Political Workers' being published, how can we know for sure that four named book manuscripts also specifically existed? Second, the fact that the two named articles were indeed published from this smuggled bundle of documents by Lala Feroz Chand does suggest that something was in all probability written during his two years in jail, although it is unlikely that he would have had the time to complete four books in their entirety. This much is fairly recognized by Chaman Lal, noting of Bhagat Singh how 'during this time, he was engaged in agitation inside the jail, as well preparing for the trial'. This being so, 'it seems unlikely that he could actually have finished writing four full-fledged books, even considering his enormous energy and willpower'.[12] Nevertheless, the belief that a treasure trove of lost Bhagat Singh documents existed refuses to die. This is perhaps best encapsulated in the journalist Bhupendra Hooja's lament that 'the vacuum of these precious manuscripts' is something which 'no amount of literature on or about Bhagat Singh . . . can fill'.[13] The result is, as Moffat points out, that at the very least the existence of 'a fragmented assemblage of personal notes' is something which today 'fuels a narrative of unconsecrated potential, opening space for rumination'.[14] Yet, if it were possible so to do, what would a consecrated potential look like? This is the perpetual question to which an answer must be sought.

42

1931, 'Mahatma Ji Is Great'

Bhagat Singh was a contender for power with Gandhi. Had he lived, Gandhi would have been forced to share power with him. When Bhagat Singh wrote to young political workers on 2 February 1931 (just over a month before he was to be executed), he urged that 'for any revolutionary party a definite programme is very essential' because 'you must know that revolution means action' and that '[i]t means a change brought about deliberately by an organised and systematic work'. He further wrote,

> We want a socialist revolution, the indispensable preliminary to which is the political revolution. That is what we want. The political revolution does not mean the transfer of state (or more crudely, the power) from the hands of the British to the Indians, but to Indians who are at one with us as to the final goal, or to be more precise, the power to be transferred to the revolutionary part through popular support. After that, to proceed in right earnest is to organise the reconstruction of the whole society on the socialist basis.[1]

Since he distrusted the middle classes, he proclaimed, 'The only forces on which you can rely to bring about any revolution, whether national or the socialist, are the peasantry and the labour. Congress leaders do not dare organise those forces,' because to 'their hearts' desire – Dominion Status', which he was against, was what they were after. He drew upon the evidence and asserted that '[y]ou can easily judge it by studying the resolutions of the last three sessions of the Congress' which were at 'Madras, Calcutta and Lahore', one can see how '[a]t Calcutta, they passed a resolution asking for Dominion Status within twelve months, otherwise they would be forced to adopt complete independence as their object . . .'.

He continued, 'It is this half-heartedness that we hate, not the compromise at a particular stage in the struggle.' He wished to protect the rural masses, arguing that 'if you say that you will approach the peasants and labourers to enlist their active support' then

> [t]hey ask you quite candidly: what are they going to gain by your revolution for which you demand their sacrifices, what difference does it make to them whether Lord Reading is the head of the Indian government of Sir Purshotamdas Thakordas? What difference for a peasant if Sir Tej Bahadur Sapru replaces Lord Irwin! It is useless to appeal to his national sentiment.

Being against such use and abuse of the masses, Bhagat Singh argued for 'the revolution of the proletariat and for the proletariat'.[2] In a veiled attack on Gandhi, he argued that 'the policy of voluntarily going to jail should altogether be abandoned'.[3]

Bhagat Singh would definitely not have endeared himself to Mahatma Gandhi when he talked of the 'mental stagnation' that inhibits 'criticism and independent thinking', which are 'the two indispensable qualities of a revolutionary' and he was scathing about a mentality whereby,

> Because MahatmaJi is great, therefore none should criticise him. Because he has risen above, therefore everything he says – may be

in the field of Politics or Religion, Economics, or Ethics – is right. Whether you are convinced or not you must say: 'Yes, that's true'. This mentality does not lead towards progress.[4]

Bhagat Singh also strongly disagreed with Gandhi's own personal attitude to the Indian peasantry whom he disfavoured over the middle-class. When advising the young political workers, Bhagat Singh was very critical of the 'middle class shopkeepers and a few capitalists' who he said 'can never dare to risk its property or possessions in any struggle.', Whilst Gandhi overlooked the poor and the disenfranchised, Bhagat Singh's view was that, 'the real revolutionary forces have not been invited into the arena'. As he explained, 'The real revolutionary armies are in the villages and in factories, the peasantry and the labourers. But our bourgeois leaders do not and cannot dare to tackle them.'[5] As a result, he is openly critical of Gandhi. This is because,

> After his first experience with the Ahmedabad labourers in 1920 Mahatma Gandhi declared: 'We must not tamper with the labourers. It is dangerous to make political use of the factory proletariat' (*The Times*, May 1921). Since then, they never dared to approach them. . . . The Bardoli resolution of 1922 clearly defines the horror the leaders felt when they saw the gigantic peasant class rising to shake off not only the domination of an alien nation but also the yoke of the landlords. [6]

So critical was Bhagat Singh of this stance that he added how 'it is here that our leaders prefer a surrender to the British than to the peasantry'. He demanded bitterly,

> Apart from Pt. Jawahar Lal can you point to any leader, who made any effort to organise the peasants or the labourers? No, they will not run the risk. There they lack. That is why I say they never meant a complete revolution. Through economic and administrative pressure they hoped to get a few more reforms [from the British],

a few more concessions for the Indian capitalists. That is why I say that this movement is doomed to die . . .[7]

It is interesting to see here how similar this view is to that of Fanon. Like Bhagat Singh, who criticized Gandhi, Fanon also wrote, 'The politicians who make speeches and who write in the nationalist newspapers make people dream dreams. They avoid the actual overthrowing of the State . . .'[8]

Bhagat Singh ultimately disagreed with Gandhi's satyagraha (a policy of passive political resistance). In an essay written in Punjabi in June 1928, when he was on the editorial board of *Kirti*, he explained why. This was the year when the biggest satyagraha was being held by the peasants of Bardoli (in Gujarat). He wrote, 'After every thirty years taxes are revised and every time the tax on the land is raised.' He continued, 'The same thing happened this year as well and the tax has been hiked . . . But what are the people to do?' The problem was acute because '[t]he peasant in any case is not able to fill his belly and how can he pay 22% more tax than before?'. As the preparations were made for satyagraha, he notes how 'Mahatma Gandhi corresponded with the Governor of Punjab to try and get the tax reduced, but Sir, this government is not about to bend only through letters. It had no effect'.

The same thing had happened some years earlier when 'in 1917-18 the crop had rotted due to excessive rains and was not even worth one fourth of the price of the normal crop'. Since '[t]he law stated that tax would not be collected if the crop was less than six annas worth in a rupee,' the people protested the demand for tax but 'the government did not heed their word. Then Mahatma Gandhiji took the matter into his hands and held a meeting. He explained to the people that if they refused to pay the tax their land would be confiscated, and asked them if they were prepared for that'.[9] It is the repeated compromise that Bhagat Singh resented, and this is why on 2 February 1931 he was still as defiant as ever and wrote that '[w]e should not have any illusion about the possibilities, failures and achievements of Congress movement' which should 'be better stamped Gandhianism'. For him, '[i]t does not stand for freedom avowedly; it is in favour of "Partnership" – a strange interpretation of what "complete independence" signifies. Its method is novel, and but for the helplessness of the people',' he was convinced that 'Gandhianism would gain no adherent . . .'. What he meant by this was that '[i]t has fulfilled the role of an intermediate party' which is 'controlled mostly by men with stakes in the country, who prize their stakes with bourgeoisie tenacity . . .'.[10] Therefore, '[in a sense Gandhianism' is a creed that 'counts on mass action, though not for the masses alone'.[11] On the other hand, Bhagat Singh's philosophy was that '[w]hat we mean by Revolution is quite plain. In this century it can only mean one thing – the capture of the political power by the masses for the masses'. Indeed, '[t]he proletariat revolution is the only weapon of India to dislodge the Imperialist'.[12] Today the imperialists have gone but not imperialist thinking. Colonialism has gone but not neo-colonialism. And India is free but remains unfree.

43

1928, Lala Lajpat Rai

One thing that is much overlooked in Bhagat Singh's avenging of Lala Lajpat Rai's death by the cold-blooded shooting of J.P. Saunders on 17 December 1928 is the extent to which Bhagat Singh himself did not agree with Lala Lajpat Rai on the question of communal coexistence. We have tended to overlook this difference because our focus has been on the barbaric use of colonial violence and the colonized people's avenging of that violence. Like Bhagat Singh, who had shot a policeman in broad daylight, Fanon too explained,

> The colonial world is a world cut into two. The dividing line, the frontiers are shown by barracks and police stations. In the colonies it is the policeman and the soldier who are the official, instituted go-betweens, the spokesmen of the settler and his rule of oppression.[1]

The fact that a policeman's lathi had killed Lala Lajpat Rai as he participated in a protest in Lahore against the Simon Commission was significant in that, in the words of Fanon:

> In the colonial countries . . . [t]he policeman and the soldier, by their immediate presence and their frequent and direct action

maintain contact with the native and advise him by means of rifle-butts and not to budge. It is obvious here that the agents of government speak the language of pure force.[2]

At another place, writing in 1952 in *Black Skin, White Masks*, Fanon had remarked how '. . . Europe has a racist structure'.[3] Fanon stridently asserts,

> The violence which has ruled over the colonial world, which has ceaselessly drummed the rhythm for the destruction of native social forms . . . that same violence will be claimed and taken over by the native at the moment when deciding to embody history in his own person, he surges into the forbidden quarters.[4]

And indeed, it is precisely this violence that Bhagat Singh puts into practical effect by assassinating J.P. Saunders. What Fanon was here putting in writing as a political philosophy had already been put into practical operation by Bhagat Singh. To that extent there is a moral necessity in the violence of Bhagat Singh and his comrades. If the Indian masses had united in a violent overthrow of their colonial subjugation there is every reason to believe that Hindus, Muslims and Sikhs would today be living together in one united country rather than in separate individual enclaves. This is why Fanon considered anti-colonial violence so important as he wrote that 'the native's violence unites the people. By its very structure, colonisation is separatist and regionalist. Colonialism does not simply state the existence of the tribes; it also reinforces it and separates them'. However, '[a]t the level of individuals, violence is a cleansing force. It frees the native from his inferiority complex and from his despair and inaction; it makes him fearless and restores his self-respect'.[5] It is this 'cleansing force' of the violence in the assassination of J.P. Saunders that has come to be applauded by those opposed to colonial rule in India. In the process, it has obscured the difference between the act of avenging and the person on whose behalf it was undertaken. It is time to set the record straight.

The extent of Bhagat Singh's disagreement with Lala Lajpat Rai is intriguing, in that although Bhagat Singh revered Lajpat Rai as a leader of the militant nationalist freedom movement in his own right, he did not always see eye-to-eye with him. Indeed, a number of his disagreements were fundamental. They went to the core of how the fight for freedom should be fought. For one thing, Bhagat Singh could not agree with Lajpat Rai 'that India should be divided into two countries: Hindu India and Muslim India'. This is because Hindus and Muslims had lived together 'side by side in thousands of towns, villages, and hamlets for hundreds of years' and 'they shared each other's sorrow and happiness, heritage and history'. In fact, 'they toiled together and suffered together' such that 'the entire country belonged to both the communities'. For this reason, 'Bhagat Singh feared that if Lajpat Rai's idea of a division of the country along religious lines ever took shape, it would be disastrous' and that 'there would be a bloodbath'. And, of course, so it came to be. Bhagat Singh was proven right. Lajpat Rai was proven wrong. This is not to say that Lajpat Rai did not in turn think Bhagat Singh to be equally mistaken in his philosophy. In fact, while Bhagat Singh 'regretted his tilt towards Hindu chauvinism', the fact was that 'Lajpat Rai, in turn, had denounced him as a "Russian agent"' and even 'regarded revolutionaries as "irresponsible" young men'.[6]

Not surprisingly Bhagat Singh, the martyr, political activist, thinker, revolutionary, took a different view. That he should do so is interesting. Deviating from a man whom he had always looked up to, however, was based on high principle. This is today unrecognized because Bhagat Singh is known for the most part only as a revolutionary firebrand. This in turn is because what we know of him comes from the stand that Bhagat Singh so boldly took before the judges of the special tribunal before whom he was beaten and humiliated and yet remained staunchly defiant to the end. But there was another Bhagat Singh. This was Bhagat Singh the writer and journalist. This is important because in his writings Bhagat Singh strongly castigated communalism in favour of a society based on tolerance, pluralism, diversity and broad-mindedness.

The main differences between the two of them arose from the
fact that Bhagat Singh was a socialist. Lala Lajpat Rai was not. In
a piece written in Punjabi in 1928, 'Lala Lajpat Rai and the Youth',
Bhagat Singh explains how Lala Lajpat Rai had dismissed, 'these
propagandist young men as misguided'.[7] He notes how 'Lalaji says
that our socialist ideas will cause the capitalists to join forces with
the government', but disagreeing with him Bhagat Singh ventures
to ask: 'How many capitalists have become harbingers of change?'.
The reality is that '[i]n a revolution anyone who fears his wealth
and property may be harmed will always oppose it', which is why
'[i]n such a situation, to abandon one's principles to appease them
and damage our own cause is not appropriate'.[8] In a searing critique,
which exposes the difference between Bhagat Singh and his mentor,
he adds: 'Lalaji himself is a great man. He travels by the first or the
second class. How would he know the people who travel in the third
class?' Indeed, '[h]ow would he know who endures kicks in the third
class waiting rooms?'.

In fact, Lala Lajpat Rai's distance from his people is only made
worse when '[h]e sits in the motor car and passes through thousands of
villages, laughing and joking with his friends'. Given this, 'how would
we know what thousands of people go through'.[9] For this reason, it
is not leaders like Lala Lajpat Rai, but the youth of India like Bhagat
Singh, who understand the plight of their people because '[w]hen we
see the peasants work in the heat, cold rain, sun, hot-low winds and
foggy day and night' and notice how 'these poor people make do with
dry crumbs – and are burdened by debt', one has to ask, '[d]on't we
burn with agony? Does not a fire rage in our hearts?'[10] What is needed
are 'new ideas in this new environment'.[11] All this emphasized how
Bhagat Singh's revolution was intended to be a revolution of ideas.
Lala Lajpat Rai's stance in this respect would only replace one form
of tyranny with another. This is why Bhagat Singh asks the rhetorical
question: 'Does Lalaji want that now we should rebel against the
English rulers and hand over the reins in the hands of the rich?'[12]

To his abiding regret, Bhagat Singh laments the fact that 'Lala
Lajpat Rai has, for some reason, from the very beginning been against

the youth movements'. This is surprising, because like Bhagat Singh, '[h]e imbibed his idea of patriotism from the great Giuseppe Mazzini of Italy', and ironically, 'Mazzini was a great admirer of the youth' for 'their voice carries magic'.[13] It would appear that one reason why Lala Lajpat Rai did not trust the youth was because of the events of 1907, when the young Ajit Singh made a fiery speech at Lyallpur. That had resulted in both him and Lala Lajpat Rai being subject to a sentence of deportation. This is why 'Lalaji expounds that people should be wary of the movements led by the hot-headed youth of today', but as Bhagat Singh asks, 'Why dig up the past of 1907-08?'[14]

In fact, such criticism of the youth was not always justified because Bhagat Singh used the pen much more than the sword. This is where his skill as a journalist came into its own, and yet it is a feature of Bhagat Singh's persona that has historically been overlooked. English, Hindi, Urdu and Punjabi were the four languages that he could turn his hand to. As a renegade on the run, he even got to grips with some Bengali. These are remarkable feats for a man who was put to death by the age of twenty-three years, when most people have barely embarked on a career in journalism. His forays in journalism were published in such journals and pamphlets as *Kirti*, *Pratap*, *Vir Arjun*, *Milap* and in *Akali*. Tantalizingly, much of his writings were signed off under pseudonyms, so we will never be able to recover what would have been the full range of his written thoughts.

The loss is incalculable when one considers how, while not yet an adult, he had succeeded at the age of seventeen at compiling a written translation of the book by revolutionary Dan Breen, *My Fight for Irish Freedom*[15] from English to Hindi. All this he was able to do because he was a consummate reader. Nothing demonstrates this more vividly than his 716 days in prison, when Bhagat Singh won the right, after going on hunger strike, to have access in prison to more than 300 books, of which 63 were in Hindi, 197 were in English, 28 were in Urdu, 17 were in Bengali and 7 were in Punjabi. He read them, digested them and made notes on them, all while living a day-by-day existence in the shadow of the hangman's noose.

He read so widely so that he could agitate all the more rigorously because, to the end, he remained wary of religious communalism. He could see how this was fanned by unscrupulous political leaders, aided and abetted by a communalized press. It made him all the more determined to use every means at his disposal to quell such developments in the community of which he was a part. It mattered not if such communal instincts were displayed by one such as Lala Lajpat Rai whom he revered. Such forces had to be opposed. Whether it was Lala Lajpat Rai's predisposition towards Hindu chauvinism that was misguided or Bhagat Singh's revolutionary fervour was a matter on which different people at the time were to take different views. It would suffice to say that the record of history as to how events were to unfold when India eventually acquired Independence in 1947 speaks for itself. The country erupted into a communal carnage, the scars of which are still visible today.

PART 9

MARTYRDOM

Ye kiska lahu hai kaun marah;
Ae rehbar e mulk o qaum bata;
Nazren to utha aankhen to mila

Whose blood is this? Whose life destroyed?
Pray, tell me, oh ruler! Oh country most pitiful!
Raise your eyes; and look me in my face.

—Sahir Ludhianvi

44

Kartar Singh Sarabha

Did Bhagat Singh set out to die from the very beginning? Was this how he planned to sacrifice himself in the cause of India's freedom? Or was he just oblivious to death? If so, could he have saved himself if he so wished? Of course, in one sense we will never know what he thought or might have intended. In another sense, however, there is the evidence. How is this evidence to be interpreted? Martyrdom was, of course, something of which Bhagat Singh had early knowledge. To be a 'martyr' was to be called a 'shaheed'. There was no nobler way to fight for India's Independence than to die in its cause. And Bhagat Singh was not the first to do so. It was the ultimate sacrifice that a freedom fighter could make for the love of his motherland, and India had an illustrious line of shaheeds'. Two incidents in particular left a lasting impression on his young mind. The first such event was when Bhagat Singh was still only a child of eight years of age. This was the hanging of seven Ghadar martyrs over 16 and 17 November 1915 by the British, in what became known as the First Lahore Conspiracy Case. Among those who were put to death was Kartar Singh Sarabha, who was barely twenty years old and was the man that Bhagat Singh grew up to adore and eventually emulate. Such was the devotion that the manner of his death commanded that when in March 1926 Bhagat Singh, Sukhdev and Bhagwati

Charan Vohra established the Naujawan Bharat Sabha in Lahore, they consciously set its tone from the outset by unveiling at its inaugural session a portrait of Kartar Singh Sarabha, in what would have been an act of extreme provocation for the authorities as well as an act of sedition. Bhagat Singh himself was known to regularly carry a photograph of Kartar Singh Sarabha in his pocket and was found carrying it when arrested in 1929. A page of the judgment sentencing Kartar Singh Sarabha to death, which bears some hand-written notes by Bhagat Singh, is on display at the Shaheed-e-Azam Bhagat Singh Museum in Katkar Kalan.

After all, Kartar Singh Sarabha was one of Bhagat Singh's childhood heroes. In 1912, he left Ludhiana in Punjab for San Francisco. Entering Berkeley University as an engineering student, he founded the Ghadar Party. This was an international political movement established in the United States on 15 July 1913. It was initially called the Pacific Coast Hindustan Association, and it was formed with the express aim of overthrowing British rule in India, under the leadership of Har Dayal along with other Indians there. When the First World War broke out, the Ghadar Party too declared its *Ailan-i-Jang* on Britain in the form of a declaration of war, following which Sarabha hastened to return to India. Upon arrival he was unfortunately betrayed by an accomplice in 1915, just as Bhagat Singh was in his time by his own comrades. Upon being captured, he was put not before a regular court for trial, but before a specially convened tribunal, just as Bhagat Singh was to be just over a decade later. It was a special tribunal that sentenced Sarabha to death in what came to be known as the First Lahore Conspiracy Case.[1] It was also of course a special tribunal which sentenced Bhagat Singh to death in what came to be known as the Second Lahore Conspiracy Case 1931. Barely an adult at 19, Sarabha was also charged with the same offence of conspiracy against the King as Bhagat Singh. The First World War was ongoing during Kartar Singh Sarabha's hanging. Tensions were high. His death in November 1915 was essential to the Raj.

Yet, death in revolution was not just a matter for the executioner. It was also a matter of importance for the executed.

It was his prerogative no less. This is best epitomized in the words of Ram Prasad Bismil, a revolutionary poet who took part in the Mainpuri Conspiracy 1918 and the Kakori Conspiracy 1925. He was hanged on 19 December 1927. Popularly known as 'Bismil' and associated with the Arya Samaj, he wrote the poem '*sarfaroshī kī tamannā ab hamāre dil meñ hai*'[2] (meaning, 'The desire for revolution is in our hearts'), where the word '*sarfaroshī*' quite literally means the giving of one's head for a higher gain. Bismil was not alone in extolling the virtues of sacrifice to the extent of embracing *shahidee*. In her insightful analysis, Simona Sawhney draws attention to 'the figure of Shaheed, the one who bears witness to the truth of the nation and stands by that truth, even unto death'. We can 'recall that the word Shaheed in Arabic, means much like "Martus" in Greek, initially refers to the witness', so that in this way, '[t]he epithet "Shaheed" is often associated with Bhagat Singh and other nationalist heroes of that time'. This allows us to understand how '[i]n Bismil's poem, the Shaheed stands out as a figure to be emulated'.[3] She continues, 'In Bismil's poem the hero gains his true life – his life as a hero – only in death.'[4] Since '[i]n such a dream, the *qatil,* or the murderer, becomes almost the accomplice of the Shaheed – less an antagonist, and more an ally', Bhagat Singh also has to die. In the same way, '[f]or one [who] must also think of the *qatil* here as love of the native land; it is the strength of this love that must be tested, not only the strength of the enemy'[5], Bhagat Singh again must die. [6]

Bismil was not alone in writing like this. Sachindra Nath Sanyal, who helped establish the HRA, wrote an open letter to Gandhi chiding him. What had removed the fear of death from the hearts of Indians, he told the great Mahatma, was not Gandhianism, but the people's own belief in 'the grandeur and the beauty that lie in dying for noble causes'.[7] This is because for the HRA, the ultimate consummation of revolutionary action was to be ready to die a martyr's death for it. Bhagat Singh's own writings leave little doubt that this was his belief as well. We know this because Yadav and Singh have translated the earlier writings[8] of Bhagat Singh. From these it is clear that even as a young college student, Bhagat Singh wrote endearingly in Indian journals, such as *Kirti*, an Amritsar weekly; *Pratap*, published in Kanpur; and in *Chand*, a monthly Hindi publication, about how such shaheeds as Kartar Singh Sarabha, Madan Lal Dhingra and the Kakori martyrs had openly welcomed death. Simona Sawhney also directs our attention to 'a poem attributed to Ashfaqullah Khan [where] we read the following verse: *"Ai pukhtakhare – ulfat hoshiyar dig na jana / yan raz ashiqi hai is dar-o-rasan mein"* [Be vigilant, and do not fall, O victorious lover/ The secret of love is in the gallows and rope]'. This affirms a devotion to *shahadat* (martyrdom). In Bismil's poem there is the line, '*aaj phir maqtal meñ qātil kah rahā hai baar baar, aa.eñ vo shauq-e-shahādat jin ke jin ke dil meñ hai*' (meaning, 'Today again on the gallows, the executioner is asking again and again / Whosoever has the heartfelt desire for martyrdom so may they step forward').

Indeed, 'from March to October 1928 Bhagat Singh wrote a serial column in the journal *Kirti* titled, *"Azadi ki bhent shahadaten"*' (meaning 'Martyrs for Freedom'). So much so that,

> In the piece about Madan Lal Dhingra (March 1928), Singh writes: 'When pain arose from seeing the chains of slavery grow more powerful day by day, many youths were unable to calm their nation-love-maddened hearts (*"deshprem mein pagal hue di"*) with mere speech and proposal-work and some broken-hearted people (*"dil-jale log"*) began the revolutionary movement.'[9]

In this way, Sawhney explains, 'Both the emotional charge of love (whether it appears as love for the motherland, love between revolutionaries, love for those who are oppressed, love for the world), as well as the madness of the one who truly experiences this love, are integrally related to the celebration of death.'[10] It is this celebration of death to which we must next turn.

45

1930, Sufferings and Sacrifices

The impact of this tradition of martyrdom on Bhagat Singh was deep and everlasting. When, at the time of the 1921–1926 Gurdwara Reform Movement, the Sikh militant organization of the Babbar Khalsa Akali order saw six of their members executed on charges of having killed government officials and informers, Bhagat Singh, who could not have been more than eighteen years old at the time, wrote of them approvingly. He described them as men 'showing great indifference to the trial' and that when 'after months, the judge gave his verdict', what was to transpire was that there were 'five to be hanged' and many others were sent 'for life imprisonment or exile' in what is described as 'their fond waiting for this day'. Such was their keenness in making the ultimate sacrifice that, upon hearing the verdicts, 'the accused heroes thundered' and 'even the skies echoed with their triumphant slogans'. Bhagat Singh would have doubtlessly learnt from this. He would have early imbibed the lesson of how death should be embraced. For the right cause it was to be welcomed and even desired. The greater the injustice, the greater the need to make that personal sacrifice. Accordingly, when in the case of the Babbar Akalis it was decided that 'an appeal was preferred', paradoxically what happened now that 'instead of five, now six were sent to the noose'. But it did not end there. More irony was to follow still when 'the same day the news came that a mercy petition was sent' then 'the Punjab Secretary declared that the hanging would be put off', but that astonishingly 'on the very day of Holi' on 27 February 1926, 'when we were getting high on our enjoyment, a terrible thing was happening in a corner of this great province'. This was that 'all of a sudden' it came to be that 'we saw a small contingent of mourners carrying the dead bodies of the heroes towards the cremation side'. They had been hanged contrary to all expectation when they were meant eventually to have been released from death.

For Bhagat Singh, 'they were fearless patriots' and 'if they were misguided, if they were frenzied, let them be so' because 'whatever they did, they did it for this wretched country'. The Babbar Khalsa Akalis had taken violent action against government officials because they simply 'could not bear injustice' and 'they could not countenance the fallen nation'.[1] Since 'they could not tolerate the exploitation of the masses, they challenged and jumped into action'. The anguish in which Bhagat Singh found himself was plain as he exclaimed, 'Oh! The terrible toll of their dedicated deeds!',[2] while still acknowledging the atrocity for what it was with the words, 'even if' it was the case that they 'might have done something hateful, their courage and the dedication shown in surrendering their lives at the altar of the nation, is something to the opposite side . . .'.[3] In anger, he upbraided those who were too preoccupied with the festivities of Holi on this day, pointing out how 'we the cowards and human wretches lack the courage of even sighing and putting off our celebrations even for a moment. What a disheartening deed!'.[4] Rhetorically, he asked, 'Where is the end of sacrifice? Where is the limit to courage and fearlessness? Where does the extremity of idealism reside?'[5] All this Bhagat Singh was pondering over when he was barely twenty years of age.

The historian Moffat, who has conducted cutting-edge research into India's revolutionary tradition, states that what Bhagat Singh is doing here is engaging in 'appeals to the global landscape of rebellion'.[6] Whereas this is undoubtedly true, it is possible to also draw the inference that at age twenty what Bhagat Singh is doing is undergoing his own transformation into a revolutionary in the mould of those who went before him. He is learning. And he is learning how to die. In fact, he is on the path of emulating those whom he described as 'fearless patriots' and 'heroes'. Just as there was no respite or reprieve for them, he begins to learn that when it comes to it, there will be no respite or reprieve for him. All the characteristics of his own life, from the day of his own arrest on 8 April 1929 to the trial, in which his sentence of deportation was confirmed before being upgraded to a sentence of death by hanging, right to the day of his execution on 23 March 1931, are present in the hanging of the Babbar Khalsa Akalis on 27 February 1926.

Whether it be police beatings, starvation through hunger strike or death by hanging, the idea of inviting untold suffering for an exalted cause such as India's freedom was ingrained in the revolutionaries. This does not mean that individuals did not break under pressure. But when they did, they were reminded of the path they had willingly themselves chosen to tread. Thus, upon the trial for the Second Lahore Conspiracy Case being concluded in October 1930, when a judgment from the special tribunal was being anxiously awaited and Sukhdev had begun contemplating suicide, Bhagat Singh reprimanded him with the words of the Naujawan Bharat Sabha: 'to suffer and sacrifice through service'. Sukhdev expected to be sent to jail for twenty years. He did not want this. He wanted either release or death. But Bhagat Singh reminded him how '[a]t the time of our imprisonment, the condition for the political prisoners of our party was very miserable' and that 'we were not aware of the technique of forced feeding and nor had we ever thought of it', but having experienced its horrors, 'we were ready to die' and yet had emerged stronger. He told Sukhdev, 'I want to tell you that obstacles make a man perfect.' 'Neither you nor I, or any of us, have suffered any pain so far,' he said.

To know pain, he draws upon its depiction in Russian literature for its realism, reminding Sukhdev, 'You will recollect that we have talked several times about realism in the Russian literature, which is nowhere visible in our own. 'We highly appreciate the situations of pain in their stories, but we do not feel that spirit of suffering within ourselves,' he said. And yet ironically, '[w]e also admire their passion and the extraordinary height of their characters, but we never bother to find out the reason'. Russian literature has much to commend it because 'the reference to their resolve to bear pain has produced the intensity, the suffering of pain, and this has given great depth and height to their characters and literature'.[7] It is well-known that Bhagat Singh often referred to the young having something unique to offer, in their energy, their hope and in their shared future.[8] In addition, the fact that Bhagat Singh, Ram Prasad Bismil and Ashfaqullah 'remained within the influence of poetry . . . even at the moment of death' is widely heralded, as Simona Sawhney makes plain. Even McKinley, the British officer at the time, recorded in his diary, 'I think it was the poetry that held their souls together, as the torture tore their bodies apart.'[9] Yet, it is clear that it was not just poetry, but literature too, and in particular Russian literature.

Bhagat Singh gave Sukhdev an example from his own life, when an attempt was made by intelligence officers to cajole him into becoming an informant and to thereby save his life. He spurned the offer contemptuously, explaining that he had ideals:

> When I was brought here from Delhi for the purpose of identification, some intelligence officers talked to me . . . in the presence of my father. They said that since I did not try to save my life by divulging secrets, it proved the presence of an acute agony in my life. They argued that death of this kind will be something like suicide. But I had replied that a man with beliefs and ideals like mine, could never think of dying uselessly. We want to get the maximum value for our lives. We want to serve humanity as much as possible. Particularly a man like me, whose life is nowhere sad or worried . . .[10]

The proceedings before the special tribunal having ended, and with the verdict awaited in keen anticipation by all, Bhagat Singh now made a revelation of remarkable sincerity, saying, 'I hope you will permit me to tell you what I think about myself. I am certain of capital punishment for me. I do not expect even a bit of moderation or amnesty.' In this sense, he was ahead of the game because it is startlingly revealing from this that he knew from the beginning what awaited him. This being so, he set out from the outset to embrace death, believing that '[a] revolution can be achieved only through sustained striving, sufferings and sacrifices. And it shall be achieved'. He wished to end his struggle in a manner whereby 'some indelible impressions are made on the hearts of the people of the country through our hanging. Only this much and nothing more'.[11] This is why Simona Sawhney is able to say that '[w]hat makes him such a powerful icon today' according to her 'is less his writing or beliefs, and more the very fact of his death – that is to say, the commitment to which that death attests'.[12] As she explains, 'what makes Bhagat Singh so compelling for people of varied hues in India is precisely his passion, manifested in his embrace of death'.[13] Yet, 'Bhagat Singh's relation to death cannot be exhausted by the phrase "dying for the nation" although that is often how he is remembered today'.[14] The 'centrality of death' to Bhagat Singh's outlook is linked to a wider 'imagination and other elements such as excessive love, delirium (*junoon*), and the explosive destructiveness and generosity of youth'.[15] In this way, '[t]he dissolution of the self in love, in this language, allegorizes the death-in-struggle of a committed political actor'.[16]

This is also why Bhagat Singh was scornful of the sort of shallow-minded Indian mysticism that induces spasms of uncontrolled sentimentalism and self-pity, emphasizing the need for rationalism, by pointing out that '[w]e become pitiable and ridiculous when we imbibe an unreasoned mysticism in our life without any natural or substantial basis'. That, he reminds Sukhdev at the time when he was contemplating suicide, is to betray the cause of the revolutionary so that '[p]eople like us, who are proud to be revolutionary in every sense, should always be prepared to bear all the difficulties, anxieties, pain and suffering which we invite upon ourselves by the struggles initiated by us and for which we call ourselves revolutionary'. In fact, appeals to God are of no avail in times like this. In the same letter to Sukhdev, Bhagat Singh is not only disarmingly frank but utterly compelling in his penetrating logic when he exclaims, 'We do not believe in God, hell and heaven, punishment and rewards, that is in any Godly accounting of human life. Therefore, we must think of life and death on materialist lines.'[17]

It is precisely this attitude to death which Moffat finds alluring in his study because it is 'not just any death' but one involving 'a spectacular self-sacrifice' that is openly 'invited and embraced by the revolutionary'.[18] When Bhagat Singh scolds Sukhdev, he does so in terms which remind him that '[t]o die in a struggle like this is an ideal death' and that 'those of us who are certain to get the death sentence should wait patiently for the day when this sentence would be pronounced, after which they will be hanged'. There is nothing to fear in this because 'even that death will be beautiful, but to commit suicide, to put an end to one's life, to escape some suffering – that is cowardice'.[19] In so saying, Bhagat Singh reaches the heights of virtue, even as he suffers with Sukhdev, and addresses him in the letter as 'dear brother'. In fact, his convictions have an aesthetic all of their own. This is clear from the way in which he admonishes Sukhdev, telling him that 'the best part of self-experiment is – endure agony oneself'.[20] He then upbraids him, saying that 'if you feel that life imprisonment is really humiliating, then why don't you agitate against it and try to reform it?'.[21] If there ever was a call to reform Indian penal policy, this was it, and it came at the time of the revolutionaries' most acute suffering. This ties in with what may be described as the particularity of revolutionary violence, as encapsulated by Giorgio Agamben where '[r]evolutionary violence is not a violence of means, aimed at the just end' but that '[r]ather, it is a violence that negates the self' and 'it awakens a consciousness of the death of the self'. This is because '[o]nly the revolutionary class can know that enacting violence against the other inevitably kills the self'.[22] How does Bhagat Singh develop such a cogent and coherent theory of death for the revolutionary? The answer lies in his time in jail. Jail time on death row was necessary to prepare oneself for the ultimate sacrifice. And time to explain one's atheism.

46

1931, 'Why I Am an Atheist'

While we can never know for certain what Bhagat Singh really thought about dying in the face of the inevitable death that awaited him, there is, nevertheless, this twentieth century moment in India to which we have already referred, where acts of self-sacrifice are deemed necessary as the revolutionaries strive to create a new world. Jail time was considered vital by Bhagat Singh because of the opportunities it afforded in reading and self-analysis. Awaiting sentence upon conclusion of the special tribunal proceedings, he put this in his letter to Sukhdev, explaining,

> I want to tell you that in jail, and in jail alone, can a person get an occasion to study empirically the great social subjects of crime and sin. I have read some literature on this and only in jail is the proper place for self-study on all these topics. The best parts of self-study is to suffer oneself.

As for any suggestion that 'jail life will crush all ideas', he questions 'whether the situation outside the jail was any bit more favourable to our ideas?'. He saw the use of the jail rules against the detainees as a source of strength to draw upon, pointing out how 'we continued our work despite the testing environment of disappointments, pressures and violence ordained by the Jail rules' and asks, 'Were these conditions not testing in the extreme?' He draws attention to 'our revolutionary comrades who suffered for their convictions in Jails and are still working on return from jails', referring to Bakunin and pointing out how '[t]oday, you find many revolutionaries occupying responsible posts in the Russian state who passed the greater part of their lives in prison, completing their sentences'.[1] Simona Sawhney observes that, notwithstanding the

> immense role in the education of Bhagat Singh, of equal if not greater significance is the literary and aesthetic space that allowed him to cast himself as part of an international brotherhood formed around the gallows. This is brought home most powerfully by references to the Russian novella, *The Seven Who Were Hanged* (1908) in the reminiscences of two of Bhagat Singh's co-prisoners in Lahore Central Jail, Shiv Verma and Jatinder Nath Sanyal. Referring to Bhagat Singh's interest in Dickens, Upton Sinclair, Hall Caine, Victor Hugo, Oscar Wilde, Gorky, Stepniak and in particular Leonid Andreyev, Shiv Verma recounts:
>
> > 'He frequently got emotionally involved with some particular characters in the novels, to the extent that he wept and laughed with them. A familiar instance was a character in Leonard Andrew's [*sic*] novel *The Seven Who Were Hanged*. This character kept on saying, "I shall not be hanged." While he was being actually led to the gallows, he was still saying, "I shall not be hanged." Upon reading this, Bhagat Singh would first laugh heartily, and then be silent and tears would start dropping from his eyes.'[2]

Simona Sawhney asks, 'What could Bhagat Singh's laughter and tears signify? We can only speculate.' She adds that surely the tears are 'a moment of identification' leading to the conclusion that 'the revolutionary does not love death because he hates life. On the contrary, it is precisely love of life that also demands love of death so that both life and death may be wrestled away from totalitarian control'. For Sawhney, 'Bhagat Singh's encounter with this novel should be read along with all the moments in his writings where he either glorifies the death of heroes, or argues against suicide (in a famous letter to Sukhdev), or gestures, through citation or allusion, towards a sweet intimacy with death'. Given his quest of overcoming the fear of death and suffering, Sawhney explains, 'The many references to the importance of enduring suffering, the prolonged practice of the hunger strike, and the defiant gesture of laughing at the moment of execution are all part of this challenge.'[3] Indeed, Sawhney goes further and even recognizes that in this sense there are in Bhagat Singh's work 'arguments similar to those made by Frantz Fanon: that at a systemic level the violence can only be confronted by the violence of the colonized, and at an individual level, violence functions as a way of restoring agency and capacity to a humiliated people'.[4]

It is this restoration of agency and capacity to a humiliated people that also accounts for Bhagat Singh's writing of his most controversial piece while he was in jail. A famous Sikh religious scholar and revolutionary, Bhai Sahib Bhai Randhir Singh, was imprisoned in Lahore Central Jail from 1930 to 1931 for his activities on behalf of the Ghadar Party. In jail he encountered Bhagat Singh in the condemned cell. Bhagat Singh was an avowed atheist. Despite being condemned to death, he refused to believe in the existence of God. Bhai Sahib Bhai Randhir Singh attempted to convince him otherwise, whereupon Bhagat Singh wrote the article titled 'Why I Am an Atheist', which was a tract released by Bhagat Singh's family several months after he had been hanged, towards the end of 1931. Adherents of Bhai Sahib Bhai Randhir strenuously insist that the great sage managed to convince Bhagat Singh to return into the fold of Sikhism as he faced the hour of his death in jail. Others think this cannot possibly have been the case. The truth is that this claim is only based on Bhai Randhir Singh's own memoirs.[5] In an attempt to reconstruct his hagiography, it is arguable that he and his supporters would have had every reason to make such a claim. In so doing, one often sees a photograph of Bhagat Singh (which is the only one of him when he was not a child), sitting manacled on a charpoy with hair unshorn in earnest discussion with an elderly man alleged to be Bhai Sahib Bhai Randhir Singh. This, however, is a 1927 photo, when Bhagat Singh was 20 years old. It is during his first arrest following the Dussehra bomb blast, when he is seen sitting with DSP Gopal Singh Pannu. It is not with Bhai Sahib Bhai Randhir Singh at all. Most important, however, is the fact that Bhagat Singh wrote 'Why I Am an Atheist' in prison. This tract was first published in September 1931. That was just six months after Bhagat Singh was executed in March. The fact that it was published with the permission of his family, and in circumstances where not a single one of his comrades in prison had suggested that during his final days he had returned to the fold of Sikhism, suggests that he did not do so and remained an atheist to the end. If his family wished to honour his memory so soon after his execution, they would not have done so by being oblivious to his moral and ethical stance which this essay so powerfully depicts.

In fact, it appears that while a meeting did take place between Bhai Sahib Bhai Randhir Singh and Bhagat Singh, it was not an amicable one. Nor does it appear to have been one which Bhagat Singh himself desired. According to Shiv Verma, the article 'Why I Am an Atheist' actually came about when the Ghadarite Bhai Randhir Singh, during his own incarceration in Lahore Jail in 1930–31, wished to see Bhagat Singh. This is because,

> Baba Randhir Singh . . . was a God-fearing religious man. It pained him to learn that Bhagat Singh was a non-believer. He somehow managed to see Bhagat Singh in the condemned cell and tried to convince him about the existence of God, *but failed*. Baba lost his temper and said tauntingly: 'You are giddy with fame and have developed an ego which is standing like a black curtain between you and God.' It was in reply to that remark that Bhagat Singh wrote this article.[6] (emphasis added).

In 'Why I Am an Atheist', Bhagat Singh sets out the gradual process by which his belief in God had begun to disintegrate, explaining, 'I had stopped believing in God when I was an obscure young man . . .' even though 'my grandfather, under whose influence I was brought up is an orthodox Arya Samajist'. When Bhagat Singh was a student at 'the D.A.V School of Lahore and stayed in its Boarding House for a full one year', he was still very much a believer and 'used to recite "Gayatri Mantra" for hours and hours' to such an extent that 'I was a perfect devotee in those days'. However, it was when, '[i]n the Non-Cooperation days I joined the National College . . . that I began to think liberally and to criticise all religious problems, even about God'.[7] Thereafter, '[l]ater on I joined the revolutionary party' but still did not totally deny the existence of God. The change in him came when later on he 'got ample opportunity to study various ideals of the world revolution', and this is when 'I studied Bakunin, the anarchist leader, something of Marx, the father of communism, and much of Lenin, Trotsky and others – men who had successfully carried out a revolution in their country. They were all atheists'. The result was that '[b]y the end of 1926 I had been convinced as to the baselessness of the theory of existence of an almighty supreme being who created, guided and controlled the universe'.[8]

By all accounts, Bhagat Singh was proud of his atheism. He did not wish to be redeemed by God. He had no belief in a paradise or an after-life. Whereas, '[a] God-believing Hindu might be expecting to be reborn a King, a Muslim or a Christian might dream of the luxuries to be enjoyed in Paradise as the reward he is to get for his suffering and sacrifices', the question for Bhagat Singh was, 'But, what am I to expect? I know the moment the rope is fitted round my neck and rafters removed from under my feet, that will be the final moment – that will be the last moment.' He did not believe that his soul would have the luxury of transmigration because, 'I, or to be more precise, my soul as interpreted in the metaphysical terminology shall be finished there', and there is to be '[n]othing further'. He had no regrets about this, no melancholic moments for him to indulge in because:

A short life of struggle with no such magnificent end, shall in itself be the reward, if I have the courage to take it in that light.

That is all. With no selfish motive or desire to be rewarded here or hereafter, quite disinterestedly, have I devoted my life to the cause of independence, because I could not do otherwise.[9]

This is not to say that Bhagat Singh is unaware of the solace of religion or of its psychological benefits for a condemned man who knows he is living on borrowed time on this earth because, 'I know in the present circumstances my faith in God would have made my life easier, my burden lighter, and my disbelief in Him has turned all the circumstances too dry, and the situation may assume too harsh a shape.' He is aware that '[a] little bit of mysticism can make it poetical. But I do not want the help of any intoxication to meet my fate. I am a realist'.[10] What a thundering dissent of religion! And what erudite defiance. No wonder that Shiv Verma, who was in jail with Bhagat Singh, wrote that he had personally witnessed Baba Randhir Singh's attempt to convince Bhagat Singh about the existence of God 'but failed'. As Bhagat Singh himself wrote in his essay, this was 'because reason is the guiding star of my life'. In fact, 'any man who stands for progress has to criticise, disbelieve and challenge every item of the old faith'.[11] He ended by leaving no doubt that even in his last hour he would not succumb to prayer because 'I will think that to be an act of degradation and demoralisation on my part. For selfish motives I am not going to pray'.[12] Today, those who extol Bhagat Singh's courage in the face of death would do well to remember that it was a courage born not out of a religious militantism but out of a belief in humanity and the goodness of the human soul. It was as simple as that.

47

1931, 'I Will Climb the Gallows Gladly'

By the end of his trial before the special tribunal, Bhagat Singh wished to die. Of that there can be no doubt. In his last letter to his father shortly before he was hanged, he even upbraided his own father for getting in the way. Kishan Singh had made a last-ditch frantic plea by writing to the tribunal on 20 September 1930 from Bradlaugh Hall in Lahore. He had claimed that his son was innocent of J.P. Saunder's murder because, 'Bhagat Singh was in Calcutta on the day of the occurrence and he actually wrote and despatched a letter . . .' from there. In fact, there were witnesses and 'I can produce them if I am given an opportunity, according to justice, or they may be called as court witnesses in the interest of justice, equity and good conscience' because '[t]he question in this case is of life and death'.[1] Bhagat Singh was incensed. Far from even putting up a defence he had never been interested in even proving his innocence. In a letter to his father which he asked to be made public and which was published in *The Tribune* on 4 October 1930,[2] he scolded his father in the sternest terms. He wrote how 'from the very beginning you have been trying to convince me to fight my case very seriously and to defend myself properly' but that 'you also know that I was opposed to it'. The reason was that 'we have been pursuing a definite policy in this trial'. This being so, '[e]very action of mine ought to have been consistent with that policy, my principle and my programme', clearly demonstrating how his approach to the trial was elaborately conceived and meticulously carried out from beginning to end. As he explained,

> I had only one idea before me throughout the trial, i.e. to show complete indifference towards the trial in spite of the serious nature of the charges against us. I have always been of the opinion that all political workers should be indifferent and should never bother about the legal fight in the law courts and should boldly bear the heaviest possible sentences inflicted upon them. They may defend themselves but always from purely political consideration and never from a personal point of view.[3]

It is clear from this that if Gandhi had a policy of 'passive resistance' to British colonial rule, then Bhagat Singh had a policy of 'active resistance'. And yet while Gandhi is known the world over, Bhagat Singh is all but forgotten. In fact, Bhagat Singh went on to tell his father, 'We have always been doing our duty quite disinterestedly.' Later on he went onto reproach his father with the words,

> My life is not so precious, at least to me, as you probably think to be. It is not at all worth buying at the cost of my principles. There are other comrades of mine whose case is as serious as that of mine. We had adopted a common policy and we shall stand to the last . . .

Even in that last letter he left his father with no doubt that 'I am still not at all in favour of offering any defence. Even if the court had accepted that petition submitted by some of my co-accused regarding my defence, I would not have defended myself'. Indeed, he then went on to reveal how the applications before the tribunal were all part of a wider strategy and a ruse in that '[m]y applications submitted to the Tribunal regarding my interview during the hunger strike, were misinterpreted and it was published in the press that I was going to offer defence, though in reality I was never willing to offer defence'.[4]

If Bhagat Singh was not going to put up a defence, what was he planning to do? Bhagat Singh has a clear answer to this. His approach was a highly sophisticated one. It was to expose the rank injustice of a judicial system of coercive colonial legalism. In this approach Bhagat Singh stood entirely vindicated because as he explained to his father,

> In the statement accompanying the text of the Lahore Conspiracy Case Ordinance, the Viceroy had stated that the accused in this case were trying to bring both the law and justice into contempt. The situation afforded to us an opportunity to show to the public whether we are trying to bring the law into contempt or whether others were doing so.[5]

The strategy was one of exposing the arrant hypocrisy of the colonial rulers. They had instigated a special trial procedure for twenty-five of the accused. Their trial before a regular magistrate was cut short and aborted while in full swing. Instead, they were put before a special tribunal. This act of desperation by the colonial authorities showed the rule of law in India to be a charade. And, this is what Bhagat Singh cleverly set out to expose. No wonder he saw his father's attempt to save him from the gallows as 'nothing short of treachery'. By intervening in this way, his father was inadvertently undoing the strategy that Bhagat Singh had so meticulously planned and worked for. This is why he told his father: 'Let me be candid. I feel as though I have been stabbed in the back.' Chastising his father, he struggled to contain his emotions, as he declared, 'I fear I might overlook the ordinary principles of etiquette, and my language may become a little bit harsh . . .'. And yet, managing to restrain himself just in time, he ends with the words, 'But, in your case, let me say that it has been a weakness – a weakness of the worst type.'[6] Coming from son to a father, these were harsh words, but Bhagat Singh was on the last leg of his journey, the journey to death. He could brook no interference, even if the interference was that of a tormented stricken father who was desperately helpless in the face of his eldest son's impending death.

The day before his hanging Bhagat Singh wrote a last letter to his 'Comrades' on 22 March 1931. Shiv Verma, who was himself detained in Ward Number 14, close to the cells of the condemned, slipped out a note to Bhagat Singh asking him if he would prefer to live. Bhagat Singh promptly wrote back,

> The desire to live is natural. It is in me also. I do not want to conceal it. But it is conditional. I don't want to live as a prisoner or under restrictions. My name has become a symbol of Indian Revolution. The ideal and sacrifices of the revolutionary party have elevated me to a height which I will never be able to rise if I live.

This vindicates Bhagat Singh's strategy of courting martyrdom which he had so carefully and painstakingly pursued right from the beginning. In fact, he was now able to also add that 'if I mount the gallows boldly and with a smile, that will inspire Indian mothers and they will aspire that their children should also become Bhagat Singh. Thus the number of persons ready to sacrifice their lives for the freedom of our country will increase enormously'. Yet, he was human, and being human pricked his conscience. Of desires that remained unfulfilled. Of what could have been had he lived. With these thoughts in mind, he ended his note sorrowfully with the words:

> Yet, one thing pricks me even today. My heart nurtured some ambitions for doing something for humanity and for my country. I have not been able to fulfil even one-thousandth part of these ambitions. If I live I might perhaps get a chance to fulfil them. If ever it came to my mind that I should die, it came from this end only.[7]

There is a sense of desolation here as one begins to fathom the feelings of a young man who knows he will die within twenty-four hours. The sense of loss of a life which could have been lived in any normal circumstance is enough to make one weep. The wretched and dismal end to a life brutally cut short is all too well understood by Bhagat Singh himself as he pens his last words. Yet, he retains his dignity. His head remains high and unbowed even when as he comes to terms with his own mortality. Almost a hundred years after India's Independence, Bhagat Singh's dream for India remains but a dream. The promise he held out remains unfulfilled. With opportunities for education, healthcare, racial, religious, and communal harmony all but squandered, as well as the threat of constant war, Independence lies barren and burnt-out.

Modern day independent India's leaders do not understand what the revolutionaries understood only too well—the need for sacrifice for a better India. Bhagat Singh remained acutely aware of this right to the very end. If sacrifice meant death, then so much the better. We can see this in Bhagat Singh's final letter written from Lahore Central Jail in November 1930 to B.K. Dutt, who had escaped the sentence of execution. The letter starkly displays his attitude to death. It was published in English originally in the now discontinued Calcutta weekly named *New Era*. Bhagat Singh begins by saying, 'The judgment has been delivered. I am condemned to death.' He then adds that '[i]n these cells, besides myself, there are many other prisoners who are waiting to be hanged', but that '[p]erhaps I am the only man amongst them who is anxiously waiting for the day when I will be fortunate enough to embrace the gallows for my ideals'. He then asserts, 'I will climb the gallows gladly and show to the world as to how bravely the revolutionaries can sacrifice themselves for the cause.' He goes onto tell B.K. Dutt, 'I am condemned to death, but you are sentenced to transportation for life' so that '[t] hose revolutionaries who have by chance escaped the gallows, should live and show to the world that they cannot only embrace the gallows for the ideal but also bear the worst type of tortures in the dark dingy prison cells'.[8]

The only wish Bhagat Singh had was a say in the manner of his going. He did not wish to go as a common criminal. Everything he had said and done from the beginning to the end demonstrated that he was a freedom fighter. He was a prisoner of war. This is because his act in the assassination of J.P. Saunders was an act of political murder in what was a war waged by the Indian nation against the King of England. And, this is exactly how he had been charged and tried. His crime did not arise from a personal vendetta. Nor was it a crime for personal gain. So, like a prisoner of state, he demanded to be shot by the state. He did not want to be hanged like a criminal. So he, together with Sukhdev and Rajguru, wrote to the Punjab governor, as the day of execution drew closer. They explained that 'we were sentenced to death on 7th October 1930 by a British Court, L.C.C. Tribunal, constituted under the Special L.C.C. Ordinance, promulgated by H.E. The Viceroy' and that this being so, 'the main charge against us was that of having waged war against H.M. King George, the King of England'. Indeed, the 'findings of the court presupposed two things', namely, that 'there exists a state of war between the British nation and the Indian nation' and that 'we had actually participated in that war and were, therefore, war prisoners'. Against this background,

> Let us declare that the state of war does exist and shall exist so long as the Indian toiling masses and their natural resources are being exploited by a handful of parasites. They may be purely British capitalists or mixed British and Indian, or even purely Indian. They may be carrying on their insidious exploitation through mixed or even purely Indian bureaucratic apparatus. All these things make no difference.[9]

For this reason, 'what we wanted to point out was that according to the verdict of your court we had waged war and we are therefore war prisoners. And we claim to be treated as such, i.e. we claim to be shot dead instead of being hanged. It rests with you to prove that you really meant what your court has said'.[10] It was a dying last wish not to be fulfilled. So relentless was the Raj's persecution of these men, so determined the state to remove all trace of their knowledge and existence, that death for them would be designed to be deliberately ignominious. The authorities were not going to grant the three the dignity of being shot as political prisoners. They were to be hanged and even that before their time. And yet, even in their hanging, Bhagat Singh, Sukhdev and Rajguru managed to cock a snook at the British Raj. They refused to be cowed. All three walked out of their cells smiling. They mounted the scaffold with alacrity, refused to have their faces masked, hugged each other warmly and grasped the rope themselves and put it around their necks. They knew how to die after all. And they died in the manner of their choosing with their heads unbowed. They died the death of a revolutionary, of an *Inqalabi*!

PART 10

EFFICIENT DESPOTISM

Qafas valon ki bhi kya zindagi hai
Chaman duur ashiyan duur asman duur

How pitiful the life of the caged—
bereft of the joys of the garden, home, and blue sky

—Firaq Gorakhpuri

48

An Apology?

One question that is on the lips of everyone who knows of Bhagat Singh's case is whether there should now be a restitution for acts done long ago in the heyday of the British Empire. Should there be an act of atonement for what happened a hundred years ago? All the evidence suggests that by the time of the Lahore Conspiracy Case in 1929, the colonial administration in Punjab knew full well that its sustained and systemic campaign of unabated physical violence on the youth of the land was not working. It was not able to break their resolve or force them to mend their errant ways. It could have granted the Lahore conspirators an amnesty and focussed its resources instead on preventing violent acts from taking place in the first place. Instead, it chose to use the law as a specific tool of colonial coercion by subjecting them to legal repression of the most severe sort through judicial reprisals. Should there not be an atonement for that, one may well ask? In fact, there is the revealing historical fact of how '[i]n November 1929, shortly after Jatin Das' death [following his hunger strike], and as the proceedings for the Lahore Conspiracy trials began, *the highest officials in the colonial government began to consider how to deal with the problem of political prisoners* as they tried to construct a way to evaluate the success of the constitutional reforms of 1919 under Montagu and Chelmsford' (emphases added). Moreover, there was, as Durba Ghosh has pointed out, 'a private letter in November 21, 1929, from Lord Irwin, the viceroy, to Wedgewood Benn, secretary of state for India and Liberal MP', in which

> 'Irwin identified two important issues in terms of dealing with political prisoners and the activities of the revolutionary terrorist movement. One issue was amnesty for political prisoners, as had been offered in 1919, and the second was whether to fully prosecute each crime using the mechanisms available through the Indian Penal Code.

What is evident from this exchange is that 'Irwin noted that severe punishments had been unsuccessful in upholding the laws against sedition, since radical materials continued to circulate; he also noted that if the government wanted to continue to enlist what he called "responsible" Indians, it should use a gentler approach in enforcing laws'.[1] Durba Ghosh notes how 'Lord Irwin noted with approval, "I recall the case of Gandhi a few months ago who was fined a rupee, which vindicated the law, which had only been technically infringed and left no bitterness"'.[2]

Why was there then no imposition of a fine on the Lahore conspirators as there was for Gandhi? Why was there no amnesty offered as was discussed by Lord Irwin? Why were the three in the Lahore Conspiracy Case hanged after a show trial? These questions are important because of the clear awareness by the governor-general and viceroy that physical repression was a fruitless and self-defeating endeavour on their part and that a different path, which had already been tried and tested, was likely to be more practically useful to the authorities. Lord Irwin sought advice from far and wide. He elicited the views of two trusted officials in Bengal who had previously served in Ireland and had the experience of dealing with unrest there. Both John Anderson and Charles Tegart told him that prevention was more effective than prosecution so that concentrating on removing the risk of violent attacks was altogether more constructive. On this basis, Irwin decided to endorse a policy of what he described as 'efficient despotism'. This was designed to discourage Indian nationalists from assembling and organizing around eye-catching prosecutions. This was often done in the full glare of the press as had been vividly demonstrated by the Lahore Conspiracy Case trials. It did not do the administration any good. Astonishingly, what one learns, however, is that '[s]everal weeks later, Irwin reported that figures such as Malaviya, *Nehru, and Gandhi had not made demands on behalf of political prisoners, as the viceroy had been expecting*' (emphases added).[3] If this is right then it demonstrates that the lamentable failure of Lord Irwin to effectively push through his policy of 'efficient despotism' and grant the Lahore conspirators an amnesty was in no small part linked to the abject failure of the leading Congress politicians to come to the assistance of their fellow countrymen and put pressure on Lord Irwin to do exactly that when it was most needed.

'Efficient despotism' worked in other respects. One learns, for example, of an event in 1933, when there was a forty-five-day hunger strike in the cellular jail in the Andaman Islands, when caution was urged in a manner that it was not in 1929–30 when the Lahore conspirators were on trial. On that occasion, the hunger strike ran from 12 May to 26 June. It involved no less than fifty-eight inmates. It was moreover accompanied by another twenty who refused to work as well. In the end, three hunger strikers died in the cellular jail. From the Indian Medical Service, there was a Lieutenant-Colonel F.A. Barker who had served in the Lahore Central Jail during the Lahore Conspiracy Case in 1929 when the hunger strike was being used by the detainees as a tool of resistance. When he was sent to the Andaman Islands half-way through the hunger strike of the prisoners there, he was able to report that there was a humane way of force-feeding the prisoners without occasioning unnecessary death by inflicting additional injury upon them. He advised that when artificial feeding was undertaken, the rubber tubes should be moistened with olive oil and only then inserted into the nasal passage as this would not interfere with their breathing.[4] This technique of humane force-feeding was largely absent in the case of the Lahore conspirators, who suffered grievously at the hands of prison wardens, who often delighted in inflicting untold pain on the hunger strikers when they resisted the forced feeding. Should there be an apology for that?

Before this question is answered, it is as well to remember that the issue of an apology is complex and controversial. Apologies have become all too commonplace these days. Jawad Iqbal has referred to Spanish atrocities in South America in a past age and the demand that Spain now apologize for such misdeeds. He pointed out that for President Andres Manuel Lopez Obrador of Mexico to be 'asking the Spanish to say sorry for their historical misdeeds is just a political gimmick, making a mockery of the actual violence committed during the Spanish conquest in 1519'. For Jawad Iqbal, 'this line of thinking also makes the mistake of confusing modern Spain with imperial Spain, as if the same state or ruling entity remained in power to this day'.[5] He argues that 'saying sorry is often a case of political expediency', so that it 'has no impact on current government policies' and is therefore an 'empty gesture'. It also 'can polarise people within the countries affected' so that 'it would be better to remember past wrongs in ways that bring people together rather than divide them'. Even so, he does accept that there is today 'the growing tendency for countries to acknowledge past crimes committed during colonisation'. This explains why in 1995 Queen Elizabeth II of England apologized for atrocities committed against the Maoris in New Zealand; in 2008, the Australian parliament formally apologized to indigenous Australians; in 2007, Tony Blair, the British PM, said sorry for the slave trade; in 2010, his successor, Gordon Brown apologized for sending 1,30,000 children to the former colonies. In a two-page letter in October 2020, Mexico's president also wrote to Pope Francis, asking for an apology for the Catholic Church's role in the oppression of indigenous people in the Spanish conquest 500 years ago.[6] Apologies and acts of atonement continue. Those wronged demand recognition of wrongdoing. They seek reparatory action. On 28 May 2021, Germany not only apologized to Namibia for its military's past violence which led to the killing of 80,000 Africans between 1904 and 1908, but also declared it to be 'genocidal', with a pledge of $1.3 billion in aid to Namibians.[7]

Nevertheless, Jawad says that 'such an approach makes no distinction between those in actual authority responsible for historical crimes and everyone else at the time', even as the clamour for an apology for colonial crimes continues to grow. One hundred years after the Amritsar Massacre, there was a brief statement in the House of Commons by Britain's Prime Minister Theresa May, who said: 'The tragedy of Jallianwala Bagh in 1919 is a shameful scar on British Indian history. As her majesty the Queen said before visiting Jallianwala Bagh in 1997, it is a distressing example of our past history with India.' She went on to add that 'we deeply regret what happened and the suffering caused. I am pleased that today the UK-India relationship is one of collaboration, partnership, prosperity and security'. In the violence of the Jallianwala Bagh Massacre, however, there was the appearance of collusion between Sikh elites at the time and the perpetrators of these crimes.[8] Should that make a difference to whether or not an apology is given? It is noteworthy that at the time the leader of the Labour opposition, Jeremy Corbyn, has nevertheless demanded a full apology: 'I am very pleased that the prime minister mentioned what happened in Jallianwala Bagh and the issues of the massacre at Amritsar a hundred years ago. I think the people in memory of those that lost their lives and the brutality of what happened deserve a full, clear and unequivocal apology for what took place on that occasion.' However, as Mark Field, the junior minister in the foreign office, told MPs seeking the apology the previous day, the issue is a 'work in progress'.[9] Does this suggest that one may still be forthcoming? Only time will tell.

49

A 'Historical Adjustment'

If there is an apology, what will it achieve? It is a question worth posing because when it comes to the Jallianwala Bagh Massacre in 1919, even at the time, Winston Churchill, the secretary of state for war, denounced General Dyer's actions as 'an extraordinary event, a monstrous event, an event which stands in singular and sinister isolation'.[1] It is debatable whether this was indeed a barbarity of 'singular and sinister isolation' in the history of the British Empire. It appears not. Nevertheless, the value and practical utility of an apology today from a global power that is no longer in the ascendancy but very much in decline is not a matter of insignificance, which can be ignored. It needs to be taken into account in the face of ever more strident calls for an apology, because as Patrick Cockburn has argued, '[f]uture historians may well pick 2019 as a decisive year in the decline of the US and UK as world powers' and that '[t]his geopolitical shift comes exactly a century after the Treaty of Versailles, in 1919, when the US and UK were at the peak of their power in determining the fate of nations after the First World War'. He points out that '[l]ike most political retreats, the present one by the US and UK is masked by patriotic bombast about "Making America Great Again" or launching a post-Brexit "Global Britain" but the reality will soon be all too clear when the mask eventually falls'. For him, the British 2019 general election is the 'election that will be the point of no return for Britain in the current phase of its decline'. He has no doubt that in the pursuit of 'Brexit as an act of self-destructive folly', what is now inevitable is that 'the country will be without real allies for the first time for over 200 years – historians say the last such moment was during some particularly dire moment during the Napoleonic wars'.[2]

In these circumstances, what is surely needed is an account of history that puts the Empire in its proper historical place which has been strangely lacking so far. In the words of Professor Edgerton, 'What's striking about postwar historiography is the lack of imperialist histories and the absence of condemnation for nationalist and anti-imperial forces.' And yet, as he explains, 'Putting the empire in its proper historical place is hugely important for understanding the sheer scale of slavery, the racialised nature of the imperial project . . .'[3] This is why at Oxford University, there has been a successful movement to remove the statue of the colonialist, Sir Cecil Rhodes, who had once given his name to the apartheid country of Rhodesia in southern Africa. As Din-Kariuki has written, the movement, however, has always been about more than a statue. Its demands are about the 'official, public and permanent acknowledgment' of the university's involvement in colonialism and slavery. This would include such things as the immediate renaming of the Codrington Library at All Souls College; the immediate renaming of the Rhodes Scholarship and of Rhodes House. However, it would include also other positive measures such as a 'reparatory scholarship scheme for Southern Africans of African descent' at Oriel; the 'establishment of a review committee for the decolonisation of the curriculum'; a 'commitment to bringing Black British undergraduate student numbers in line with the British population'; a 'commitment to doubling the number of Black faculty' and an 'anti-racism and implicit bias training' for students and staff.[4]

So, we can do two things. First, we can start by rejecting the end of Empire in India as a story of high politics. The fact is that the Empire in India was fundamentally undermined and destabilized from below. Young radicals from across Asia used new technologies of the printing press and global travel to communicate and interact as never before. Witness the example of Ajit Singh, Bhagat Singh's uncle, who went to Latin America and from there communicated with Har Dayal's Ghadar Party in San Francisco in 1918 before meeting with Subhas Chandra Bose in Europe in 1939, as the Second World War raged on. As clandestine networks spanned across the world's imperial metropolises, from London to Paris to the Americas and then to Moscow, 'an extraordinary world of stowaways, false identities, secret codes, cheap firearms, assassinations and conspiracies'[5] emerged, as Prof. Tim Harper's magnificent new book makes clear. The point is, Bhagat Singh was not apart from this furtive world. From false identities to conspiracies to assassinations, he indulged in all these in order to bring down the Empire in India. Quite contrary to the traditional accounts of that such as Dr Pattabhi Sitaramayya, whose official history of the Congress Party we are all familiar with, it is this history from below that needs to be understood now if an accurate and realistic story of Independence is to be told. Second, and not unrelated to this, it is time to acknowledge how changes in our history, brought about by transformative radical movements, have failed to recognize the role played by the anarchist. This is a problem not just in India but in Europe as well. John Quail, in his lost history of British anarchists,[6] has explained how the British anarchist movement developed between the years of 1880 to 1930 but has today been largely obscured. He argues for the resurrection of the vibrant stories of these unsung heroes, tumultuous political activities and searing manifestos. Of course, the last ten years of the period that John Quail sets out was also the period of Bhagat Singh's blistering manifestoes, radical dissent and withering denunciation of the Raj. For John Quail, the story of British anarchism is still being written today. For India, it has not even begun. Even the great historical works on India by such British stalwarts as Percival Spear[7], C.H. Philips[8] and Judith Brown[9] are silent about Bhagat Singh.

Returning to the increasingly fashionable practice of seeking apologies, what we can say from the perspective presented above is that the practically useful step would be to have changes in school curricula, the teaching of history from below, the mainstreaming of the revolutionary freedom struggle in our narratives and recognition of the role of the anarchist. The potential of such accounts for connecting with and confronting current ideologies of racism, xenophobia and the intolerance of minorities will otherwise go unappreciated. As it is, '[b]oth Congress and Sangh Parivar vigorously attempt to deny Bhagat Singh's revolutionary ideology and politics, and in the process they try to distort his memory and his legacy'.[10] This is why a mere apology not followed by a remedial behavioural change back in India is entirely inconsequential and of no use to anyone. When others such as Hardeep Singh have asked 'shouldn't memorialisation and education about the darker aspects of colonialism (along with the good) take precedent?',[11] what they are all asking for is a 'historical adjustment' of a past misrepresentation of history. In this sense, a sincere apology may well work because it can work to perform three functions, namely, that it will recognize the errors of the past, it will express regret over such errors and it will make it clear that the same error will not be repeated in the future. In this way, it avoids the misapprehension in the future of continuing to treat racially and religiously varied minorities differently. It helps to defeat the 'legacy of racism' that still endures from the past to this day. This is why Anita Anand explains that '[t]he way history was and continues to be taught in Britain does a disservice to all . . .' and that 'the ignorance has been shown into sharp relief by the centenary anniversary of the Jallianwala Bagh Massacre', which was to be commemorated in 2019. She is in no doubt that '[a]n honest appraisal of colonial history will, however, make all the difference to my children and theirs'.[12] The young Indian historian, Manu S. Pillai, puts it rather well when writing about the Jallianwala Bagh Massacre. He argued that 'a sincere expression of remorse would not only offer closure for relatives of those who suffered Dyer's bullets, but could encapsulate all other acts of injustice sponsored by the

Raj'.[13] Could the same be said in relation to Bhagat Singh's hanging? Ultimately, the deliberate repression of history's most significant events, and what questions they raise today about human existence, is what needs to be overcome.

For those who argue that the Empire had some upsides as well as downsides, Prof. Priya Satia, in her enticingly titled *Time's Monsters*, has recently disabused them of this notion by explaining, 'The problem with weighing pros and cons is that it presumes there is a point at which the story is over, the accounts are closed, and we can actually tot up the balance.' Such an argument 'also depends on the premise that empire was a legitimate political form'. The difficulty here is that '[t]his premise subverts the laborious work of generations who fought to end empire on the grounds that it was illegitimate – the imposition of racist, violent, and extractive form of rule'. Prof. Satia makes an important comparison which has never been made in the same manner before, namely, that '[h]istorical evaluation of racist despotisms in Europe – for instance, fascist regimes – are never written about as legitimate, and yet many write about empire as though it can be evaluated neutrally'. Driving her point home, she refers to the absurd irony of how '[n]o historian would say, yes, Hitler was horrible to the Jews, but, on the other hand, he built the autobahn!'[14] In this sense, historical adjustment is political. What is needed is political redress, or at least political acknowledgement, but otherwise apologies mean little or nothing. The wrong done to Bhagat Singh and his comrades, in the sense of putting them before a Tribunal, the sole purpose of which was to hang them speedily is arguably one that requires a political adjustment.

In fact, if the imperial project was conceived as a 'civilising mission' against an uncivilized people, as many such as Kim Wagner have argued, then at one level it is surely impossible to ask an apology of someone who did not believe that what he was doing was wrong at all. For such a person, those who refused to be 'civilised' in this manner, as Bhagat Singh and many others did during the Raj, were met with 'divine retribution' rooted deeply in a fundamentalist Christian tradition. The setting up of a special tribunal was deliberate. It was a way of inflicting such 'divine retribution' on those who stepped out of line. It was eminently visible for all to see and learn from. Its 'justice' was exalted and celebrated by the colonizer. It was not something to be ashamed of. That is why it was not hidden. That is also why trial by special tribunal was not such an anomaly as appears at first sight but used frequently as a means of dispensing 'colonial justice'. An apology can only be demanded of someone who recognizes what they are doing to be wrong. In this case, there was no such recognition, and indeed, very little of the same in the following decades. In one sense, therefore, it is arguable that it is far more important to remember the verdicts of the past, right and wrong, rather than to try to expunge them. An attempt to expunge is futile, it may well be argued, unless of course there are legal consequences for living people. In Bhagat Singh's case, he has descendants, such as his nephew, Prof. Jagmohan Singh,[15] who has an interest in seeing Bhagat Singh's legacy fully protected. It may, nevertheless, still be possible to say that it is better to remember Bhagat Singh's trial by special tribunal and the Privy Council's ready acceptance of it for what it is—a system of colonial 'justice' and of coercive colonial legalism that does not even pretend to apply the established common law cannons of the rule of law to a trial of young men before it. If this argument has traction, then it does not add anything to Bhagat Singh's historical fame or significance to have his sentence annulled. It is far more important to make Bhagat Singh's ideas better known instead. That is a far more fruitful venture.

On the other hand, it is surely equally arguable that if the possibility exists, then there is no reason why one cannot pursue a legal case for a 'Royal Pardon' from the Queen of England which would set aside Bhagat Singh's conviction and sentence. There is a well-established precedent for this. It comes from the 1993 case of Derek Bentley,[16] which established that the prerogative of mercy is no longer 'an arbitrary monarchical right of grace and favour' but 'a constitutional safeguard against mistakes'. In that case, the High Court in England held that 'we would invite the Home Secretary to look at the matter again and to examine whether it would be just to exercise the prerogative of mercy in such a way as to give full recognition to the now generally accepted view that this young man should have been reprieved'. Fears that 'even a limited form of pardon might lead to a flood of other applications seeking to re-open past convictions' was no justification for not doing so just because 'of the broad scope of the prerogative of mercy', because what needed to be looked at was that 'the matter is exceptional and requires further consideration'. As Lord Justice Watkins explained in that case, 'It should be possible to devise some formula which would amount to a clear acknowledgement that an injustice was done.' The same surely applies in Bhagat Singh's case today. A formula can be devised for all similar miscarriage of justice cases during the days of the Empire. It is worth reminding ourselves that Bhagat Singh was hanged by the sentence of a special tribunal constituted under Section 72 of the Government of India Act. But Lord Irwin had failed both to demonstrate the existence of an 'emergency' and that 'peace and good government' of British India was at stake. It was therefore a clear mistake of law. The conferment of 'a posthumous conditional pardon where a death sentence has already been carried out' is arguably today the right remedy because '[t]he grant of such a pardon is a recognition by the state that a mistake was made and that a reprieve should have been granted'. This is all the more so given that an application for a reprieve had indeed already been made back then. It was made by D.N. Pritt before the judicial committee of the Privy Council in February 1931, but it was summarily dismissed without being admitted to a full hearing.[17] Referring to the Governor-General, Lord Dunedin had ruled that it was not 'in any way incumbent on him as a matter of law'[18] for Lord Irwin to give reasons for bringing the accused to trial under the ordinance, which is quite simply wrong. As Lord Justice Neuberger made clear in a recent case, 'decisions without reasons are certainly not justice; indeed they are scarcely decisions at all'.[19] It was wrong then, and it is wrong now.

50

The Gandhi–Irwin Pact 1931

The quest to make Bhagat Singh's ideas better known, however, is mired in the enigma of whether his death was preventable. And if so, by whom? A growing body of evidence suggests that Gandhi did not do all he could to save Bhagat Singh from being executed. The late V.N. Datta, in his book *Gandhi and Bhagat Singh*, has recounted the raging debate from its earliest days, as he drew attention to each of the protagonists, for and against, the role of Gandhi, in whether he could or could not have saved Bhagat Singh. Taking a nuanced approach, he did not flinch from accepting that 'Gandhi regarded Singh's mode of militant nationalism, and the extreme left-wing political activity as the most injurious to the cause of Indian independence'.[1] However, he was nevertheless clear that Bhagat Singh could not have been saved by Gandhi because 'the assumption that Gandhi and Irwin were sovereign shapers of events . . . is questionable' in that 'they were working under constraints, which set limits to their actions'.[2] He is in no doubt that 'Gandhi put the maximum pressure on the Viceroy Lord Irwin for the commutation of the death sentence of Bhagat Singh and his comrades',[3] but that tragically it was all to no avail. However, a markedly different view was taken much earlier by G.S. Deol, when writing in 1969 he suggested that 'Mahatma Gandhi did not make it a condition of the settlement, though he could have done' because 'Gandhi himself wrote in his *Young India*, "I might have made commutation a term of the settlement. It could not be so made . . . The Working Committee had agreed with me in not making commutation a condition precedent to truce. I could, therefore, only mention it."' Deol goes on to say, 'But a "leader" who could go to the extent of stating to the Viceroy, that "if the boys should be hanged, they had better be hanged before the Congress (Karachi) Session, not after it"[4] could hardly be expected to secure commutation of the death sentences of Bhagat Singh and his comrades'.[5]

One original source which has curiously been all too often overlooked is that of the Indian nationalist Subhas Chandra Bose's *The Indian Struggle (1920–1942)*, which he wrote while in exile in Europe. Described by Sisir Bose and Sugata Bose as a 'major political study of the movement for independence in which he himself was a leading participant',[6] the book was immediately banned by the secretary of state for India, Sir Samuel Hoare, on grounds that it 'tended generally to encourage methods of terrorism and direct action'.[7] That did not stop *The Manchester Guardian* from bestowing upon it an even better accolade when it said of it that '[t]his is perhaps the most interesting book which has yet been written by an Indian politician on Indian politics' and that it 'is as nearly fair to all parties and everyone else [as] can reasonably be expected of an active politician'.[8] It is for this reason why what this account has to say of Bhagat Singh is so significant. Bose gives a stirring description of the time in 1929 when in India '[t]here was an under-current of revolutionary activity' together with 'an unrest in the Labour world which extended to every part of the country' as well as 'an awakening among the middle-class youths which was manifest everywhere'. He explains how '[t]he visible expression' of this 'was afforded by two incidents which occurred at Lahore and at Delhi', the first being the assassination of the police inspector, Mr Saunders, who was believed to be responsible for the attack on Lala Lajpat Rai in 1928, and the second being the throwing of the bomb in the assembly in Delhi by Bhagat Singh and Batukeshwar Dutt,[9] which led to their arrest, detention and trial by the authorities.

This was the time of the Gandhi–Irwin Pact 1931, which was important because it marked the end of the period of civil disobedience, known as satyagraha, that Gandhi had invoked with the Salt March against British Rule during the months of March and April 1930, and which led to his incarceration for illegally making salt. By the end of that year, tens of thousands of his followers were arrested. Under the glare of international publicity, the Viceroy Lord Irwin was keen to find a way out. By January 1931, Gandhi was released from custody. Two men now set about discussing a negotiated settlement of their dispute, in eight meetings involving twenty-four hours. Gandhi undertook to relinquish his quest for satyagraha and Lord Irwin agreed to release all those who had been imprisoned during the protests. Indians were also to be allowed to make salt for domestic use. Winston Churchill, together with others in the British establishment back in London, was incensed and scandalized '. . . at the nauseating and humiliating spectacle of this one-time Inner Temple lawyer, now seditious fakir, striding half-naked up the steps of the Viceroy's, there to negotiate and parley on equal terms with the representative of the King Emperor'.[10] However, Gandhi saw satyagraha as a 'non-violent struggle', with the emphasis being on self-suffering at the hands of an oppressor, thus making it morally impracticable for the oppression to continue indefinitely. However, modern-day criticism, such as from Justice Katju, is that what this succeeded in doing was 'diverting the genuine revolutionary independence struggle against the British in India to harmless . . . channels like "Satyagrah"'.[11]

As for Subhas Chandra Bose, in a separate chapter on 'The Gandhi-Irwin Pact And After (1931),'[12] he explains how the terms of this pact included on the one hand 'the suspension by Mahatma Gandhi of the Civil Disobedience Movement' and 'the participation in the deliberations of the forthcoming conference for drafting a constitution for India on the basis of Federation' while on the other hand, on the part of the viceroy of India, it included a concomitant undertaking 'to release simultaneously all political prisoners incarcerated in connection with the non-violent movement' as well as 'to withdraw the emergency ordinances'. While it is certainly true that Bhagat Singh was not seen as a prominent exponent of the non-violent movement, it was equally the case that he was being tried as the most famous revolutionary freedom-fighter known in India at the time, under emergency ordinances, namely, the Lahore Ordinance No. 3 of 1930. In the circumstances, therefore, one would have expected Mahatma Gandhi to insist on his release precisely because that release fell within the terms of the Gandhi-Irwin Pact (1931) that he had negotiated. Those who claim that the Mahatma could not, as a matter of principle, have insisted that the pact would stand dishonoured on the part of Lord Irwin if Bhagat Singh was not released fail to recognize that the agreement between Gandhi and Irwin required the withdrawal and consequent nullification of the emergency ordinances. If Gandhi did try to intervene on behalf of Bhagat Singh, but not determinedly enough so as to actually insist on his release, then that made all the difference between securing his freedom from the gallows and seeing him hang.

When Bose and Gandhi arrived in New Delhi from Bombay, Bose proceeds to describe how 'we received a bombshell in the shape of news, to the effect that the government had decided to execute Sardar Bhagat Singh and two of his comrades in the Lahore conspiracy case'. In the circumstances, therefore, '[p]ressure was brought to bear upon the Mahatma to try to save the lives of these young men and *it must be admitted that he did try his very best*' (emphasis added). Bose then goes on to say, 'I ventured the suggestion that he should, if necessary, break with the Viceroy on the question, because the execution was against the spirit, if not the letter, of the Delhi Pact.' Bose had good reason to take this line, because as he recollected, 'I was reminded of the similar incident during the Armistice between the Sinn Fein party and the British government, when the strong attitude adopted by the former, had secured the release of Irish political prisoners sentenced to the gallows.' However, the fact that Bose then adds the proviso that '*[b]ut the Mahatma did not want to identify himself with the revolutionary business*, (emphasis added)' only serves to confirm that the Mahatma did not in fact wish to go any further than he had already done. This casts doubt on Bose's own earlier statement that the Mahatma 'did try his very best', which plainly he did not if Gandhi was not prepared to break with the Viceroy on the question of those sentenced to the gallows as Bose had exhorted him to. Indeed, Bose was clear that the Mahatma '*would not go so far and naturally that made a great difference when the Viceroy realised that the Mahatma would not break on that question*'[13] (emphases added). This is the clearest evidence from Bose about what the Mahatma did and did not do. It was the deliberate failure of the Mahatma to push his point home that prevented the lives of these young men from being saved. The Mahatma could have saved them in a way that only he knew given the power that he wielded at the time. He chose not to do so. That was his decision. It was a deliberate decision. And the reason for this was that he wished to have nothing to do 'with the revolutionary business'.

Yet, a thousand miles away in Calcutta from the Punjab, when two fifteen-year-old girls, Santi Ghosh and Suniti Choudhry, quietly walked into the office of a British District Magistrate, Charles Geoffrey Buckland Stevens, and shot him dead whilst still in their school uniforms, on a simmering hot day in December 1931, in revenge for the hanging of Bhagat Singh in March 1931, Gandhi found his voice. At their trial, the girls were unrepentant, making fiery speeches, and asking of the judge to be put to death. Given their tender ages, they were sentenced to transportation for life, but served only seven years, because Gandhi intervened on their behalf in 1938 and agreed an amnesty with the Government.[14] Yet, Gandhi took no such step with Bhagat Singh, even though that too was a killing in cold blood of a government official.

51

'If the Boys Are to be Hanged'

The suggestion that Gandhi wished to dissociate himself from 'the revolutionary business' in a way that it made 'a great difference' to the viceroy has been much overlooked by those who say that Gandhi spared no effort. The fact that the viceroy realized that the Mahatma 'would not break [the accord] on that question' is the most compelling indication of Gandhi not doing enough to save Bhagat Singh. This was at precisely the moment when he could have done so. Gandhi well knew that the viceroy himself did not wish the accord to break. So why did he not dig his heels in? Was he complicit in the viceroy's decision? If so, that is a grave allegation to make. Nevertheless, the enormity of the Mahatma's act of omission is all the more glaring considering, as Bose recalls, that by the time the Congress was to meet at Karachi on 26 March 1931, 'the general expectation was that the execution would be cancelled.' This is why '[i]t was therefore a most painful and unexpected surprise when on March 24, while we were on our way to Karachi from Calcutta, the news was received that Sardar Bhagat Singh and his comrades had been hanged the night before'.[1] Clearly horrified, he recounts how '[i]t is impossible to understand the poignant grief which stirred the country from one end to the other'. This is because by now, '[s]omehow or other,

Bhagat Singh had become the symbol of the new awakening among the youths' so that '[w]hen the Mahatma alighted near Karachi, there was a hostile demonstration, and several young men received him with black flowers and black garments. The feeling among a considerable section of the youths was that the Mahatma had betrayed the cause of Bhagat Singh and his comrades'.[2] Did the Mahatma then really betray the cause of Bhagat Singh? Did his pusillanimous approach to saving him actually contribute in the end to Bhagat Singh's death at the hands of Lord Irwin? One needs only look at two specific pieces of evidence.

First, after the governor-general in council had rejected the petition of mercy for Bhagat Singh, Home Secretary, H.W. Emerson met with Mahatma Gandhi on 19 March 1931. A recent commentary by Utpal Aich, a diplomat who served as the first secretary in the Indian embassy in Addis Ababa, is revealing.[3] Aich takes the view that with the execution now more likely than not, what we learn from Emerson's minutes of that meeting, as reproduced in Volume XLV of the *Collected Works of Mahatma Gandhi* (CWMG)[4], is that he told Gandhi that 'the question as to whether it should take place before or after the Karachi Congress had been very seriously considered by Government who realized the difficulties of either course'. This, according to Emerson's note (which is produced in that volume at p. 440), would have been 'unfair to the condemned persons to postpone execution' but curiously 'also not fair to Gandhi'. What is startling about this account, however, is that Emerson records of Gandhi, 'He agreed that of the two alternatives it is better not to wait, but he suggested, *though not seriously*, that the third course of commutation of the sentence would have been better still. *He did not seem to me to be particularly concerned about the matter . . .*' (emphases added). Why, on a matter as serious as saving the life of Bhagat Singh, is Emerson suggesting here that Gandhi was not serious about the commutation of the sentence of death on Bhagat Singh and his comrades? And, why does Emerson record that Gandhi was not particularly concerned about this issue? In fact, it does not end there because Emerson then goes on to say of Gandhi in the same breath, 'I asked him to do all that he could to prevent meetings being held in Delhi . . . *He promised to do what he could*' (emphases added).[5] Why is Gandhi agreeing in the aftermath of Bhagat Singh's execution to actively assist Emerson in the maintenance of law and order? If what Emerson writes is correct, then this is truly extraordinary because it shows the Mahatma being in active discussions with Irwin about how Bhagat Singh should be executed. This is a grave charge, which is why it must be pointed out that Gandhi's own version of his personal meeting with Emerson is not reproduced in the *CWMG* regarding the meeting with the viceroy on 19 March 1931. But Utpal Aich has argued that 'since the versions of the Viceroy are in English and duly validated by his initials at the end of the texts, these appear to be more authentic . . .'.[6]

Utpal Aich may well not be wrong because less than two weeks earlier, on 7 March 1931, Gandhi addressed a public meeting in New Delhi.[7] What he said here makes it abundantly clear that he had already given up on Bhagat Singh because he did not agree with his ways: 'If you pin your faith to violence, take it from me that you will not only not secure Bhagat Singh's release but will have to sacrifice thousands of Bhagat Singhs. I was not prepared to do so, and hence I preferred the way of peace, of non-violence.'[8] On 19 March, Gandhi had an interview with the viceroy on his return from Bombay on the matter of India's financial credit and stability. We learn that he says of the viceroy that '[h]is general attitude was friendly' and that at the end of the meeting '[a]s he was leaving, he asked if he might mention the case of Bhagat Singh, saying that he had seen in the Press the intimation of his execution for March 24th'. His concern, however, was that '[t]his was an unfortunate day, as it coincided with the arrival of the new President of the Congress at Karachi and there would be much popular excitement'. The viceroy assured him, saying,

> I told him I had considered the case with most anxious care, but could find no grounds on which I could justify to my conscience

commuting the sentence. As to the date, I had considered the possibility of postponement till after the Congress, but had deliberately rejected it on various grounds . . . He appeared to appreciate the force of these arguments, and said no more.[9]

And two days before Bhagat Singh was hanged, Gandhi in his interview to the press on 21 March 1931, when asked, 'Do you entertain any hope that Bhagat Singh may be saved at the last minute?', answered that 'Yes, but it is a very distant hope'.[10]

Second, we have the damning statement of Dr Pattabhi Sitaramayya. A gifted polymath, he was the official historian of the Congress Party. He was also Gandhi's protégé and was nominated by him as president of Congress in 1939. He was nominated over Subhas Chandra Bose. When Bose was nevertheless elected president of the Congress Party for the second consecutive term in 1939, Gandhi bewailed 'Pattabhi's defeat is my defeat'. So Pattabhi Sitaramayya can hardly have been anything other than sympathetic to Gandhism. What Sitaramayya has to say about Gandhi's actions over Bhagat Singh's death sentence is revealing for he explains in his *The History of the Indian National Congress*, 'The Karachi Session was to meet in the last week of March but Gandhi himself definitely stated to the Viceroy that if the boys are to be hanged, they had better be hanged before the Congress, than after.' Definitely stated? Why the desire for such certainty over Bhagat Singh's death? The reason for this, as he makes clear, is that '[t]he position of affairs in the country would be clear. There would be no false hopes lingering in the breasts of the people'. Chillingly, it is then also added that '[t]he Gandhi–Irwin Pact would stand or fall on its own merits at the Congress, and on the added fact that the three boys had been hanged'.[11] Shockingly, the hanging of the three condemned men was to be turned to Congress' advantage. It is in these circumstances that Bhagat Singh ended up being hanged on the night of 23 March 1931.[12] This was not by accident. Although the opening day of the Karachi Congress was on 26th March, the stalwarts of the Congress Party were all to be

in Karachi on 24 March. Not only were Gandhi and Bose to take
the train across the thousand mile breadth of India from Calcutta
to arrive in Karachi on 24 March, but Sardar Vallabhbhai Patel,
the newly elected President of the Indian National Congress Party
was also to arrive on the same day. Amid the pomp and fanfare
of the day, the one distraction that the leadership did not want
was to have to deal with Bhagat Singh's hanging. Gandhi would
move heaven and earth to prevent this. This is why a telegram was
sent on 18 March 1931 by the home secretary of Punjab, H.W.
Emerson to the Delhi government, five days before, confirming
that the hanging will be brought forward by eleven hours contrary
to protocol and take place in Lahore jail at 7pm at night instead
(as confirmed in the Appendix herewith).

No wonder that upon his arrival in Karachi, Gandhi was met by
several angry young men. The ruse had fooled no one. Ordinarily,
the arriving entourage would have been received with brightly
coloured flowers of all shades and varieties. Instead, the angry men
chose to present him with black clothes and black flowers. This is
the ultimate mark of disgrace and disrespect for a man otherwise
known as the 'Mahatma'.

Gandhi's ignominy in Karachi at the hands of these several
young men is an event that stands in stark contrast to how Bose
described him immediately after the pact when,

> From the ovation he received everywhere it was quite apparent
> that his popularity had reached the high watermark. It had
> surpassed even the record of 1921, when after the departure of
> Jinnah in 1920 from the Congress Party, he had reorganized the
> Party's Constitution around the principle of "Swaraj" or complete
> political independence from the British, and become its leader'.

He was the 'Mahatma' because as Bose explained,

> The spiritual man has always wielded the largest influence in
> India and he is called a 'Sant' or 'Mahatma' or 'Sadhu'. For various

reasons, Gandhiji came to be looked upon by the mass of the people as a Mahatma before he became the undisputed political leader of India. At the Nagpur Congress in December 1920, Mr. M.A. Jinnah, who was till then a Nationalist leader, addressed him as 'Mr. Gandhi', and he was shouted down by thousands of people who insisted that he should address him as 'Mahatma Gandhi'.[13]

The fact that several young men could now purport to bestow black clothes and flowers upon him, and so soon after the Gandhi–Irwin Pact (1931), especially just before the Karachi Congress of 1931 was to take place, shows that there had been serious failings on the part of the Mahatma in his dealings with Viscount Irwin in relation to Bhagat Singh.

These failings are nowhere more vividly recognized than in Bose's book *The Indian Struggle (1920–1942)*, which refers to 'a lack of diplomacy' as being also 'responsible' for the implementation of the Gandhi–Irwin Pact (1931). This is clear from how 'on the demand for an inquiry into the police atrocities, the Mahatma had been informed that if he stuck to it till the breaking-point, the Government would yield' and yet 'he voluntarily gave up the demand on an appeal from the Viceroy'.[14] This is so difficult to believe so as to be almost incomprehensible. Mahatma Gandhi was an equal partner in negotiations with Lord Irwin. Police atrocities were one of three items specifically enumerated as requiring Viscount Irwin's investigation. Yet the Mahatma gave up on it. As Bose goes on to lament, 'With better bargaining, even in March 1931, one could have expected more from the government, because they were really anxious for the settlement.' If the government were really that anxious, why did the Mahatma not drive the point home? Bose has an answer which places the blame squarely on the Mahatma. He explains that 'men with fixed ideas are not well qualified for political bargaining' and that '[s]o far as the Mahatma is concerned, he alternates between obstinacy and leniency and moreover, he is too susceptible to personal appeals – and with such habits of mind, it is difficult to get the better of one's opponent in political bargaining'.[15] That is quite a damning indictment of the Mahatma's failure to deploy his much-vaunted political skills in the case of Bhagat Singh. If this is right, at the very least, Gandhi gave up on saving Bhagat Singh because Irwin impressed upon him that this is what he should do in a personal appeal. This is clear from Gandhi's declaration (not mentioned by Bose in his book), 'If the boys are to be hanged let them be hanged before the Karachi Congress', which is exactly what came to pass on the night of 23 March 1931.

It is unsurprising, therefore, that others have argued that in the final analysis Gandhi actually made no effort at all to save the life of Bhagat Singh and his two condemned comrades. Mr Makandey Katju is a former judge, spending much of his time presently in southern California in comfortable retirement. He served as chief justice of both the Allahabad High Court and the Delhi High Court before being elevated to the Supreme Court of India in 2006, where he remained for the next five years. He hails from an illustrious lineage of Hindu Pandits. The Katjus lived in the enclosure of the ancient Kathlishwar Temple, from which they derive their name, and from where for generations they had served the nawabs of Jaora. In more modern times, Mr Markendey's grandfather was Dr Kailas Nath Katju. He became the union home and law minister under Prime Minister Jawaharlal Nehru, who was also another Kashmiri Pandit. It was his great-grandfather, Mansa Ram Katju, who had in fact some 200 years ago left the valley of Kashmir to seek his fortunes elsewhere in India. One can therefore presume that Mr Makandey Katju speaks with some authority when he states,

> When the British sentenced Bhagat Singh to death, Gandhi made no effort to save his life. He never wrote any letter to the British Viceroy to commute his sentence, nor did he issue any public appeal for this purpose, and he never went to meet Bhagat Singh in jail when the latter was on hunger strike.[16]

The same criticism cannot be made of India's first prime minister, Jawarharlal Nehru. As Irfan Habib notes, many in Congress privately approved of the assembly bomb explosion in April 1929, and Gandhi was all too aware of this, as is clear from the actions of none other than Nehru. As Habib states, 'Jawaharlal informed the Viceroy that "it is absurd to talk of unqualified condemnation of the young men who did it".' In fact, Nehru 'ridiculed the rulers' attempt to connect the bombs with Moscow, saying that "for them everything they (rulers) do not like comes from Moscow"'.[17] Nehru had gone so far as to 'publish the statements of Bhagat Singh and Dutt in the Congress Bulletin for which he was duly reprimanded by the Mahatma' after which '[a]pologising, Nehru wrote to Gandhi, "I am sorry you disapproved my giving Bhagat Singh and Dutt's statement in the Congress Bulletin"', but the fact was, as is clear from the *Selected Works of Jawaharlal Nehru*, he felt that he was 'compelled to publish the statement because there was very general appreciation of it among Congress circles'.[18]

Others, such as Subhas Chandra Bose, also saw the Lahore assembly bomb explosion as 'a visible expression of the revolutionary movement', such that it 'excited not only the public interest but public sympathy well'.[19] The inescapable fact, therefore is that given its lofty embrace of martyrdom, '[t]he second Lahore Conspiracy Case of 1929-30 occupied a place of pride in the liberation movement', in the words of S. Irfan Habib, because 'the principal accused' were revolutionaries who 'chose death in order to propagate their ideology and programme'.[20] Even though no one was killed and, indeed, there was no intention to kill, the impact of the Assembly bomb blast of April 1929 was, as Habib has put it, such that it 'rocked the foundations of the imperialist government'. But the difference with the Gandhian approach was clear from the outset in that immediately 'Gandhi's reaction was a bitter denunciation: "The bomb-throwers have discredited the cause of freedom"' and that 'Congressmen should not give, even in secret, any approval to the deed'".[21] The 'mad worship' of Bhagat Singh had 'led to goondaism and degradation'.[22] Habib therefore refers to 'the Mahatma's unqualified hostility towards the revolutionaries'.[23] The suggestion that the throwing of two harmless smoke bombs in the Delhi Assembly had 'discredited the cause of freedom' does Gandhi no credit whatsoever. It fundamentally misunderstands what is in the nature of a national freedom struggle against a brutal colonial oppressor from a far-off land. It treats the event of the throwing of smoke bombs as if India was already a free democracy, with equal partners vying for power in a mature democracy before an elected legislative assembly. A reference to the 'mad worship' of Bhagat Singh— as if Gandhi himself was free from such foibles—as leading to 'goondaism and degradation' is as further from the truth as can be. In the 1920s, the demand for a people's revolution was a quest for emancipation. Its inspiration came not from *goondas* on the street but from the October Revolution of 1917 in Russia. The Russian example would be emulated across the world for many years yet to come. Bhagat Singh and his comrades were only the first to have done so.

52

A 'Clean Fighter'

Nehru did not hesitate to recognize that Bhagat Singh became 'a symbol' of the honour of the nation and how a myriad songs grew about him after he avenged the death of Lala Lajpat Rai.[1] Indeed, three days after he was hanged, Pattabhi Sitaramayya, a high-ranking Congress leader and staunch Gandhi supporter, observed, 'It is no exaggeration to say that at the moment Bhagat Singh's name was as widely known all over India and was as popular as Gandhi's.'[2] This was a concession he could hardly not have made, given that upon Gandhi's arrival at the Karachi Session on 25 March 1931, he was openly insulted and faced the humiliation of having black flags waved in his face, with demonstrating youths chanting 'Down with Gandhi'.[3] Subhas Chandra Bose noted how, overnight, 'Bhagat Singh had become the symbol of the new awakening among the youths . . .'.[4] What distinguished him, over and above everyone else even in the violence that he had used, was as Nehru acknowledged, 'He was a clean fighter who faced his enemy in the open field . . . He was like a spark which became a flame in a short time and spread from one end of the country to the other dispelling the prevailing darkness everywhere.'[5]

If Bhagat Singh was a spark, then his kind of spark was sorely needed in the India of the time, because as Prof. Pritam Singh has pointed out, 'in the late 1920s and early 1930s, there were two serious ideological contenders for leadership of India's national movement' and that of these '[o]ne was Gandhism and the other was what may fairly be termed Bhagat Singhism'. Yet, 'Gandhism and Bhagat Singhism should not be reduced to the polarity of non-violence vs violence' because it is important to be aware that 'Gandhism was a perspective of minimal socio-economic transformation as a replacement of British imperial rule' and that as such '[i]t was focused on transfer of political power'. Pritam Singh continues, 'There is ample historical evidence to show that Gandhi was even willing to accept a subordinate dominion status for India under the broad structure of imperial rule.' This is a perspective to which Justice Markandey Katju has recently added his voice. Gandhi was opposed in this by Subhas Chandra Bose from within the Congress Party itself, and as Pritam Singh observes, he was opposed 'in muted voices even from Nehru', but it is nevertheless Gandhism that has prevailed and become the popular narrative of the Indian Independence movement to the exclusion of all else.

The reason for Gandhi's 'compromising stance towards British imperialism was the serious involvement of the top layers of India's capitalist class (Birla, Purushottamdas Thakurdass, and Walchand Hirachand etc.) in the influencing of, if not making of, the Gandhian and Congress perspective.' These major Indian industrialists, who formed the backbone of the Indian economy, had curried much favour during the years of the British Raj and did not wish to see the goose that laid the golden egg for them put so peremptorily to death. If there were reasons for Gandhi's moderation, they were entirely practical and self-serving and not noble, as the popular image of the salt marches and ahimsa (non-violence) have come to denote over the last hundred years. This is echoed by the noted Bhagat Singh specialist, Chaman Lal, who has referred to the 'moral indictment of Gandhian principles' when alluding to the 'national bourgeoisie interests involved' so that '[e]veryone knows that Gandhi was very close to business magnate, G.D. Birla' and that 'much of the funds for the Congress Party came from business houses . . .'.[6] Chaman Lal even goes further, however. Lord Irwin's biography itself, he points out, shows him in the following position:

> Irwin says that during their discussion of the Bhagat Singh issue Gandhi had asked him if he would mind if he (Gandhi) publicly claimed that he put a lot of pressure on the Viceroy on this issue. Irwin had replied that he wouldn't mind that. So "the best efforts" made by Gandhi "to save the lives of Bhagat Singh" and his comrades, were planned with full knowledge of the British administration.[7]

And yet Gandhi had undoubted virtues which enabled him to attract the accolade of a 'Mahatma'. What these were have withstood the test of time. Pritam Singh, however, has explained, 'Gandhi's strength was his unflinching, even arrogant, commitment to non-violence and what he considered to be truth.' On the other hand, Gandhi's weakness was 'his utter lack of understanding of the process of global capital accumulation and imperialism and the insertion of India into the global capitalist framework.'[8] Gandhi was mercilessly ridiculed for his beliefs by socialists such as Yusuf Meherali, who was unequivocal in his assertion, 'We do not believe in the change of heart theory, to which Mahatmaji attaches so much importance.' This was because '[t]o our mind, imperialism has no heart to change, it has only pockets to fill'.[9] Gandhi may have displayed his genius in understanding 'Hinduism', the religion of the majority of India's population, when coining the phrase 'Ram Rajya' (i.e., rule by the Hindu god 'Ram'), but in so doing he distanced himself from and isolated the Muslim population of India, thus paving the way to the eventual creation of Pakistan. He was even less charitable to the Sikhs of India, such that, as Pritam Singh observes, 'he never had any influence, whatsoever, amongst the Sikhs after his arrogant characterisation of Guru Gobind Singh as a misguided leader', and it is also 'doubtful if he had any serious influence amongst the Christians'. Gandhi's view of Guru Gobind Singh stands in stark contrast to that of Rabindranath Tagore (1861–1941), a man of letters and the first Indian to be awarded the Nobel Prize in Literature for his compilation *Gitanjali*, who was knighted by the British in 1915 but only for him to later renounce the accolade bestowed upon him after the Jallianwala Bagh Massacre in 1919. He wrote of Guru Gobind's moments of joy and sorrow, of his triumphs and empathy, with considerable empathy. In *Bir Guru*, his first work, written when he was in his twenties, Tagore wrote that the Guru fought for 'oppressed humanity' and laid down his life in order to bring an end to Mughal authority in Punjab. When Tagore was later disillusioned with what he called the 'degrading mendicancy policy' of the Indian National Congress of the 1880s, he wrote *Guru Gobinda*, where he made no secret of his admiration of Guru Gobind Singh, and in *Nishpal Upahar*, he noted the Guru's contempt for wealth and projected him as his ideal Indian leader. Indeed, he was not alone. A host of Bengalis, living a thousand miles away from Punjab, had written in praise of Guru Gobind Singh, admiring the spirit of martyrdom and of self-sacrifice of the Sikhs. Bengali monographs like *Sikher Balidan* (1904), *Sikhi–Itihas* (1907) and *Sikher Jagaran* (1929) provided an added stimulus to India's fight for freedom, so that many of these works were rigorously suppressed by the British for their avowed appeal to the militant nationalists of Bengal. *Sikher Athmauti*, for example, was so effectively proscribed by the colonial government that not a single copy of it can be found in any leading library in India.[10]

Unlike Gandhi, who alienated not only the Muslims of India but also the Sikhs, Bhagat Singh made no such mistake when it came to the various communities of India. He and his colleagues in the HSRA understood the imperatives of the world capitalist economy, and this is what gave him his popular appeal. Where they were vulnerable was in their weaker organizational structure compared to what Gandhi had achieved in the Congress Party. Nevertheless, their mass popularity meant that they could cut across caste, creed, race and religion so that they were popular no less with Muslims and Sikhs as they were with the majority Hindu population, and this was their distinctive and under-appreciated strength. Their political radicalism was born out of an acute understanding of the class structure of colonialism, which they had dissected by way of a non-religious and analytical discourse. As such, unlike the Congress Party, they had no wish to see the substitution of a foreign imperialist capitalist class by an indigenous Indian capitalist class. On the contrary, what they envisioned was the advent of the rule of labour over what had previously been the rule of capital.[11] It was underpinned by the fact that unlike the revolutionary zeal of the communists of India, Bhagat Singh's radicalism had the advantage over other left-wing movements of being home grown and anchored in the Indian psyche. What the 1931 hanging of Bhagat Singh deprived an emerging India of, as Pritam Singh reminds us, was 'a serious contest between the Gandhi-led Congress vision and the Bhagat Singh-led socialist vision' as India embarked upon a determined quest for Independence. With the idea of a post-independent India still undetermined, undefined and unimagined, Bhagat Singh posed a powerful challenge to a pro-capitalist vision of a Gandhi-led Congress Party, as he positioned himself within a solid Indian socialist tradition that posed a simple bipolar choice for the people of India between Gandhian post-imperial capitalism and Bhagat Singh's independent Indian socialism.

This should be contrasted with what became under Gandhi a contest between the Congress Party and the Muslim League or between the Hindus and Muslims (as being their erstwhile Muslim conquerors who had arrived to usurp a long-enduring indigenous culture), which not only led to the formation of a Muslim-dominated Pakistan in 1947, but which also sowed the seeds of discontent within a Hindu-dominated India, with such tensions continuing with increasing ferocity to this day. Pritam Singh maintains that it is entirely possible that had Bhagat Singh lived there would have been a 'large scale migration of the Congress cadre to the fold of the Bhagat Singh-led radical alternative', but unfortunately '[t]hat possibility died with the hanging of Bhagat Singh'. He maintains what many even today will simply not admit: 'Gandhi and the colonial authorities understood the critical historical importance of

Bhagat Singh.' This meant that 'Gandhi did not protest against the decision of the colonial authorities to hang Bhagat Singh', and that,

> This decision of Gandhi was not simply the result of the moralist/ pacificist Gandhi not endorsing violence because by allowing hanging he was endorsing another kind of violence; it was the result of an extremely sharp tactician and strategist Gandhi realising that if Bhagat Singh survived, that would sound the death knell of his (Gandhi's) political leadership of India's independence movement.

In fact, Bhagat Singh was the only one who stood to threaten Gandhi's hegemony on the political landscape. Gandhi knew that, and if Gandhi, who was not averse to going on a hunger strike, had done the same for Bhagat Singh, it is inconceivable that Lord Irwin, at the time of the three Round Table Conferences between 1930 and 1932, would not have released him!

That is quite a bold claim to make but it has increasingly now been echoed by others. As for the British government, the choice was no less clear in whether Bhagat Singh should live or die because '[f]or the colonial authorities, the survival of Bhagat Singh could have meant facing a revolutionary movement against them in competition with the ever compromising Gandhi-led Congress movement'. Professor Pritam Singh has been uncompromising in his denunciation, as has Justice Markandey Katju of late, that '[t]he Indian National Congress and the Indian State know and understand that Gandhi and the Congress party were deeply implicated in the colonial hanging of Bhagat Singh', and that is the reason, according to Pritam Singh, why it is the case that 'while 1857 and 1947 anniversaries continue to be commemorated, the 100th birth anniversary of Bhagat Singh will remain an embarrassing and, therefore, a marginal affair for the Congress-led Indian government'. After all, '[t]he political economy of the current Indian nation state necessitates this stance'.[12] In short, as Pritam Singh has more recently argued, whereas the 'Gandhian path was focused only on the transfer of political power', 'Bhagat

Singh's vision was to transform independent India into a socialist and an egalitarian society'. And herein lay the problem.[13]

Criticism of Gandhi from other sources also abounds. In what he describes as his 'most sensitive chapter of the volume', M.M. Juneja in his *Biography of Bhagat Singh* also examines 'Gandhi's attitude'[14] to the release of Bhagat Singh. Juneja's focus is on the week after the rejection by the Privy Council of Bhagat Singh's petition against the penalty of death by hanging. This is when on 17 February 1931 there were negotiations between Viceroy Lord Irwin and Mahatma Gandhi over the release of political prisoners who had taken part in Gandhi's non-cooperation movement. Gandhi found time on the afternoon of 18 February 1931 to raise the question of Bhagat Singh, who was not one of the political prisoners in Gandhi's movement. The viceroy made a detailed written note of what transpired between the two of them. What we learn of Gandhi is that '[h]e did not plead for commutation, although he would, being opposed to all taking of life, take that course himself'. However, what the viceroy does say of Gandhi is that given that he 'thought it would have an influence for peace', for this reason 'he did ask for postponement'.[15] Juneja points out that Gandhi's own version, which is available from an extract of Mahadev Desai's diary, 'does not conflict with that of the Viceroy'. In fact, what transpires is that Gandhi had no wish to prioritize the issue of Bhagat Singh's death sentence over other more pressing matters, because the meetings of 17–18 February 1931 between Gandhi and Viceroy Irwin were about the Gandhi-Irwin Pact. This led to the agreement between the two of them on 5 March 1931, marking the end of the Civil Disobedience Movement in India. Under this agreement Irwin agreed to release those who had been imprisoned for taking part in the Salt March and to allow Indians to make salt for domestic use.

At best, Gandhi took a disinterested view on Bhagat Singh. He himself records how with respect to Bhagat Singh he told Irwin that '[t]his has no connection with our discussion, and it may even be inappropriate on my part to mention'. One is bound to ask why, if Gandhi was so concerned to ensure the release of all those political prisoners who at his behest had taken part in the Salt March, he was not also at pains to seek the immediate release of one such as Bhagat Singh? After all, Gandhi managed to secure the freedom of no less than some 90,000 detainees. Yet, his words to Irwin clearly suggest that he was in cahoots with the viceroy. Outwardly, he would give the favourable appearance of doing something. Behind the scenes he was engaged in a discreditable design with Irwin to let the matter of Bhagat Singh lie exactly where it was. Nothing brings this home more clearly than Gandhi's own words to Irwin. He has no doubt that it would be inappropriate to bring the issue of Bhagat Singh up at this time. On the other hand, does the statement '[b]ut if you want to make the present atmosphere more favourable, you should suspend Bhagat Singh's execution' make the present atmosphere more favourable? Is that what it was all about? Creating a favourable atmosphere rather than saving the life of a condemned man? We learn that unsurprisingly '[t]he Viceroy liked this very much and Irwin even said, "I am grateful to you that you have put this thing before me in this manner. Commutation of sentence is a difficult thing, but suspension is certainly worth considering'. The two of them were clearly patting each other on the back. Together they were working through a process of helping each other out from their respective predicaments. In the process they stitched up Bhagat Singh. So long as they could create the impression that they had done all that they could, that was all that mattered.

The truth is that at no stage did Mahatma Gandhi insist that the need of the hour was the release of Bhagat Singh. The political agreement in the Gandhi–Irwin Pact was reached on 5 March 1931. Bhagat Singh went to the gallows eighteen days later on 23 March 1931. At no stage did Gandhi say to Irwin that a price for the agreement reached at that time was not the suspension, but the commutation of the sentence of death passed on the three young men in the Lahore Conspiracy Case. Yet, Gandhi happily went on thereafter to participate in the Second Round Table Conference which started six months later in London on 7 September 1931. If the Mahatma in the Gandhi-Irwin Pact was able to ask for the release of tens of thousands of prisoners who had been involved in the non-cooperation movement, he could also have asked for the release of Bhagat Singh on death row. That he did not venture to do so is a damning indictment of the Mahatma. To this day, there are people who hold him singularly responsible. In fact, if truth be told, Gandhi's efforts on behalf of Bhagat Singh were next to nothing. His efforts serve only to show his cynicism. We know this because while speaking about Bhagat Singh to Irwin, he needlessly condemns him with the words, 'He is undoubtedly a brave man but I would certainly say that he is not in his right mind.'[16] Why would anyone want to save a person who is not in his right mind? In fact, anyone with a scintilla of knowledge of what Bhagat Singh believed in and stood for in his life in revolution would not use these words while asking for clemency from the viceroy. Still less would he have described him as such to the viceroy because to do so was to show him as being less than human and to diminish his humanity. To crown it all, Gandhi then told the viceroy, 'I am putting this matter before you as a humanitarian issue . . . in order that there may not be unnecessary turmoil in the country. *I would not take it ill even if you do not give any reply to this issue.*'(emphases added)[17] Is that how one pleads for a person's life? That one would not take it remiss even if despite one's earnest entreaties and supplication Irwin need give no consideration to the issue at all? And this, at exactly the time that Gandhi was negotiating with Irwin in the matter of calling off the Civil Disobedience Movement. Take it or leave it is what Gandhi was suggesting to Irwin. He was doing so in a perfunctory and half-hearted manner. The technique was designed to backfire. It was calculated not to work, for otherwise there was no need for Gandhi to have expressed himself in this way. And backfire it did.

The only difficulty for Gandhi lay in the date of 24 March 1931, which was the day that Gandhi and Bose would arrive on a train from Calcutta to Karachi. Karachi Congress on 26 March where the Gandhi–Irwin Pact was up for ratification. So he spoke again about Bhagat Singh. The meeting is recounted by Irwin. The

viceroy refers to Gandhi and records how following a discussion on
the pact on 19 March 1931, '[a]s he was leaving, he asked if he
might mention the case of Bhagat Singh' again. Gandhi had learnt
from the press that 24 March was the planned date of execution.
However, '[t]his was an unfortunate day as it coincided with the
arrival of the new President of the Congress at Karachi and there
would be much popular excitement'.[18] If this is right, then Gandhi's
only concern throughout seems to have been, not whether the young
men were spared but when they should be hanged, and if they were
hanged at the time of the Karachi Congress session, that would
take the limelight off the session. For Gandhi, it was politically
convenient if the death sentence was carried out before the Karachi
Congress session. And so it was. Small wonder that Irwin then saw
no need to commute Bhagat Singh's death sentence. Small wonder
that within a week of this meeting Irwin promptly proceeded with
the execution on the night of 23 March 1931 before the President
of Congress arrived in Karachi on 24th March. Tantalizingly, at the
eleventh hour, Gandhi realized that he was still not off the hook as
far as public opinion would be concerned. History would judge him
harshly for his ambivalence. Contemporary India too would damn
him. He had to now ask for commutation directly, even if the hour
was late. So Gandhi wrote a final bizarre letter on the day of the
execution on 23 March 1931 to the viceroy. In this he asked 'if there
is any room left for reconsideration' because 'popular opinion rightly
or wrongly demands commutation'.

The letter is bizarre not only because it came far too late after
his vacillations over the issue on 18 February and 19 March 1931,
when he ended the discussion saying that he would leave the matter
entirely in Irwin's hands to decide as he would. It is bizarre also
because while he reminds the viceroy for the first time how 'political
murders have been condoned before now' and can be condoned
now, he, nevertheless, does not make a complete uncompromising
demand for release of the condemned in the Lahore Conspiracy
Case. It is no good for anyone to say that Irwin would have remained
unmoved at this late hour. How can we know? We cannot know

that without a firm demand first for release being made. There was no solid demand. And yet, the expectation of the people of India during the prolonged negotiations with the British for the release of political prisoners was precisely that he be seen to at least be making a robust and unflinching demand of the viceroy of India that the Lahore conspirators also be released. If those languishing as political prisoners in India's jails could be released on Gandhi's demand, this was all the more reason that those condemned to die as political prisoners on the gallows should also be released on Gandhi's demand. That was the expectation of the people. It did not happen. What we have is a muffled and muddled request from the Mahatma. The reason is that it was public opinion that the Mahatma was worried about. He was not making his own heartfelt demand of the viceroy. He was not imposing his own personal condition and saying that any agreement with Irwin will have to be subject to that condition. And Irwin knew that. Consequently, the Mahatma ended up taking the bite out of his request to Irwin. He made the request conditional. The condition was one over which the Mahatma himself had no control. He asked for 'suspension of sentence *pending cessation of revolutionary murders*' (emphases added).[19] How could Gandhi guarantee to Irwin that those whom he dismissed as 'deluded patriots' would stop the revolutionary struggle? If he could not, then what assurance did Irwin have from the young revolutionaries themselves that there would be an immediate cessation of revolutionary murders? He had none. So how could Irwin proceed to suspend the sentence on a promise which was without foundation and stood unsubstantiated? He could not. To be effective, Gandhi had to ask not for a 'suspension of sentence' but an outright commutation as he had done in the other cases of prisoner release. This he did not do.

In the end Gandhi did not escape the harsh judgement of providence. While many have praised his efforts, many others have not. Juneja writes, 'Gandhi alone could have intervened effectively to save Bhagat Singh's life. He did not, till the very last.' In fact, he is clear that 'Gandhi was not candid . . . on saving Bhagat Singh's life'.[20] If this is so, then it is hardly surprising because Gandhi himself mockingly wrote that '. . . I want the greater bravery . . . of the meek, the gentle and the non-violent, the bravery that will mount the gallows without injuring, or harbouring any thoughts of injury to a single soul'.[21] This is so unrealistic that it is ludicrous. Why on earth would anyone have to mount the gallows if they had not even harboured so much as a thought of injuring a soul? The Mahatma in his sanctimoniousness does not deign to explain. This is Indian mysticism, pure and simple, which bears no relevance to the reality on the ground where people hang from the gallows for the injury they have caused. No one in the real world hangs for the sin of non-injury to a single soul. Gurdev Singh Deol had little doubt that Gandhi had no expectation of commutation of death, and did not want one, if what he had said to Irwin was that the boys could be hanged before the Karachi session but not after it.[22] After the boys were indeed hanged, Gandhi released a statement in *The Tribune* the next day on 24 March 1931. He described Bhagat Singh as if he was a person of only transient and fleeting memory unknown to him, someone quite distant from his own life as a crusader for India's freedom. Gandhi's words were that, '[t]here never has been, within living memory, so much romance round any life as has surrounded that of Bhagat Singh', even as he struggled to remember how '. . . I must have seen him as a student while at Lahore many times', but that 'I cannot recall Bhagat Singh's features'. Such was his fading recollection of him even as the young Bhagat Singh had bravely mounted the gallows with Sukhdev and Rajguru. He could not have known him very well if it was the case only that 'during the past month, it was a privilege to listen to the story of Bhagat Singh's patriotism, his courage and his deep love for Indian humanity'.[23] And yet, Gandhi still could not resist the opportunity of a jibe at his erstwhile rival on grounds that 'he misused his extraordinary courage . . . .'.[24] The truth is that it was not Bhagat Singh who misused his courage but Gandhi who did not use his courage to save Bhagat Singh. Gandhi was not slow to acknowledge, however, how he stood to benefit from what he described as Irwin's 'grave blunder'. Bhagat Singh's death, he declared, 'has increased our power for winning the freedom for which Bhagat Singh and his comrades have died'.[25] Perhaps Gandhi had a strategy after all. If so, it was an astute one.

PART 11

RESTITUTION

Tumhari yaad ke jab zakhm bharne lagte hain
Kisi bahane tumhein yaad karne lagte hain

Tormented by the pain of your memories as I am,
The pain is a cause to remember you by.

—Faiz Ahmed Faiz

53

'Prayaschitta'

Given Mahatma Gandhi's joint culpability with Lord Irwin in the death of Bhagat Singh, what India needs today more than a mere apology is a psychic process of decolonization, similar to what the Germans have undergone in the 'de-nazification' of their past. It is for this reason that an apology on its own would serve no purpose unless it is also accompanied by such a process within India itself. This is manifest from how in 2019 the German president asked the Poles to forgive Germany for the Second World War at an event in Warsaw to mark the eightieth anniversary of the Nazi attack on Poland, a country which suffered the most war-related deaths per capita of any country. Some 17% of the nation's population was wiped out when six million Poles, half of whom were Jews, were killed. In the face of the Polish prime minister's clamour for an enhanced apology, the German president was disarmingly apologetic: 'I bow before the victims of the attack. I bow before the Polish victims of German tyranny. And I ask your forgiveness,' he pleaded. He then continued, with the words, 'We want to, and we will, remember. And we will bear the responsibility that our history imposes on us.'[1]

There is a lesson to be learnt here. Germany is able to do this because it has committed itself to making amends for the wrongs and injuries that it committed during the Second World War. It even has a specific term for it. The word, *'Vergangenheitsbewältigung'* implies a 'struggle to overcome the [negatives of the] past' or 'working through the past'. It is said that there isn't a native equivalent for this word in any other language. Yet, beginning in the 1960s, it has engaged in a decades-long exercise in examining, analysing and ultimately learning to live with an evil chapter in Germany's history. This is done through monuments, teachings, art, architecture, protocols and public policy. In fact, as Michele L. Norris explained in June 2021, 'The country looks at its Nazi past consistently, almost obsessively, memorialising the victims of that murderous era, so much so that it is now a central feature of the nation's cultural landscape.'[2] It refers to the national process of self-analysis and self-examination that consists of a public debate within Germany on a problematic period of its recent history during the time of National Socialism that led to traumatic events, which raised for the Germans sensitive questions of collective culpability. The term originally connoted the German people's remorse for their complicity in the war crimes of the Wehrmacht and the Holocaust. As such, the word *'Vergangenheitsbewältigung'* refers also to a psychic process of denazification and is a way by which Germany sets out to come to terms with the excesses and human rights abuses of its past. Would it be too much to expect the same with respect to what happened during a hundred years of the British Raj?

Before this question is answered, it is worth remembering that there is significant historic evidence of feelings of penance, atonement and reparation being expressed by individual persons long before decolonization was ever on the horizon. The premise, therefore, that we cannot judge the standards of the past from the vantage point of the present is a false one. This is because there already exists a reference point of people in the past, speaking in precisely the same historical epoch, who disagreed with the 'civilising' mission of the colonizer, to which we can turn for revealing insights. These show how evil was still described as evil by many in those days. It was not just Churchill who described the Jallianwala Bagh as 'monstrous' and chose to publicly disagree with General Dyer on that one occasion. There were others. And they were consistent in their opposition to this so-called 'civilising' mission. These feelings were expressed amongst the colonizers themselves during the British Raj. If that is so, is it so altogether unrealistic to speak of atonement and restitution now? One needs only look at Charles Freer Andrews, a Christian educator and social reformer, who perhaps put it best when, in writing about the Jallianwala Bagh Massacre in 1919, he lamented, 'Every day that I have been working side by side with my Indian fellow-workers, the deep sense of the wrong done has come home to me, and each act has been in very truth an act of penance, of atonement, an act of reparation for my country.'[3]

In fact, in a much-forgotten masterpiece, Edward Thompson, as early as 1925 in his aptly named *The Other Side of the Medal* wrote in the preface that his book 'will change the attitude of every Englishman who reads it to the end', pointing out that 'if that belief is justified, then I have no choice but to trust to the magnanimity of my own people . . .' in what he described as a work which 'has long been suppressed'.[4] This is because for him '[t]he East India Company was the successor of the Mughal Empire, and it wrought after its ways. Instead of impaling and flaying alive, it put to death in other fashion; under both rules, districts where rebellion had taken place were depopulated and pillaged'.[5] Significantly, he did not regard British colonial brutality as being exceptional at all. Referring for example to what is popularly known as the Indian Mutiny of 1857, he remarked, 'It is our glorification of the Mutiny that is exceptional, not its brutality.'[6]

With respect to the Amritsar Massacre of 1919, he wrote, 'It is impossible to overestimate the harm by the hysterical way in which the European community rushed to the defence of the Punjab repressions, and especially Jallianwalla.'[7] For this reason, Edward Thompson ends his highly controversial work with the observation, 'There is no commoner word on Indian lips today than *atonement*. England, they say, has never made atonement; and she must do it before we can be friends. The word in their minds is the Sanskrit word *prayaschitta*, usually translated *atonement*; but its meaning is rather *a gesture.*' In fact, he even suggests at the time, 'It is not larger measures of self-government for which they are longing, it is the magnanimous gesture of a great nation, so great that it can afford to admit mistake and wrong-doing, and is too proud to distort facts.'[8] With the passage of nearly a hundred years, since when Thompson penned these words, it is even more important today that the facts are not distorted, even as the passage of time makes the risks manifestly greater, for as Thompson himself noted, 'Truth has an eternal title to our confession, though we are sure to be the sufferers by it.'[9]

In fact, slowly but surely we are moving into the direction not only of a more fulsome apology in place of a simple expression of words but also of demonstrable acts of atonement. Perhaps the way to do it has been shown most recently by the Archbishop of Canterbury Justin Welby. He did not apologize. But he achieved something more than what a bare apology would have done. On 10 September 2019, he physically prostrated himself before the Jallianwala Bagh memorial in Amritsar, lying level on the ground before it, as a mark of respect for the victims of the 1919 massacre, declaring that he was ashamed and sorry that such an incident took place. His words are a testament to the power of words in the quest for atonement and reconciliation: 'I have no status to apologise on behalf of the UK, its government or its history,' he said, 'but I am personally very sorry for this terrible atrocity.' He added, 'Coming here arouses a sense of profound shame at what happened in this place. It is one of a number of deep stains on British history. The pain and grief that has transcended the generations since must never be dismissed or denied.'

His Facebook post after the visit went further: 'When there is something on the scale and horror of this massacre, and done so many years ago, words can be cheaply bandied around, as if a simple apology would ever be enough.'[10] His words on the day provide a practical example of how atonement is to be undertaken, for he lamented the misuse of power when he described how '[t]he souls of those who were killed or wounded, of the bereaved, cry out to us from these stones and warn us about power and the misuse of power'. He went on to say, 'I cannot speak for the British government . . . but I can speak in the name of Christ and say this is a place of both sin and redemption, because you have remembered what they have done and their names will live, their memory will live before God. And I am so ashamed and sorry for the impact of this crime committed here.'

His words showed more than a determined stride towards real reconciliation when he said, 'Learning of what happened, I recognise the sins of my British colonial history, the ideology that too often subjugated and dehumanised other races and cultures. We have a great responsibility to not just lament this horrific massacre but most importantly to learn from it in a way that changes our actions.'[11] Indeed, during Britain's 2019 parliamentary election, the Labour Party 'promised to tender a "formal apology" on behalf of the British government for the 1919 Jallianwala Bagh massacre, and hold a "public review" into the UK's role in the 1984 Operation Bluestar if it is voted to power in the December 12 elections', when its leader, Jeremy Corbyn, distanced himself from the simple expression of 'deep regret', which had been given by PM Theresa May when she was in office earlier in 2019.[12]

54

The Rule of Law

While these are all no doubt positive developments in individual acts of atonement, what will ultimately help secure societies across the world that are free from the whims of those who would wish to suppress the inalienable rights and freedoms of mankind will be to ensure that the wrongs of the past are not repeated. Two examples suffice. First, it is important that those being tried for acts of terrorism are not denied the full protection of regular law as Bhagat Singh was. The rule of law is not an imaginary land out of the reach of those accused of the most serious crimes, and cases of terrorism are still subject to the due process of law. Khalid Sheikh Mohammed, the accused Al-Qaeda mastermind of the 11 September 2001 attacks detained in Guantanamo, is facing the death penalty. In a lawsuit filed by victims seeking damages from Saudi Arabia, he has indicated a willingness to cooperate with the authorities, provided that the United States does not seek capital punishment against him. In 2003, he was subjected to waterboarding by the CIA no less than 183 times. This was personally authorized by former US President George W Bush.[1]

In the summer of 2019, a military judge set a trial date for Khalid Sheikh Mohammed with four other men, which would be held at Guantanamo. It is now twenty years after these unspeakable atrocities were committed in September 2001, and there have already been more than thirty pre-trial hearings and endless procedural arguments, with proceedings moving at the pace of a tortoise. During this time, witnesses have died, lawyers have grown old and victims' families have seen their patience unreasonably tested. Yet, although Barack Obama tried to close the prison on Guantanamo Bay, his successor Donald Trump pledged to 'load it up with some bad dudes'—hardly a shining commitment to ensuring that justice is done and is seen to be done.[2]

Compare that to Lord Steyn, who served as a senior judge in the UK throughout the 1990s. An implacable critic of the claim to immunity from prosecution of the former Chilean head of state Augusto Pinochet in 1998, he reserved his most fierce ire for the detention of prisoners at Camp X-ray at Guantánamo Bay. He was forced by the UK government to stand down and not be available for the hearings in the House of Lords on the indefinite detention of terrorist suspects in 2004. When he died, the Times of London described Lord Steyn in its obituary as '[o]ne of the most liberal judges ever to enter the House of Lords', who had 'branded the US regime at Guantanamo Bay "a monstrous failure of justice" and declared that the system of trial by military tribunal was no more than a "kangaroo court" that "makes a mockery of justice"'. Such was the impact of this statement, in giving the Twenty-Seventh F.A. Mann Lecture on 25 November 2003 at Lincoln's Inn, that '[i]n 2004 the senior law lord, Lord Bingham of Cornhill, was asked not to include Steyn on the nine-judge panel to decide on the legality of detaining foreign terror suspects without trial' and 'Steyn agreed to stand down, but later told The Times that the government had raised a "truly flimsy objection"'. He was, as a law lord, 'one of the most outspoken – so much so that the New Labour government broke with precedent to block his appointment to a House of Lords judicial committee'. Lord Steyn was described by Anthony Lester QC as a champion of human rights law who had 'transformed our country into a rights-based democracy' such that '[h]e's going to be extraordinarily difficult to replace'.[3] There is, after all, a different way of doing trials that have a bearing on national security and public order.

Second, it is important that those in the subcontinent who suffered from coercive colonialism in all its multifarious forms take a stand against its continuance and repetition. The quest for transitional justice, in the sense of the redress of the legacies of human rights abuses through avenues of reparation programmes and truth commissions, does not begin and end with an apology from a former imperial power alone, particularly if one bears in mind the role of Mahatma Gandhi. What is most important in the long run is not what others do, but what the people of the Indian subcontinent themselves do. Before there can be calls for atonement elsewhere, there must first be atonement amongst the people of the subcontinent to include those who collaborated in the injustices wreaked upon the Indian people by the Raj. Bhagat Singh must first be rehabilitated in the minds and hearts of the people where it most matters. The reason for this is quite simply that before one can call upon others to honour their heroes, they must first be honoured at home. We must avoid ethnonationalist accounts of our histories quite simply because they are not true. Cheap gimmickry is not a substitute for real societal change. No wonder Justice Markandey Katju has said that current Indian policies and issues surrounding events like Yoga Day, movements like Swatchh Bharat Abhiyan and controversial debates regarding Ram Mandir and cow protection are not the ideal representations of the India that Bhagat Singh stood for.[4] In the land of the sacred cow, India's pluralist identities stand in question today. Its liberal democracy, its secularism, its rush to globalization and even its economic growth have been abandoned in the ruthless pursuit of an ideology of homogenized nationalism that has led to obsessive self-harm. Professor David Edgerton has referred to 'the racialised nature of the imperial project' in Britain with which it has yet to come to terms. If this is so, then India has had a 'casteist' political and religiously discriminatory project which is still not altogether recognized. As Edgerton says that in Britain 'all our national history needs rethinking',[5] so in India too this is no less true.

The countries of the Indian subcontinent were born out of a frenzied bout of ethnic bloodletting. Instead of coming together as one in a violent revolutionary struggle against imperial rule they used violence against each other at precisely the moment of their liberation from foreign rule. The violence of Partition has still not been put to bed. Theirs was not an immaculate conception but a benighted one. It paved the way for the birth of two countries where previously there was one. The distinguishing hallmark was religion. Religion it was that was the reason for the savage and merciless killing of one neighbour by the other. The violence of Partition was not addressed by either side. In that sense, the violence of Partition is not over. It continues today and it has come to haunt the Indian subcontinent. Ethnic divisions are still being stoked. Some see it is 'unfinished business' where the mixity, hybridity and cosmopolitanism of its millenia old society continue to be cleansed of their individual communities, which together had always enriched it like a richly embroidered mosaic. Bhagat Singh is relevant because he opposed sectarianism. Had Partition not happened, his legacy would have had a better chance of survival than it has otherwise done. India would have been different.

That is why Bhagat Singh remains as relevant today as he was during the days of imperial rule. For these reasons, it is in many ways rather pointless for India or Pakistan to be seeking atonement from Britain if the memorialization of their respective celebrated freedom has taken the form of a claim to freedom, which is as much a freedom from each other as it is a freedom from the coercive colonial rule of a foreign power. Today's governing party in India is formed from the political arm of the RSS. This is the organization to which Gandhi's assassin, Nathuram Godse, belonged. The banality of communal violence based on religious hatred is evident once again, as it was three-quarters of a century ago, when the Raj left ignominiously, having committed its own heresies. Mob killings, such as that of the dairy farmer Pehlu Khan, who was dragged and humiliated on a busy road in broad daylight even while he is seen on mobile video footage pleading for his life, are all too commonplace and frequent in their occurrences now. Instead of dealing with socio-economic disparities that grow incessantly by the day, India, in 2022, stands obsessed, in the words of Pratap Bhanu Mehta, with the 'Hijab debate', which is nothing but 'a pretext for institutionalising state cruelty.'[6] Elsewhere the celebrated public intellectual, Noam Chomsky has lamented at how 'the pathology of Islamophobia' is 'taking its most lethal form in India' today where 'Indian secular democracy' was being dismantled in order to turn the country into 'a Hindu ethnocracy.'[7] Others have decried the rise in India today of 'a state devoted to the humiliation of muslims.'[8] The ethnic cleansing at the time of Independence, which has never been treated as the central narrative of Partition by mainstream historians, has now ricocheted with a vengeance and returned to haunt the subcontinent, which appears to have learnt nothing from the forced migration of 15 million on account of their religion. Citizenship and the right to be in a homeland, the very essence of belongingness, are being bestowed on one group of migrants but denied to others of a different faith. It was not for this that Bhagat Singh mounted the scaffold, so willingly, with such conviction, and in such great hope for the future. What India most urgently needs in the circumstances of today is not so much an apology from Britain but a '*Vergangenheitsbewältigung*' of its own where it can strive to overcome its own negatives and work through not only its own past but also its own present – its here and now. It needs, in the words of Edward Thompson, its own *prayaschitta*. Its *atonement* for its own deeds.

55

Indic Hybridity

What needs reclaiming in the name of Bhagat Singh is the hybrid Indo-Islamic world that is fast disappearing. This is a world where Sanskrit-based languages charmingly and teasingly intermingle with Turkish, Persian and Arabic dialects, and this world needs to be rescued for the good of India's cosmopolitan society. A world where it was not unknown for a Rajput princess to marry a Mughal ruler—replaced now with a moral universe where even the pictorial depiction of such historic events is deemed to be nothing short of sacrilege and infamy.[1] Let us not forget how after an ill-thought-out fast-track citizenship law was passed for non-Muslim migrants from three neighbouring countries, which excluded the right of Muslim migrants to register as citizens of India, protests broke out across. A Hindu nationalist agenda to marginalize the 200 million Indians who follow Islam led to the death of six people in the north-east and reports of up to a 100 injured in Delhi in December 2019.[2]

The last thing that Bhagat Singh's India could have been associated with was sectarianism. It was not for this that he sacrificed his young life. Kama Maclean explains this well when she asserts, 'The HSRA and Naujawan Bharat Sabha worked on a very different trajectory, eschewing communalism with a strident secularist critique which forbade its members from membership of religious

or communal organisations . . .'.[3] Jinnah defended Bhagat Singh
in Parliament for this reason. Yet, as Maclean points out, it was 'a
revelation to many when A.G. Noorani wrote at length in his book
of M.A. Jinnah's defence of Bhagat Singh, Rajguru and Sukhdev in
the Legislative Assembly in 1929, objecting to the bill introduced
to allow the business of the Lahore conspiracy case to be tried in
absentia by a special tribunal'.[4] What united all these people at the
time was a belief in India's diversity. This was its crowning glory. So
distinctive is this trait that as recently as June 2021, tribute has been
paid by the British Indian sculptor, Sir Anish Kapoor, to 'India's
capacity for diversity, India's inescapable multi-layered complexity,
India's refusal of singularity'.[5]

Yet today, as Amy Kazmin points out, India is set upon a path to
follow 'the example of Myanmar, which is battling genocide claims at
the International Court of Justice over the crackdown on the country's
Muslim minority' because at the end of 2019 India 'approved new
citizenship rules that redefine – a pluralistic secular democracy with
a sizeable Muslim minority – as a natural homeland for Hindus
and adherents of other "Indic" faiths, from which Islam is pointedly
excluded'.[6] This is the first time that India has incorporated a religious
criterion into its naturalization and refugee policies. It has done so by
allowing any Hindu, Sikh, Jain, Buddhist, Parsee or Christian who
entered India prior to December 2014 a fast-track route to citizenship,
from countries such as Pakistan, Afghanistan and Bangladesh where,
as minorities in a Muslim country, they faced discrimination. Muslim
immigrants, including Muslim minorities such as Ahmadiyas and
Shias, are excluded. While Prime Minister Modi regarded this as 'the
unfinished business of the traumatic 1947 partition of the Indian subcontinent', critics see this as the renunciation of the pledge by India's
founding fathers 'as a home for all faiths and signalling to India's 200m
Muslims that they do not fully belong'[7] in India. This risks creating
two tiers of citizenship, with one created for a privileged community
and the other for a marginalized one.

If the idea is not very clever, it is not very original either. It is
borrowed directly from Myanmar, which in 1982 adopted a citizenship

law that recognized eight different ethnic groups as 'national races' entitled to citizenship but excluded the Rohingya Muslims, who were vilified by the Burmese as illegal immigrants from Bangladesh. To acquire citizenship, they had to show 'conclusive evidence' that prior to Independence in 1948 their ancestors had already lived in Burma. This proved impossible for many poor immigrants to prove in much the same way that it will be impossible for many Muslim immigrants to India to prove under its Citizenship (Amendment) Act 2019.[8] What unfolded in Myanmar is all too well known, and it augurs badly for what risks unfolding in India. There were decades of discrimination against the Rohingya in education, housing and employment, before it culminated in 2017 in the mass expulsion of 7,00,000 of them to Bangladesh. India too now wants to embark on a futile and costly exercise of determining which of its 1.3 billion residents are eligible for citizenship, fearing that it is being swamped by illegal Muslim migration from Bangladesh.

As in Myanmar, Indian Muslims will have to prove that they were resident in India upon Independence in 1947 or risk detention and deportation as illegal immigrants, whereas other religious groups will not. The entire scheme is an exercise of monumental folly. Not only will it be impracticable to remove millions of Muslims from their communities of sustainable livelihood at a time when the Indian economy is in the doldrums and place them in detention camps where they will be fed and maintained at public expense, but it will be well nigh impossible to deport those who have no documentation to a country of which they are not citizens. Yet, India's first and largest detention centre at Goalpara in Assam, the size of seven football grounds, has already been built to hold up to 3,000 illegal immigrants, and ten further centres are planned across this north-eastern state of India.[9] Small wonder then that Professor Chaman Lal has felt inclined to point out that, 'in present situation when a saffron build-up was trying to choke up the very Constitution of India and the concept of a nation' that Bhagat Singh and his comrades fought and died for, especially given that men like 'Bhagat Singh were undoubtedly patriotic and secular but the current fascist build-up in the country was trying to promote him by subverting his hallmark – rationalism and scientific temper'.[10] In fact, the actions of the Myanmar government suitably saw it in the dock when on 11 November 2019, the International Court of Justice at the Hague heard an application by the Gambia against it, alleging violation of the obligations under the Genocide Convention in which it succeeded.[11] It is not inconceivable that the same may happen to the Indian government were it to persist in this programme of disenfranchising vast swathes of its population and turning them into an un-people. This is why Professor Chaman Lal has remarked that 'there is good reason to hold on to [Bhagat] Singh's principles, owing to the current political atmosphere in the country'.[12]

The student protests which have followed have been met with unprecedented state brutality through the invocation of Section 144 of the Indian Code of Criminal Procedure. This, like the power used to deal with Bhagat Singh and his comrades, is an 'emergency power' designed to prevent public disorder and to protect human life. The existence of the power itself is a throwback to colonial times as it prevents any more than three persons from congregating in a public place. Thereafter, wide-ranging powers are bestowed upon the district magistrate to use his/her discretion to order any person to 'abstain from a certain act' or to 'take certain order with respect to certain property in his possession or under his management'. The slapdash use of Section 144 across the country to deal with peaceful student protests, without the slightest regard being given to the fact that they posed no threat to public disorder whatsoever, led to a needlessly merciless repressive action by the police authorities. 'Such repression by the police was not witnessed on the Aligarh Muslim University campus even during the time of the British,'[13] said the eminent eighty-eight-year-old Indian historian, Irfan Habib. He recalled how when he was a professor at Aligarh Muslim University, which saw the worst of the government repression against students, protesting against the Citizenship (Amendment) Act (CAA), that even '. . . the time when students had closed down the university for three days after Pakistan's Prime Minister Liaquat Ali Khan was assassinated in 1951' and even when ' India had nothing to do with it, still there had been no action against the students'. He could not forget 'the gracious attitude of the first Prime Minister Jawaharlal Nehru towards students', when 'in the 1950s some right-wing MPs in Parliament had asked Nehru to conduct a survey to find out how many AMU engineering students migrated to Pakistan after completing their course'. The curt reply that Nehru gave to them was, 'Wherever they go, they serve humanity,' which left them all reeling in speechless stupour.[14]

When the Bar Council of India ('BCI') passed a resolution on 22 December 2019 urging the lawyers, bar associations, state bar councils and students' associations of all law colleges to ensure that law and order is maintained throughout the country, nearly a thousand lawyers from across the country immediately distanced themselves from its statement on the Citizenship (Amendment) Act, 2019 and the National Register of Citizens (NRC). This is because it had chosen to thoughtlessly add the words of its chairman Manan Kumar Mishra,

> The Leaders of the Bar and young students are requested to take active role in diffusing the disturbances and violence in the country: We are to convince the people and the illiterate ignorant mass, who are being misled by some so-called leaders [that] the matter with regard to Citizenship Amendment Act is under consideration of our Supreme Court, therefore everyone should await the decision of apex court.

This led N. Manoj Kumar, the vice-chairman of the executive committee of the BCI to dissent vehemently in these terms:

> The protests against CAA and NRC are the attempt of the Indian citizens to save their Constitution from being trampled upon by an authoritarian regime on the strength of their brute majority in the Legislature. Being the real torch bearers of the constitution, it is the duty of every self-esteemed lawyer to lead the struggle to defend the constitution.

The dissent was then signed by close to 1,000 lawyers who wished to make it emphatically clear 'that the BCI has not spoken for the Bar'. Indeed, it went on to remark that

> it is amiss that the BCI, a body which is supposed to stand up for the Bar, did not deem it fit to express solidarity with advocates such as Mr. Mohd. Shoaib who has been detained in Lucknow or the hundreds of advocates fighting across the country to uphold the rights of citizens as recognised by the constitution.[15]

Yet, when protests broke out in the southern city of Bangalore, one of the banners being proudly waved in the throng featured none other than Bhagat Singh. By April 2022, however, the worsening situation saw homes of the poor and marginalized Muslims being razed by the authorities in Delhi's Jahangirpuri, which had witnessed communal violence on April 16 during a Hanuman Jayanti procession. The only mainstream politician to oppose this was the CPI(M) leader Brinda Karat, who dramatically stood in front of a bulldozer as she denounced the government's 'communal political game plan' and moved the Indian Supreme Court to order a stay on grounds that she described as `selective and discriminatory action'.[16] In this way, unlike others, she as a politician has proved herself a worthy successor to the legacy of Bhagat Singh.

For the most part, however, hope for the future must come in the shape of the youth in both countries. It was so in the febrile atmosphere of the 1920s, and it is so now. The future lies with them. Their student movements protesting against the government have shaken both New Delhi and Lahore. Following a four-week-long agitation by students of New Delhi's Jawaharlal Nehru University against an increase in hostel fees which would put a squeeze on the ability of poorer students to join India's elite research university, hundreds of people decided to take part in a 'Citizen's March' in support of them at the end of 2019. Students from neighbouring states concerned about rising education costs also joined in, as did members of political parties. Standing beside Parliament Street

Police Station, where Bhagat Singh and Batukeshwar Dutt were kept under arrest after they had exploded bombs at the central Legislative Assembly in 1929, Sitaram Yechury, a former president of the JNU Students' Union, quoted Bhagat Singh's reply when questioned about the actions of the students: 'If the deaf are to hear,' he repeated the memorable words of Bhagat Singh, 'the sound has to be very loud.'[17]

In Pakistan too there have been long-standing student concerns. These have included a ban on their unions, absence of protocols to deal with sexual harassment, rise in annual fees, as well as a general lack of satisfaction with the quality of education offered. All these led to the formation in 2016 of the Progressive Students' Collective in Lahore. When in June 2019, a 37% budget cut to the country's higher education development programme was announced by the government, the Students' Solidarity March took to the streets on 29 November 2019 in at least fifty locations, with the principal activity being in Lahore. Their grievances went back to the reign of the military dictator Zia ul-Haq. It was he who banned student unions across the country in 1984, as he had become alarmed at their increasingly emboldened resistance. For thirty years, this ban had proscribed political activity on university and college campuses. It had imposed a culture of silence. The students were calling into question thirty years of silence, and their cause was being channelled through progressive student organizations which emulated the 2016 Lahore Students' Collective in its resolve to do the same. So now, dressed in black with red motifs and holding placards, the students fearlessly shouted slogans against the authorities, right across cities in Pakistan. They rose up unflinchingly to demand the restoration of a series of basic rights—from the right to form student unions to an end to sexual harassment. Among the student banners being euphorically paraded by the young in Lahore was one that carried the image of Bhagat Singh.[18]

In India, a protest erupted against three ordinances on agricultural marketing passed by the Modi government on 5 June 2020. The new laws passed hurriedly and without parliamentary consultation under cover of the dreadful COVID-19 pandemic were aimed at 'modernizing' Indian agriculture. The intention was to open it up to market forces. As the largest labour movement in human history began to gain momentum along Delhi's border in late 2020, Bhagat Singh's dead hand once again reached out to place itself reassuringly on the shoulders of the poor and the destitute. Before long, the numbers of the protestors had swelled to 1,25,000 farmers. Along the Tikri border in Delhi and Haryana's Bahadurgarh, the sea of humanity soon stretched to several kilometres. One in thirty of India's population now became embroiled in the agitation. With the farmers pouring in from all directions, a new-found cultural unity of Punjab and Haryana suddenly found expression in songs, dances and musical performances. The name of Bhagat Singh once again rang out in shrill expectant tones. Performances were held of the Haryanvi Raginis[19] to buoy up miraculously the morale of the drained and the deprived as one of the most bitterly freezing winters on record descended upon the protesters. By the opening months of 2021, there sprang up a Bhagat Singh Library at Dakha Singhu on Delhi's border with Haryana. With no less than an astonishing 3,500 books in Punjabi and Hindi, the ones which were most in demand were the writings and biographies of freedom fighters. Amongst the most cherished were those of Udham Singh, Kartar Singh Sarabha and Bhagat Singh.[20]

The dead clearly live among us. The past inhabits the present. We just need to look harder to see it. For now, we would do well to remember India's Ali Sardar Jafri: *'Ab bhi zindan-e-ghulami se nikal sakte hain, Apni taqdir ko hum aap badal sakte hain.'* ('Even now we can cast aside our chains / Even now we can build our own destiny').

~~~~~~~~~~~~~~~~~~~~

Appendix

In the Court of the Special Magistrate, Lahore.

113

Crown   Versus   Jatindra Nath Sanyal, etc.

Application under Section 337 (3) Criminal Procedure Code, respectfully sheweth :-

1. That it is understood that the approvers in the case to whom the pardon is said to have been granted under Section 337 have been detained in Police custody for over 4 months.

2. That the said persons were kept in Police custody from the time of their arrest till the time when they turned approver and ever since have been detained in the same custody.

3. That the petitioners apprehend that the detention of the approvers in Police custody for such a long time will defeat the ends of justice, the approvers being under the constant pressure of the Police.

4. That it is a well-known fact that the various accused persons, including the approvers, during their confinement in Police lock-up were not allowed to have access to their relatives, friends, and legal advisers and afterwards, when the High Court ruled that these facilities should be afforded to them some obstacles were still put in their way with the result that they were kept under the influence of the Police and subjected to considerable unjustifiable pressure.

5. That there is no reason why the approvers should not be kept in judicial lock-up pending the enquiry and the trial, and it is accordingly prayed, in the interests of justice, that the approvers be removed from the Police custody and kept in a judicial lock-up at any place.

Sd/- A.H. Kapur,

Advocate for Accused.

3-10-1929.

1

355

In the Court of the special magistrate,
Lahore

Crown Vs. Sukhdeo & others.

Charged under Section 121 A, 302 + 120B

This humble petition of the accused Bhagat Singh most humbly sheweth: —

1. That the petitioner is going unrepresented in this case,

2. That evidence has been produced in this court entangling the petitioner in the murders of Mr. Saunders and Sardar Chanan Singh,

3. That the petitioner may be able to effectively cross-examine the witnesses, it is necessary that the petitioner may be given an opportunity to visit the spot and see the roads and other surroundings in connection with the alleged incident.

4. That the petitioner therefore prays that proper facilities be afforded him for the said purpose and that the production of further witnesses regarding the particular incident may be postponed till the petitioner has been able to examine the locality.

Dt. 4th Nov. 29

Bhagat Singh
Petitioner

2

To   The Special Magistrate,
                       Lahore.

Case.- Crown   vs.   Sukh Dev and others.
      Charge:- Under Section 302, I.P.C., etc.

343

Sir,
        I learn that the accused have applied for a c
of the statement made by ~~Surindra Nath~~ *Phani Dutta* Gosh , appro
before the Police. Certain portions of the statemen
made by the approver before the Police are in my
opinion inexpedient in the public interests to be
furnished to the accused, and I therefore request
that while referring to the above mentioned state
you may kindly exclude such parts as you find inexpedient in the public interests to be furnished
the accused, under Section 162, Cr.P.C.

                    I beg to remain,
                         Sir,
            Your most obedient servant,

17.3.1930.

                         Dina mñ
                    Prosecuting Inspector.

3

1

In the Court of the Special Magistrate, Lahore.

Crown   Vs   Sukh Dev & others.

Charged under Sections 120+ 302, 121 A

The petitioners respectfully submit the following:—

1. That the majority of the petitioners have been in confinement for the last nine months in the above case and the rest have been so confined for terms varying from two to six months, and the case will yet take a very long time.

2. That the charges against the petitioners are of a very serious nature.

3. That the petitioners are being deprived of the fundamental right of being defended by a counsel as they are not permitted to see their attorneys and friends, a matter which the learned Court has delegated to the jail authorities who have refused to allow their interview with their attorneys and friends.

4. That although the police and other officials are permitted to come freely into the court room, the petitioners friends are not even permitted to enter the court room.

5. That the dock in which the petitioners are kept in the course of the inquiry is always surrounded by police and jail officials and even those petitioners who are represented by counsel feel handicapped in communicating with and giving full instructions to them.

6. That an unprecedented practice of keeping an assistant jailor and some jail officials present always around the dock is being pursued.

7. That the petitioners have been deprived of the right of having access to newspapers which they need very badly in connection with their defence.

8. That they are being prosecuted and punished by the jail authorities for matters which have occurred in the court.

9. That the petitioners are unable to take legal steps in respect of the illegal punishment inflicted on them and the illegal treatment meted out to them by the jail authorities.

10. That definite complaints filed by some of the petitioners in respect of the ill-treatment and assault by the police officials have not been attended to by the authorities and while in custody the petitioners are unable to prosecute them.

5(a)

5(b)

The court of the Special Tribunal Lahore Conspiracy Case, Lahore.

15

Crown vs. Sukhdeo and others.
Charged under Sec. 302, 120 B, 121.A. 15 P.C.

The humble petition of the undersigned accused persons Bejoy Kumar Sinha and others, most respectfully sheweth:—

(1) That the petitioners have been brought on trial before this learned court without sufficient notice.

(2) That the petitioners have at present no counsel to defend them.

(3) That it has not been possible for these reasons to draw up their line of defence.

(4) That it is therefore prayed that the hearing be adjourned for a fortnight to enable the petitioners to prepare their line of defence and further to make necessary arrangements for defence.

Dy. 5/5/30.

Bejoy Kumar Sinha
Shiva Varma
Jai Deva Kapur
Surhandi and others.

Petitioners

5/5/31

5

In the Court of the Special
Tribunal,
Lahore

Respectfully sheweth. —

1. That it is prayed that
an interview allowed to me with
my father during the lunch
interval. and oblige.

Bhagat Singh
Petitioner

D/5·5/30

Arrangements for interviews during
Court hours cannot be made
unless there are any # urgent
grounds which should be stated.

5/5/30   J. Coldstream

From

        Major P.D. Chopra I.M.S.,
           Superintendent Central Jail,
           LAHORE.

To

        The Registrar,
           Special Tribunal,
           Lahore Conspiracy Case,
           LAHORE.
           No. 262-G dated 6.5.1930.

Sir,

      With reference to your letter No.6T
without date received today. I have the honour
to state that the two accused Bhagat Singh and
B.K. Dutt being undertrials in the Lahore Conspiracy Case are allowed interviews at the Jail
with their relatives once a week and with legal
counsel whenever their accredited counsels have
applied for an interview.

2.   In addition to above when the case was
being tried by the Special magistrate in the
Lahore Central Jail Court the two above accused
were allowed interviews with their relatives
daily during luncheon interval. The application
were for such interviews were sent to me for
sanction through the special magistrate.

               I have the honour to be,
                   Sir,
            Your most obedient servant,

                   Major I.M.S.,
       Superintendent Central Jail, Lahore.

In the court of the Special Tribunal
Lahore Conspiracy Case, Lahore.

Crown vs. Sukhdeo and others
Charged under Sec 302 read with Sec 109, 120B, & 121/121A.A.

31

The humble petition of the accused Bhagat
Singh most respectfully sheweth:—

(1) That he got fever in the court yesterday
at 11 A.M.

(2) That in the evening he had 103° temp as
recorded in the jail.

(3) That he was given a very strong purgative
last night and consequently he is feeling
extremely weak.

(4) That it is therefore prayed that a
reclining seat be arranged for him just behind
the defence counsels or if that cannot be
arranged, he be sent back to jail and the
trial be proceeded with in his absence, to which
the petitioner has got no objection whatsoever.

8/5/30.

Bhagat Singh
Petitioner.

Police in charge about whether
such arrangements are possible

8/5/30.

9

(47)

To,

      The Registrar,
      The Special Tribunal,
      Lahore Conspiracy Case,
        Lahore

Sir,

      Kindly supply me with an attested copy of the order of the Special magistrate dated 3rd May 1930, according to which the inquiry proceedings in that court were stayed.

          Thanking you in anticipation,

            Yours Etc.

            Bhagat Singh
            Undertrial,
Dy 09th June 1930.   Lahore Conspiracy Case
            Lahore

To,

      The Registrar,
      Special Tribunal, Poonch House,
        Lahore

Through

      The Superintendent,
      Central Jail, Lahore.

No 767 D/24th June 1930 Special Tribunal, Poonch House. Forwarded to the Registrar, High Court, Lahore, for favour of necessary action as he deems fit.

Let a copy be given

             Major J.M.S.
             Superintendent Central Jail,
             Lahore
20/6/30

173

In the Hon'ble High Court of Judicature (Punjab) Lahore

Crown Vs Bhagat Singh & others
[Lahore Conspiracy Case, Lahore]

Charged under Section 302, 121, 121A Etc & I.P.C.

Most respectfully Sheweth:—

1. That the petitioner ~~and~~ is an accused in the Lahore Conspiracy case, being tried by the Special Tribunal constituted under the Lahore Conspiracy Ordinance.

2. That the petitioner and his consceness refused to attend the court in protest of a certain order passed and treatment meted out to the accused.

3. That the petitioner went on hunger strike on July 29th '30 in protest against certain regulations of the jail department.

4. That the trial is entering a new stage i.e. the Prosecution evidence is about to be closed and the petitioner is to be called upon to make his statement and to offer any defence if desired.

5. That the jail authorities have altogether stopped all the interviews of the petitioner with his relatives and legal advisers.

6. That this purely executive affair is hampering the cause of justice and these orders of the executive are highly illegal.

7. That the petitioner wants the help of his relatives and legal advisers in deciding the most delicate question of defence.

8. That there is a special provision in the Lahore Conspiracy case Ordinance to the effect that if any accused voluntarily disables himself by hunger-striking or otherwise or resists his production before the Court, he shall still have the right to be represented by a counsel in his absence.

9. That in the present circumstances the accused feels quite handicapped due to the above mentioned orders of the jail authorities.

10. That it is prayed that in the interest of justice and fair play, the court be pleased to intervene in this affair and to issue such instructions to the authorities concerned, as would if be necessary to give full and proper facilities for arranging defence adequately in a case where the petitioner is being tried for such serious offences ~~which~~ as may bring the extreme penalty of law.

11. That it is prayed that the court be pleased to issue urgent orders for allowing interviews etc at the earliest convenience.

9) 11/8/30

Bhagat Singh
convict & undertrial
Lahore Conspiracy Case,
Lahore
Central Jail Lahore

Through
The Supdt
no. 127–9/11/8/30 Central jail,
Lahore

Forwarded to the Registrar to the High Court of Judicature for
forum of disposal.   Lahore,   M. Fazluddin
                            11. 8.30   Major IMS

Let us see a copy of the conspiracy case ordinance.

Said Commr.
12.5.30.

175

D.T.

Herewith

Ryot   M.C.
                        17 P

Hon'ble vacation Judge might please say what
he would like done with this petition from Bhagat
Singh, one of the accused in the Lahore Conspiracy
case. The man states (para 5) that the jail
authorities have stopped his interviews with
pleaders and relatives; he claims in para 6 that
this is hampering the ~~cause~~ course of justice and is also
illegal; in paras 10 and 11 he prays that the High
Court will be pleased to issue orders that he
should be allowed interviews again.

2.   Ordinance No: III of 1930 is to "provide
specially for the trial of the accused in the
cases known as the Lahore conspiracy case" and
under section 11 thereof the High Court has no
jurisdiction in respect of any proceeding under it.
The forbidding of interviews by the jail authorities
does not seem to have much to do with the trial
of the accused and I should say on the whole that
it is not a proceeding under the Ordinance unless
of course the jail authorities were directed to

159

To,

    The Special Commissioners,
        Lahore Conspiracy Case Tribunal,
            Lahore

Through,

      The Supdt.
        Central Jail,
          Lahore

Sirs,

    I have just been informed by the jail-authorities that the learned Court was pleased to pass order on my application dated 11th Aug '30, to the effect that interviews with legal adviser alone may be allowed. I was at a loss to understand the reason of such an order. Why should I not be allowed to see my relatives, when the said interviews are very essential for defence purposes? If the order is meant simply to make a show that the accused are given proper facilities regarding their defence, though in reality nothing of the sort is done, on the contrary, the defence is hampered at every step, then all my petitions and representations are useless.

    My legal adviser, L. Duni Chand Barrat Law is in jail. I want to engage a new one, which I can not without the help and advice of my father. Therefore the interview is very essential. I have to consult my father about offering the defence. I want to ascertain how far he can help me in this respect. If interviews will not be allowed, the court and jail authorities shall stand responsible for the serious conse-quences that I might have to bear for this high-handedness.

    With no stretch of imagination can I understand as to why should the court of law join hands with the executive in such matters as are immediately concerned with the administration of justice and be a party to the unnecessary harassment of the accused.

    I most earnestly request the court to reconsider their orders passed on my said application and to issue instructions to the jail authorities to allow all my interviews so long as the trial is going on. They shall have time enough to treat us as they like after conviction.

    Hoping to be favoured with an early decision,

              Yours Etc.
              Bhagat Singh
              Convict - under trial

D 15th Aug 30

161

With reference to his applications

of 11th August, 1930, and 15th August,1930,

on the subject of interviews between him-

self and friends or relatives in the

Jail let Bhagat Singh be supplied by

the Registrar with a copy of the remarks

made by the Tribunal on his application

of 11th August, 1930. Let Bhagat Singh

also be informed that if he wishes to
                    further
make any/representation to the Tribunal

in connection with the matter the Tribunal

will be prepared to hear him personally

or through counsel on the subject at

Poonch House on 25th August,1930, at

3 p.m.

22/8/30.

14

we adjourn the taking up of
this application to tomorrow
26th August, Bhagat Singh's
presence having been
dispensed with today
under section 9 of the
Ordinance for reasons
given in the order
passed under that
section.

25.8.30 Abdul Qadir

26/8/30. Bhagat Singh's presence has been
dispensed with owing to his resistance
to production in Court. In view of
his absence we take no further
action on his application.

207

In the Court of the Special Tribunal,
Lahore Conspiracy Case, Lahore.

Crown Vs Sukhdeo & others.

Charged under Sections 302, 120B,
121, 121A Etc g 9P.C.

Most respectfully Sheweth :—

1. That the petitioner has just been
furnished with a copy of the order of the learned
Court regarding the close of the prosecution
evidence.

2. That, since the accused — petitioner — has not
been given any opportunity to interview his relatives
and particularly his father, who is the only person
interested in his defence, he is not in a position to
engage any counsel or legal adviser, and without
whose help he can not decide any thing regarding
such a delicate matter as the defence.

3. That it is prayed that the Court be
pleased to see if it is proper in these circumstances to deprive a man of all facilities of
defence, and to do what ever is thought proper
to meet the ends of justice.

Bhagat Singh

Petitioner
Central Jail,
Lahore

26/8/30

Seen by all the members of Tribunal

Placed on the record

27/8/30.

ORDER.

The Tribunal has no objection if the petitioners are permitted to interview any or all of the accused in the Lahore Conspiracy Case in the prisons in which the accused are respectively incarcerated.

28. 3. 1930.   Sd/- G. C. Hilton.

17a

COPY.   215

To

    The Special Tribunal,
    Lahore Conspiracy Case,
                    LAHORE.

Sirs,

        We understand the accused in the Conspiracy Case have been called upon by the Tribunal to enter on their defence. This being a crucial stage in the case, as members of the Defence Committee that arranged for the defence of the accused in the Special Magistrate's Court and has all along looked to their needs in various other matters, we beg to apply to your Lordships for some special facilities for deciding upon the defence arrangements. As the accused are not at present coming to court, the only course for us to put our point of view before them is to interview them in the jails. We shall feel much obliged if we are permitted to see Mr. Bhagat Singh in the Central Jail and the other accused in the Borstal Jail, and then, if necessary, both sets of accused together, so that we may effectively put our point of view before them and enable them to take a decision in their best interests. We hope Your Lordships will grant this request.

                    We beg to remain,

                    Your Lordships obedient servants

                    Sd/- Lajja Vati

                    Sd/- Feroz Chand

17b

209

To The President.
Lahore Conspiracy Case Tribunal.
Lahore.
(Through the Supdt. Borstal Jail, Lahore.)

Sir,

An order of the court dated 27th Aug '30
calling upon me to enter upon my defense,
was served on me yesterday in jail.

In this connection I beg to request
your favour of allowing me an inter-
-view with comrade Bhagat Singh; after
consulting whom regarding the giving of defence
I will intimate my decision to the court
whether I would enter upon my defence
or not. I hope this request will
not be refused in view of the facts that
we had such interviews regularly in the
past according to the standing order of
the local govt. in the matter.

In conclusion I reiterate that I cannot
decide about the said point without consulting
with comrade Bhagat Singh, because it is a
conspiracy case and so far the evidence produced
against me is mostly of conspiracy

Kindly send a copy of your order on
this application to me.

Yours obediently
Borstal Jail
20th Aug 30.

P.T.O.

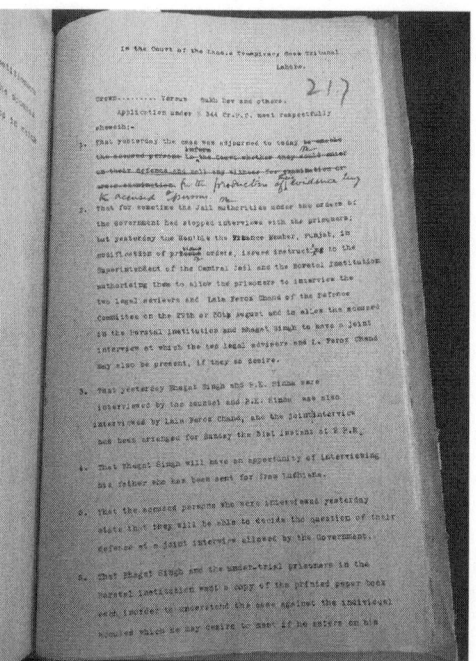

19(a)

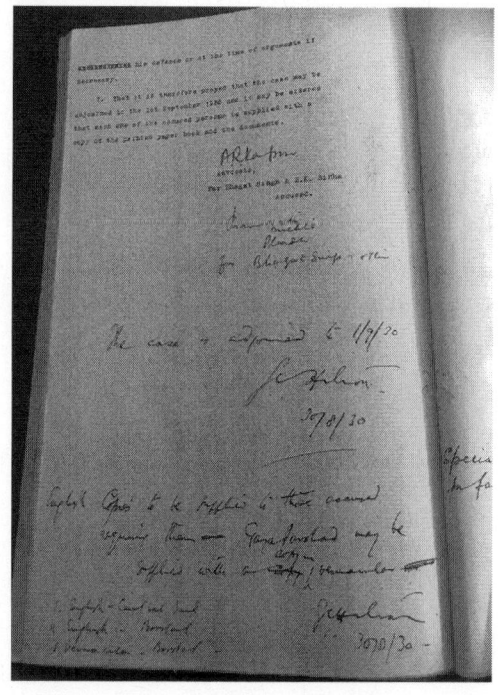

19(b)

To

The President
Special Tribunal
Lahore Conspiracy Case
Lahore

199

Sir,

Most respectfully I beg to
state that I want to study the
nature of the evidence as recorded
against me. This has been my practice in the lower court as well.
I hope you will be kind enough to
supply me with a copy # (english)
of the record of the proceedings.

Thanking in anticipation

I am

Yours obediently,

Prithi Singh Varma
the unrepresented accused
Lahore Conspiracy Case
Lahore

22nd Sep. 1930

Forwarded

23/8/30 . A. S-335
Major, I.M.S.
Superintendent
Borstal Institution
Lahore.

Telegram XX No. P11., dated (and recd.)18th March 1931,
From . . . .Home Secretary, Punjab.
To . . . . .Home Department,New Delhi.

872.

CLEAR LINE.

Your telegram of the 17th instant No. 797-S.
Bhagat Singh Rajguru and Sukh Dev will be executed at 7 on
evening of March 23rd. The news will be made known in Lahore
on early morning of March 24th. Ends.

. . . .

(Secy. Home Dept.)

1. Bhagat Singh was arrested on 8 April 1929. His trial before a regular magistrate, Rai Sahib Pandit Sri Kishen Kapur, began on 10 July 1929 and ran for ten months. But by 3 October 1929, and three months into the trial, his lawyer, Amolak Ram Kapur, was already complaining of the unfairness: (i) the pardoned 'approvers' were being kept in police custody, where they could be tutored by the police, rather than judicial custody, such that this 'will defeat the ends of justice'; (ii) the accused on the other hand are not allowed 'access to their relatives, friends and legal advisers' even 'when the High Court rules that those facilities should be afforded', because 'some obstacles were still put in their way'; and (iii) with four months now gone, the approvers 'should be kept in judicial lock-up pending the inquiry and the trial' (Lahore Archives, previously unpublished).

2. Once it became clear that Bhagat Singh would be tried not only for the Delhi Assembly Bomb Blast of 8 April 1929 but also for the earlier assassination of Special Constable J.P. Saunders on 17 December 1928, ever the skilled tactician, he petitioned the court on 4 November 1929. The FIR did not mention his name and the identification parade failed to identify him. At the same time, Bhagat Singh remained unrepresented. So, he asked that he 'may be able to effectively cross-examine the witnesses, it is necessary that the petitioner may be given an opportunity to visit the spot and see the roads and other surroundings in connection with the alleged incident' (Lahore Archives, previously unpublished).

3. Well into the ten-month trial in the magistrate's court, gross trial irregularities were being committed, which undermined the rule of law. A fundamental rule of criminal procedure is that the prosecution must disclose its evidence to the accused, including that which is unfavourable to the prosecution, so as to ensure that an innocent man is not wrongly convicted. Yet here, on 17 March 1930, one finds the prosecuting inspector having the audacity of writing directly to the magistrate to say of the arch-approver, Phonindranath Ghosh, that he 'may kindly exclude such evidence [given to the Police] that you may find inexpedient in the public interests to be furnished to the accused'. The public interest, however, is in disclosure, and nothing damages that public interest than the realization that the magistrate is working with the prosecution behind the backs of the accused and his lawyers (Lahore Archives, previously unpublished).

4. Nine months into the trial before the special tribunal, and just as it was to end and be transferred to a specially constituted tribunal on 5 May 1930, a legion of demands from the accused had built up. Nothing demonstrates this better than these ten grievances. By now, it had dawned on the prisoners, in what will be a case which 'will yet take a very long time' with charges 'of a very serious nature', that it was important to recognize 'that the petitioners are being deprived of the fundamental right of being defended by a counsel as they are not permitted to see their attorneys and friends'. Yet, this was remarkably 'a matter which the learned court had delegated to the jail authorities'. It did not end there, because 'although the police and other officials are permitted to come freely into the court room, the petitioners' friends are not even permitted to enter the court-room'. Moreover 'the dock in which the petitioners are kept . . . is surrounded by police and jail officials' such that the 'counsel feel handicapped in communicating with and giving full instructions to them'. There is the 'unprecedented practice of keeping an assistant jailor . . . always around the dock'. As if this were not enough, there were 'illegal punishment inflicted on them . . . by the jail authorities', and although there have been 'definite complaints filed by some of the petitioners in respect of the ill-treatment and assault by the police', these 'have not been attended to by the authorities . . .' (Lahore Archives, previously unpublished).

5. It is a little-known fact that throughout his trial, both before the magistrate and later before the special tribunal, Bhagat Singh's relatives were determined to visit him in jail despite the heavy restrictions imposed on them by the jail authorities. An attendance record [Image 5(a)] shows how Bhagat Singh's grandfather, Arjan Singh, visited him in jail on 9 December 1929, and how later his younger aunt, Harnam Kaur (the wife of the deceased Swaran Singh), visited him on 23 April 1930 [Image 5(b)] (Lahore Archives, previously unpublished).

6. On the first day of the new trial before the special tribunal at Poonch House, on 5 May 1930, Bejoy Kumar Sinha, Shiv Verma and Jai Dev Kapoor, and the others, complained to the tribunal that they 'have been brought to trial without sufficient notice' and that 'petitioners have at present no Counsel to defend them', so that 'it has not been possible for these reasons to draw up their line of defence'. This is why they were now requesting 'that the hearing

be adjourned for a fortnight' so that they can 'make necessary arrangements for defence'. Despite this request being an eminently reasonable one, the special tribunal did not grant an adjournment. The gross violation of the fundamental tenets of the rule of law therefore continued unabated (Lahore Archives, previously unpublished).

7. On the first day of the new trial before the special tribunal, on 5 May 1930, Bhagat Singh asked for 'an interview allowed to me with my father during the lunch interval', but Justice Coldstream ruled immediately that 'arrangements for interview during court hours cannot be made . . .' (Lahore Archives, previously unpublished).

8. On the second day of the new trial before the special tribunal at Poonch House, on 6 May 1930, the superintendent of Lahore Central Jail, Major Chopra, wrote to the registrar of the special tribunal, giving him a categoric assurance 'that the two accused, Bhagat Singh and B.K. Sinha, being undertrials in the Lahore Conspiracy Case, are allowed interviews at the Jail with their relatives once a week, and with legal counsel whenever their accredited counsels have applied for interview'. The practice, however, would be different, as subsequent events were to show (Lahore Archives, previously unpublished).

9. Within a week of the trial starting before the special tribunal, Bhagat Singh had on 8 May 1930 complained of being down with fever and of 'feeling extremely weak' as he had been put on 'very strong' medicines the night before. He requested that 'a reclining seat be arranged for him just behind defence counsel or, if that cannot be arranged, he be sent to jail and that the trial be proceeded with in his absence to which the petitioner has got no objection whatsoever'. However, even if such an application was submitted by the accused, it behoved the court to provide him with proper seating arrangements rather than be content with despatching him back to jail. In a case where the liberty of the subject is at stake, holding a trial in his absence is against the canons of justice (Lahore Archives, previously unpublished).

10. Even with the new trial before the special tribunal having commenced on 5 May 1930, the ever-astute Bhagat Singh remained troubled by how regular proceedings before a magistrate, running for nearly ten months and with over 200 witnesses already having been called, could just be abandoned on the spur of the moment. This is why on

19 June 1930, over a month after the Poonch House tribunal had begun to hear the case again, he asked for 'the copy of the order of the Special Magistrate' which was 'dated 3 May 1930, according to which the inquiry proceedings in that court were stayed'. It seems remarkable that if proceedings were adjourned before the special magistrate, an order to that effect was not served on Bhagat Singh, especially when he was unrepresented (Lahore Archives, previously unpublished).

11. Some three months into the trial before the special tribunal, and with matters going from bad to worse, on 11 August 1930, Bhagat Singh petitioned the high court in Lahore. He explained that he and the co-accused were now refusing to attend court 'in protest' given 'the treatment meted out to the accused'. In fact, 'the petitioner went on hunger strike on July 28th, 1930 in protest against certain regulations of the jail department'. But 'the trial is entering a new stage, i.e. the Prosecution evidence is about to be closed and the Petitioner is to be called upon to make his statement and to offer any defence . . .'. However, 'the jail authorities have altogether stopped all the interviews with his relatives and legal advisers'. But 'this purely executive affair is hampering the cause of justice and these Orders of the executive are highly illegal'. The fact is that 'the Petitioner wants the help of his relatives and legal advisers in deciding the most delicate question of his defence'. After that, Bhagat Singh's flair for the legal niceties of trial advocacy becomes thunderously clear. He argues that 'that there is a special provision in the Lahore Conspiracy Case Ordinance to the effect that if any accused voluntarily disables himself by hunger striking, or otherwise, or resists his production before the court, he shall still have the right to be represented by Counsel in his absence'. Thus, unless the jail authorities grant him access to his relatives and legal advisers, 'the accused feels quite handicapped'. Therefore, 'in the interests of justice and fair play, the court be pleased to intervene in this affair and to issue such instructions to the authorities concerned, as would be necessary to give full and proper facilities for arranging defence adequately in a case where the petitioner is being tried for such serious offences as may bring the extreme penalty of law'. Bhagat Singh pleaded that the high court therefore 'issue urgent orders for allowing interviews etc. . . .'. It was to be all in vain. The next day the jail authorities stopped all interviews and declared that the

high court had no jurisdiction to get involved in the matter (Lahore Archives, previously unpublished).

12. Following Bhagat Singh's petition of 11 August 1930 to the Lahore High Court that it intervene to pass an order guaranteeing the restoration of interviews for the proper preparation of his trial now that he had to put up a defence before the special tribunal, there was an immediate response from the jail authorities after the close of the prosecution case on 12 August 1930. This was that 'Ordinance No. III of 1930 is to provide specially for the trial of the accused . . .' in this case. Under Section 11 of that ordinance, 'the High Court has no jurisdiction in respect of any proceeding under it'. Moreover that, 'the forbidding of interviews by jail authorities does not seem to have much to do with the trial of the accused'. This is quite simply wrong, because the preparation of one's defence in one's own trial is part of the proceedings before the court, and it cannot be otherwise. In fact, the folly of this adopted position is made clear when the writer of the same document goes on to say that 'I should say that on the whole that it is not a proceeding under the Ordinance unless of course the jail authorities were directed' to make interviews available. This is sophisticated casuistry that bears no relation to the facts on the ground and serves only to undermine the requirements of due process and natural justice which are so integral to the rule of law (Lahore Archives, previously unpublished).

13. Such was the underhanded and duplicitous way that the jail authorities conducted themselves that even when they acceded to Bhagat Singh's request of 11 August, they only did so to the extent that 'interviews with legal advisers alone may be allowed'. So on 15 August 1930, Bhagat Singh wrote to say that he was 'at loss to understand the reason of such an order [since] why should I not be allowed to see my relatives since the said interviews are essential for defence purposes?'. He accordingly rather suspected that 'the Order is meant simply to make a show that the accused are given proper facilities regarding their defence, but in reality nothing of the sort is done, on the contrary the defence is hampered at every step . . .' which means that 'all my petitions and representations are useless'. He was not very wrong, for such are the myriad ways in which the façade of the rule of law exposes itself to be a sham. Here was Bhagat Singh, as he explained, with his current lawyer,

Dunni Chand, who also was now in jail. So Bhagat Singh argued that 'I want to engage a new one, which I cannot without the help and advice of my father'. His patience wears thin as he admonishes the authorities with the words that 'with no stretch of imagination can I understand as to why should the court of law join hands with the executive in such matters as immediately concerned with the administration of justice and be a party to the unnecessary harassment of the accused'. He ends with erudite eloquence and matchless acerbic wit as he 'earnestly requests the court to reconsider their Orders' and then 'to issue instructions to the jail authorities to allow all my interviews as long as the trial is going on' because the jail authorities 'will have time enough to treat us as they like after conviction' (Lahore Archives, previously unpublished).

14. On 22 August 1930, Mr Justice Hilton once again allowed Bhagat Singh's applications of 11 August and 15 August for 'interviews between himself and friends or relatives in the Jail' (Lahore Archives, previously unpublished). So a pattern was clearly emerging whereby the judges would make the requested orders and formally publicize them as such to create the spectre of the rule of law, but one which was promptly hollowed out by the authorities on the ground refusing to abide by such orders. With no judicial sanctions being employed by the courts against the jail authorities, this is a classic way in which the rule of law was habitually undermined.

15. Eventually, even the pretence of a trial in accordance with the dictates of the rule of law was no longer being maintained, and it stood as an apparition fully exposed, when on 25 August 1930 Mr Justice Hilton even dispensed with Bhagat Singh's presence in court. Nor of course was his lawyer present in court (Lahore Archives, previously unpublished).

16. Despite being already subject to a dispensation order by Justice Hilton on 25 August 1930, the following day Bhagat Singh is seen to be still complaining about the fact that 'since the accused – petitioner – has not been given any opportunity to interview his relatives and particularly his father, who is the only person interested in his defence, he is not in a position to engage any Counsel or legal adviser, and without whose help he cannot decide anything regarding such a delicate matter as the defence'. It is clear that he is not voluntarily choosing to absent himself from the proceedings but is being forced out because he implores the judicial authorities

'that the court be pleased to see if it is proper in the circumstances to deprive a man of all facilities of defence; and to do whatever is thought proper to meet the ends of justice' (Lahore Archives, previously unpublished). The ends of justice? Normally, it is the court which is studiously conscious of preserving the ends of justice. Here, remarkably, it is a defendant appearing before it.

17. On 28 August 1930, the lawyer Feroz Chand, on behalf of Bhagat Singh's defence committee, which had 'arranged for the defence of the accused in the Special Magistrates Court and has all along looked to their needs in various other ways', now pleaded with the special tribunal 'for some special facilities for deciding upon the defence arrangements'. It was a critical moment in the trial, because the accused had now been called upon to enter their defence. So, given that this was 'a crucial stage in the case', what was being demanded was that 'as the accused are not at present coming to court, the only course for us to put our point of view before them is to interview them in the jails' (Lahore Archives, previously unpublished). A trial that had started over a year ago before the special magistrate had now been reduced to this. An order by Mr Justice Hilton promptly acceded to this request. It was a different matter whether the court's order would be carried out in full.

18. In this 'conspiracy' case, where the elements of the conspiracy were being made up as the trial progressed, there was much dissatisfaction on the part of the accused as to the state of the evidence against them. This is why when on 27 August 1930 Bejoy Kumar Sinha was ordered to enter a defence, he requested first 'an interview with Comrade Bhagat Singh' on 28 August 1930. As he explained, 'I cannot decide about the said point without consultation with Comrade Bhagat Singh because it is a conspiracy case and so far the evidence produced against me is mostly conspiracy' (Lahore Archives, previously unpublished). Bejoy Kumar Sinha escaped death and was sentenced to transportation for life.

19. On 30 August 1930, the distinguished lawyer Amolak Ram Kapur openly penned the words to the special tribunal that 'for some time the Jail authorities under orders from the government had stopped interviews with the prisoners' so that it was only a day before that the finance minister of Punjab (rather than an order from a court of law) 'issued instructions to the Superintendent of the Central Jail and the Borstal institution authorising them to allow the prisoners

to interview the two legal advisers . . .'. As per these instructions, both Bhagat Singh and B.K. Sinha were to be afforded 'a joint interview' now with their legal advisers. More importantly, 'Bhagat Singh will have an opportunity of interviewing his father who has been sent for from Ludhiana'. In the meantime, 'Bhagat Singh and the under-trial prisoners in the Borstal institution want a copy of the printed paper-book each, in order to understand the case against the individual accused which he may desire to meet . . .' (Lahore Archives, previously unpublished).

20. Less than a month before the sentence of death was pronounced on Bhagat Singh, there was an application on 22 September 1930 by Shiv Verma that he 'wanted to study the nature of the evidence as recorded against me' so that he required the tribunal 'to supply me with a copy (English) of the record of proceedings' (Lahore Archives, previously unpublished). Like B.K. Sinha, he too escaped death and was sentenced to transportation for life.

21. How was it that Bhagat Singh's execution, scheduled for the morning of 24 March 1931, was brought forward by eleven hours and carried out, contrary to all protocol, at 7 p.m. on the evening of 23 March 1931? This telegram of 18 March 1931 (courtesy of Gurdev Singh Sidhu), sent by the home secretary of Punjab, H.W. Emerson, to the Delhi government, just five days before he was hanged, makes clear that it was once again government pressure which determined the manner of his going. That is how Bhagat Singh was hanged.

Notes

Epigraph

1. Chaman Lal, 'No Hanging, Please Shoot Us', in *Bhagat Singh: The Jail Notebook and Other Writings* (New Delhi: Leftword, Reprinted 2014), p. 181.

Prologue

1. These five under-trials who signed were J.N. Sanyal, Mahavir Singh, B.K. Dutt, Bejoy Kumar Sinha and Kundan Lal.
2. Shiv Verma, *Sansmritiyan* (Delhi, 2002), p. 37.
3. Jawaharlal Nehru, *An Autobiography* (Delhi, 1962), pp. 175 176.
4. Asaf Ali, *The Commonweal* (Pune, 23 March 1949), cited in M.M. Juneja, *Biography of Bhagat Singh* (Modern Publishers, 2nd reprint 2016), pp. 157–158.

Chapter 1

1. Bhagat Singh, 'Emergence of the Punjab in the Freedom Movement'. *Bandemataram* (1931). Reprinted in Jagmohan Singh and Chaman Lal, eds., *Bhagat Singh Aur Unke Sathion Ke Dastavez* (Ludhiana, 1987).
2. See https://www.revolutionarydemocracy.org/rdv3n1/bsingh.htm.
3. Statement by Dr Jagmohan Singh during an interview, as published in *Frontline* on 2 November 2007.

4. Ian A. Talbot, The Punjab Under Colonialism: Order and
    Transformation in British India, pp. 3–10, p. 3.
5. Ibid., p. 4.

Chapter 2

1. Ian A. Talbot, 'The Punjab Under Colonialism: Order and
    Transformation in British India', pp. 3–10, at p. 3. Also see, D.A.
    Washbrook, 'Law, State and Agrarian Society in Colonial India',
    Modern Asian Studies, 15, 3 (1981), pp. 653–4.
2. Ian A. Talbot, 'The Punjab Under Colonialism: Order and
    Transformation in British India', pp. 3–10, at p. 9.
3. Ibid., p. 8.
4. Ibid., p. 9.
5. Ibid., p. 6.
6. Ibid., p. 7.
7. Virendra Sindhu, *Yugdrishta Bhagat Singh Aur Unke Mrityuanjay
    Purakhe* (Delhi, 1997), p. 6.
8. Imran Ali, *The Punjab under Imperialism, 1885–1947* (Princeton
    University Press, 1988), p. viii.
9. M.M. Juneja, *Biography of Bhagat Singh* (Modern Publishers, 2nd
    Reprint 2016), p. 10.

Chapter 3

1. N. Gerald Barrier, 'The Punjab Disturbances of 1907: The
    Response of the British Government in India to Agrarian Unrest',
    in David Hardiman ed., *Peasant Resistance and the Raj* (New Delhi,
    1992).
2. Ibid.
3. Ibid., p. 7.
4. D. Gilmartin, 'Migration and Modernity: The State, the Punjabi
    Village and the Settling of the Canal Colonies', in I. Talbot
    and S. Thandi eds., *People on the Move, A Century of Punjabi
    Local, Regional and International Migration* (Karachi, 2003),
    p. 13.
5. N. Gerald Barrier, 'The Punjab Disturbances of 1907: The
    Response of the British Government in India to Agrarian Unrest',
    in David Hardiman ed., *Peasant Resistance and the Raj* (New Delhi,
    1992), p. 245. He makes the point that approximately 30,000 Sikhs

(23 per cent of the army) and 18,000 Punjabi Muslims (13 per cent of the army) were in the army.

6. James Campbell Ker, *Political Trouble in India, 1907–1917* (Calcutta, 1917), p. 23.

7. See Pandit Pearay Mohan, *The Punjab 'Rebellion' of 1919, and How It Was Suppressed: An Account of the Punjab Disorders and the Working of Martial Law* (in two volumes) (1920; 1999 edition).

8. Ibid., p. 3–4.

9. Sudha Narayan, 'The Three Farm Bills: Is This the Market Reform Indian Agriculture Needs?', *The India Forum*, 2 October 2020. (Available at https://www.theindiaforum.in/article/three-farm-bills).

10. Raakhi Jagga, 'Farm Protests Eating Into Economy, Will Harm Punjab More Than Centre', *The Indian Express*, 12 November 2020. (Available at https://indianexpress.com/article/india/farm-protests-eating-into-economy-will-harm-punjab-more-than-centre/). On the repeal of the farms laws, see Hannah Ellis-Peterson, 'Indian PM Narendra Modi to Repeal Farm Laws After Year of Protests', (Available at https://www.theguardian.com/world/2021/nov/19/indian-pm-narendra-modi-to-repeal-farm-laws-after-year-of-protests).

11. See 'Congress Kicks Off Nation-Wide Campaign Against Farm Bills, Says Govt Misleading People', *The Times of India*, 25 September 2020. (Available at https://timesofindia.indiatimes.com/india/congress-kicks-off-nation-wide-campaign-against-farm-bills-says-govt-misleading-people/articleshow/78306668.cms).

12. Shekhar Gupta, 'Shambles over Farmers' Protest Shows Modi-Shah BJP Needs a Punjab Tutorial', *The Print*, 28 November 2020. (Available at https://theprint.in/national-interest/shambles-over-farmers-protest-shows-modi-shah-bjp-needs-a-punjab-tutorial).

13. Ravinder Vasudeva, 'Punjab Assembly Polls: BJP Plans Come a Cropper, Reduced to Just Two Seats'. *Hindustan Times*, 11 March 2022. (Available at https://www.hindustantimes.com/cities/chandigarh-news/bjps-attempts-to-mark-presence-in-punjab-comes-a-cropper-101646920007838.html).

14. Jatin Anand, 'Farmers Erect Stage to Honour Bhagat Singh', *The Hindu*, 19 December 2020. (Available at https://www.thehindu.

com/news/cities/Delhi/farmers-erect-stage-to-honour-bhagat-singh/article33369873.ece).

15. Shekhar Gupta, 'Modi Govt Has Lost Farm Laws Battle, Now Raising Sikh Separatist Bogey Will be a Grave Error', *The Print*, 6 February 2021. (Available at https://theprint.in/national-interest/modi-govt-has-lost-farm-laws-battle-now-raising-sikh-separatist-bogey-will-be-a-grave-error/599860/).

16. Hannah Ellis-Peterson, '"*We Are More Powerful Than Modi*": *Indian Farmers Celebrate U-turn on Law*', *The Guardian*, 19 November 2021 (Available at https://www.theguardian.com/world/2021/nov/19/we-are-more-powerful-than-modi-indian-farmers-celebrate-laws-repealing)

17. Amandeep Sandhu, '*How India's Farmers Launched a Movement Against Modi's Farm Bills—and Won*', *Yes Magazine*, 19 January 2022 (Available at https://www.yesmagazine.org/social-justice/2022/01/19/india-farmers-movement)

Chapter 4

1. For a critique of this legislation, see Gerald N. Barrier, 'The Punjab Disturbances of 1907: The Response of the British Government in India to Agrarian Unrest', *Modern Asian Studies*, 1, 4 (1967), pp. 353–83. Further, see Imran Ali, 'Malign Growth? Agricultural Colonization and the Roots of Backwardness in the Punjab', *Past & Present*, no. 114 (1987): pp. 110–32. Also see subsequent land reforms in Altaf Hussain, The *Colonization of Government Lands (Punjab) Act, 1912* (as amended up to April 1964) (Lahore: Pakistan Law Times Publications, 1964) (Available at http://punjablaws.gov.pk/laws/22.html).

2. Gerald N. Barrier, 'The Punjab Disturbances of 1907: The Response of the British Government in India to Agrarian Unrest', *Modern Asian Studies*, 1, 4 (1967), pp. 353–83, p. 353.

3. Ian A. Talbot, 'The Punjab Under Colonialism: Order and Transformation in British India', pp. 3–10, p. 6.

4. Gerald N. Barrier, 'The Punjab Disturbances of 1907: The Response of the British Government in India to Agrarian Unrest', *Modern Asian Studies*, 1, 4 (1967), pp. 353–83, p. 355.

5. Ibid., p. 360.

6. Ibid., p. 359.

7. Ibid., p. 361.

8. It is sometimes said that it was Prab Dyal who recited the poem. The better view appears to be that it was Lala Bankay Dyal; see Tahir Kamran, 'Pagri Sambhal O Jatta – II', *The News on Sunday*, 19 March 2017. (Available at https://www.thenews.com.pk/tns/detail/562862-pagri-sambhal-o-jatta).

9. 'Shaheed: The Definite Bhagat Singh Film Which Almost Didn't Get Made, Listen to Its Songs', *The Indian Express*, 23 March 2017. (Available at https://indianexpress.com/article/entertainment/bollywood/shaheed-the-definite-bhagat-singh-film-manoj-kumar-which-almost-didnt-get-made-listen-to-its-songs-4581778/).

10. Chris Moffat, *India's Revolutionary Inheritance* (Cambridge University Press, 2019), p. 140, fn.68.

11. Gerald N. Barrier, 'The Punjab Disturbances of 1907: The Response of the British Government in India to Agrarian Unrest', *Modern Asian Studies*, 1, 4 (1967), pp. 353–83, p. 367.

12. James Campbell Ker, *Political Trouble in India: 1907–1917* (Calcutta, 1917), p. 23.

13. 'Shaheed: The Definite Bhagat Singh Film Which Almost Didn't Get Made, Listen to Its Songs', *The Indian Express*, 23 March 2017. (Available at https://indianexpress.com/article/entertainment/bollywood/shaheed-the-definite-bhagat-singh-film-manoj-kumar-which-almost-didnt-get-made-listen-to-its-songs-4581778/).

14. Gerald N. Barrier 'The Punjab Disturbances of 1907: The Response of the British Government in India to Agrarian Unrest', *Modern Asian Studies*, 1, 4 (1967), pp. 368 -369. Barrier refers here to Ibbetson's minute.

15. James Campbell Ker, *Political Trouble in India: 1907-1917* (Calcutta, 1917), p. 23.

16. Ibid.

17. Ibid., p. 423.

18. Ibid., p. 350.

19. Ibid., p. 352.

Chapter 5

1. Chris Moffat, *India's Revolutionary Inheritance* (Cambridge University Press, 2019), p. 23.

2. Here Moffat draws attention to Malwinder Jit Singh Warraich's *Bhagat Singh: The Eternal Rebel* (Delhi, 2007), which he states devotes an entire chapter to Bhagat Singh's 'roots' (see Moffat at fn. 24).

3. Chris Moffat, *India's Revolutionary Inheritance* (Cambridge University Press, 2019), p. 24.

4. See James Campbell Ker, *Political Trouble in India, 1907–1917* (Calcutta, 1917), p. 423.

5. Chris Moffat, *India's Revolutionary Inheritance* (Cambridge University Press, 2019), p. 24.

6. Ibid., p. 25.

7. 'Letter to father, Kishan Singh', 1923. Reproduced in *The Bhagat Singh Reader*, Chaman Lal ed., (Noida: Harper Collins, 2019), p. 8.

8. See, Bhagat Singh, 'Why I Am an Atheist', 5–6 October 1930. Reprinted in Chaman Lal ed., *The Bhagat Singh Reader* (Noida: Harper Collins, 2019), p. 195–209.

9. Kishan Singh had written on 20 September 1930 from Bradlaugh Hall, Lahore.

10. Bhagat Singh's letter was published in *The Tribune* on 4 October 1930.

11. Chris Moffat, *India's Revolutionary Inheritance* (Cambridge University Press, 2019), p. 25.

12. The full letter is reproduced in Chaman Lal, *Bhagat Singh: The Jail Notebook and Other Writings* (Leftword, 2007) pp. 147–148, p. 148.

13. Chris Moffat, *India's Revolutionary Inheritance* (Cambridge University Press, 2019), p. 25.

14. Ibid., p. 26.

15. The word *swadeshi* is derived from the combination of the two Sanskrit words *Swa*, which means self or own, and *desh*, which means country. One's own country is referred to as *swadesh*. The adjectival word is *swadeshi*, and this can generally be taken to mean self-sufficiency for one's country.

16. James Campbell Ker, *Political Trouble in India: 1907–1917* (Calcutta, 1917), p. i.

17. Ibid., p. 350.

Chapter 6

1. Anita Anand, *The Patient Assassin: A True Tale of Massacre, Revenge and the Raj* (London: Simon and Schuster, 2019), p. 128.

2. Malwinder Jit Singh Waraich, *Bhagat Singh: The Eternal Rebel* (Delhi: Unistar Books, 2014), p. 33.

3. Kama Maclean, *A Revolutionary History of Interwar India: Violence, Image, Voice and Text* (London: Hurst & Co, 2015), p. 30.

4. Ibid., p. 31.

5. Naved Hamid, 'Dispossession and Differentiation of the Peasantry in the Punjab During Colonial Rule', *The Journal of Peasant Studies*, 10, 1 (1982), pp. 52–72.

6. Ian A. Talbot, 'The Punjab under Colonialism: Order and Transformation in British India', pp. 3–10, p. 7.

7. Tim Murphy, Underground Asia: Global Revolutionaries and the Assault on Empire (Penguin Random House, 2020), p. 136

8. James Campbell Ker, *Political Trouble in India: 1907-1917* (Calcutta, 1917), p. 267.

9. Ibid.

10. M.M. Juneja, *Biography of Bhagat Singh* (Modern Publishers, Second Reprint 2016), p. 13

11. Virendra Sindhu, *Yugdrishta Bhagat Singh Aur Unke Mrityuanjay Purakhe* (Delhi, 1997), p. 124. Quoted also in M.M. Juneja, *op. cit.*, at p. 14.

12. See Jordanna Bailkin, 'The Boot and the Spleen: When Was Murder Possible in British India?', *Comparative Studies in Society and History*, vol. 48, no. 2, 2006, pp. 462–93. Here, she refers to 'the centrality of race in constructing ideas of homicide and violence itself' (at p. 465).

13. *The Punjabee* (Lahore), 11 April 1906. Also see, V.C. Joshi, ed., *Lajpat Rai: Autobiographical Writings* (Delhi, 1965), p. 99.

14. James Campbell Ker, *Political Trouble in India: 1907–1917* (Calcutta, 1917), p. 352.

15. M.M. Juneja, *op. cit.*, p. 12.

16. Virendra Sindhu, *Yugdrishta Bhagat Singh Aur Unke Mrityuanjay Purakhe* (Delhi, 1997), p. 124. Quoted also in M.M. Juneja, *op. cit.*, p. 12.

17. 'Letter to Aunt Hukam Kaur', October 1921 in Punjabi. Reproduced in *The Bhagat Singh Reader*, Chaman Lal ed., (Noida: Harper Collins, 2019), p. 6.

18. Ibid., p. 7.

Chapter 7

1. Malwinder Jit Singh Waraich, *Bhagat Singh: The Eternal Rebel* (Delhi: Unistar Books, 2014), p. 27.

2. Ibid., p. 28, where Waraich quotes from her grand-daughter, Verinder.

3. 'Letter to grandfather Arjun Singh', 22 July 1918. Reproduced in Chaman Lal (ed.), *The Bhagat Singh Reader* (Noida: Harper Collins, 2019), p. 3.

4. 'Letter to grandfather Arjun Singh', 27 July 1919. Reproduced in *The Bhagat Singh Reader*, Chaman Lal ed., (Noida: Harper Collins, 2019), p. 4.

5. Manmathnath Gupta, *Bhagat Singh and His Times* (Delhi, 1977), p. 79.

6. M.J.S. Waraich, *Bhagat Singh: The Eternal Rebel* (Unistar Books, Delhi, 2014), p. 35.

7. Lala Lajpat Rai, *The Problem of the Education in India* (New York, 1920).

8. Chris Moffat, *India's Revolutionary Inheritance* (Cambridge University Press, 2019), p. 31.

9. Ibid., p. 29.

10. Ibid., p. 28.

11. Ibid., p. 32.

12. 'Letter to grandfather Arjun Singh', 14 November 1921 Reproduced in *The Bhagat Singh Reader*, Chaman Lal ed., (Noida: Harper Collins, 2019), p. 5.

13. Chris Moffat, *India's Revolutionary Inheritance* (Cambridge University Press, 2019), p. 27.

14. Yashpal, *Sinhavalokan Vol. 1* (Lucknow, 1951), p. 18 (Available in Hindi at https://archive.org/details/in.ernet.dli.2015.342678).

15. Ajoy Ghosh, *Bhagat Singh and His Comrades* (Bombay: People's Publishing House, 1945). An online version is available at http://www.sankalpindia.net/bhagat-singh-i-knew-him-ajoy-ghosh.

16. Vachnesh Tripathi, *Krantimurti Durga Bhabhi* (Delhi, 1996), p. 10.

Chapter 8

1. Shoaib Daniyal, '"The Man Who Goes on a Hunger Strike Has a Soul": When Jinnah Defended Bhagat Singh', *Scroll.in*, 23 March 2016, (Available at https://scroll.in/article/805568/the-man-who-goes-on-a-hunger-strike-has-a-soul-when-jinnah-defended-bhagat-singh).

2. Jinnah's speech at the Legislative Assembly on 12 September 1929. It was A.G. Noorani who first most memorably brought Jinnah's

historic speech to light in modern India. See, A.G. Noorani, *Jinnah and Tilak: Comrades in the Freedom Struggle* (Oxford University Press, 2010), p. 75. Also see, A.G Noorani, *The Trial of Bhagat Singh: Politics of Justice* (Oxford, 1996) at p.84.

3. Shoaib Daniyal, 'The Man Who Goes on a Hunger Strike Has a Soul: When Jinnah Defended Bhagat Singh', *Dawn*, 23 March 2017. (Available at https://www.dawn.com/news/1322361)

4. A.G. Noorani, *Jinnah and Tilak: Comrades in the Freedom Struggle* (Oxford University Press, 2010), p. xiii.

5. Ibid., p. xiv.

6. Ibid., p. 76.

7. Ibid., p. 74.

8. Ibid., p. 75.

9. Ibid., p. xvii.

10. Dr Ishtiaq Ahmed, Jinnah: His Successes, Failures and Role in History (Penguin, 2019). For a review see, Amit Cowshish, *'A Book That Busts Many Myths Surrounding Jinnah'*, *The Wire*, 27 March 2021. (Available at https://thewire.in/uncategorised/book-review-jinnah-ishtiaq-ahmed-pakistan).

11. Ibid., p. 77.

12. Ibid., p. 269.

13. Ibid., p. 270.

14. Ibid.

Chapter 9

1. Ammara Ahmad, '#ShaheedBhagatSingh: An Answer to Pakistan's Search for a National Hero', *NewsLaundry*, 28 September 2017. (Available at https://www.newslaundry.com/2017/09/28/shaheed-bhagat-singh-pakistan-national-hero-lahore).

2. S. Irfan Habib, 'A Shared Hero for India and Pakistan?', *The Hindu*, 1 May 2018. (Available at http://www.thehindu.com/opinion/op-ed/a-shared-hero-for-india-and-pakistan/article23732329.eceMORE-INHistory's heroes).

3. S. Irfan Habib, 'Revolutionary Ideas That Live On', *The Hindu*, 23 March 2019 (Available at https://www.thehindu.com/opinion/op-ed/revolutionary-ideas-that-live-on/article26613250.ece).

4. S. Irfan Habib, 'Bhagat Singh: A Revolutionary Thinker and Not Just a Martyr', *News Central*, 23 March 2018. (Available

at https://newscentral24x7.com/bhagat-singh-a-revolutionary-thinker-and-not-just-a-martyr/).

5. Manimugdha S. Sharma, 'Bhagat Singh Was Always a Revolutionary Nationalist . . . Indian Cultural Ethos Was Deeply Ingrained in Him', *The Times of India*, 20 March 2019. (Available at https://timesofindia.indiatimes.com/blogs/parthian-shot/bhagat-singh-was-always-a-revolutionary-nationalist-indian-cultural-ethos-was-deeply-ingrained-in-him/).

6. S. Irfan Habib, 'Bhagat Singh and Us', *The Indian Express*, 25 March 2017 (Available at https://indianexpress.com/article/opinion/columns/bhagat-singh-iconic-revolutionary-and-us-martyrs-day-march-23-4584306/).

Chapter 10

1. Intikhab Hanif, 'Archives of Bhagat Singh Case Trial to be Exhibited', *Dawn*, 25 March 2018 (Available at https://www.dawn.com/news/amp/1397297).

2. Ibid.

3. Pippa Virdee, *From the Ashes of 1947: Reimagining Punjab* (Cambridge University Press, 2018).

4. Fakir S. Aijazuddin, *The Resourceful Fakirs: Three Muslim Brothers at the Sikh Court of Lahore* (New Delhi: Three Rivers Publishers, 2014), p.3.

5. Ibid., p. xiii.

6. Ibid., p. 2.

7. Ibid., p. xix.

8. Ibid., p. 2.

9. Ibid., p. 2.

10. Chris Moffat, 'India's Revolutionary Inheritance: The Political Afterlives of Shaheed Bhagat Singh', *Hypotheses*, 15 June 2017. (Available at https://revbio.hypotheses.org/675).

11. Chris Moffat, 'Infinite Inquilab', *The Caravan*, 1 August 2013. (Available at https://caravanmagazine.in/lede/infinite-inquilab).

12. Chris Moffat, *India's Revolutionary Inheritance: Politics and the Promise of Bhagat Singh* (Cambridge University Press, 2019).

13. Chaman Lal, *The Bhagat Singh Reader* (Noida: Harper Collins, 2019), p. xliii.

Chapter 11

1. 'Pulwama Terror Attack: Suicide Bomber Drives SUV Packed With 300 kg Explosives Into CRPF Bus, 44 Men Martyred', *India Today Webdesk*, 16 February 2019. (Available at https://www. indiatoday.in/india/story/twelve-crpf-jawans-injured-in-ied-blast-in-j-k-1456037-2019-02-14).

2. '"Operation Bandar" Was IAF's Code Name for Balakot Airstrike', *Mint*, 21 June 2019 (Available at https://www.livemint.com/ news/india/-operation-bandar-was-iaf-s-code-name-for-balakot-airstrike-1561119715509.html). Also see, *"We Had the Bull's Eye. All over in 90 Seconds", Balakot Airstrike Pilots Confirm That They Had Hit the Terror Camps'*, OpIndia Staff, 25 June 2019. (Available at https://www.opindia.com/2019/06/we-had-the-bulls-eye-all-over-in-90-seconds-balakot-airstrike-pilots-confirm-that-they-had-hit-the-terror-camps/).

3. Teesta Prakash, 'Pulwama and Its Aftermath: What Is Different This Time?', *Australian Institute of International Affairs*, 4 March 2019. (Available at https://www.internationalaffairs.org.au/ australianoutlook/pulwama-aftermath-different-this-time/).

4. Happyman Jacob, 'After Balakot: India-Pakistan Relations Heading Nowhere', *The India Forum*, 7 May 2019. (Available at https:// www.theindiaforum.in/article/after-balakot-india-pakistan-relations-heading-nowhere).

5. Kallol Bhattarchajee, 'India Boycotts Pakistan National Day Event', *The Hindu*, 22 March 2019. (Available at https://www.thehindu. com/news/national/india-boycotts-pakistan-national-day-event/ article26612743.ece).

6. The earliest films had indeed been soon after Independence.

7. This was demanded by the Memorial Foundation in January 2018 (see, http://breaknews.in/world/in-pakistan-bhagat-singh-memorial-foundation-demands-highest-gallantry-medal-nishan-e-haider-for-bhagat-singh).

8. Neel Kamal, 'Bhagat Singh Links Pakistanis, Indians', *The Times of India*, 24 March 2019. (Available at https://timesofindia. indiatimes.com/city/amritsar/bhagat-singh-a-hero-in-pakistan-too/articleshow/68542375.cms).

9. 'Two Groups in Pakistan Want Bhagat Singh to be Declared a National Hero', *The Economic Times*, 24 March 2018. (Available at

https://economictimes.indiatimes.com/news/politics-and-nation/ two-groups-in-pakistan-want-bhagat-singh-to-be-declared-a-national-hero/articleshow/63441488.cms).

10. Qaswar Abbas, 'Pakistani Authorities Do a U-turn on Renaming a Chowk After Freedom Fighter Bhagat Singh', *Daily Mail*, 1 November 2012. (Available at https://www.dailymail.co.uk/ indiahome/indianews/article-2226553/Pakistani-authorities-U-turn-renaming-chowk-freedom-fighter-Bhagat-Singh.html).

Chapter 12

1. Known as the Indictment in the West.
2. It would appear that Bhagat Singh's name was not mentioned in the FIR for the murder of Saunders.
3. 'Lahore Lawyer Gets Copy of 1928 Saunders' Murder FIR, It Doesn't Name Bhagat Singh, Rajguru, Sukhdev', *Express News Service*, 10 June 2019. (Available at https://indianexpress.com/ article/cities/ludhiana/lahore-lawyer-gets-copy-of-1928-saunders-murder-fir-it-doesnt-name-bhagat-singh-rajguru-sukhdev/). The case against Bhagat Singh was registered under Sections 302, 120 and 109 of the Indian Penal Code (IPC). An inspector of the Lahore police's legal branch on 8 June handed over the attested copy of the FIR in a sealed envelope to the additional district and sessions judge of Lahore, Tariq Mahmood Zargham. This was following a petition by the Lahore-based advocate Imtiaz Rashid Qureshi, the chairman of Bhagat Singh Memorial Foundation, who is reported as having vowed, 'I want to establish Bhagat Singh's innocence in the Saunders case.' The Lahore High Court has referred the case to the chief justice for the constitution of a larger bench to hear the case.
4. Radhika Singha, *A Despotism of Law: Crime and Justice in Early Colonial India* (Oxford University Press, 1998), p. 289.
5. Ibid., p. 291.
6. Ibid., p. 293.

Chapter 13

1. *District and Miscellaneous Reports on The Punjab Disturbances*, Sr. A33 (4), April 1919.
2. Ibid., para 4.
3. Ibid., para 5.

4. Ibid., p. 4.
5. Ibid., p. 119.
6. Ibid., p. 119, Section XII, para 1.
7. Ibid., p. 119, Section XII, para 2.
8. Ibid., p. 165, AMRITSAR DISTRICT: Report on the Disturbances at Amritsar, 1919 – Survey of Pre-disposing Causes.
9. Ibid., p. 165, para 1.
10. Ibid., p. 165, para 2.
11. Ibid., p. 166, para 8.
12. Ibid., p. 165, para 4.
13. Ibid., p. 165, para 3.
14. Ibid., p. 165, para 5.
15. Ibid., p. 165, para 6.
16. Durba Ghosh, *Gentlemanly Terrorists: Political Violence and the Colonial State in India, 1919-1947* (Cambridge University Press, 2017), p. 31.
17. Ibid., p. 95.
18. *District and Miscellaneous Reports on The Punjab Disturbances*, Sr. A33 (4), April 1919, p. 166, para 9.
19. Ibid., p. 166, para 9.
20. Ibid., p. 166, para 10.
21. Ibid., p. 167, para 13.
22. Ibid., p. 167 para 14.
23. Ibid., p. 167, para 14.
24. Ibid., p. 167, para 15.
25. Ibid., p. 167, para 16.

Chapter 14

1. Durba Ghosh, *Gentlemanly Terrorists: Political Violence and the Colonial State in India 1919-1947* (Cambridge University Press, 2017), p. 27.
2. Ibid.
3. Mary Dudziak, *Wartime: An Idea, Its History, and Its Consequences* (Oxford University Press, New York, 2012), p. 107.
4. *Defence of the Realm (No. 2) Regulations, 1914, section 4 (No 28887).* In fact, a wide range of disparate and perfectly innocuous activities, such as flying kites, feeding wild animals bread, buying alcohol on public transport were also banned, as was the discussion of naval and military matters.

5. *Sedition Committee Report, No. 2884, Resolution*, Government of India, (Home Department, Delhi, 10 December 1971), p. i.

6. Durba Ghosh, *Gentlemanly Terrorists: Political Violence and the Colonial State in India, 1919-1947* (Cambridge University Press, 2017), p. 32.

7. *Rowlatt Commission's Report*, Ch. XVII; Robb, Government of India, p. 153.

8. Ibid., p. 3.

9. Durba Ghosh, *Gentlemanly Terrorists: Political Violence and the Colonial State in India, 1919-1947* (Cambridge University Press, 2017), p. 95.

Chapter 15

1. Kim Wagner, 'Savage Warfare: Violence and the Rule of Colonial Difference in Early British Counterinsurgency', *History Workshop Journal*, 85 (1 April 2018), pp. 217–37, p. 218 (Available at https://doi.org/10.1093/hwj/dbx053). For instance, see Jordanna Bailkin, 'The Boot and the Spleen: When Was Murder Possible in British India?', *Comparative Studies in Society and History*, 48, 2 (2006); Taylor Sherman, *State Violence and Punishment in India, 1919-1956* (London: Routledge, 2010); Elizabeth Kolsky, *Colonial Justice in British India: White Violence and the Rule of Law* (Cambridge University Press, 2011); Martin Thomas, *Violence and the Colonial Order: Police, Workers and Protest in the European Colonial Empires, 1918-1940*, (Cambridge University Press, 2012); and William Gallois, *A History of Violence in the early Algerian Colony* (Houndsmills, 2013).

2. Kim Wagner, op. cit., pp. 271–18.

3. Ibid., p. 231.

4. *Bhagat Singh v. The King Emperor* (1931) 33 BOMLR 950. Indeed, Kim Wagner cites legal sources himself (at fn. 83) to demonstrate the point; Mark Condos, 'Licence to Kill: The Murderous Outrages Act and the Rule of Law in Colonial India, 1867-1925', *Modern Asian Studies* (June 2015), pp. 479–517; and Elizabeth Kolsky, 'The Colonial Rule of Law and the Legal Regime of Exception: Frontier 'Fanaticism' and State Violence in British India', The *American Historical Review*, 120, 4 (20150, pp. 1,218–46.)

5. Kim Wagner, op. cit., p. 231. He refers to his own work, '"Calculated to Strike Terror": The Amritsar Massacre and the Spectacle of

Colonial Violence', *Past & Present*, 233, 1 (1 November 2016), pp. 185–225 (Available at https://doi.org/10.1093/pastj/gtw037). Military historians such as Calwell had reminded his readers of 'the distinction between "civilised" and "un-civilised" people', suggesting that 'Uncivilised races attribute leniency to timidity'. (See C.E. Calwell, *Small Wars: Their Principle and Practice* (London: Tales End Press, 1896, 1899, 1906, p. 147; cited by Wagner at p. 230).

6. Mark Condos, *The Insecurity State* (Cambridge University Press, 2017), pp. 2–3.
7. Taylor C. Sherman, 'Tensions of Colonial Punishment: Perspectives on Recent Developments in the Study of Coercive Networks in Asia, Africa and the Caribbean', *History Compass*, 7, 3, pp. 659–77. DOI: 10.1111/j.1478-0542.2009.00597.x (Available at http://eprints.lse. ac.uk/32801/1/Sheman_Tensions_colonial_punishment_2009.pdf).
8. Ibid., p. 658.
9. Ibid., p. 659.
10. Taylor C. Sherman, 'From Hell to Paradise? Voluntary Transfer of Convicts to the Andaman Islands, 1921–1940', *Modern Asian Studies*, 2, 2 (March 2009), pp. 367–88, p. 385. She refers to the government response to the new nationalist campaign: see, D.A. Low, '"Civil Martial Law": The Government of India and the civil disobedience movements 1930-1934', in D.A. Low (ed.), *Congress and the Raj: Facets of the Indian Struggle 1917-1947* (London, Heiemann, 1977), pp. 165–98. On the revival of terrorism, she refers to Tanika Sarkar, *Bengal 1928-1934: The Politics of Protest* (Delhi: Oxford University Press, 1997), p. 97.

Chapter 16

1. See Public Records Office, Kew, Great Britain, (PRO) CO 537/935, 'Report of the Interdepartmental Committee on Eastern Unrest.' Copies of the report can also be found at APAC, L/P&J/12/120. For the evidence of these international connections, see Kris Manjapra, 'Communist Internationalism and Transcolonial Recognition', in Sugata Bose and Kris Manjapra, eds., *Cosmopolitan Thought Zones: South Asia and the Global Circulation of Ideas* (New York: Palgrave Macmillan, 2010), pp. 159–77.
2. J. Daniel Elam, The "Arch Priestess of Anarchy" Visits Lahore: Violence, Love and the Worldliness of Revolutionary Texts',

Postcolonial Studies, 16, 2 (2013), pp. 140–54, p. 141. As Daniel Elam makes clear, 'This definition is originally from Goldman's pamphlet, "Anarchism: What It Really Stands For", (published in Mother India in 1917). The British Raj proscribed the pamphlet in 1911, but clearly a few copies escaped the grasp of the colonial censors.' (p. 141).

3. Farida Zakaria, *'Putin's invasion of Ukraine marks the beginning of a post-American era,' Washington Post*, 10 March 2022 (Available at https://www.washingtonpost.com/opinions/2022/03/10/why-the-west-cant-let-putin-win-in-ukraine/)

4. Kama Maclean, *A Revolutionary History of Interwar India: Violence, Image, Voice and Text* (London: Hurst & Co, 2015), p. 2.

Chapter 17

1. Tim Murphy, Underground Asia: Global Revolutionaries and the Assault on Empire (Penguin Random House, 2020), p. 448.

2. Amulya Gopalakrishnan, 'Why Mahatma Gandhi Rejected Chauri Chaura's Crime of Passion', *The Times of India* (30 September 2019) (Available at http://timesofindia.indiatimes.com/articleshow/71372232.cms?utm_source=contentofinterest&utm_medium=text&utm_campaign=cppst).

3. Rakhahari Chatterji, *'The Swarajist Revolt: A Forgotten Chapter of Indian Movement,'* The Indian Journal of Political Science, 29/4 (1968), pp. 398-404 at p. 400.

4. Tim Murphy, Underground Asia: Global Revolutionaries and the Assault on Empire (Penguin Random House, 2020) at pp. 448-449

5. Kama Maclean, *A Revolutionary History of Interwar India: Violence, Image, Voice and Text* (London: Hurst & Co, 2015), p. 4.

6. Chris Moffat, *India's Revolutionary Inheritance: Politics & the Promise of Bhagat Singh* (Cambridge University Press, 2019), p. 66, where he draws upon Yashpal, *Yashpal Looks Back*.

7. Ibid., p. 64.

8. See Asok Kumar Ray, *Revolutionary Parties of Bengal: Dacca Anushilan, New Violence, and Jugantar, 1919-1930* (Kolkata: Papyrus Books, 2013), pp. 21–34.

9. Kama Maclean, *A Revolutionary History of Interwar India: Violence, Image, Voice and Text* (London: Hurst & Co, 2015), p. 1.

10. Ibid.

11. Ibid.

12. Ibid., p. 3.
13. Ibid., p. 1.
14. Faisal Devji, *The Impossible Indian: Gandhi and the Temptation of Violence* (Harvard University Press, 2012), p. 163. See also Chapters 1, 2 and 6.

Chapter 18

1. The full poem reads: '*sarfaroshī kī tamannā ab hamāre dil meñ hai, dekhnā hai zor kitnā bāzū-e-qātil meñ hai / ai shahīd-e-mulk-o-millat maiñ tire uupar nisār, le tirī himmat kā charchā ghair kī mahfil meñ hai / vaa.e qismat paañv kī ai zo.af kuchh chaltī nahīñ, kārvāñ apnā abhī tak pahlī hī manzil meñ hai / rahrav-e-rāh-e-mohabbat rah na jaanā raah meñ, lazzat-e-sahrā-navardī dūrī-e-manzil meñ hai / shauq se rāh-e-mohabbat kī musībat jhel le, ik khushī kā raaz pinhāñ jāda-e-manzil meñ hai / aaj phir maqtal meñ qātil kah rahā hai baar baar, aa.eñ vo shauq-e-shahādat jin ke jin ke dil meñ hai / marne vaalo aao ab gardan kaTāo shauq se, ye ghanīmat vaqt hai khanjar kaf-e-qātil meñ hai / māne-e-iz.hār tum ko hai hayā, ham ko adab, kuchh tumhāre dil ke andar kuchh hamāre dil meñ hai / mai-kada sunsān khum ulTe paDe haiñ jaam chuur, sar-nigūñ baiThā hai saaqī jo tirī mahfil meñ hai / vaqt aane de dikhā deñge tujhe ai āsmāñ, ham abhī se kyuuñ batā. eñ kyā hamāre dil meñ hai / ab na agle valvale haiñ aur na vo armāñ kī bhiiD, sirf miT jaane kī ik hasrat dil-e-'bismil' meñ hai*'.

2. The full translation of the poem in English is as follows: 'The desire for revolution is in our hearts, Let us see what strength there is in the arms of our executioner / Why do you remain silent thus?, Whoever I see, is gathered quiet so . . . / O martyr of country, of nation, I submit myself to thee, For yet even the enemy speaks of thy courage The desire for struggle is in our hearts . . . / When the time comes, we shall show thee, O heaven, For why should we tell thee now, what lurks in our hearts? / We have been dragged to service by the hope of blood, of vengeance, Yea, by our love for nation divine, we go to the streets of the enemy, The desire for struggle is in our hearts . . . / Armed does the enemy sit, ready to open fire, Ready too are we, our bosoms thrust out to him, With blood we shall play Holi, if our nation need us The desire for struggle is in our hearts . . . / No sword can sever hands that have the heat of battle within, No threat can bow heads that have risen so . . . / Yea, for in our insides has risen a flame, and the desire for

struggle is in our hearts . . . / Set we out from our homes, our heads shrouded with cloth, Taking our lives in our hands, do we march so . . . / In our assembly of death, life is now but a guest, The desire for struggle is in our hearts . . . /Stands the enemy in the gallows thus, asking, "Does anyone wish to bear testimony?" . . . / With a host of storms in our heart, and with revolution in our breath, We shall knock the enemy cold, and no one shall stop us . . . / What is that body that does not have hot blood in it, How can a person conquer a Typhoon while sitting in a boat near the shore / The desire for struggle is in our hearts, We shall now see what strength there is in the boughs of the enemy.

3. Aparna Vaidik, Waiting for Swaraj: Inner Lives of Indian Revolutionaries (Cambridge University Press, 2021).

4. Chris Moffat, *India's Revolutionary Inheritance: Politics & the Promise of Bhagat Singh* (Cambridge University Press, 2019), p. 53.

5. Kama Maclean, *A Revolutionary History of Interwar India: Violence, Image, Voice and Text* (London: Hurst & Co, 2015), p. 28.

6. Chris Moffat, *India's Revolutionary Inheritance: Politics & the Promise of Bhagat Singh* (Cambridge University Press, 2019), p. 55.

7. S Irfan Habib, *To Make the Deaf Hear* (Three Essays Collective, 3rd Print, 2015) at p. xiii.

8. Ibid

9. Ibid

10. See the 'Preface' to S Irfan Habib, *To Make the Deaf Hear: Ideology and Programme of Bhagat Singh and His Comrades* (New Delhi: Three Essays Collective, 3rd edn., 2015), p. xv.

11. Durba Ghosh, *Gentlemanly Terrorists: Political Violence and the Colonial State in India, 1919-1947* (Cambridge University Press, 2017), p. 94. She quotes the sources as APAC, L/P&J?6/1910, *Kakori Train Dacoity and Conspiracy Case*, L/P&J/6/1962, *Deoghar Conspiracy Case*; APAC L/P&J/12/327, 'Meerut Conspiracy Case in Comparative and International Perspective', *Comparative Studies of South Asia, Africa and the Middle East*, 33, 3 (2013), pp. 310–15; A.G. Noorani, *Indian Political Trials*, (Oxford University Press, 2005), Ch. 10.

12. For an account, see Karish K. Puri, *Ghadar Movement: Ideology, Organisation and Strategy* (Amritsar: Guru Nanak Dev University, 1983). Also see, James Campbell Ker, *Political Trouble in India, 1907-1917* (India: Oriental Publishers, 1973).

13. Chaman Lal, *The Bhagat Singh Reader* (Noida: Harper Collins, 2019), pp. 320–21.

14. Ibid.

15. Ibid., p. 336.

16. Anita Anand, *The Patient Assassin* (London: Simon & Schuster, 2019), p. 291.

17. Ibid., p. 290.

18. Ibid., p. 291.

19. Ibid., p. 291.

20. Ibid., p. 292.

21. Ibid., p. 292–93.

22. Ibid., p. 293.

23. Ibid., p. 308.

24. Extract from New Scotland Yard report, dated 12 June 1940, *P.&J. (S.) 466/36*, which refers to the Public & Judicial (S) Department, pp. 48–48A.

25. Ibid., p. 42.

26. See, *P.&J. (S.) 466/36* at the British Library.

27. Extract from New Scotland Yard Report at IOR: 4/PLJ/12/500 where *P.&J. (S.) 466/36* refers to the Public & Judicial (S) Department.

28. Kim A. Wagner, *Amritsar 1991: An Empire of Fear & the Making of a Massacre* (Princeton University Press, 2019), pp. 264–65.

29. *Shaheed Udham Singh, Hindustan Times*, 31 July 2013 (Available at https://www.pressreader.com/india/hindustan-times-jalandh ar/20130731/282913793115629)

30. *Ashok* Dhawale, 'Bhagat Singh: A Perennial Saga of Inspiration' People's Democracy, vol. xxx, No. 40, 1 October 2006. (Available at https://archives.peoplesdemocracy.in/2006/1001/10012006_ ashok%20dhawale.html)

31. M.J.S. Waraich, *Bhagat Singh: The Eternal Rebel* (Delhi: Unistar Books, 2014), p. 13.

32. The six who were hanged were (i) Babbar Kishan Singh Gargajj (Varing, Jalandhar); (ii) Babbar Karam Singh (Manko, Jalandhar); (iii) Babbar Nand Singh (Ghurial, Jalandhar); (iv) Babbar Santa Singh (Chhoti Harion, Ludhiana); (v) Babbar Dalip Singh (Dhamian, Hoshiarpur) and (vi) Babbar Dharam Singh (Hayatpur Rurki, Hoshiarpur).

33. Chaman Lal, *The Bhagat Singh Reader* (Noida: Harper Collins, 2019), p. 246.

34. Ibid., p. 247.

Chapter 19

1. Omesh Saigal, *Shaheed Bhagat Singh: Unique Martyr in Freedom Struggle* (Delhi: Gyan Publishing House, 2002), p. 52.

2. Vachnesh Tripathi, *Krantimurti Durga Bhabhi* (Delhi: Hindi Akademi, 1996), p. 31.

3. Tim Murphy, Underground Asia: Global Revolutionaries and the Assault on Empire (Penguin Random House, 2020) at p. 80, where the reference by Professor Tim Murphy is to Bhai Parmanand, *The Story of My Life, Lahore*: The Central Hindu Yuvak Sabha, 1934, pp. 31-35.

4. James Campbell Ker, *Political Trouble in India: 1907-1917* (Calcutta, 1917), p. 352–53.

5. Ibid., p. 353.

6. Ibid., p. 353.

7. Ibid., p. 371.

8. Ibid., p. 371.

9. Ibid., p. 372.

10. Ibid., p. 350.

11. Manorama Dewan, *Inquilabi Yatra: Sita Devi Aur Principal Chhabil Das Ki Jeevani* (Delhi: National Book Trust, 2006), p. 119.

12. See, Raja Ram Shastri, *Amar Shahidon ke Sansmaran* (Kanpur, 1981), pp. 82–83. Bhagat Singh is said to have remarked to Raja Ram Shastri, a close associate, that '. . . *main bhi naujawan hoon. Meri raigon mein bhi garm khoon bahta hae. Mere mun mein bhi prem ki bhavnayen zor mara karati hain. Par ve itani balwati nahin ki mujhe kartavya-vimukh kar sake*'. ('I too am young and full-blooded in my veins / I too feel the pangs of love in my heart/ But I am not so weak as to give in to such temptations').

13. M.M. Juneja, *Biography of Bhagat Singh* (Delhi: Modern Publisher, 2nd Reprint, 2009), p. 39.

14. Ibid., p. 300.

15. Sachindra Nath Sanyal, *Bandi Jeevan* (Delhi: Atmaram, 1963), pp. 270–71.

Chapter 20

1. See, Pandit Pearay Mohan, *The Punjab 'Rebellion' of 1919, and How It Was Suppressed: An Account of the Punjab Disorders and the Working of Martial Law* (Gyan Publishing House, 1999).
2. Ibid., 23.
3. Mahesh Sharma, *The Life and Times of Bhagat Singh* (Prabhat Prakashan, 2021), p. 35. Also see S.S. Paul, *Great Men of India: Bhagat Singh* (New Delhi: Sterling Publishers, 2003), Chapter 4.
4. Priya Ramani, 'Bhagat Singh Comes to Delhi', *Mint* (20 November 2008), (Available at https://www.livemint.com/Leisure/BNlft0AiWNfGdkntHb3fSK/Bhagat-Singh-comes-to-Delhi.html). She gives an eye-witness account of having seen them. A page of the first Lahore Conspiracy Case's judgement in which Kartar Singh Sarabha was sentenced to death and on which Singh put some notes is also displayed.
5. Mahesh Sharma, *The Life and Times of Bhagat Singh* (Prabhat Prakashan, 2021), p. 35.
6. 'First letter by Bhagat Singh to postmaster of Lahore', 1 November 1926. Reproduced in Chaman Lal, *The Bhagat Singh Reader* (Noida: Harper Collins, 2019), p. 10.
7. 'Second letter to the Secretary, Punjab Government', 17 November 1926. Reproduced in Chaman Lal, *The Bhagat Singh Reader* (Harper Noida: Collins, 2019), p. 11.
8. 'Letter to the Secretary, Punjab Government', 16 November 1926. Reproduced in Chaman Lal, *The Bhagat Singh Reader* (Noida: Harper Collins, 2019), p. 12.
9. The Selected Works of Bhagat Singh (Introduction by Aka Rico) Big Red Oak, 2009, at p. 71.
10. Chaman Lal, *Bhagat Singh: The Jail Notebook and Other Writings* (New Delhi: Leftword, Reprinted 2014), p. 167.

Chapter 21

1. 'Letter to friend Amar Chand', 1927. Reproduced in Chaman Lal, *The Bhagat Singh Reader* (Noida: Harper Collins, 2019), p. 14–15
2. 'Letter to Superintendent of C.I.D., Lahore', 19 June 1928. Reproduced in Chaman Lal, *The Bhagat Singh Reader* (Noida: Harper Collins, 2019), p. 17.

3. Sachindra Nath Sanyal, *Bandi Jeevan* (Atmaram, Delhi, 1963), pp. 277–78.

4. Manorama Dewan, *Iquilabi Yatra: Sita Devi Aur Principal Chhabil Das Ki Jeevani* (Delhi, 2006), p. 119.

5. Raja Ram Shastri, *Amar Shahidon ke Sansmaran* (Kanpur, 1981), pp. 82–83, where the author explains how Bhagat Singh told him: '. . . *main bhi naujawan hoon. Meri ragon mein bhi khoon bahta hai. Mere mun mein prem ki bhavnayen zor mara karati hain. Par ve itani balwati nahin ki mujhe kartavya-vimukh kar sake*'. Quoted in M.M. Juneja, *Biography of Bhagat Singh* (Delhi: Modern Publisher, 2nd Reprint, 2009), p. 44.

6. Virendra Sindhu, *Yugdrishta Bhagat Singh Aur Unke Mrityuanjay Purke* (Delhi, 1997), p. 309.

7. A.B. Bardhan, *Bhagat Singh: Pages from the Life of a Martyr* (Delhi: All India Youth Federation, 2006), p. 31.

8. Jagmohan Singh and Chaman Lal eds., *Bhagat Singh Aur Unke Sathion Ke Dastavej* (Delhi, 2003), p. 56.

9. 'Letter to Sukhdev', 5 April 1929 in Hindi. Reproduced in Chaman Lal, *The Bhagat Singh Reader* (Noida: Harper Collins, 2019), p. 18–19.

10. Ibid., p. 20.

Chapter 22

1. Kuldip Nayar, *The Martyr: Bhagat Singh – Experiments in Revolution* (New Delhi: Har-Anand Publications, 2000), p. 33–34.

2. Ibid., p. 35.

3. Kamlesh Mohan, *Militant Nationalism in the Punjab, 1919-35* (Delhi: Manohar, 1985), p. 345.

4. Kuldip Nayar, *The Martyr: Bhagat Singh – Experiments in Revolution* (New Delhi: Har-Anand Publications, 2000), p. 36.

5. Kama Maclean, *A Revolutionary History of Interwar India: Violence, Image, Voice and Text* (London: Hurst & Co, 2015), p. 31.

6. M.J.S. Waraich, *Bhagat Singh: The Eternal Rebel* (Chandigarh: Unistar, 2014), p. 149.

7. R.K. Kaushik, 'Missed Target of Bhagat Singh', *The Tribune*, 18 September 2002. (Available at https://www.tribuneindia.com/2002/20020918/edit.htm#5).

8. Jagmohan Singh and Chaman Lal eds., *Bhagat Singh Aur Unke Sathion Ke Dastavej* (Delhi, 2003), pp. 284–85.

9. Malwinder Jit Singh Waraich and Dr Gurdev Singh, *The Hanging of Bhagat Singh: Complete Judgment and Other Documents* (Chandigarh:

Unistar Books, 2005), p. 51. Also see Chapter 24 on Ferozeshah Kotla at p. 141.

10. Born as Durgavati Devi in 1907, she lived right up to 1999 and was the wife of the HSRA revolutionary Bhagwati Charan Vohra. The HSRA revolutionaries generally referred to her as *Bhabhi* (meaning elder brother's wife), by which name she became popular in Indian revolutionary circles.

11. Shiv Verma, *Sansmritiyan* (Delhi, 2002), p. 37.

12. M.M. Juneja, *Selected Collections on Bhagat Singh* (Hisar: Modern Publishers, 2007), p. 96.

13. Shiv Verma, *Sansmritiyan* (Delhi, 2002), p. 39.

14. Jawaharlal Nehru, *An Autobiography* (Delhi: Allied Pub, 1962), pp. 175–76.

15. Telegram from the viceroy to the secretary of state for India in London dated 10 January 1929, British Library, (P&J, 79, 1929).

Chapter 23

1. See, M.J.S. Waraich, *Bhagat Singh: The Eternal Rebel* (Chandigarh: Unistar, 2014), p. 173–74. Also see, M.M. Juneja, *Biography of Bhagat Singh* (Mohali: Modern Publishers, 2nd Reprint, 2016), p. 76.

2. Exhibit P.E. X/2 statement made before the additional district magistrate, Delhi, on 8 May 1929, British Library.

3. Malwinder Jit Singh Waraich, *Profile of a Martyr Jatin Dass: A First Hand Account by his Brother Kiron Das* (Chandigarh: Unistar Press, 2nd ed., 2015), p. 26.

4. See now, however, Satvinder Singh Juss, *The Execution of Bhagat Singh: Heresies of the Raj* (Amberley, 2020), pp. 191–226.

5. The judgement is reproduced in Satvinder Singh Juss, *The Execution of Bhagat Singh: Heresies of the Raj* (Amberley, 2020), pp. 265–66.

6. Both were charged under Section 307 of the Indian Penal Code and under Section 3 of the Explosive Substances Act.

Chapter 24

1. For fuller details see, Shiv Verma, *Sansmritiyan* (Delhi, 2002), pp. 33–34; Virendra Sindhu, *Yugdrishta Bhagat Singh Aur Unke Mrityuanjay Purkhe* (Delhi, 1997), pp. 159–60; K.K. Khullar, *Shahid Bhagat Singh* (Delhi, 1975), p. 39.

2. Justice Markandey Katju, 'Who Was Right, Gandhi or Bhagat Singh? — II', *Daily Times* (28 November 2018) (Available at

https://dailytimes.com.pk/326921/who-was-right-gandhi-or-bhagat-singh-ii/).

3. See the 'Preface' to S. Irfan Habib, *To Make the Deaf Hear: Ideology and Programme of Bhagat Singh and His Comrades* (New Delhi: Three Essays Collective, 3rd edn., 2015), p. xi.

4. Ibid., p. xii.

5. Comrade Ram Chandra, Naujawan Bharat Sabha and Hindustan Socialist Republican Association Army (HSRA) 2nd edition 2003, (Lakshmi Printing Works, 2003) at p.18

6. Ibid., at p. 17

7. Ibid., See the Preface.

8. Simona Sawhney, 'Death in Three Scenes of Recitation', *Postcolonial Studies*, 16, 2 (2013), pp. 202–15, p. 203.

9. S.K. Mittal and I. Habib, 'Towards Independence and Socialist Republic: Naujawan Bharat Sabha', *Social Scientist*, 8, 2 (September 1969), pp. 18–29, p. 20.

10. Ibid., p. 21.

Chapter 25

1. 'Manifesto of the Naujawan Bharat Sabha' (6 April 1928), in Shiv Verma, (2nd Ed., 1996) *Selected Writings of Shaheed Bhagat Singh*, (Kanpur: Samajwadi Sahitya Sadan, 1996, [1985]) p. 150. Also available at https://theanarchistlibrary.org/mirror/b/bc/bhagawati-charan-vohra-manifesto-of-naujawan-bharat-sabha-punjab.html)

2. 'Manifesto of the HSRA' (1929), in Shiv Verma, (2nd Ed., 1996) *Selected Writings of Shaheed Bhagat Singh*, (Kanpur: Samajwadi Sahitya Sadan, 1996, [1985]) p. 154

3. The slogan, *Inquilab Zindabad*, was published in *The Tribune* of 24 December 1929.

4. See *Home Pol. File KW II of 130/1930* at the National Archives of India.

5. Chris Moffatt, 'Experiment in Political Truth', *Postcolonial Studies*, 16, 2 (2013), pp. 185–201, p. 198.

6. Kama Maclean, *A Revolutionary History of Interwar India: Violence, Image, Voice and Text* (London: Hurst & Co, 2015), p. 6.

7. Ibid., p. 15.

8. Durba Ghosh, *Gentlemanly Terrorists: Political Violence and the Colonial State in India, 1919-1947* (Cambridge University Press, 2017), p. 244.

9. Ibid., p. 248. See also R.C. Majumdar, *History of the Freedom Movement in India* (South Asia Books, 1998).

10. R.C. Majumdar, 'Foreword', in Uma Mukherjee, *Two Great Indian Revolutionaries: Rash Behari and Jyotindra Nath Banerjee* (Calcutta: Firma K.L. Mukhopadhyay, 1966).

11. Aparna Vaidik, 'History of a renegade revolutionary: revolutionism and betrayal in colonial India', *Postcolonial Studies*, 16, 2, pp. 216–29, p. 217.

12. Durba Ghosh, *Gentlemanly Terrorists: Political Violence and the Colonial State in India, 1919-1947* (Cambridge University Press, 2017), p. 248.

13. Ibid., p. 253.

14. See the *Working Class Movement Library* ('WCML') at https://www.wcml.org.uk/maccoll/maccoll/theatre/the-red-megaphones/.

15. Durba Ghosh, *Gentlemanly Terrorists: Political Violence and the Colonial State in India, 1919-1947* (Cambridge University Press, 2017), p. 131.

Chapter 26

1. See S. Irfan Habib, *To Make the Deaf Hear: Ideology and Programme of Bhagat Singh and His Comrades* (New Delhi: Three Essays Collective, 3rd edn., 2015).

2. Durba Ghosh, *Gentlemanly Terrorists: Political Violence and the Colonial State in India, 1919-1947* (Cambridge University Press, 2017), p. 94.

3. Kama Maclean, *A Revolutionary History of Interwar India: Violence, Image, Voice and Text* (London: Hurst & Co, 2015), p. 35.

4. 'India and the Simon Commission', *The Commonwealth Journal of International Affairs* (April 2008), pp. 301–20, p. 301.

5. Taylor C. Sherman, 'State Practice, Nationalist Politics and the Hunger Strikes of the Lahore Conspiracy Case Prisoners, 1929–39', *Cultural and Social History*, 5, 4 (2008), pp. 497–508, p. 498, (Available at https://www.tandfonline.com/doi/abs/10.2752/147800408X341686).

6. Nine of the twenty-five had, as Taylor Sherman reminds us, absconded and were at large when the trial began.

7. Christopher Pinney, *Photos of the Gods: The Printed Image and Political Struggle in India* (London: Oxford University Press, 2004), p. 126.

8. Taylor C. Sherman, 'State Practice, Nationalist Politics and the Hunger Strikes of the Lahore Conspiracy Case Prisoners, 1929–39', *Cultural and Social History*, 5, 4 (2008), pp. 497–508, p. 498, (Available at https://www.tandfonline.com/doi/abs/10.2752/147800408X341686).

9. Ibid.

10. Ibid., p. 500.

11. Chris Moffatt, 'Experiment in Political Truth', *Postcolonial Studies*, 16, 2 (2013), pp. 185–201, p. 185.

12. Ibid., p. 186.

13. Shubhankar Dam, *Presidential Legislation in India: The Law and Practice of Ordinances* (Cambridge University Press, 2014), p. 5.

14. This was a body consisting of six to twelve non-official members (under S. 10), but the Council's legislative powers were greatly limited because in many cases the governor-general's prior sanction was required (under S. 19).

15. Shubhankar Dam, *Presidential Legislation in India: The Law and Practice of Ordinances* (Cambridge University Press, 2014), pp. 38–39.

16. Indian Councils Act 1861, S. 23.

17. Shubhankar Dam, *Presidential Legislation in India: The Law and Practice of Ordinances* (Cambridge University Press, 2014), p. 44.

18. Anon, 'Public Safety Ordinance: Preventive Purpose', *The Strait Times*, 1 May 1929.

19. Shubhankar Dam, *Presidential Legislation in India: The Law and Practice of Ordinances* (Cambridge University Press, 2014), pp. 44–45.

20. Ibid., p. 46.

21. Ibid., p. 46, quoting from the statement of Lord Irwin appended to the Lahore Conspiracy Case Ordinance, 1 May 1930, Shimla.

22. (1931) 55 Ind. App. 169.

23. Ibid., 172. Dam writes, 'This exclusionary rule quickly became standard reasoning, see e.g., *King-Emperor v. Benoari Lal Sharma And Others* (1945) 72 Ind. App. 57; *Hubli Electricity Co. Ltd v. Province of Bombay L.R.* (1948) 76 Ind. App. 57; *Lakhi Narayna Das v. The Province of Bihar* [1949] F.C.R 693. But even so, we now know from *Bancoult* that this is wrong reasoning and Bhagat Singh's case is merely the precursor to all these others, which is why it should be revisited in the courts again.

24. Shubhankar Dam, *Presidential Legislation in India: The Law and Practice of Ordinances* (Cambridge University Press, 2014), p. 47.

25. Ibid., p. 47.

26. Neeti Nair, *'Bhagat Singh as "Satyagrahi": The Limits to Non-violence in Late Colonial India'*, Modern Asian Studies (vol. 43, Issue 3, May 2009, at p. 649).

27. S Irfan Habib, *To Make the Deaf Hear: Ideology and Programme of Bhagat Singh and His Comrades* (New Delhi: Three Essays Collective, 3rd edn., 2015), p. xi.

28. Radhika Singha, *A Despotism of Law: Crime and Justice in Early Colonial India* (Oxford University Press, 1998), p. viii.

29. Ibid., p. 29.

30. In the landmark UK Supreme Court case of *Bancoult [2008] UKHL 61*, consideration was given to the question of how a colonial power can '*make laws for the peace, order and good of the Territory*', which was the issue in relation to the UK government's expulsion of the Chagos Islanders from the atoll of Diego Gracia in the Indian Ocean. Various judges, as the case progressed through the courts, took the view that UK ministers could not properly legislate in the interests of the UK as a whole (including its dependent territories), but only in the interests of the particular territory itself (per Laws LJ in *Bancoult (No. 1) [2001] QB 1067*) para 43). It was also suggested that '*even if its subject-matter is incontestably the colony, it is capable of being rendered invalid by jurisdictional error or malpractice . . . In the second place, it must also be open to challenge if its subject-matter, on examination, is manifestly not the peace, good order and good government of the colony*' (per Sedley LJ in *Bancoult [2007] EWCA Civ. 498*).

31. For a discussion on Canada, see Dara Lithwick, '"Welfare" of a Nation: The Origins of "Peace, Order and Good Government"' (Available at https://hillnotes.ca/2017/04/26/welfare-of-a-nation-the-origins-of-peace-order-and-good-government/).

32. For a discussion on Australia, see Ian D. Killey, '"Peace, Order and Good Government": A Limitation on Legislative Competence', *Melbourne University Law Review*, 17 (June 1989), pp. 24–55.

33. Mark Condos, *The Insecurity State* (Cambridge University Press, 2017), pp. 223.

34. Neeti Nair, 'Bhagat Singh as "Satyagrahi": The Limits to Non-violence in Late Colonial India', *Modern Asian Studies*, 43, 3 (2009), pp. 649–81, p. 649.

35. Kama Maclean, *A Revolutionary History of Interwar India: Violence, Image, Voice and Text* (London: Hurst & Co, 2015), p. 2.

Chapter 27

1. Reproduced in Chaman Lal, *The Bhagat Singh Reader* (Noida: Harper Collins, 2019) p. 114.
2. *Crown v. Bhagat Singh & B.K. Dutt*; Charge S.S. 307 I.P.C. & 3&4 Explosive Substance Act.
3. 'Statement in the Sessions Court' (6 June 1929), Reproduced in Chaman Lal, *The Bhagat Singh Reader* (Noida: Harper Collins, 2019), p. 114; Aka Rico, 'Introduction' in *Selected Works of Bhagat Singh* (Big Red Oak, 2009), p. 33.
4. Ibid.
5. 'Statement in the Sessions Court' (6 June 1929), which was read in court by Asaf Ali, the defence lawyer, who was also a leading light in the Congress Party. Reproduced in Chaman Lal, *The Bhagat Singh Reader* (Noida: Harper Collins, 2019), p. 114; Aka Rico, 'Introduction' in *Selected Works of Bhagat Singh* (Big Red Oak, 2009), p. 30.
6. Gregory Shaya, 'How to Make an Anarchist-Terrorist: An Essay on the Political Imaginary in Fin-de-Siecle France', *Journal of Social History*, 44, 2 (Winter 2010), pp. 521–43 (Available at https://www.jstor.org/stable/25790369).

Chapter 28

1. Chaman Lal, *Bhagat Singh: The Jail Notebook and Other Writings* (Leftword, New Delhi, Reprinted 2014), p. 131.
2. Ibid., p. 134 (para 6 of *Statement before the Sessions Court*).
3. Ibid., p. 136 (para 8 of *Statement before the Sessions Court*).
4. Ibid., p. 131-134 (para 3 of *Statement before the Sessions Court*).
5. Ibid.
6. Ibid., p. 131-134 (para 5 of *Statement before the Sessions Court*).
7. Ibid., p. 131-134 (para 3 of *Statement before the Sessions Court*).
8. Ibid.
9. Ibid., p. 133 (para 4 of *Statement before the Sessions Court*).
10. Ibid., p. 135 (para 7 of *Statement before the Sessions Court*).
11. Ibid., p. 136 (para 8 of *Statement before the Sessions Court*).
12. Ibid.

13. Ibid., p. 135.
14. Kama Maclean, *A Revolutionary History of Interwar India: Violence, Image, Voice and Text* (London: Hurst & Co, 2015), p. 36; Shiv Verma & Bhupinder Hooja, *Bhagat Singh: On the Path of Liberation* (Indian Universities Press, 2011); see 'Statement Before the Lahore High Court Bench' at pp. 147–48.
15. Mark Condos, 'Licence to Kill: The Murderous Outrages Act and the Rule of Law in Colonial India, 1867-1925', *Modern Asian Studies*, 50, 2 (2016), pp. 479–517, p. 479. Also see Mark Condos, '"Fanaticism" and the Politics of Resistance along the North-West Frontier of British India', *Comparative Studies in Society and History*, 58, 3 (2016), pp. 717–45, which refers to the practice of 'criminalising fanaticism' (at p. 724).
16. Neeti Nair, 'Bhagat Singh as "Satyagrahi": The limits to non-violence in late colonial India', *Modern Asian Studies*, 43, 3 (2009), pp. 649–81, p. 649.

Chapter 29

1. Reproduced in Chaman Lal, *The Bhagat Singh Reader* (Noida: Harper Collins, 2019), p. 116–17.
2. Ibid., p. 118.
3. Ibid., p.118.
4. Ibid., p. 119.
5. Ibid., p. 119.
6. Ibid., p. 119.
7. Kama Maclean, *A Revolutionary History of Interwar India: Violence, Image, Voice and Text* (London: Hurst & Co, 2015), p. 32.
8. Malwinder Jit Singh Waraich, *Profile of a Martyr Jatin Das: A First Hand Account by his Brother Kiron Das* (Chandigarh: Unistar Press, 2nd ed., 2015), p. 33.
9. Kama Maclean, *A Revolutionary History of Interwar India: Violence, Image, Voice and Text* (London: Hurst & Co, 2015), p. 32.
10. A.G. Noorani, *The Trial of Bhagat Singh* (Oxford University Press, 1996).
11. Satvinder Singh Juss, *The Trial of Bhagat Singh: Heresies of the Raj* (Amberley, 2020; HarperCollins, 2021).
12. Christopher Pinney, 'The Body and the Bomb: Technologies of Modernity in Colonial India', in Richard Davies ed., *Picturing*

the Nation: Iconographies of Modern Indian (New Delhi: Orient BlackSwan, 2007), p.60. Quoted from C. Moffat at p. 8.

13. Also see Kama Maclean, *A Revolutionary History of Interwar India: Violence, Image, Voice and Text* (London: Hurst & Co, 2015), p. 32.

Chapter 30

1. Kama Maclean, *A Revolutionary History of Interwar India: Violence, Image, Voice and Text* (London: Hurst & Co, 2015), p. 305.

2. Kuldip Nayar, *The Martyr: Bhagat Singh – Experiments in Revolution* (New Delhi: Har-Anand Publications, 2000), p. 105.

3. R.K. Kaushik, 'Bhagat Singh, the Final Hours', *The Hindustan Times*, 9 October 2011. (Available at https://www. hindustantimes.com/india/bhagat-singh-the-final-hours/story-oHHsDEhtugs4wSI7dfWuzO.html).

4. DIB Report, 24 June 1926, IOR, L/PJ/12/ 375, p. 1. Quoted in Kama Maclean, *A Revolutionary History of Interwar India: Violence, Image, Voice and Text* (London: Hurst & Co, 2015), p. 33.

5. DIB Report, 20 December 1928. IOR, L/P&J/12/60, p. 3. Quoted in Kama Maclean, *A Revolutionary History of Interwar India: Violence, Image, Voice and Text* (London: Hurst & Co, 2015), p. 33.

6. Kama Maclean, *A Revolutionary History of Interwar India: Violence, Image, Voice and Text* (London: Hurst & Co, 2015), p. 32.

7. Ibid.

8. Shiv Verma (ed.), *Bhagat Singh: On the Path of Liberation*, p. 78. Quoted in Kama Maclean, *A Revolutionary History of Interwar India: Violence, Image, Voice and Text* (London: Hurst & Co, 2015), p. 34.

9. Max Harcourt, 'Revolutionary Networks in North Indian Politics, 1907-1935', unpublished D.Phil thesis, University of Sussex, 1974, p. 264. Quoted in Kama Maclean, *A Revolutionary History of Interwar India: Violence, Image, Voice and Text* (London: Hurst & Co, 2015), p. 34.

10. Shiv Verma (ed.), *Bhagat Singh: On the Path of Liberation*, NMMl, OHT, p.87. Quoted in Kama Maclean, *A Revolutionary History of Interwar India: Violence, Image, Voice and Text* (London: Hurst & Co, 2015), p. 34.

11. DIB Report, 12 January 1928. IOR, L/P&J/12/59, p. 17. Also see report by Fryer, 19 April 1929. NAI, HP, 192/1929, K.W.II, p. 14. Quoted in Kama Maclean, *A Revolutionary History of Interwar India: Violence, Image, Voice and Text* (London: Hurst & Co, 2015), p. 35.
12. Statement of Lalit Kumar Mukherji, Confession Exhibit PBV/1/28.6.29, in Waraich & Jain (eds.), *The Hanging of Bhagat Singh*, Vol. III, p. 247. Quoted in Kama Maclean, *A Revolutionary History of Interwar India: Violence, Image, Voice and Text* (London: Hurst & Co, 2015), p.35.

Chapter 31

1. SR 21 at the Lahore Archives
2. Ibid., para 50–51.
3. Ibid, para 51
4. Folio 23. The letter was signed off on 5 May 1930 by J.N. Sanyal, Mahabir singh, B.K. Nath, D.G. Nigham, and Kundan Lal.
5. See Craig Murray, 'Your Man in the Public Gallery: The Assange Hearing Day 6', *Uncategorised*, 8 September 2020 (Available at https://www.craigmurray.org.uk/archives/2020/09/your-man-in-the-public-gallery-the-assange-hearing-day-6/).

Chapter 32

1. See, 'In Defence of Bhagat Singh', *The Hindustan Times*, 9 August 2005.
2. Binda Preet Sahni, 'Effects of Emergency Law in India 1915-1931', *Studies on Asia*, 2, 2 (Series IV, October 2012), pp. 146–179, p.148, see fn10.
3. Under S. 307 of the Indian Penal Code, whoever does any act with such intention or knowledge, and under such circumstances that, if he by that act caused death, he would be guilty of murder, shall be punished with imprisonment of either description for a term which may extend to ten years, and shall also be liable to fine; and, if hurt is caused to any person by such act, the offender shall be liable either to imprisonment for life, or to such punishment as is herein before mentioned.
4. Kennedy, Charles, 'The Creation and Development of Pakistan's Anti-terrorism Regime, 1997-2002', *Religious Radicalism and Security in South Asia* (2004), pp. 387–411.

5. 'Pakistan hangs sectarian bomber', *BBC News*, 11 August 1998 (Available at http://news.bbc.co.uk/1/hi/world/south_asia/149215.stm, Accessed 22 July 2019).

6. Charles Kennedy, 'The Creation and Development of Pakistan's Anti-terrorism Regime, 1997-2002', *Religious Radicalism and Security in South Asia* (2004), pp. 387–411.

7. Kama Maclean, *A Revolutionary History of Interwar India: Violence, Image, Voice and Text* (London: Hurst & Co, 2015), p. 32.

8. Clare Anderson, 'Execution and its Aftermath in the Nineteenth-Century British Empire' in *A Global History of Execution and the Criminal Corpse* (Palgrave Macmillan, 2015), pp.170–98.

Chapter 33

1. See Section 69 of the Government of India Act 1919.

2. There was a 'Statement' provided by Governor-General Irwin which accompanied the ordinance. It had five paragraphs, but none demonstrated an 'emergency' or the necessity to act for the 'peace and good government' of British India. All Irwin did was to give a narrative account of how 'on the 11th July 1929 the enquiry in the proceedings known as the Lahore Conspiracy Case commenced before a Magistrate . . .' and proceeded to state, '. . . The offence alleged against the accused are both in their own nature and in their relation to the public security of unusually serious character. They include the murder of Mr Saunders, Assistant Superintendent of Police, and head Constable Chanan Singh in Lahore, on the 17th December 1928, the establishment of bomb factories at Lahore and Saharanpur, the conspiracy leading to the throwing of two bombs in the Legislative Assembly on the 8th April 1929, and various other revolutionary activities. For the purpose of establishing these charges which were concerned with many different places and with events occurring over a considerable period of time, the prosecution considered it would be necessary to produce 600 witnesses.'

3. A.G. Noorani, The Trial of Bhagat Singh: Politics of Justice (Oxford University Press, 1996) at p. 87. The entire chapter Noorani's classic work, headed *'When Jinnah defended Bhagat Singh'* (at pp. 76–96) pays careful reading for the lengths that Jinnah went to in his defence of Bhagat Singh, even when their politics differed so widely from each other.

4. Lahore Ordinance No III of 1930, §3.
5. Lahore Ordinance No III of 1930, §4.
6. Lahore Ordinance No III of 1930, §5(2).
7. Lahore Ordinance No III of 1930, §9 (1).
8. Lahore Ordinance No III of 1930, §6(1).
9. Lahore Ordinance No III of 1930, § 6(3).
10. Lahore Ordinance No III of 1930, § 11.

Chapter 34

1. But Section 65 of the 1915 act says: In the first place it does not take into consideration the other provisions of the Government of India Act, 1915, particularly the provision contained in sections 65 and 72. By section 65(1) of the Government of India Act, 1915, the Governor-General in Legislative Council was given power to make laws for all persons, for all courts, and for all places and things, within British India. By section 72 he was also given power for promulgating ordinances in cases of emergency. By the Charter Act of 1915 therefore the High Court possessed all the jurisdiction that it had at the commencement of the Act and could also exercise all such jurisdiction that would be conferred upon it from time to time by the Legislative power conferred by that Act.
2. See the judgment in Satvinder Singh Juss, *The Execution of Bhagat Singh: Heresies of the Raj* (Amberley Press, 2020), p. 266.
3. *Secretary of State for the Foreign & Commonwealth Affairs v Bancoult, R (on the application of) [2007] EWCA Civ 498* (Available at http://www.bailii.org/ew/cases/EWCA/Civ/2007/498.html).
4. Ibid., paras 50–51.
5. Ibid., para 46.
6. *Bancoult* (no 2) [2008] UKHL 61; [2009] 1 AC 453, para 71.
7. Ibid., para 157.

Chapter 35

1. Ajoy Ghosh, *Bhagat Singh and His Comrades: A Page from Our Revolutionary History* (Bombay: People's Publishing House, 1945), p. 16.
2. See the notice of Shadi Lal CJ in Satvinder Singh Juss, *The Execution of Bhagat Singh: Heresies of the Raj* (Amberley Press, 2020), p. 139.

3. A.G. Noorani, The Trial of Bhagat Singh: Politics of Justice (Oxford University Press, 1996) at p. 87.
4. *The Tribune*, 6 October 1929. Also see A.G. Noorani, *Indian Political Trials*, (Oxford University Press, 2005), p. 189.
5. See, Proceedings of the Lahore Conspiracy Case (PLCC), p. 14.

Chapter 36

1. 'The Trial of Bhagat Singh', *India Law Journal* (2007) (Available at https://www.indialawjournal.org/archives/volume1/issue_3/bhagat_singh.html).
2. The incident is described in graphic detail by A.G. Noorani in his chapter, *'The Magisterial Farce'* in The Trial of Bhagat Singh: Politics of Justice (Oxford University Press, 1996, pp 97-129) where he writes of the detainees how on that day, 'they had been caned and abused. Some had received injuries. All had been roughly handled' (at p. 109)
3. *The Tribune*, 22 October 1929, p. 3.
4. *The Tribune*, 25 October 1929, pp. 1–7.
5. A.G. Noorani, The Trial of Bhagat Singh: Politics of Justice (Oxford University Press, 1996) at p. 113-115.
6. *The Tribune*, 14 May 1930.
7. A.G. Noorani, The Trial of Bhagat Singh: Politics of Justice (Oxford University Press, 1996) at p. 146
8. This is directly from Page 38 of the Tribunal Proceedings.
9. A.G. Noorani, The Trial of Bhagat Singh: Politics of Justice (Oxford University Press, 1996) at p. 87-89
10. See *The Tribune*, 26 June 1930, at p. 7.
11. Chaman Lal, *Bhagat Singh: The Jail Notebook and Other Writings* (New Delhi: Leftword, Reprinted 2014), p. 24.

Chapter 37

1. Much is owed by the author in this Part Seven to Dr Chris Moffat's penetrating evaluation of how Bhagat Singh's thinking is to be interpreted. See Chris Moffat, *India's Revolutionary Inheritance* (Cambridge University Press, 2019), Chapters 2 and 4.
2. Bipan Chandra, *'The Ideological Development of the Revolutionary Terrorists of Northern India in the 1920s'*, Nationalism and Colonialism in Modern India, *(Hyderabad: Orient Longman, 1979, pp. 223-251)* p. 167.

3. *Times of India*, 22 September 2010.
4. Chris Moffat, *India's Revolutionary Inheritance* (Cambridge University Press, 2019), p. 148.
5. Ibid., p. 148.
6. Ibid., p. 154.
7. Ibid., p. 150.
8. Ibid., p. 151.
9. Ibid., p. 150.
10. Cited by Moffat at p. 151.
11. *Mima v. Singh (2002)* 186 ALR 393 (at paras 64–67, esp. para 67).
12. J. Callinan (dissenting), para 167.
13. See, Mr Gleeson CJ Kirby in *Mima v. Singh (2002)* 186 ALR 393, para 21.
14. See, Ibid., para 16.
15. See, Ibid., para 18.
16. Frantz Fanon, *The Wretched of the Earth* (Penguin Classics, 2001), pp. 27–84.
17. Ibid., p. 27.
18. Ibid., pp. 27–28.
19. See, '*Young India*', 2 January 1930, in *Collected Works of Mahatma Gandhi, Vol. XLII*, pp. 361–64.
20. Thus, '*In its first twenty years, known as a "moderate phase", Congress was not interested in campaigning for independence or self-rule but for greater political autonomy within empire.*' 'Making Britain: Discover How South Asians Shaped the Nation', 1870-1 (Available at https://www.open.ac.uk/researchprojects/makingbritain/content/indian-national-congress). Perhaps the reason for this is that, as Jona Aravind Dohrmann points out, '*This is probably the only instance in modern history in which a nationalist party in a colonial territory was organised and led for many years by a member of the ruling authority, which was the British Empire*'. The Congress Party as the Creator, Preserver and Destroyer of the Indian State?' at p. 54 (Available at 1496-Artikeltext-3012-1-10-20170404.pdf). Indeed, Priya Satia, in her detailed review of Dinyar Patel's remarkable book on Naoroji has explained how Congress 'earlier [an] agenda of piecemeal reform' within the Empire only (see Priya Satia, '*A Few Heroic Men*', The London Review of Books, (vol. 43, No. 17, 9 September 2021). This is how, '*Nationalist organisations such as the Indian National Congress and the South African Native National Congress clung to the language of imperial citizenship into the early decades of the twentieth*

century' '"Positively cosmopolitan": Britishness, Respectability, and Imperial Citizenship' at p. 125 (Available at https://www.jstor.org/stable/j.ctv64h705.10?seq=1#metadata_info_tab_contents)

21. Chaman Lal, *The Bhagat Singh Reader* (Noida: Harper Collins, 2019), p. ix.
22. Ibid., p. x.
23. Ibid., p. xi.
24. Ibid., p. xi.
25. Vivek Chibber, *Postcolonial Theory and the Specter of Capital* (London: Verso, 2013), p. 290.
26. Ibid., p. 152.
27. Ibid., p. 153.

Chapter 38

1. Simona Sawhney, 'Death in Three Scenes of Recitation', *Postcolonial Studies*, 16, 2 (2013), pp. 202–15, p. 205.
2. Bhagat Singh, 'Why I Am an Atheist', in D.N. Gupta (ed.) *Select Speeches and Writings* (New Delhi: National Book Trust, 2007), p. 54. Quoted from Simona Sawhney, 'Death in Three Scenes of Recitation', *Postcolonial Studies*, 16, 2 (2013), pp. 202–15), p. 213.
3. Bhagat Singh, 'Why I Am an Atheist' (4–5 October 1939). Reproduced in Chaman Lal, *The Bhagat Singh Reader* (Noida: Harper Collins, 2019), p.196–209.
4. Ajoy Ghosh, *Bhagat Singh and His Comrades* (Bombay: People's Publishing House, 1945) as quoted from M.M. Juneja, *Selected Collections on Bhagat Singh* (Hisar: Modern Publishers, 2007), p. 122–23.
5. A.G. Noorani, *The Trial of Bhagat Singh: Politics of Justice* (Oxford University Press, Delhi, 1996), p. xxxvi.
6. Shiv Verma, *Sansmritian* (Delhi, 2002), pp. 49–50. Quoted in M.M. Juneja, *Selected Collections on Bhagat Singh* (Hisar: Modern Publishers, 2007), p. 49–50.
7. Jatinder Nath Sanyal, *Bhagat Singh: A Biography*, edited by K.C. Yadav & Babar Singh (Gurgaon, 2006), pp. 105–06.
8. M.M. Juneja, *Selected Collections on Bhagat Singh* (Hisar: Modern Publishers, 2007), p. 125.
9. Yashpal, *Sinhavalokan Vol. I* (Lucknow, 1951), p. 91.

10. Raja Ram Shastri, *Amar Shahidon Ke Sansmaran* (Kanpur, 1981), pp. 89–90. Quoted in M.M. Juneja, *Selected Collections on Bhagat Singh* (Hisar: Modern Publishers, 2007), pp. 89–90.

11. Ibid., pp. 125–27.

12. Shiv Verma, *Sansmritian* (Delhi, 2002), pp. 26. Quoted in M.M. Juneja, *Selected Collections on Bhagat Singh* (Hisar: Modern Publishers, 2007), p. 129.

13. Vidhyawati Papers, Quoted in M.M. Juneja, *Selected Collections on Bhagat Singh* (Hisar: Modern Publishers, 2007), p. 129–30.

14. Raja Ram Shastri, *Amar Shahidon Ke Sansmaran* (Kanpur, 1981), pp. 89–90. Quoted in M.M. Juneja, *Selected Collections on Bhagat Singh* (Hisar: Modern Publishers, 2007), pp. 131.

15. Bhagat Singh, 'Why I Am an Atheist' (4–5 October 1939). Reproduced in Chaman Lal, *The Bhagat Singh Reader* (Noida: Harper Collins, 2019), p. 195-209.

16. Manmathnath Gupta, *Bhagat Singh and His Times* (Delhi: Lipi Prakashan, 1977), p. 196. Quoted in M.M. Juneja, *Selected Collections on Bhagat Singh* (Hisar: Modern Publishers, 2007), p. 132.

17. Virendra Sindhu, *Yugdrishta Bhagat Singh Aur Unke Mrityuanjay Purkhe* (Delhi, 1997), p. 286.

18. M.M. Juneja, *Selected Collections on Bhagat Singh* (Hisar: Modern Publishers, 2007), p. 131.

19. Raja Ram Shastri, *Amar Shahidon Ke Sansmaran* (Kanpur, 1981), p. 113. Quoted in M.M. Juneja, *Selected Collections on Bhagat Singh* (Hisar: Modern Publishers, 2007), p. 136.

Chapter 39

1. Bipin Chandra, *Nationalism and Colonialism in Modern India* (Orient Longman, 1979), p. 223.

2. Ibid., p. 229

3. Ibid., p. 228

4. 'New Leaders and Their Different Ideas', *Kirti*, July 1928. Reproduced in Chaman Lal, *The Bhagat Singh Reader* (Noida: Harper Collins, 2019), p. 128.

5. 'Statement in the Sessions Court' (6 June 1929). Reproduced in Chaman Lal, *The Bhagat Singh Reader* (Noida: Harper Collins, 2019), p. 112. Also see Aka Rico, 'Introduction' in *Selected Works of Bhagat Singh* (Big Red Oak, 2009), p. 30.

6. Chris Moffat, *India's Revolutionary Inheritance: Politics & the Promise of Bhagat Singh* (Cambridge University Press, 2019), p. 76.

7. Ibid., p. 76–77.

8. Ibid., p. 77.

9. Ibid., p. 83.

10. Ibid., p. 83–84.

11. Chaman Lal, *Bhagat Singh: The Jail Notebook and Other Writings* (New Delhi: Leftword, Reprinted 2014), p. 152.

12. Ibid., p. 156.

13. Ibid., pp. 155–56.

14. Ibid., p. 156.

15. Ibid., p. 160–61.

16. Ibid., p. 161.

17. Ibid., p. 157.

18. Ibid., p. 158.

19. Chris Moffat, *India's Revolutionary Inheritance: Politics & the Promise of Bhagat Singh* (Cambridge University Press, 2019), p. 68.

20. Chaman Lal, *Bhagat Singh: The Jail Notebook and Other Writings* (New Delhi: Leftword, Reprinted 2014), p. 160.

21. Ibid., p. 161.

22. Ibid., p. 159.

23. Bipan Chandra, 'The Ideological Development of Revolutionary Terrorists in North India in the 1920s', in his *Nationalism and Colonialism in Modern India* (Delhi: Orient Longman, 1979).

24. Bhagwan Josh, 'Paradox of Armed Revolution', in Jagtar Singh Grewal (ed.), *Bhagat Singh and His Legend*, (World Punjabi Center, 2008), pp. 64–74.

25. P.M.S. Grewal, *Bhagat Singh: Liberation's Blazing Star*, (Leftword, 2007), p. 94. (See p. 153 of Moffat).

26. Vivek Gupta, *'Why an AAP 'Tsunami' – and Not Just Wave – Has Come Over Punjab'* The Wire, 10 March 2022. Interestingly, Bhagwant Mann, the in-coming 17th chief minister of the province, was himself from Khatkar Kalan. (Available at https://thewire.in/politics/why-an-aap-tsunami-and-not-just-wave-has-come-over-punjab).

Chapter 40

1. See, M.M. Juneja, *Selected Collections on Bhagat Singh* (Hisar: Modern Publishers, 2007), pp. 125–26. This was during the eighteenth

death anniversary of Bhagat Singh in March 1949 when Asaf Ali's article appeared in *Commonweal*, a Pune-based publication. Cited by Chris Moffat, *India's Revolutionary Inheritance: Politics & the Promise of Bhagat Singh* (Cambridge University Press, 2019), p. 140.

2. G.S. Deol, *Shaheed-e-Azam Sardar Bhagat Singh: The Man and His ideology* (Nabha, 1978), p. 132. Cited by Chris Moffat, *India's Revolutionary Inheritance: Politics & the Promise of Bhagat Singh* (Cambridge University Press, 2019), p. 141.

3. Hooja, Bhagat Singh – In Jail and His 'Diary', 13/F. Cited by Chris Moffat, *India's Revolutionary Inheritance: Politics & the Promise of Bhagat Singh* (Cambridge University Press, 2019), p. 141.

4. Ashok Dhawale, 'Shaheed Bhagat Singh: An Immortal Revolutionary', *The Marxist*, 22, 2–3 (April–September 2006).

5. Chris Moffat, *India's Revolutionary Inheritance: Politics & the Promise of Bhagat Singh* (Cambridge University Press, 2019), p. 128.

6. Jagmohan (ed.), *Bhagat Singh Ate Uhna De Saathian Diyan Likhtaan* (Ludhiana, 2006, 1982).

7. K.C. Yadav, 'Editorial Note', in Sachindra Nath Sanyal, *Bhagat Singh: A Biography* (2006), p. 14.

8. 'Interview with Jagmohan Singh', *Frontline*, 2 November 2007, p. 16. Cited in Chris Moffat, *India's Revolutionary Inheritance: Politics & the Promise of Bhagat Singh* (Cambridge University Press, 2019), p. 141.

9. Shamsul Islam, 'No to Bhagat Singh's Second Hanging', *Countercurrents.org*, 12 October 2013 (Available at www.countercurrents.org/shamsul112013.htm). The cause of this concern was the occasion of Narendra Modi's invitation for the purposes of releasing a new edition of Bhagat Singh's jail book in 2013. Cited in Chris Moffat, *India's Revolutionary Inheritance: Politics & the Promise of Bhagat Singh* (Cambridge University Press, 2019), p. 141.

10. Chris Moffat, *India's Revolutionary Inheritance: Politics & the Promise of Bhagat Singh* (Cambridge University Press, 2019), p. 144.

11. Ibid., pp. 145–46.

12. Krishna Pratap Singh, 'Still Waiting for Chandrashekhar's "Azad" Vision After All These Years', *The Wire*, 23 July 2020 (Available at https://thewire.in/history/still-waiting-for-chandrashekhars-azad-vision-after-all-these-years).

13. Shiv Verma, 'Preface', in *Selected Writings of Shaheed Bhagat Singh*. Reproduced in *Selected Works of Shaheed Bhagat Singh*, 14, 16. Cited

in Chris Moffat, *India's Revolutionary Inheritance: Politics & the Promise of Bhagat Singh* (Cambridge University Press, 2019), p. 138.

14. P.C. Joshi, *Mainstream,* 25 March 1969, included in ACH-JNU Books and Pamphlets on History; Cited in Chris Moffat, *India's Revolutionary Inheritance: Politics & the Promise of Bhagat Singh* (Cambridge University Press, 2019), p. 142.

15. Chaman Lal, *Bhagat Singh: The Jail Notebook and Other Writings* (Leftword, New Delhi, Reprinted 2014), 'Introduction', p. 23.

16. Chris Moffat, *India's Revolutionary Inheritance: Politics & the Promise of Bhagat Singh* (Cambridge University Press, 2019), p. 143.

17. He is referring here to S. Irfan Habib, *To Make the Deaf Hear* (Three Essays Collective, 2007).

18. He is referring here to S.R. Bakshi, *Bhagat Singh and His Ideology* (New Delhi, 1981).

19. He is referring here to Chaman Lal, *Understanding Bhagat Singh* (Aakar Books, 2013.)

20. Chris Moffat, *India's Revolutionary Inheritance: Politics & the Promise of Bhagat Singh* (Cambridge University Press, 2019), p. 143.

21. Ibid., p. 144.

22. Ibid., p. 145.

23. Ibid., p. 146.

24. Chaman Lal, *Bhagat Singh: The Jail Notebook and Other Writings* (New Delhi: Leftword, Reprinted 2014), p. 139.

Chapter 41

1. Navtej Singh, *Challenge to Imperial Hegemony: The Life Story of a Great Indian Patriot Udham Singh* (Patiala: Punjab University, 1998), p. ix.

2. Dr Bhuvan Lall, *The Great Indian Genius: Har Dayal* (Chennai: Notion Press, 2020).

3. Ibid., p. 364.

4. Chris Moffat, *India's Revolutionary Inheritance: Politics & the Promise of Bhagat Singh* (Cambridge University Press, 2019), p. 148.

5. Chaman Lal, *Bhagat Singh: The Jail Notebook and Other Writings* (New Delhi: Leftword, Reprinted 2014), p. 150.

6. Malcolm Lyall Darling, *Punjab Peasants in Prosperity and Debt* (Oxford University Press, 1928).

7. Ibid., p. xiv.

8. Chaman Lal, *Bhagat Singh: The Jail Notebook and Other Writings* (New Delhi: Leftword, Reprinted 2014), 'Introduction', p. 22.

9. Ibid., p. 22.
10. Ibid., pp. 22–23.
11. Ibid.
12. Ibid., p. 22.
13. Bhupendra Hooja, *Bhagat Singh – In Jail and His 'Diary': An Introductory Note about a Martyr's Notebook* (Jaipur, 1994), 5/F. Cited in Chris Moffat, *India's Revolutionary Inheritance: Politics & the Promise of Bhagat Singh* (Cambridge University Press, 2019), p. 129.
14. Chris Moffat, *India's Revolutionary Inheritance: Politics & the Promise of Bhagat Singh* (Cambridge University Press, 2019), p. 129.

Chapter 42

1. Bhagat Singh, 'Why I Am an Atheist'. In Chaman Lal, *Bhagat Singh: The Jail Notebook and Other Writings* (New Delhi: Leftword, Reprinted 2014), p. 162.
2. Ibid.
3. Ibid., p. 163.
4. Ibid., p. 171.
5. Ibid., p. 158
6. Chaman Lal, *Bhagat Singh: The Jail Notebook and Other Writings* (New Delhi: Leftword, Reprinted 2014), p. 158.
7. Ibid., p.159
8. Frantz Fanon, *The Wretched of the Earth* (Penguin Classics, 2001), p. 53.
9. Bhagat Singh, 'Satyagraha and Strikes', 1928 (originally in Punjabi) in Chaman Lal, *The Bhagat Singh Reader* (Noida: Harper Collins, 2019), pp. 156–60, p. 157.
10. Ibid., pp. 156–60, pp. 235–36.
11. Ibid., p. 237.
12. Ibid., p. 238.

Chapter 43

1. Frantz Fanon, *The Wretched of the Earth* (Penguin Classics, 2001), p. 29.
2. Ibid., p. 29.
3. Frantz Fanon, Chapter Four: 'The So-called Dependency Complex of the Colonised' in *Black Skin, White Masks* (New York: Gove Press, 2008), p. 72.

4. Frantz Fanon, Chapter 1, *The Wretched of the Earth* (Penguin Classics, 2001), p. 31.
5. Ibid., p. 74.
6. Ibid., pp. 32–33.
7. Reprinted in Chaman Lal, *The Bhagat Singh Reader* (Noida: Harper Collins, 2019), pp. 168–72, pp. 169–170.
8. Ibid., p. 172.
9. Ibid., p. 170.
10. Ibid., p. 170.
11. Ibid., p. 171.
12. Ibid., p. 171.
13. Ibid., p. 168. Indeed, Lala Lajpat Rai had written a biography of Mazzini, as well as of Garibaldi and Shivaji.
14. Ibid., p. 169.
15. This is the story of the man who fired the first shot in the Irish War of Independence, who was the leader of the 3rd Tipperary Brigade. In 1919, a group of young men, barely out of their teens, poorly armed, with no money and little training, renewed the fight that had begun in 1916 to drive the British out of Ireland. Dan Breen was to become the best known of them. At first, they were condemned on all sides. They became outlaws and *My Fight for Irish Freedom* describes graphically what life was like 'on the run,' with 'an army at one's heels and a thousand pounds on one's head'. A burning belief in their cause sustained them through many a dark and bitter day and slowly support came from the people. (See, Dan Breen, My Fight for Irish Freedom, Mercier Press, New Edition, 16 July 2021).

Chapter 44

1. For an account, see Karish K. Puri, *Ghadar Movement: Ideology, Organisation and Strategy* (Amritsar: Guru Nanak Dev University, 1983). Also see, James Campbell Ker, *Political Trouble in India, 1907-1917* (India: Oriental Publishers, 1973).
2. The full poem reads: '*sarfaroshī kī tamannā ab hamāre dil meñ hai, dekhnā hai zor kitnā bāzū-e-qātil meñ hai / ai shahīd-e-mulk-o-millat maiñ tire uupar nisār, le tirī himmat kā charchā ghair kī mahfil meñ hai / vaa.e qismat paañv kī ai zo.af kuchh chaltī nahīñ, kārvāñ apnā abhī tak pahlī hī manzil meñ hai / rahrav-e-rāh-e-mohabbat rah na jaanā*

raah meñ, lazzat-e-sahrā-navardī dūrī-e-manzil meñ hai / shauq se rāh-e-mohabbat kī musībat jhel le, ik khushī kā raaz pinhāñ jāda-e-manzil meñ hai / aaj phir maqtal meñ qātil kah rahā hai baar baar, aa.eñ vo shauq-e-shahādat jin ke jin ke dil meñ hai / marne vaalo aao ab gardan kaTāo shauq se, ye ghanīmat vaqt hai khanjar kaf-e-qātil meñ hai / māne-e-iz.hār tum ko hai hayā, ham ko adab, kuchh tumhāre dil ke andar kuchh hamāre dil meñ hai / mai-kada sunsān khum ulTe paDe haiñ jaam chuur, sar-nigūñ baiThā hai saaqī jo tirī mahfil meñ hai / vaqt aane de dikhā deñge tujhe ai āsmāñ, ham abhī se kyuuñ batā. eñ kyā hamāre dil meñ hai /ab na agle valvale haiñ aur na vo armāñ kī bhiiD, sirf miT jaane kī ik hasrat dil-e-'bismil' meñ hai'.

3. Simona Sawhney, 'Death in Three Scenes of Recitation', *Postcolonial Studies*, 16, 2 (2013), pp. 202–15, p. 206.
4. Ibid., p. 207.
5. Ibid.
6. See also, Simona Sawhney, 'Bhagat Singh: A Politics of Death and Hope' in Anshu Malhotra and Farina Mir eds., *Punjab Reconsidered* (Delhi: Oxford University Press, 2012), pp. 377–408.
7. Sachindra Nath Sanyal, 'Open Letter to Gandhi', *Young India*, 12 February 1925. Also available in Manmath Nath Gupta, *They Lived Dangerously: Reminiscences of a Revolutionary* (People's Pub House, 1969).
8. K.C. Yadav and Babar Singh eds., *Fragrance of Freedom: Writings of Bhagat Singh* (Gurgaon: Hope India Publications, 2006).
9. Simona Sawhney, 'Death in Three Scenes of Recitation', *Postcolonial Studies*, 16, 2 (2013), pp. 202–15, p. 208. Quoted from Chaman Lal ed., *Bhagat Singh ke Sampurna Dastavez* (Panchkula: Adhar Prakashan, 2004), pp. 70, 65.
10. Simona Sawhney, 'Death in Three Scenes of Recitation', *Postcolonial Studies*, 16, 2 (2013), pp. 202–15), p. 208.

Chapter 45

1. 'Blood Sprinkled on the Day of the Holi Babbar Akalis on the Crucifix', *Pratap*, 15 March 1926. Reproduced in Aka Rico, 'Introduction', *Selected Works of Bhagat Singh* (Big Red Oak, 2009), p. 11.
2. Ibid., p. 12.
3. Ibid., p. 12.

4. Ibid., p. 12.

5. Ibid., p. 14.

6. Chris Moffat, *India's Revolutionary Inheritance: Politics & the Promise of Bhagat Singh* (Cambridge University Press, 2019), p. 72.

7. Chaman Lal, *Bhagat Singh: The Jail Notebook and Other Writings* (New Delhi: Leftword, Reprinted 2014), p. 145–46.

8. Simona Sawhney, 'Death in Three Scenes of Recitation', *Postcolonial Studies*, 16, 2 (2013), pp. 202–15, p. 210. Also See, Dr Chris Moffat, 'Experiments in Political Truth', Political Studies, (vol. 16, 2013, Issue 2) at pp. 185-201.

9. Simona Sawhney, 'Death in Three Scenes of Recitation', *Postcolonial Studies*, 16, 2 (2013), pp. 202–15, p. 210.

10. Chaman Lal, *Bhagat Singh: The Jail Notebook and Other Writings* (New Delhi: Leftword, Reprinted 2014), p. 145-146

11. Ibid., p. 146.

12. Simona Sawhney, 'Death in Three Scenes of Recitation', *Postcolonial Studies*, 16, 2 (2013), pp. 202–15, p. 202.

13. Ibid., p. 202–03.

14. Ibid., p. 203.

15. Ibid., p. 204. She refers to Bhagat's Singh's exhortatory article 'Yuvak' (a young man, a youth), which was published in May 1925. Bhagat Singh 'explicitly connects the generosity of youth with its potential for both self-sacrifice and violence'. See, Chaman Lal ed., *Bhagat Singh ke Sampurna Dastavez* (Panchkula: Adhar Prakashan, 2004), pp. 52–54.

16. Simona Sawhney, 'Death in Three Scenes of Recitation', *Postcolonial Studies*, 16, 2 (2013), pp. 202–15, p. 204.

17. Chaman Lal, *Bhagat Singh: The Jail Notebook and Other Writings* (New Delhi: Leftword, Reprinted 2014), p. 145.

18. Chris Moffat, *India's Revolutionary Inheritance: Politics & the Promise of Bhagat Singh* (Cambridge University Press, 2019), p. 147.

19. 'Regarding Suicide: Letter to Sukhdev' (1930). Reproduced in Chaman Lal, *The Bhagat Singh Reader* (Noida: Harper Collins, 2019), p. 71.

20. Ibid., p. 72.

21. Ibid., p. 73.

22. Georgio Agamben, 'On the Limits of Violence' (1970), Lorenzo Fabbri (ed.) and Elisabeth Fay (trans.), diacritics 39 (4), 2009, pp. 103–11, p. 108. Quoted by Simona Sawhney, 'Death in Three

Scenes of Recitation ', *Postcolonial Studies*, 16, 2 (2013), pp. 202–15, p. 209.

Chapter 46

1. Chaman Lal, *Bhagat Singh: The Jail Notebook and Other Writings* (New Delhi: Leftword, Reprinted 2014), p.144–45.
2. M.M. Juneja, *Biography of Bhagat Singh* (Haryana: Modern Publishers, 2008), p. 124. Quoted in Simona Sawhney, 'Death in Three Scenes of Recitation', *Postcolonial Studies*, 16, 2 (2013), pp. 202–15, p. 211.
3. Simona Sawhney, 'Death in Three Scenes of Recitation', *Postcolonial Studies*, 16, 2 (2013), pp. 202–15, p. 212.
4. Ibid., p. 212.
5. Trilochan Singh, *Autobiography of Bhai Sahib Randhir Singh: Freedom Fighter, Reformer, Theologian, Saint and Hero of the Second Lahore Conspiracy Case* (Ludhiana: Bhai Randhir Singh Publishing House, 1971).
6. Chaman Lal, *Bhagat Singh: The Jail Notebook and Other Writings* (New Delhi: Leftword, Reprinted 2014), p. 166.
7. Bhagat Singh, 'Why I Am an Atheist'. Reproduced in Chaman Lal, *Bhagat Singh: The Jail Notebook and Other Writings* (New Delhi: Leftword, Reprinted 2014), p.167.
8. Ibid. p. 169.
9. Ibid., p. 170.
10. Ibid., p. 171.
11. Ibid., p. 172.
12. Ibid., p. 177.

Chapter 47

1. Reproduced by A.G. Noorani, *The Trial of Bhagat Singh* (Oxford University Press, 1996), pp. 302–05, p. 304.
2. Ibid., p. 304.
3. Ibid., p. 306.
4. Ibid., p. 307.
5. Ibid., p. 307.
6. Ibid., p. 307.
7. Bhagat Singh, 'No Hanging, Please shoot us'. Reproduced in Chaman Lal, *Bhagat Singh: The Jail Notebook and Other Writings* (New Delhi: Leftword, Reprinted 2014), p.181.

8. Chaman Lal, *Bhagat Singh: The Jail Notebook and Other Writings* (New Delhi: Leftword, Reprinted 2014), p.149.

9. Bhagat Singh, 'No Hanging, Please shoot us'. Reproduced in Chaman Lal, *Bhagat Singh: The Jail Notebook and Other Writings* (New Delhi: Leftword, Reprinted 2014), p. 178.

10. Ibid., p. 179.

Chapter 48

1. Durba Ghosh, *Gentlemanly Terrorists: Political Violence and the Colonial State in India, 1919-1947* (Cambridge University Press, 2017), p. 132.

2. Ibid., referring to APAC, L/PO/6/51 (iii), p. 154.

3. Durba Ghosh, Ibid., here refers to 'APAC, L/PO/6/51 (iii), "Extract from Private Letter from Lord Irwin to Mr. Wedgewood Benn, January 23, 1930"', p. 130.

4. Ibid., p. 193.

5. Jawaid Iqbal, 'Mexico's Request That Spain Say Sorry for 1519 Is Absurd', *The Sunday Times*, 27 March 2019, p. 28.

6. 'Mexico Asks Pope Francis for Apology for Church's Role in Spanish Conquest', *The Guardian*, 11 October 2020 (Available at https://www.theguardian.com/world/2020/oct/11/mexico-asks-pope-francis-for-apology-for-churchs-role-in-spanish-conquest?CMP=Share_AndroidApp_Other).

7. Steven Press, 'As Germany Acknowledges Its Colonial-era Genocide in Namibia, the Brutal Legacy of Diamond Mining Still Needs a Reckoning', *Time*, 10 June 2021 (Available at https://time.com/6072145/namibia-germany-apology-diamonds/).

8. The Union Cabinet minister of food processing in the Government of India and member of Parliament in the Lok Sabha from Bathinda is Harsimrat Kaur Badal. She is also the daughter-in-law of Prakash Singh Badal, who served as chief minister of Punjab many times. Her brother is Bikram Singh Majithia, who is a former cabinet minister in the Punjab government. Their great-great-grandfather was Sir Sunder Singh Majithia, who hosted a special dinner for General Dyer on the evening following the Jallianwala Bagh Massacre, on 13 April 1919, and then went on to be knighted in 1926 for services to King and Empire. Both these politicians have asked for apologies from the British government for past atrocities.

Even more striking is the example of Giani Arur Singh, who was a former *jathedar* (head priest) of Sri Akal Takht (the Amritsar Sikh temple). After the Jallianwala Bagh Massacre, he presented to Lieutenant Governor O'Dwyer a *'siropa'*, the word being adapted from Persian 'sar-o-pa' (meaning 'head and foot') or 'sarapa' (head to foot), which denotes an honorary dress. It is used by Sikhs to refer to the award of a garment, scarf or a length of cloth when it is bestowed on someone as a mark of honour. He is the maternal grandfather of Simranjit Singh Mann, who is the president of the Shiromani Akali Dal, Punjab's Sikh political party, having twice also been a member of Parliament. He too has demanded that the British government atone for the actions of General Dyer in 1919. One of the most glamorous of Sikh maharajas was from the existing Royal House of Patiala, by the name of Maharaja Bhupinder Singh, and he was indeed a close friend of Lieutenant-Governor O'Dwyer, often wining and dining with him. After the Jallianwala Bagh Massacre, he visited O'Dwyer at London's Caxton Hall, where eventually in 1934 Shaheed Udham Singh was to assassinate him in an effort to avenge the 1919 massacre. Captain Amrinder Singh, erstwhile chief minister of Punjab, is his grandson and also a person seeking recompense for past imperial atrocities.

9. Prasun Sonwalkar, 'Jallianwala Bagh: PM May repeats "deep regret", no apology', *The Hindustan Times*, 11 April 2019 (Available at https://www.hindustantimes.com/world-news/british-pm-theresa-may-voices-regret-over-jallianwala-bagh-massacre/story-owyh1wPwchwCEvX7gC620J.html).

Chapter 49

1. What he had said in the debate in Parliament on that occasion was, 'However we may dwell upon the difficulties of General Dyer during the Amritsar riots, upon the anxious and critical situation in the Punjab, upon the danger to Europeans throughout that province, upon the long delays which have taken place in reaching a decision about this officer, upon the procedure that was at this point or at that point adopted, however we may dwell upon all this, one tremendous fact stands out – I mean the slaughter of nearly 400 persons and the wounding of probably three to four times as many, at the Jallian Wallah Bagh on 13th April. That is an

episode which appears to me to be without precedent or parallel in the modern history of the British Empire. It is an event of an entirely different order from any of those tragical occurrences which take place when troops are brought into collision with the civil population. It is an extraordinary event, a monstrous event, an event which stands in singular and sinister isolation.' See *Hansard House of Commons (U.K.) Proceedings*, 8 July 1920, Supply-Committee, Punjab Disturbances, pp. 1719–34 (Available at http://hansard.millbanksystems.com/commons/1920/jul/08/army-council-and-general-dyer). (Also see https://www.indiaofthepast. org/contribute-memories/read-contributions/major-events-pre-1950/365-churchill-on-jallianwala-bagh-massacre-1919).

2. Patrick Cockburn, 'Britain's Reign as a World Superpower Is Over – and It's All Thanks to Brexit', *The Independent*, 8 December 2019, p. 29.

3. David Edgerton, 'Britain's Persistent Racism Cannot Simply be Explained by Its Imperial History', *The Guardian*, 24 June 2020 (Available at https://www.theguardian.com/commentisfree/2020/jun/24/britain-persistent-racism-imperial-history).

4. Natalya Din-Kariuki, 'After Rhodes Falls', *London Review of Books*, 29 June 2020 (Available at https://www.lrb.co.uk/blog/2020/june/after-rhodes-falls).

5. Tim Harper, *Underground Asia: Global Revolutionaries and the Assault on Empire* (Penguin, 2020).

6. John Quail, *The Slow Burning Fuse: The Lost History of the British Anarchists* (Flamingo, 1978).

7. Percival Spear, *The Oxford History of Modern India: 1740-1947* (Oxford University Press, 1965).

8. C.H. Philips, *The Evolution of Indian and Pakistan, 1858-1947* (Cambridge University Press, 1964).

9. Judith Brown, *Modern India: The Origins of an Asian Democracy*, (The Short Oxford History of the Modern World) (Oxford University Press, 1991).

10. 'Bhagat Singh Reigns in the Hearts of Indian People', *Liberation*, May 2008.

11. Hardeep Singh, 'The Problem with Apologising for the Amritsar Massacre', *The Spectator*, 9 April 2019 (Available at https://blogs.spectator.co.uk/2019/04/the-problem-with-apologising-for-the-amritsar-massacre/).

12. Anita Anand, 'Jallianwala: Regret Isn't Enough. An Honest Appraisal of the Raj Can Do So Much More', *The Times of India*, 14 April 2019 (Available at https://timesofindia. indiatimes.com/articleshow/68868082.cms?utm_source=twitter. com&utm_medium=social&utm_campaign=TOIDesktop&utm_ source=contentofinterest&utm_medium=text&utm_campaign=cppst).

13. Manu S. Pillai, 'The Ghosts of Amritsar', *The New Statesman*, 12–17 April 2019, pp. 42–44, p. 44.

14. Priya Satia, *Time's Monsters* (Harvard University Press, 2019), p. 277.

15. Bharat Dogra, 'Jagmohan Singh—Life Devoted to Carrying Forward the Legacy of Shahid Bhagat Singh', *Mainstream Weekly*, 14 August 2020 (Available at https://mainstreamweekly.net/article9791.html).

16. *R v Secretary of State for the Home Department ex p. Bentley* [1993] EWHC Admin 2 (Available at *http://www.bailii.org/ew/cases/ EWHC/Admin/1993/2.html*). See also, McGeough, *Re Judicial Review* [2012] NIQB 11 (Available at http://www.bailii.org/nie/ cases/NIHC/QB/2012/11.html).

17. For a full account, see Satvinder Singh Juss, *The Execution of Bhagat Singh: Legal Heresies of the Raj* (Noida: Harper Collins, 2021), pp. 191–208.

18. Ibid, p. 266.

19. See, the recent British judgment of Neuberger LJ in Allport v. Wilboram [2004] EWCA Civ 1668.

Chapter 50

1. V.N. Datta, *Gandhi and Bhagat Singh* (New Delhi: Rupa & Co., 2008), p. xv.

2. Ibid., p. 11.

3. Ibid., p. 92.

4. See P. Sitarmayya, *The History of the Indian National Congress, Vol. I* (Bombay, 1946), p. 442.

5. Gurdev Singh Deol, *Shaheed Bhagat Singh: A Biography* (Patiala University Press, 1985), p. 93.

6. Ibid., p. ix.

7. Ibid., p. ix.

8. Ibid., p. x.

9. Sisir K. Bose and Sugata Bose, *The Indian Struggle 1920-1942* (Netaji: Collected Works, Vol. 2, Oxford University Press, 2015), p. 177.

10. *'Why Did Winston Churchill Call Mahatma Gandhi a Fakir?'* India Today, 19 February 2015. (Available at https://www.indiatoday. in/india/story/mahatma-gandhi-fakir-winston-churchill-kingsley-hall-london-240933-2015-02-19)

11. Justice Markandey Katju, 'Who Was Right, Gandhi or Bhagat Singh?—II', *Daily Times*, 28 November 2018 (Available at https:// dailytimes.com.pk/326921/who-was-right-gandhi-or-bhagat-singh-ii/).

12. Ibid., Chapter xi.

13. Sisir K. Bose and Sugata Bose, *The Indian Struggle 1920-1942* (Netaji: Collected Works, Vol. 2, Oxford University Press, 2015), p. 226.

14. For a fuller account, see Anita Rani, *The Patient Assassin* (London, 2019), p. 297.

Chapter 51

1. Sisir K. Bose and Sugata Bose, *The Indian Struggle 1920-1942* (Netaji: Collected Works, Vol. 2, Oxford University Press, 2015), pp. 226–27.

2. Ibid., p. 227.

3. Utpal Aich, 'Did Gandhi Try for the Commutation of Bhagat Singh's Death Penalty?', *Different Truths* (Last accessed on 22 May 2022).

4. *Collected Works of Mahatma Gandhi ('CWMG')*, published by the Publication Division, Ministry of Information & Broadcasting, Government of India, Gandhi Heritage Portal. This 100-volume record of Gandhi's speeches, letters, editorials and other writings was compiled over a period of thirty-eight years.

5. Utpal Aich, 'Did Gandhi Try for the Commutation of Bhagat Singh's Death Penalty?' *Different Truths* (Last accessed on 22 May 2022).

6. Ibid.

7. This appeared under the title 'Delhi Speech', with an introductory note by Mahadev Desai which read: 'Addressing a mass meeting attended by over 50,000 people at Delhi on the 7th of March, Gandhiji delivered a speech in Hindi of which the following is a condensed rendering.'

8. See *The Collected Works of Mahatma Gandhi Vol. 51*, 6 January 1931–28 April 1931, pp. 226–31, p. 229 (Available at https://www. gandhiashramsevagram.org/gandhi-literature/collected-works-of-mahatma-gandhi-volume-1-to-98.php).

9. Ibid., p.272

10. Ibid., p.276

11. Dr P. Sitarmayya, *The History of the Indian National Congress, Vol. I* (Bombay, 1946), p. 442.

12. Ibid., pp. 226–27.

13. Ibid., p. 125.

14. Ibid., p. 232.

15. Ibid., p. 232.

16. Justice Markandey Katju, 'Who Was Right, Gandhi or Bhagat Singh?—II', *Daily Times*, 28 November 2018 (Available at https://dailytimes.com.pk/326921/who-was-right-gandhi-or-bhagat-singh-ii/).

17. S. Irfan Habib, *To Make the Deaf Hear: Ideology and Programme of Bhagat Singh and His Comrades* (New Delhi: Three Essays Collective, 3rd edn., 2015), p. 93. Habib here cites *CWMG*, Vol. 40, pp 259–60.

18. See the *Selected Works of Jawaharlal Nehru* (SWJN), Vol. 4, at p. 157. Cited S. Irfan Habib, *To Make the Deaf Hear: Ideology and Programme of Bhagat Singh and His Comrades* (New Delhi: Three Essays Collective, 3rd edn., 2015), p. 93

19. Subhas Chandra Bose, p. 160. Cited by S. Irfan Habib, *To Make the Deaf Hear: Ideology and Programme of Bhagat Singh and His Comrades* (New Delhi: Three Essays Collective, 3rd edn., 2015), p. 93.

20. S. Irfan Habib, *To Make the Deaf Hear: Ideology and Programme of Bhagat Singh and His Comrades* (New Delhi: Three Essays Collective, 3rd edn., 2015), p. 73.

21. Ibid., p. 93. Habib here cites *CWMG*, Vol. 40, pp. 259–60.

22. Ibid., at p. 104. Habib here quotes from The Tribune of August 1, 1931.

23. Ibid., p. 103.

Chapter 52

1. I.D. Gaur, *Martyr as Bridegroom* (Anthem Press, 2008) at p. 5

2. S. Irfan Habib, *To Make the Deaf Hear: Ideology and Programme of Bhagat Singh and His Comrades* (New Delhi: Three Essays Collective, 3rd edn., 2015), p. 70.

3. Ibid., p. 71.

4. Ibid., p. 102.

5. Ibid., p. 102–03.

6. Chaman Lal, *Understanding Bhagat Singh* (Delhi: Aakar Books, 2013), p. 98.

7. Ibid., p. 99.

8. See Pritam Singh, 'Why the Story of Bhagat Singh Remains on the Margins', *South Asia Citizens Web*, 4 September 2008, where he reviews the 2008 publication of Irfan Habib's *To Make the Deaf Hear: Ideology and Program of Bhagat Singh and His Colleagues* (Available at http://www.sacw.net/article22.html).

9. Quoted in S. Irfan Habib, *To Make the Deaf Hear: Ideology and Programme of Bhagat Singh and His Comrades* (New Delhi: Three Essays Collective, 3rd edn., 2015), p. 103.

10. For an account see, Satvinder S. Juss, 'Sikhism' in Catherine Cookson, *Encyclopedia of Religious Freedom* (Routledge, 2003), pp. 442–45, p. 445.

11. S. Irfan Habib, *To Make the Deaf Hear: Ideology and Programme of Bhagat Singh and His Comrades* (New Delhi: Three Essays Collective, 3rd edn., 2015), Appendix B5.

12. See Pritam Singh, 'Why the story of Bhagat Singh Remains on the Margins', *South Asia Citizens Web*, 4 September 2008, where he reviews the 2008 publication of Irfan Habib's *To Make the Deaf Hear: Ideology and Program of Bhagat Singh and His Colleagues* (Available at http://www.sacw.net/article22.html). Also see Pritam Singh, 'Competing Contestations over the Appropriation of Bhagat Singh' (Paper presented at the bi-annual seminar of the Punjab Research Group at the University of Manchester on 27 October 2007 to celebrate the 100th birth anniversary of Bhagat Singh).

13. Pritam Singh, 'Bhagat Singh, Gandhi, and the British', *The Tribune*, 25 March 2015 (Available at https://www.researchgate.net/publication/274375372_Bhagat_Singh_Gandhi_and_the_British_httpepapertribuneindiacom465501The-TribuneTT_25_March_2015page111).

14. M.M. Juneja, *Biography of Bhagat Singh* (2016), Chapter 14, pp. 159–71, p. 159.

15. Quoted in M.M. Juneja, Ibid., p. 162. Citing *File No. 5-45/1931* KW2, Home Department Political Branch; also *Collected Works of Mahatma Gandhi, Vol. 45*, pp. 196–97.

16. A.G. Noorani, *The Trial of Bhagat Singh* (Oxford University Press, 1996), at p. 239

17. Citing *File No. 5-45/1931* KW2, Home Department Political Branch; in M.M. Juneja Ibid., p. 163, quoting directly from *Collected Works of Mahatma Gandhi, Vol. 45*, p. 209.
18. *Collected Works of Mahatma Gandhi, Vol. 45*, pp. 438–40. Also see *File No. 5-45/1931* KW2, Home Department Political Branch.
19. *Collected Works of Mahatma Gandhi, Vol. 45*, pp. 333–34.
20. M.M. Juneja, *Biography of Bhagat Singh* (2016), p. 168.
21. *Collected Works of Mahatma Gandhi, Vol. 45*, p. 344.
22. Gurdev Singh Deol, *Shaheed-e-Azam Sardar Bhagat Singh: The Man and His Ideology* (Nabha, 1978), p. 94.
23. M.M. Juneja, *Biography of Bhagat Singh* (2016), p. 169.
24. Ibid., p. 170.
25. *The Tribune*, 26 March 1931.

Chapter 53

1. Bruno Waterfield, 'Forgive Us for Starting the Second World War, Germany begs Poles', *The Times*, 2 September 2019.
2. Michele L. Norris, 'Germany Faced Its Horrible Past. Can We Do the Same?', *The Washington Post*, 3 June 2021.
3. Amandeep Singh Madra and Parmjit Singh, *Eyewitness at Amritsar* (London: Kashi House, 2019), p. 144.
4. Edward Thompson, *The Other Side of the Medal* (London: Hogarth Press, 1925). See 'Preface', p. 5.
5. Ibid., p. 128.
6. Ibid., p. 130.
7. Ibid., p. 110.
8. Ibid., pp. 131–32.
9. Ibid., p. 5.
10. 'Archbishop of Canterbury Prostrates before Jallianwala Bagh Memorial', *The Week*, 10 September 2019 (Available at https://www.theweek.in/news/india/2019/09/10/archbishop-canterbury-prostrates-before-jallianwala-bagh-memorial.html?fbclid=IwAR1ggE6ni9EbvpNXM_fa4qwQ9B7nsBzEUlAhev85OIc3se-Tzba9QXG56FM).
11. Harriet Sherwood, 'Justin Welby Prostrates Himself in Apology for British Massacre at Amritsar', *The Guardian*, 10 September 2019 (Available at https://www.theguardian.com/world/2019/sep/10/justin-welby-apologises-in-name-of-christ-british-massacre-amritsar).

12. Prasun Sonwalker, 'Will Apologise for Jallianwala Bagh Massacre if Voted to Power: Labour Party's Manifesto', *Hindustan Times*, 21 November 2019 (Available at https://www.hindustantimes. com/world-news/will-apologise-for-jallianwala-bagh-massacre-if-voted-to-power-labour-party-s-manifesto/story-5YOTcNR1oxJeBBnRdfCpuI.html).

Chapter 54

1. See 'Accused 9/11 mastermind open to testimony against Saudi Arabia', *Al-Jazeera* (Available at https://www.aljazeera.com/ news/2019/07/accused-911-mastermind-open-testimony-saudi-arabia-190729231512390.html).

2. David Smith, 'Trial for Five men Charged with Planning 9/11 to Start in 2021, 20 Years after Attack', *The Guardian*, 30 August 2019. Also see, Carol Rosenberg, 'Trial for Men Accused of Plotting 9/11 Attacks Is Set for 2021', *New York Times*, 30 August 2019. (Available at https://www.nytimes.com/2019/08/30/us/politics/ sept-11-trial-guantanamo-bay.html).

3. See, 'Lord Steyn, Outspoken Law Lord Whose Liberal Views Became a Thorn in the Side of the Blair Government, Especially over Iraq and Guantanomo Bay', *The Times*, 1 December 2017, p. 59. For the full lecture see, Johan Steyn, 'Guantanamo Bay: The Legal Black Hole', Twenty-Seventh F.A. Mann Lecture, 25 November 2003. (Available at http://www.statewatch.org/ news/2003/nov/guantanamo.pdf).

4. See his posts at https://www.facebook.com/justicekatju/.

5. David Edgerton, 'Britain's Persistent Racism Cannot Simply be Explained by Its Imperial History', *The Guardian*, 24 June 2020. (Available at https://www.theguardian.com/commentisfree/2020/ jun/24/britain-persistent-racism-imperial-history).

6. Pratap Bhanu Mehta, *'Hijab Debate Is a Pretext for Institutionalising State Cruelty'*, Indian Express, 23 February 2022. (Available at https://indianexpress.com/article/opinion/columns/hijab-debate-is-a-pretext-for-institutionalising-state-cruelty-muslim-students-islam-7786330/).

7. '"Pathology of Islamophobia" Taking Lethal Form, Says Noam Chomsky'. The Telegraph *online*, 23 February 2022. (Available at https://www.telegraphindia.com/india/pathology-of-islamophobia-taking-most-lethal-form-in-india-noam-chomsky/cid/1851456).

8. Rafia Zakari, *'Intolerant India'*, The Baffler, 18 February 2022. (Available at https://thebaffler.com/latest/intolerant-india-zakaria).

Chapter 55

1. There were strong reactions to the two films *Jodha Akbar* and *Padmavat*; see 'Rajputs, Their Women, & Muslim Rulers', *The Tribune*, 6 January 2018.
2. Agence France-Presse, 'India: Protests against Citizenship Law Seen as Anti-Muslim Spread', *The Guardian*, 16 December 2019 (Available at https://www.theguardian.com/world/2019/dec/16/india-protests-six-dead-as-demonstrators-vow-to-continue-to-fight-citizenship-changes).
3. Kama Maclean, *A Revolutionary History of Interwar India: Violence, Image, Voice and Text* (London: Hurst & Co, 2015), p. 46.
4. Ibid., p. 46.
5. Anish Kapoor, 'Modi's Bulldozing of Parliament Shows Him as the Architect of a Hindu Taliban', *The Guardian*, 4 June 2021 (Available at https://www.theguardian.com/artanddesign/2021/jun/04/modi-parliament-taliban-anish-kapoor?CMP=twt_gu&utm_source=Twitter&utm_medium#Echobox=1622817913-1).
6. Amy Kazmin, 'Modi Citizenship Stirs Memories of Myanmar's Dark Path', *Financial Times*, 17 December 2019, p. 8.
7. Amy Kazmin, *'India's Citizenship Bill Has Echoes of Myanmar's Dark Path'* Financial Times, 16 December 2019 (Available at https://www.ft.com/content/b9767a42-1cfb-11ea-97df-cc63de1d73f4)
8. Rajshree Chandra, 'Has India Descended Into a Constitutional Theocracy?', *The Wire*, 17 December 2020 (Available at https://thewire.in/government/india-hindutva-constitutional-theocracy-caa).
9. Zamira Rahim, 'India Builds Detention Camps for up to 1.9m People "Stripped of Citizenship" in Assam', *The Independent*, 10 September 2019. (Available at https://www.independent.co.uk/news/world/asia/assam-india-detention-camps-bangladesh-nrc-list-a9099251.html).
10. Sandip Chakraborty, *Chaman Lal*, 21 October 2019, where Prof. Chaman Lal was speaking at the Seagull Bookstore in Kolkata with respect to his forthcoming book (Available at https://www.newsclick.in/fearlessness-bhagat-singh-needed-fight-fascist-build-chaman-lal).
11. Owen Bowcott, 'Gambia Files Rohingya Genocide Case against Myanmar at UN Court', *The Guardian*, 11 November 2019.

12. Varun Das, 'Bhagat Singh Re-visited', *The Indian Express*, 26 December 2019, (Chandigarh edition).

13. Shahira Naim in Aligarh, 'Such Repression Not Seen Even In Colonial Period: Irfan Habib', *The Tribune*, 22 December 2019 (Available at https://www.tribuneindia.com/news/such-repression-not-seen-even-in-colonial-period-irfan-habib-15296?fbclid=IwAR2bDR2X_AP2Vvugod5IR HK8Fj0zLOTsp9Q8iQIpLbHQ8kSYo7bcAnh3EsQ).

14. Ibid.

15. 'Nearly 1,000 Lawyers Distance Themselves from Bar Council's Resolution on Protests', *The Wire*, 26 December 2019. (Available at https://thewire.in/law/lawyers-bar-council-resolution-caa-protests).

16. Poulomi Ghosh, 'Brinda Karat Moves Supreme Court against Jahangirpuri Demolition Drive, Says "Political, Communal Game Plan"', Hindustan Times, 21 April 2022. (Available at https://www. hindustantimes.com/india-news/brinda-karat-moves-supreme-court-against-jahangirpuri-demolition-drive-says-political-communal-game-plan-101650511345207.html).

17. Pheroze L. Vincent, 'Citizens Join JNU March', *The Telegraph*, 24 November 2019 (Available at https://www.telegraphindia.com/india/citizens-join-jnu-march/cid/1721603).

18. Natasha Japanwala, '"Love and Power": The Revival of People's Politics in Pakistan', *Aljazeera*, 3 December 2019 (Available at https://www.aljazeera.com/indepth/features/power-revival-people-politics-pakistan-191204103203422.html).

19. Jatin Anand, 'Farmers Erect Stage to Honour Bhagat Singh', *The Hindu*, 19 December 2020 (Available at https://www.thehindu. com/news/cities/Delhi/farmers-erect-stage-to-honour-bhagat-singh/article33369873.ece).

20. Pheroze L. Vincent, 'Schools of Thought Sprout at Farm Protest Sites', *The Telegraph*, 13 January 2021 (Available at https://www. telegraphindia.com/india/schools-of-thought-sprout-at-farm-protest-sites/cid/1803494).

Select Bibliography

Books

1. Aijazuddin, Fakir S. *The Resourceful Fakirs: Three Muslim Brothers at the Sikh Court of Lahore.* 2014.
2. Ali, Asaf. *The Commonwealth.* 1949.
3. Ali, Imran. *The Punjab under Imperialism, 1885-1947.* 1988.
4. Anand, Anita. *The Patient Assassin.* 2019.
5. Bardhan, A.B. *Bhagat Singh: Pages from the life of a Martyr.* 2006.
6. Bose, Sisir K., and Sugata Bose, eds. *The Indian Struggle 1920– 1942,* Netaji: Collected Works, Vol. 2. 2015.
7. Brown, Judith. *Modern India: The Origins of an Asian Democracy,* The Short Oxford History of the Modern World. 1991.
8. Chandra, Comrade Ram. *Naujawan Bharat Sabha and Hindustan Socialist Republican Association Army.* 2003.
9. Chibber, Vivek. *Postcolonial Theory and the Specter of Capital.* 2013.
10. Condos, Mark. *The Insecurity State.* 2017.
11. Darling, Malcolm Lyall. *Punjab Peasants in Prosperity and Debt.* 1928.
12. Datta, V.N. *Gandhi and Bhagat Singh.* 2008.
13. Deol, G.S. *Shaheed-e-Azam Sardar Bhagat Singh: The Man and His Ideology.* 1978.
14. Devji, Faisal. *The Impossible Indian: Gandhi and the Temptation of Violence.* 2012.

15. Dewan, Manorama. *Inquilabi Yatra: Sita Devi Aur Principal Chhabil Das Ki Jeevani.* 2006.

16. Dudziak, Mary. *Wartime: An Idea, Its History, and Its Consequences.* 2012.

17. Fanon, Frantz. *Black Skin, White Masks.* 2008.

18. Fanon, Frantz, *The Wretched of the Earth.* 2001.

19. Gallois, William. *A History of Violence in the Early Algerian Colony.* 2013.

20. Gandhi, Mahatma. *The Collected Works of Mahatma Gandhi ('CWMG')* (Publication Division, Ministry of Information & Broadcasting, Government of India, Gandhi Heritage Portal). 1999.

21. Ghosh, Ajoy. *Bhagat Singh and His Comrades: A Page from Our Revolutionary History.* 1945.

22. Ghosh, Durba. *Gentlemanly Terrorists: Political Violence and the Colonial State in India, 1919–1947.* 2017.

23. Gupta, Manmath Nath. *Bhagat Singh and His Times.* 1977.

24. Gupta, Manmath Nath. *They Lived Dangerously: Reminiscences of a Revolutionary.* 1969.

25. Hussain, Altaf. *Colonization of government lands (Punjab) Act, 1912.* 1964.

26. Habib, S. Irfan. *To Make the Deaf Hear: Ideology and Programme of Bhagat Singh and His Comrades.* 2015.

27. Harcourt, Max. 'Revolutionary Networks in North Indian Politics, 1907-1935', unpublished D.Phill. thesis, University of Sussex, 1974.

28. Harper, Tim. *Underground Asia: Global Revolutionaries and the Assault on Empire.* 2020.

29. Hooja, Bhupendra. *Bhagat Singh – In Jail and His 'Diary': An Introductory Note about a Martyr's Notebook.* 1994.

30. Noorani, A.G. *Jinnah and Tilak: Comrades in the Freedom Struggle.* 2010.

31. Josh, Bhagwan. 'Paradox of Armed Revolution' in Grewal (ed.), *Bhagat Singh and His Legend.* 2008.

32. Joshi, P.C. *Mainstream,* 25 March 1969, included in ACH-JNU Books and Pamphlets on History http://www.mainstreamweekly.net/breve25.html

33. Juneja, M.M. *Biography of Bhagat Singh.* 2009.

34. Juneja, M.M. *Selected Collections on Bhagat Singh.* 2007.

35. Juss, Satvinder S. *The Execution of Bhagat Singh: Legal Heresies of the Raj*. 2021.
36. Juss, Satvinder S. 'Sikhism', in Catherine Cookson (ed.), *Encyclopedia of Religious Freedom*. 2003.
37. Kamal, Neel. 'Bhagat Singh links Pakistanis, Indians', *The Times of India*, 24 March 2019.
38. Kennedy, Charles. 'The Creation and Development of Pakistan's Anti-terrorism Regime, 1997-2002'. *Religious Radicalism and Security in South Asia. 2004.*
39. Kerr, James Campbell. *Political Trouble in India,1907–1917*. 1917.
40. Khullar, K.K. *Shahid Bhagat Singh*. 1975.
41. Kolsky, Elizabeth. *Colonial Justice in British India: White Violence and the Rule of Law*. 2011.
42. Lall, Bhuvan. *The Great Indian Genius: Har Dayal*. 2020.
43. Lal, Chaman (ed.). *The Bhagat Singh Reader*. 2019.
44. Lal, Chaman. *The Selected Works of Bhagat Singh*. 2009.
45. Lal, Chaman. *Bhagat Singh – The Jail Notebook and Other Writings*. 2007.
46. Lal, Chaman. *Understanding Bhagat Singh*. 2013.
47. Low (ed.), *Congress and the Raj: Facets of the Indian Struggle 1917–1947*. 1977.
48. Maclean, Kama. *A Revolutionary History of Interwar India: Violence, Image, Voice and Text*. 2015.
49. Manjapra, Kris. 'Communist Internationalism and Transcolonial Recognition' in Sugata Bose and Kris Manjapra (eds.). *Cosmopolitan Thought Zones: South Asia and the Global Circulation of Ideas*. 2010.
50. Mukherjee, Uma. *Two Great Indian Revolutionaries: Rash Behari and Jyotindra Nath Banerjee*. 1966.
51. Moffat, Chris. *India's Revolutionary Inheritance: Politics & the Promise of Bhagat Singh*. 2019.
52. Mohan, Kamlesh. *Militant Nationalism in the Punjab, 1919–35*. 1985.
53. Mohan, Pandit Pearay. *The Punjab 'Rebellion' of 1919, and How It Was Suppressed: An Account of the Punjab Disorders and the Working of Martial Law*. 1999.
54. Nayar, Kuldip. *The Martyr: Bhagat Singh – Experiments in Revolution*. 2000.
55. Nehru, Jawahar Lal. *An Autobiography*. 1962.
56. Noorani, A.G. *The Trial of Bhagat Singh: Politics of Justice*. 1996.

57. Philips, C.H. *The Evolution of India and Pakistan, 1858–1947.* 1964.

58. Pinney, Christopher. *Photos of the Gods: The Printed Image and Political Struggle in India.* 2004.

59. Pinney, Christopher. 'The Body and the Bomb: Technologies of Modernity in Colonial India', in Richard Davies (ed.), *Picturing the Nation: Iconographies of Modern Indian.* 2007.

60. Puri, Karish K. *Ghadar Movement: Ideology, Organisation and Strategy.* 1983.

61. Quail, John. *The Slow Burning Fuse: The Lost History of the British Anarchists.* 1978.

62. Rai, Lala Lajpat. *Autobiographical Writings.* Delhi: University Publishers, 1965.

63. Rai, Lala Lajpat. *The Problem of National Education in India.* 1920.

64. Ray, Asok Kumar. *Revolutionary Parties of Bengal: Dacca Anushilan, New Violence, and Jugantar, 1919–1930.* 2013.

65. Saigal, Ias Omesh. *Shaheed Bhagat Singh: Unique Martyr in Freedom Movement.* 2002.

66. Sanyal, Jitendra Nath. *Bhagat Singh: A Biography*, K.C. Yadav and Babar Singh (eds.). 2006.

67. Sanyal, Sachindra Nath. *Bandi Jeevan.* 1963.

68. Satia, Priya. *Time's Monsters.* 2019.

69. Sawhney, Simona. 'Bhagat Singh: A Politics of Death and Hope' in Anshu Malhotra and Farina Mir (eds.), *Punjab Reconsidered.* 2012.

70. Sharma, Mahesh. *The Life and Times of Bhagat Singh.* 2012.

71. Shastri, Raja Ram. *Amar Shahidon Ke Sansmaran.* 1981.

72. Sindhu, Virendra. *Yugdrishta Bhagat Singh Aur Unke Mrityuanjay Purkhe.* 1997.

73. Sarkar, Tanika. *Bengal 1928–1934: The Politics of Protest.* 1997.

74. Sherman, Taylor C. *State Violence and Punishment in India, 1919–1956.* 2010.

75. Singh, Jagmohan, and Chaman Lal, (*eds.) Bhagat Singh Aur Unke Sathion Ke Dastavez.* 1987.

76. Singh, Jagmohan (ed.). *Bhagat Singh Ate Uhna De Saathian Diyan Likhtaan.* 2006.

77. Singh, Jagmohan and Lal, Chaman (ed) *Bhagat Singh Aur Unke Sathion Ke Dastavej.* 2003.

78. Singh, Navtej. *Challenge to Imperial Hegemony: The Life Story of A Great Indian Patriot Udham Singh.* 1998.

79. Singha, Radhika. *A Despotism of Law: Crime and Justice in Early Colonial India.* 1998.
80. Singh, Trilochan. *Autobiography of Bhai Sahib Randhir Singh: Freedom Fighter, Reformer, Theologian, Saint and Hero of the Second Lahore Conspiracy Case.* 1971.
81. Sitarmayya, P. *The History of the Indian National Congress Vol. I.* 1946.
82. Spear, Percival. *The Oxford History of Modern India: 1740-1947.* 1965.
83. Talbot, I, & S. Thandi (eds.). *People On the Move, A Century of Punjabi Local, Regional and International Migration.* 2003.
84. Thompson, Edward. *The Other Side of the Medal.* 1925.
85. Thomas, Martin. *Violence and the Colonial Order: Police, Workers and Protest in the European Colonial Empires, 1918–1940.* 2015.
86. Tripathi, Vachnesh. *Krantimurti Durga Bhabhi.* 1996.
87. Verma Shiv. *Selected Writings of Shaheed Bhagat Singh.* 1986.
88. Verma, Shiv. *Sansmritiyan.* 2002.
89. Virdee, Pippa. *From the Ashes of 1947: Reimagining Punjab.* 2018.
90. Wagner, Kim A. *Amritsar 1991: An Empire of Fear & the Making of a Massacre.* 2019.
91. Waraich, M.J.S. *Bhagat Singh: The Eternal Rebel.* 2014.
92. Waraich, M.J.S. *Profile of a Martyr Jatin Das: A First Hand Account by His Brother Kiron Das.* 2015.

Book Chapters and Articles in Journals

1. Anderson, Claire. 'Execution and its Aftermath in the Nineteenth-Century British Empire', in R. Ward (ed.) *A Global History of Execution and the Criminal Corpse.* Palgrave Historical Studies in the Criminal Corpse and its Afterlife. 2015.
2. Bailkin, Jordanna. 'The Boot and the Spleen: When Was Murder Possible in British India?', *Comparative Studies in Society and History*, vol. 48, no. 2, 2006. Available at http://www.jstor.org/stable/3879358.
3. Lithwick, Dara. '"Welfare" of a Nation: The Origins of "Peace, Order and Good Government"'. Available at https://hillnotes.ca/2017/04/26/welfare-of-a-nation-the-origins-of-peace-order-and-good-government/.

4. Barrier, Gerald N. 'The Punjab Disturbances of 1907: The Response of the British Government in India to Agrarian Unrest', *Modern Asian Studies*, vol. 1, no. 4 (1967), pp. 353–383. Available at http://www.jstor.org/stable/312066.

5. Condos, Mark. 'Licence to Kill: The Murderous Outrages Act and the Rule of Law in Colonial India, 1867-1925', *Modern Asian Studies* 50, no. 2 (2016), pp. 479–517. Available at http://www.jstor.org/stable/24734795.

6. Condos, Mark. '"Fanaticism" and the Politics of Resistance along the North-West Frontier of British India', *Comparative Studies in Society and History* 58, 3 (2016), pp. 717–45. Available at doi:10.1017/S0010417516000335.

7. Elam, Daniel J. 'The "Arch Priestess of Anarchy" Visits Lahore: Violence, Love and the Worldliness of Revolutionary Texts', *Postcolonial Studies* 16, 2 (2013), pp. 140–154. Available at https://www.tandfonline.com/doi/abs/10.1080/13688790.2013.823258.

8. Hamid, Naved. 'Dispossession and Differentiation of the Peasantry in the Punjab during Colonial Rule', *The Journal of Peasant Studies* 10, 1 (1982). Available at https://doi.org/10.1080/03066158208438189.

9. Imran, Ali. 'Malign Growth? Agricultural Colonization and the Roots of Backwardness in the Punjab', *Past & Present*, 114 (February 1987), pp. 110–132. Available at https://doi.org/10.1093/past/114.1.110.

10. Kamran, Tahir. 'Pagri Sambhal O Jatta – I', *The News on Sunday*, 19 March 2017. Available at https://www.thenews.com.pk/tns/detail/562862-pagri-sambhal-o-jatta.

11. Killey, Ian D. '"Peace, Order and Good Government": A Limitation on Legislative Competence', *Melbourne University Law Review* (Vol. 17, June 1989), pp. 24–55. Available at http://classic.austlii.edu.au/au/journals/MelbULawRw/1989/2.pdf.

12. Kolsky, Elizabeth. 'The Colonial Rule of Law and the Legal Regime of Exception: Frontier 'Fanaticism' and State Violence in British India', *American Historical Review* 120, 4 (2015), pp. 1,218–46. Available at http://www.jstor.org/stable/43696899.

13. Nair, Neeti. 'Bhagat Singh as "Satyagrahi": The Limits to Non-Violence in Late Colonial India', *Modern Asian Studies*, 43, 3 (2009), pp. 649–681. Available at https://theprg.co.uk/2009/04/15/bhagat-singh-as-'satyagrahi'-the-limits-to-non-violence-in-late-colonial-india-by-neeti-nair/

14. Mittal, S.K., and Irfan Habib. 'Towards Independence and Socialist Republic: Naujawan Bharat Sabha', *Social Scientist* 8, 2 (September 1969), pp. 18–29. Available at https://doi.org/10.2307/3516698.

15. Moffatt, Chris. 'Experiment in Political Truth', *Postcolonial Studies* 16, 2 (2013), pp. 185–201). Available at https://doi.org/10.1080/1 3688790.2013.823262.

16. Prakash, Teesta. 'Pulwama and its Aftermath: What is Different this Time?', *Australian Institute of International Affairs*, 4 March 2019. Available at https://www.internationalaffairs.org.au/ australianoutlook/pulwama-aftermath-different-this-time/.

17. Sahni, Binda Preet. 'Effects of Emergency Law in India 1915-1931', *Studies on Asia*, Series IV, 2, 2 (October 2012), pp. 146–179. https://papers.ssrn.com/sol3/papers.cfm?abstract_id=2174900

18. Shaya, Gregory. 'How to Make an Anarchist-Terrorist: An Essay on the Political Imaginary in Fin-de-Siecle France', *Journal of Social History*, 44, 2, The Arts in Place (Winter 2010), pp. 521–543. Available at https://www.jstor.org/stable/25790369.

19. Sherman, Taylor C. 'From Hell to Paradise? Voluntary Transfer of Convicts to the Andaman Islands, 1921–1940', *Modern Asian Studies*, 2, 2 (March 2009), pp. 367–388). Available at http://www. jstor.org/stable/20488087.

20. Sherman, Taylor C. 'State Practice, Nationalist Politics and the Hunger Strikes of the Lahore Conspiracy Case Prisoners, 1929–39' Cultural and Social History, 5, 4 (2008), pp. 497–508. Available at https://doi.org/10.2752/147800408X341686.

21. Sherman, Taylor C. 'Tensions of Colonial Punishment: Perspectives on Recent Developments in the Study of Coercive Networks in Asia, Africa and the Caribbean', *History Compass*, 7, 3, pp. 659–677. Available at https://doi.org/10.1111/j.1478-0542.2009.00597.x.

22. Singh, Pritam. 'Why the Story of Bhagat Singh Remains on the Margins', *South Asia Citizens Web* (4 September 2008). Available at http://www.sacw.net/article22.html.

23. Singh, Pritam. 'Competing Contestations over the Appropriation of Bhagat Singh' (Paper presented at the bi-annual seminar of the Punjab Research Group at the University of Manchester on 27 October 2007 to celebrate the 100th birth anniversary of Bhagat Singh).

24. Sawhney, Simona. 'Death in Three Scenes of Recitation', *Postcolonial Studies*, 16, 2 (2013), pp. 202–215, at p. 20. Available at https://doi.org/10.1080/13688790.2013.823263.

25. Singh, Bhagat. 'Why I Am an Atheist', in D.N. Gupta (ed.) *Select Speeches and Writings*. 2007.
26. Steyn, Johan. 'Guantanamo Bay: The Legal Black Hole', Twenty-Seventh F.A. Mann Lecture, 25 November 2003. (Available at http://www.statewatch.org/news/2003/nov/guantanamo.pdf).
27. Talbot, Ian A. 'The Punjab Under Colonialism: Order and Transformation in British India'. Available at https://www.researchgate.net/publication/240630737_The_Punjab_under_Colonialism_Order_and_Transformation_in_British_India.
28. Vaidik, Aparna. 'History of a Renegade Revolutionary: Revolutionism and betrayal in colonial India', *Postcolonial Studies* 16, 2, pp. 216–229. Available at https://doi.org/10.1080/1368879 0.2013.823264.
29. Wagner, Kim A. 'Savage Warfare: Violence and the Rule of Colonial Difference in Early British Counterinsurgency', *History Workshop Journal*, 85, 1 (April 2018), pp. 217–237. Available at https://doi.org/10.1093/hwj/dbx053.
30. Wagner, Kim A. '"Calculated to Strike Terror": The Amritsar Massacre and the Spectacle of Colonial Violence', *Past & Present*, 233, 1 (1 November 2016). Available at https://doi.org/10.1093/pastj/gtw037.

Newspaper Articles and Periodicals

1. Ammara, Ahmad. '#ShaheedBhagatSingh: An Answer to Pakistan's Search for a National Hero', *News Laundry*, 28 September 2017. Available at https://www.newslaundry.com/2017/09/28/shaheed-bhagat-singh-pakistan-national-hero-lahore.
2. Anand, Anita. 'Jallianwala: Regret Isn't Enough. An Honest Appraisal of the Raj Can Do So Much More', *The Times of India*, 14 April 2019. Available at https://timesofindia.indiatimes.com/articleshow/68868082.cms?utm_source=twitter.com&utm_medium=social&utm_campaign=TOIDesktop&utm_source=contentofinterest&utm_medium=text&utm_campaign=cppst.
3. Anand, Jatin. 'Farmers Erect Stage to Honour Bhagat Singh', *The Hindu*, 19 December 2020. Available at https://www.thehindu.com/news/cities/Delhi/farmers-erect-stage-to-honour-bhagat-singh/article33369873.ece.

4. Bhattarchajee, Kallol. 'India boycotts Pakistan national day event', *The Hindu*, 22 March 2019. Available at https://www.thehindu.com/news/national/india-boycotts-pakistan-national-day-event/article26612743.ece.

5. Bowcott, Owen. 'Gambia Files Rohingya Genocide Case against Myanmar at UN Court', *The Guardian*, 11 November 2019. Available at https://www.theguardian.com/world/2019/nov/11/gambia-rohingya-genocide-myanmar-un-court.

6. Chandra, Rajshree. 'Has India Descended into a Constitutional Theocracy?' *The Wire*, 17 December 2020. Available at https://thewire.in/government/india-hindutva-constitutional-theocracy-caa.

7. Cockburn, Patrick. 'Britain's Reign as a World Superpower Is Over – and It's All Thanks to Brexit', *The Independent*, 8 December 2019. Available at https://www.independent.co.uk/voices/brexit-uk-britain-boris-johnson-us-saudi-syria-nato-a9236286.html.

8. Dhawale, Ashok. 'Shaheed Bhagat Singh: An Immortal Revolutionary', *The Marxist* 22:2-3 (April–September 2006).

9. Din-Kariuki, Natalya. 'After Rhodes Falls', *London Review of Books*, 29 June 2020 Available at https://www.lrb.co.uk/blog/2020/june/after-rhodes-falls.

10. Dogra, Bharat. 'Jagmohan Singh—Life Devoted to Carrying Forward the Legacy of Shahid Bhagat Singh', *Mainstream Weekly*, 14 August 2020. Available at https://mainstreamweekly.net/article9791.html.

11. Edgerton, David, '*Britain's Persistent Racism Cannot Simply be Explained by Its Imperial History*', *The Guardian*, 24 June 2020. Available at https://www.theguardian.com/commentisfree/2020/jun/24/britain-persistent-racism-imperial-history.

12. Gopalakrishnan, Amulya. 'Why Mahatma Gandhi Rejected Chauri Chaura's Crime of Passion', *The Times of India*, 30 September 2019. Available at http://timesofindia.indiatimes.com/articleshow/71372232.cms?utm_source=contentofinterest&utm_medium=text&utm_campaign=cppst.

13. Gupta, Shekar. 'Shambles over Farmers' Protest Shows Modi-Shah BJP Needs a Punjab Tutorial', *The Print*, 28 November 2020. Available at https://theprint.in/national-interest/shambles-over-farmers-protest-shows-modi-shah-bjp-needs-a-punjab-tutorial.

14. Gupta, Shekar. 'Modi Govt Has Lost Farm Laws Battle, Now Raising Sikh Separatist Bogey Will be a Grave Error', *The Print*, 6 February 2021. Available at https://theprint.in/national-interest/ modi-govt-has-lost-farm-laws-battle-now-raising-sikh-separatist-bogey-will-be-a-grave-error/599860/.

15. Habib, S. Irfan. 'Bhagat Singh and Us', *The Indian Express*, 25 March 2017. Available at https://indianexpress.com/article/ opinion/columns/bhagat-singh-iconic-revolutionary-and-us-martyrs-day-march-23-4584306/.

16. Habib, S. Irfan. 'Bhagat Singh: A Revolutionary Thinker and Not Just A Martyr', *News Central*, 23 March 2018. Available at https:// newscentral24x7.com/bhagat-singh-a-revolutionary-thinker-and-not-just-a-martyr/.

17. Habib, S. Irfan. 'Revolutionary Ideas That Live On', *The Hindu*, 23 March 2019. Available at https://www.thehindu.com/opinion/ op-ed/revolutionary-ideas-that-live-on/article26613250.ece.

18. Habib, S. Irfan. 'A Shared Hero for India and Pakistan?', *The Hindu*, 1 May 2018. Available at http://www.thehindu.com/opinion/ op-ed/a-shared-hero-for-india-and-pakistan/article23732329. eceMORE-IN.

19. Jacob, Happymon. 'After Balakot: India-Pakistan Relations Heading Nowhere', *The India Forum*, 7 May 2019. Available at https:// www.theindiaforum.in/article/after-balakot-india-pakistan-relations-heading-nowhere.

20. India Today Webdesk, 'Pulwama Terror Attack: Suicide Bomber Drives SUV Packed With 300 kg Explosives into CRPF Bus, 44 Men Martyred', *India Today*, 16 February 2019. Available at https:// www.indiatoday.in/india/story/twelve-crpf-jawans-injured-in-ied-blast-in-j-k-1456037-2019-02-14.

21. 'Interview with Jagmohan Singh', *Frontline*, 2 November 2007, p. 16.

22. Hanif, Intikhab. 'Archives of Bhagat Singh Case Trial to be Exhibited', *Dawn*, 25 March 2018. Available at https://www.dawn. com/news/amp/1397297.

23. Islam, Shamsul. 'No to Bhagat Singh's Second Hanging', *Countercurrents.org*, 12 October 2013. Available at www. countercurrents.org/shamsul112013.html.

24. Iqbal, Jawaid. 'Mexico's Request That Spain Say Sorry for 1519 Is Absurd', *The Sunday Times*, 27 March 2019. Available at https://

www.thetimes.co.uk/article/mexico-s-request-that-spain-say-sorry-for-1519-is-absurd-7gj9r9b0b.

25. Jagga, Raakhi. Farm Protests Eating into Economy, Will Harm Punjab More Than Centre', *The Indian Express*, 12 November 2020. Available at https://indianexpress.com/article/india/farm-protests-eating-into-economy-will-harm-punjab-more-than-centre/.

26. Japanwala, Natasha. "'Love and Power": The Revival of People's Politics in Pakistan', *Aljazeera*, 3 December 2019. Available at https://www.aljazeera.com/indepth/features/power-revival-people-politics-pakistan-191204103203422.html.

27. Kapoor, Anish. 'Modi's Bulldozing of Parliament Shows Him as the Architect of a Hindu Taliban', *The Guardian*, 4 June 2021. Available at https://www.theguardian.com/artanddesign/2021/jun/04/modi-parliament-taliban-anish-kapoor?CMP=twt_gu&utm_source=Twitter&utm_medium#Echobox=1622817913-1.

28. Katju, Makandey. 'Who Was Right, Gandhi or Bhagat Singh? — II', *Daily Times*, 28 November 2018. Available at https://dailytimes.com.pk/326921/who-was-right-gandhi-or-bhagat-singh-ii/.

29. Kaushik, R.K. 'Bhagat Singh, the Final Hours', *The Hindustan Times*, 9 October 2011. Available at https://www.hindustantimes.com/india/bhagat-singh-the-final-hours/story-oHHsDEhtugs4wSI7dfWuzO.html.

30. Kaushik, R.K. 'Missed Target of Bhagat Singh', *The Tribune*, 18 September 2002. Available at https://www.tribuneindia.com/2002/20020918/edit.htm#5.

31. 'Mexico asks Pope Francis for Apology for Church's Role in Spanish Conquest', *The Guardian*, 11 October 2020. Available at https://www.theguardian.com/world/2020/oct/11/mexico-asks-pope-francis-for-apology-for-churchs-role-in-spanish-conquest?CMP=Share_AndroidApp_Other.

32. Moffat, Chris. 'Infinite Inquilab', *The Caravan*, 1 August 2013. Available at https://caravanmagazine.in/lede/infinite-inquilab.

33. Murray, Craig. 'Your Man in the Public Gallery: The Assange Hearing Day 6', *Uncategorised*, 8 September 2020. Available at https://www.craigmurray.org.uk/archives/2020/09/your-man-in-the-public-gallery-the-assange-hearing-day-6/.

34. Naim, Shahira, 'Such Repression Not Seen Even in Colonial Period: Irfan Habib', *The Tribune*, 22 December 2019. Available

at https://www.tribuneindia.com/news/features/such-repression-not-seen-even-in-colonial-period-irfan-habib-15296.

35. Narayan, Sudha. 'The Three Farm Bills: Is This the Market Reform Indian Agriculture Needs?', *The India Forum*, 2 October 2020. Available at https://www.theindiaforum.in/article/three-farm-bills.

36. Norris, Michele L. 'Germany Faced Its Horrible Past. Can We Do the Same?', *The Washington Post*, 3 June 2021. Available at https://www.washingtonpost.com/opinions/2021/06/03/slavery-us-germany-holocaust-reckoning/

37. '"Operation Bandar" Was IAF's Code Name for Balakot Airstrike', *Mint*, 21 June 2019. Available at https://www.livemint.com/news/india/-operation-bandar-was-iaf-s-code-name-for-balakot-airstrike-1561119715509.html.

38. Ashok Dhawale, *'Bhagat Singh: A Perennial Saga of Inspiration' People's Democracy*, vol. xxx, No. 40, 1 October 2006. Available at https://archives.peoplesdemocracy.in/2006/1001/10012006_ashok%20dhawale.html.

39. Pillai, Manu S. 'The Ghosts of Amritsar', *The New Statesman*, 12–17 April 2019, pp. 42–44, at p. 44.

40. Qaswar, Abbas. 'Pakistani Authorities Do a U-turn on Renaming a Chowk after Freedom Fighter Bhagat Singh', Daily Mail, 1 November 2012. Available at https://www.dailymail.co.uk/indiahome/indianews/article-2226553/Pakistani-authorities-U-turn-renaming-chowk-freedom-fighter-Bhagat-Singh.html.

41. Rahim, Zamira. 'India Builds Detention Camps for up to 1.9m People "Stripped of Citizenship" in Assam', *The Independent*, 10 September 2019. (Available at https://www.independent.co.uk/news/world/asia/assam-india-detention-camps-bangladesh-nrc-list-a9099251.html).

42. Ramani, Priya. 'Bhagat Singh Comes to Delhi', *Mint*, 20 November 2008. Available at https://www.livemint.com/Leisure/BNlft0AiWNfGdkntHb3fSK/Bhagat-Singh-comes-to-Delhi.html.

43. 'Shaheed: The Definite Bhagat Singh Film Which Almost Didn't Get Made, Listen to Its Songs', *The Indian Express*, 23 March 2017. Available at https://indianexpress.com/article/entertainment/bollywood/shaheed-the-definite-bhagat-singh-

film-manoj-kumar-which-almost-didnt-get-made-listen-to-its-songs-4581778/.

44. Sharma, Manimugdha S. 'Bhagat Singh Was Always a Revolutionary Nationalist . . . Indian Cultural Ethos was Deeply Ingrained in Him', *The Times of India*, 20 March 2019. Available at https://timesofindia.indiatimes.com/blogs/parthian-shot/bhagat-singh-was-always-a-revolutionary-nationalist-indian-cultural-ethos-was-deeply-ingrained-in-him/.

45. Sherwood, Harriet. 'Justin Welby Prostrates Himself in Apology for British Massacre at Amritsar', *The Guardian*, 10 September 2019. Available at https://www.theguardian.com/world/2019/sep/10/justin-welby-apologises-in-name-of-christ-british-massacre-amritsar.

46. Singh, Hardeep. 'The Problem with Apologising for the Amritsar Massacre', *The Spectator*, 9 April 2019. Available at https://blogs.spectator.co.uk/2019/04/the-problem-with-apologising-for-the-amritsar-massacre/.

47. Singh, Krishna Pratap. 'Still Waiting for Chandrashekhar's "Azad" Vision After All These Years', *The Wire*, 23 July 2020. Available at https://thewire.in/history/still-waiting-for-chandrashekhars-azad-vision-after-all-these-years.

48. Smith, David. 'Trial for Five Men Charged with Planning 9/11 to Start in 2021, 20 Years after Attack', *The Guardian*, 30 August 2019. Available at https://www.theguardian.com/us-news/2019/aug/30/khalid-shaikh-mohammad-9-11-trial-start-date.

49. Carol Rosenberg, 'Trial for Men Accused of Plotting 9/11 Attacks Is Set for 2021', *The New York Times*, 30 August 2019. Available at https://www.nytimes.com/2019/08/30/us/politics/sept-11-trial-guantanamo-bay.html.

50. Sonwalkar, Prasun. 'Jallianwala Bagh: PM May Repeats "Deep Regret", No Apology', *The Hindustan Times*, 11 April 2019. Available at https://www.hindustantimes.com/world-news/british-pm-theresa-may-voices-regret-over-jallianwala-bagh-massacre/story-owyh1wPwehwCEvX7gC620J.html.

51. Sonwalker, Prasun. 'Will Apologise for Jallianwala Bagh Massacre If Voted to Power: Labour Party's Manifesto', *Hindustan Times*, 21 November 2019. Available at https://www.hindustantimes.com/world-news/will-apologise-for-jallianwala-bagh-

massacre-if-voted-to-power-labour-party-s-manifesto/story-5YOTcNR1oxJeBBnRdfCpuI.html.

52. 'Two Groups in Pakistan want Bhagat Singh to be Declared a National Hero', *The Economic Times*, 24 March 2018. Available at https://economictimes.indiatimes.com/news/politics-and-nation/two-groups-in-pakistan-want-bhagat-singh-to-be-declared-a-national-hero/articleshow/63441488.cms.

53. Vincent, Pheroze L. 'Schools of Thought Sprout at Farm Protest Sites', *The Telegraph online*, 13 January 2021. Available at https://www.telegraphindia.com/india/schools-of-thought-sprout-at-farm-protest-sites/cid/1803494.

54. Vincent, Pheroze L. 'Citizens Join JNU March', *The Telegraph*, 24 November 2019. Available at https://www.telegraphindia.com/india/citizens-join-jnu-march/cid/1721603.

55. Waterfield, Bruno. 'Forgive Us for Starting the Second World War, Germany Begs Poles', *The Times*, 2 September 2019. Available at https://www.thetimes.co.uk/article/forgive-us-for-starting-the-second-world-war-germany-begs-poland-96f9vhfjq.

Cases

(1) *Bancoult* (no 2) [2008] UKHL 61; [2009] 1 AC 453 at para 71.

(2) *R v Secretary of State for the Home Department ex p. Bentley* [1993] EWHC Admin 2. (Available at http://www.bailii.org/ew/cases/EWHC/Admin/1993/2.html). See also, McGeough, Re Judicial Review [2012] NIQB 11 (Available at http://www.bailii.org/nie/cases/NIHC/QB/2012/11.html).

(3) *Bhagat Singh v. The King Emperor* (1931) 33 BOMLR 950.

(4) *Mima v. Singh* (2002) 186 ALR 393.

(5) *Secretary of State for the Foreign & Commonwealth Affairs v Bancoult, R (on the application of)* [2007] EWCA Civ 498 (Available at http://www.bailii.org/ew/cases/EWCA/Civ/2007/498.html).

Index